**Voluntary Action Research:
1973**

This book is part of the "Voluntary Action Research Series" of the Center for a Voluntary Society (1507 M St., N.W., Washington, D.C. 20005), under the General Editorship of David Horton Smith. This series will not only include future annual review volumes like the present one, but will also include research and theoretical monographs on specific projects/topics contributed by scholars in various fields and countries. The Center for a Voluntary Society is organized for charitable, scientific, and educational purposes to promote and expand the awareness, understanding, and effective utilization of volunteers and voluntary associations in coping with human and social problems in the United States and elsewhere, and to evaluate the quality and effectiveness of the voluntary sector in making our society more humane, just, open, nonviolent, and uncoerced.

Voluntary Action Research: 1973

Edited by
David Horton Smith
Center for a Voluntary Society
and Boston College

Lexington Books
D.C. Heath and Company
Lexington, Massachusetts
Toronto   London

THIS VOLUME IS GRATEFULLY DEDICATED TO

James Luther Adams, in recognition of his lifetime of dedication and concern, both personal and scholarly, for voluntary action and its significance in human society and history. Among his many contributions have been his inspiration of two generations of students at the universities of Chicago and Harvard, and his major help in the formation of the Association of Voluntary Action Scholars and the *Journal of Voluntary Action Research*.

Contents

List of Figures

List of Tables

Foreword

Memory, understanding, and will. These three terms come from our history as do faith, hope and charity. In a time such as the present when the bulldozers of the developer mangle into oblivion our archaeological heritage and the chilling spectacle of newspaper reporters being imprisoned conjures memories of the days of the Five Knights in the time of King Charles, we all too urgently need the discipline and grace these six terms articulate.

Part One of *Voluntary Action Research: 1973* addresses itself to the memory of our past and how we articulate it as history. Without memory, there can be no understanding; without understanding, there can be no will to change. It is no accident that the tyrannical forces of any society attempt to obliterate memory and to deny history to people and their associations.

During the winter of 1972-73, the Center for a Voluntary Society in conjunction with a local television station in Washington, D.C. presented WOMAN: CHOICES AND CHALLENGES, thirteen half-hour shows on the role of women in contemporary society. The program presented controversial subjects and discussions on female sexuality, abortion, legal rights of women, marriage. It is instructive that the program which generated the greatest viewer response had to do with the history of the women's movement in the United States. Women telephoned and wrote saying they hadn't realized there was a past and a history to their protest, to their dissent, and to their fight to present their view of reality.

This book reminds us that voluntary action has a history—indeed a very long history. This history is vital, not only to the independent voluntary sector but to the society as a whole. This book speaks of life in different associational forms at a time of rapid and surprising and unpleasant change. We need to know our roots.

Without memory we become shallow, flighty and succumb to despair. Memory leads to understanding and understanding, hopefully, leads to the courage to be. The courage to be and the will to act imply a grappling with reality—an attempt to have an impact on the world. Part Two of this volume deals precisely with this problem. Through voluntary action of all kinds mankind works out its will to action, as through other means and structures. We know so much about the impact of business and government on human society yet so little about the impact of voluntary groups. That is why the beginnings made here toward a comprehensive look at the latter issue are so important.

The Center for a Voluntary Society is pleased to continue its sponsorship of this important series. We hope the papers presented in this volume will provoke increased attention to memory, understanding, and will in the sphere of voluntary action. The quality of our lives and even the continuation of human life itself may depend on it.

John Dixon, Director
Center for a Voluntary Society

Preface

The Voluntary Action Research Annual Series represents a conscious attempt to encourage more synthesis and stock-taking in this emerging interdisciplinary and interprofessional scholarly field. As in the previous volume of this series (*Voluntary Action Research: 1972*), the present volume does *not* attempt to review what has occurred in the field in the preceding *year*. Instead, an attempt is made to present an up-to-date overview of two broad subfields of the larger field of voluntary action theory and research.

The two subfields chosen for the present volume are the space and time variations in the prevalence of voluntary associations, and the impact of voluntary action at various system levels. These two subfields were chosen partly on the grounds that they were both of substantial importance to understanding voluntary action, but at the same time they have received relatively little scholarly attention. Under these circumstances, the papers in the present volume do *not* purport to present an exhaustive review and synthesis of the relevant empirical and theoretical literature on these topics—much as we would like to be able to do so. Some of the papers are able to approach this ideal, where the research literature is relatively more copious, though in most cases we must be content with some literature review, some theory, and occasional presentations of new primary data.

Since we could not hope to achieve completeness given the present state of research, we have instead given a good deal of emphasis to attempting to provide some range and balance to both Part One and Part Two of this volume. Instead of digging deeply into the nature of a particular society or time period, for instance, with a series of chapters on that topic, we have rather requested and selected for Part One a set of papers that cover the gamut of voluntary action in space and time from the origins of man to the present day. Similarly, instead of presenting a series of chapters that focus narrowly and in-depth on the variety of impacts of a particular kind or system level of voluntary action, we have requested papers for Part Two that cover a wide range of levels and types of impact of voluntary action, all the way from impact on the individual to impact on the society as a whole.

Our primary aim in this volume is to stimulate further research and theory in these two major subfields of voluntary action. We are more concerned with trying to sketch out the possible boundaries and types of approach that may be taken than we are concerned with covering every scrap of relevant literature. We are more concerned with drawing conclusions that are actually suggestive hypotheses for future testing than we are concerned with making statements whose validity will remain unchallenged for years to come. We are more concerned with raising important questions, drawing on whatever literature and evidence we can find, than we are concerned with answering these questions definitively. Our success will be measured by the degree to which this volume arouses in the reader an eagerness to improve on or extend the kinds of analyses we present, hopefully through the performance of thoughtful new empirical research as well as theory.

As with the first volume in this series, the present volume includes some revised and expanded versions of papers prepared for the September 1970 Seminar Session on "Voluntary Action Theory and Research: Steps Toward Synthesis," organized by the editor and Burt R. Baldwin at the Annual Meeting of the American Sociological Association. Other papers were requested and written specifically for this volume, and one paper was selected from another published source and reprinted here because of its appropriateness. Some of the other papers, especially ones that were revised from the Seminar Session noted above, have also been previously published in the journal literature of the last year or two.

As this annual series of volumes develops in future years, we are hopeful of increasing the participation of scholars from various disciplines and from countries other than the United States. Toward that end, we actively *encourage* interested scholars to contact the Association of Voluntary Action Scholars or the Center for a Voluntary Society (1507 M St. N.W., Washington, D.C. 20005) if they would be willing to consider writing a chapter for some future volume. The topical areas are established about two years prior to publication; but the project is a long term one, so that the rotation of topics is likely to match with the interests of any voluntary action scholar eventually.

This series of volumes is intended primarily for readers who are either themselves engaged in research or teaching dealing with voluntary action, or who would like to keep up with the results of voluntary action theory and research in order to improve their own voluntary organizations and voluntary action in general. Students in advanced courses on voluntary associations, social movements, interest groups, voluntary organization management/leadership, and related voluntary action topics are also likely to find these volumes of use. Foundation and government funding agency officials may also find this series to be helpful, insofar as they are concerned with the support of voluntary organizations and/or voluntary action research.

No major attempt has been made in this volume to define what is meant by voluntary associations or voluntary action. The whole of Part One of the *prior* (1972) volume was concerned with such matters, and the interested reader is referred to that source. A correlative source would be the *Journal of Voluntary Action Research*, the official journal of the Association of Voluntary Action Scholars, from whose articles the nature of voluntary action and voluntary groups can be inductively derived. As a rough capsule definition for the reader new to the field, we may say that voluntary action is what an individual is neither paid nor made to do, but rather does from a sense of psychic commitment, from common (often non-economic) interest with others, or from dedication to some kind of meaningful public interest or self interest goal or value.

Finally, the editor would like to thank the contributors for making this volume possible. Special thanks are also due Ms. Barbara MacLaury, who was responsible for a great deal of the typing and many practical details of bringing this volume to publication, Mr. Charles Brain, who assisted in the proofing, and Ms. Nancy Theberge, who was responsible for final proofing and the checking of many references.

David Horton Smith
Washington, D.C.
February 1973

Voluntary Action Research:
1973

Part One
Voluntary Associations
through Space and Time

Introduction to Part One

David Horton Smith

The theme of Part One of this volume is how voluntary associations are distributed through time and space—over the whole of man's history and among the societies of the world. We make no pretense at comprehensive coverage here. Instead, we are concerned with introducing interested readers to an area of voluntary action research that deserves a great deal more concentration of interdisciplinary, interprofessional scholarly inquiry.

In requesting and selecting chapters for this section, we have tried to provide examples of both breadth and some depth, although our first interest has been to sketch the broadest demarcations of voluntary associations in time and space. The chapters in Part One therefore attempt to give answers to such questions as the following: How old are voluntary associations in terms of man's total history? Did ancient societies have anything approximating voluntary associations? How is the process of modernization related to the presence of voluntary associations? What factors seem to be associated with the prevalence of voluntary associations on a worldwide scale? What do we know about the growth of transnational or international voluntary organizations as an especially important form of voluntary associations?

In Chapter 1, Robert T. Anderson gives us a really broad anthropological view of voluntary associations in human history. When he talks of "human history," he is referring to history in the loose sense of the whole period of man on earth, rather than in the strict sense of "history recorded in symbols by man" (recorded history). From various kinds of physical evidence and sophisticated inferential techniques, anthropologists can make educated guesses about the million years or so of man's existence as a species, even though recorded history only goes back several thousand years.

As it happens, there seem to have been no voluntary associations for most of human history, the roughly one-million-plus years our species has existed. But voluntary associations have been around for about ten thousand years (since the beginning of the Neolithic period), Anderson concludes from his review of the literature. This will be a surprising conclusion to most people, even to most scholars of voluntary action (though not to most anthropological scholars of voluntary action). Many people, indeed, seem to think that voluntary associations were an American invention of a century or two ago, encouraged in this belief by the famous descriptive work of de Toqueville, DEMOCRACY IN AMERICA. Nothing could be further from the truth, although the contemporary United States, along with many other highly modernized countries, tends to have (and to have had for at least 150 years) a substantial number of voluntary associations.

3

In order to make it very clear that voluntary associations have been around for millenia, even in forms fairly similar to present day forms, we have included Chapter 2 by Jack Ross dealing with the kinds of voluntary associations present in four selected ancient societies. This chapter is not meant to be an exhaustive review of the literature on voluntary associations in ancient society (especially the "high civilizations" of antiquity). Nor is it intended to be a comprehensive survey of voluntary association activity even in the four ancient societies selected for review—China, India, Rome, and Greece. Instead, Ross has selected these societies as representative of different types of basic structuring principles of ancient society (e.g., familism, caste, etc.). And within each society he has attempted to discern the presence and functions of various kinds of voluntary associations. In three of the four societies examined, he was able to find evidence in the literature regarding the existence of significant numbers of voluntary associations, with ancient India being a doubtful case, depending partly on one's definition of "voluntary association."

Where Anderson's chapter explores the earliest beginnings of voluntary associations in human history, Ross' chapter examines four rather elaborate ancient states or civilizations to find specific evidence of voluntary associations in a millenium or two after the beginning of recorded history (depending on where and when one dates this). Anderson's review suggests that voluntary associations are somehow associated with social evolution, being characteristic of more settled agricultural societies rather than the nomadic hunting-gathering tribes that represent an earlier stage of human social evolution. His review also suggests, however, that voluntary associations are much more prevalent in industrialized societies than in either "primitive" or "preindustrial" societies.

In Chapter 3 Smith takes up the latter theme and attempts, first of all, to bring to bear some empirical data regarding the nations of the contemporary world. The nations of the world today provide a kind of testing ground for theories about the relationship between modernization and the growth of voluntary associations. There are nations that are very underdeveloped, traditional agricultural societies, little changed in their basic social structure and culture for hundreds of years or more. At the other extreme, there are a number of highly developed, industrialized, modern nations that have experienced rapid and extensive social change over the past decades or even centuries. Between these two extremes there are nations representing all intermediate stages of development. And although comparisons among the contemporary nations of the world are not the same as historical comparisons by any means, it is nevertheless instructive to examine how such comparisons may shed some light on historical processes.

After showing that modernization is indeed closely and positively related to the prevalence of voluntary associations in the contemporary nations of the world, Smith goes on to discuss why this might be the case. He presents a simple theory or model that is intended to account for this relationship in terms of such social structural variables as societal goal differentiation and structural differentiation, the development level of the communication and transportation network, and the degree of collective action orientation of the society (including government permission or facilitation, aggregate individual resources for collective action, and objective payoffs for collective action). While no data are presented to test this model directly, Smith offers illustrative examples of how and why these factors are so important in explaining voluntary association prevalence. The potential value of this model lies in its attempt to go beyond some of the conventional categories of modernizing factors and get at the roots of voluntary association prevalence.

In Chapter 4 Baldwin complements Smith's presentation by reviewing several of the factors conventionally adduced to explain the differential prevalence of voluntary associations among nations or societies. A number of scholars have remarked on the general growth of formal organizations and bureaucracies as part of the modernization process. Most of these have not commented separately on the growth of voluntary associations as a special subtype of formal group or organization. However, there have been a few scholars who have been particularly interested in voluntary association prevalence in relation to modernization processes, and still others interested in the relation between modernization and participatory democracy, which involves the presence of pluralistic interest groups, including voluntary associations.

Baldwin reviews the relationship between the growth of voluntary associations and such elements of modernization as industrialization, degree of urbanization, rate of urbanization, mass media development, development of laws and the legal system, social heterogeneity, organizational density, and political revolution. These factors can be tied together by the broad perspective of "convergence theory," as Baldwin terms it, which argues that these cumulative changes in society—any society—are conducive to the growth of voluntary associations. The contrasting view of "historical specificity theory" argues that growth of voluntary associations does not follow automatically from the presence of these factors. Instead, it is argued that special historical conditions and cultural traits can foster or hinder voluntary association prevalence over and above (or instead of) the kinds of social structural factors reviewed.

As with so many dichotomies in the social sciences, both perspectives have some merit. On the whole the social structural factors do indeed conduce toward greater voluntary association prevalence, but they are also affected by historical and cultural peculiarities. In another place, Smith and Fisher (1971) attempt to illustrate how social structural, cultural, environmental, and individual factors can all combine in unique ways to have an impact on the incidence and prevalence of particular kinds of voluntary associations.

The last three chapters of Part One take up more specific aspects of the time/space variations in voluntary associations. For each of three types of voluntary associations, recent trends are examined. Naturally, these three chapters do not purport to cover all kinds of voluntary groups, nor all countries and time periods. In barely scratching the surface of the broad emerging subfield of the incidence-prevalence of voluntary action, we mean to suggest here simply that a tremendous amount of comparative research remains to be done for all kinds of voluntary groups in all countries and time periods. The three chapters included in this volume (5, 6, and 7), then, are illustrations of the kind of specific trend research on voluntary associations that has been rare until now, but that needs to become more frequent if we are to understand what is happening in this arena of activity.

In Chapter 5 Skjelsbaek describes and discusses various aspects of the growth of international voluntary associations in the twentieth century. He gives particular attention to the number of such organizations, the number of national representations in them, the scope and intensity of associational activity of this type, the interconnections among these groups, and their distribution by field of activity, by country, and through time in this century.

Not content just to give the facts of activity through time, Skjelsbaek goes on to discuss some causes of the development of international voluntary associations. His principal conclusions fit with those of Smith (Chapter 3) and Baldwin (Chapter 4). He sees the prevalence of these associations as being especially related to the level of technological and economic development of a nation, and also to the presence of a pluralistic ideology (part of Smith's factor of "collectivity orientation" or Baldwin's factor of "organizational density/collectivity experience"). Then, foreshadowing Part Two of this volume, Skjelsbaek considers briefly the impact of international or transnational voluntary associations upon world peace.

In Chapter 6 Peterson gives us an even more specific kind of trend analysis in the area of voluntary association prevalence. He focuses specifically on what has been happening to collegiate voluntary associations in the United States in the twentieth century. Lacking a substantial scholarly literature on the topic to review, Peterson, like Skjelsbaek, is mainly concerned with reporting data that he has accumulated especially for this chapter. Although data are often spotty and incomplete, he is still able to show rather clearly that the more expressive (interpersonal or honorific, directly gratifying, "end-in-itself") kind of collegiate voluntary association seems to be declining proportionately as of about 1960, while more instrumental (goal attaining, "means-to-an-end") kinds of collegiate voluntary action have been generally growing rapidly since about 1960 in the United States.

He also presents data to show the intense political voluntary activity in the 1960s by college students and their groups. He further suggests, following Riesman, that such collegiate political voluntary activity may be cyclical, with the 1930s as an earlier period of similar intense activity. Thus not all trends in voluntary association prevalence are toward simple increases over time. There are decreases in certain areas and possibly recurrent cyclical patterns that might allow us to predict the resurgence of certain kinds of voluntary activity (collegiate or otherwise) in future decades. We must have a great deal more research of the present kind, however, before any firm conclusions about such cycles will be warranted. At present these cycles must remain essentially hypotheses for further testing—intriguing possibilities rather than established facts.

Schmidt and Babchuk, in Chapter 7, discuss complementary trends for a different kind of U.S. voluntary group—the fraternal association. Fraternal associations, as they are referred to here, include all kinds of exclusive, adult (noncollegiate, nonyouth), social or expressive formal groups that emphasize solidarity, brotherhood (sisterhood), and mutual fellowship rather than any instrumental goals. Examples of this kind of group are the Elks, Masons, Moose, and so forth. Schmidt and Babchuk find that these kinds of groups, by and large, have been declining in relative importance and in numbers in the twentieth century, especially in the last few decades. This is consistent with the finding of Peterson (in Chapter 6) that collegiate voluntary associations of an expressive sort (especially fraternities and sororities) have gone into a proportional or relative decline during the past decade in the United States.

The fact that most of these United States fraternal orders were founded in the late nineteenth or early twentieth centuries makes it clear that we are looking at a kind of cycle here too. Schmidt and Babchuk argue that the growth of fraternal associations was associated with the relatively massive foreign immigration to the United States that took place in the growth period. They suggest that these groups played important functions such as the enhancing of social integration, conferring of prestige, provision of mutual benefits (aid, insurance, etc.), and practice of religion in American society. Yet these functions have gradually atrophied in the last few decades as a result of urbanization, increasing anonymity, secularization, organizational change, and other trends. Wherever fraternal associations are incapable of adapting to changing societal conditions by changing their goals and perspectives, these groups are likely to decline.

But this does not mean that expressive voluntary associations in general necessarily will decline. New forms of expressive associations may arise to take the place of older ones; or instrumental associations may tend to take on more expressive functions for their members. If more comprehensive research is performed on these kinds of trends in the future, we shall be better placed to settle such questions. And we shall also be better able to indicate whether and why fraternal associations or their equivalent might grow and flourish for a period in other cultures. Little (1965) has shown, for instance, that voluntary associations play an important role in helping immigrants from rural areas adjust to the urban milieu in West Africa. Perhaps some of the associations he has described are an African cultural equivalent of fraternal associations, meet similar needs, and will decline at some time in the future for similar reasons.

8

References

Little, Kenneth
1965 WEST AFRICAN URBANIZATION: A STUDY OF VOLUNTARY ASSOCIATIONS IN SOCIAL CHANGE. Cambridge, England: Cambridge University Press.
Smith, David Horton, with Allon Fisher
1971 "Toward a Comparative Theory of the Incidence-Prevalence of Voluntary Associations in Territorial Social Systems." Mimeo. Washington, D.C.: Center for a Voluntary Society.

1

Voluntary Associations in History: From Paleolithic to Present Times

Robert T. Anderson

Where societies today are experiencing rapid social change, formal voluntary associations typically are found. Yet associations have also been prominent in the past, not only in preindustrial nations such as those of Rome and medieval Europe, but equally in societies which were less complex politically and economically, including tribes on the American plains and communities in Oceania, parts of Africa, or along the Pacific coast of native North America. There is much we still need to know about voluntary associations. Even so, enough has been done, particularly in the last couple of decades, to allow some preliminary assessment of the place they have in the evolution of society.

Paleolithic-Mesolithic Bands

The history of formal common interest associations during the first million years or so of human existence lends itself to brief statement: there were virtually none.[1] We can say this with confidence, even though the evidence is what a court of law would term circumstantial. Because they normally lived in small bands scattered thinly across forests and plains, Paleolithic and Mesolithic men would not normally have formed groups on the basis of common interest rather than of territory or kinship.[2] Their needs could have been totally met as societies of small bands of related families roving circumscribed territories.

What we know of living hunters and foragers of a Mesolithic sort confirms this assumption. Walter Goldschmidt in dealing with the issue points out that, in a few instances, a kind of religious sodality may have cut across band and family ties, as in the totemic groups of some Australian aborigines today. Such groups, however, are rare (Goldschmidt 1959, pp. 155-56). It is true that where they do occur, they may constitute an important part of the social system. In the example of the native Australians, totemic group members have fundamental responsibilities in a complex of rituals believed necessary for the cyclical replenishment of game and plants.

This chapter was originally prepared for the seminar session on "Volunteer Action Theory and Research: Steps Toward Synthesis," as organized by David Horton Smith for the 65th Annual Meeting of the American Sociological Association in Washington, D.C., August 31-September 3, 1970. It was later published in the AMERICAN ANTHROPOLOGIST 73 (1971), and has been somewhat revised for inclusion here.

Totem groups also lubricate intertribal communication, since membership requires movement for ritual purposes (Elkin 1964, pp. 151-58). But normally among living nomadic hunters, social activities are individual, family, or band matters.

Although rare, the common interest associations of hunting nomads invariably unite individuals in terms of religious beliefs. This tie to religion provides an additional clue to the early history of sodalities. Inferences concerning the origins of religion become, by extension, inferences concerning the early history of common-interest associations and lead to a somewhat more refined reconstruction.

The expected tie to religion makes it extremely unlikely that sodalities existed in the lower Paleolithic period, when man apparently had not yet developed any kind of religious habits, or in the middle Paleolithic, when the earliest glimmerings of religion took shape in the archeological record, as purposeful but still crude burial customs. Not until well into the upper Paleolithic period in western Europe, when men first practiced art and used caves for rituals of uncertain nature, probably no earlier than 25,000 B.C., only then is it at all likely that the first primitive sodalities flickered into life. That possibility increases with the Mesolithic, though even then common interest groups must have been rare as Goldschmidt has argued.

The description Harold E. Driver gives of the Indians of North America reinforces this conclusion. He documents the absence of any kind of common interest groupings among most Arctic, sub-Arctic, Plateau, Great Basin, and Northeast Mexican peoples (Driver 1961, p. 406). Moreover, the unusual cases which do occur among these hunting and gathering societies are invariably in places closest to other areas from which such practices might have been borrowed. At least in part, the rare occurrences among living Mesolithic societies seem the result of diffusion from more advanced neighbors.

Not all Mesolithic societies have been nomadic. In a few favored places, natural food resources have been rich enough and localized enough to allow permanent villages, a form of settlement otherwise possible only with plant husbandry. In prehistoric Denmark, for example, the Ertebølle people were able to settle this way because they could exploit a bountiful resource of fish and crustaceans. From the shell mounds they piled up over generations of sedentary life, however, the archeologist finds no clue as to the presence or absence of sodalities.

We do have information about the social organization of recent and contemporary Mesolithic villages. Indians of the Northwest Pacific Coast, for example, established permanent settlements on the basis of enormous salmon runs, and the central California Indians lived in hamlets supported by a variety of wild foods, including a plentitude of acorns. These Indians, we know, had what Driver refers to as "relatively important sodalities" (Driver 1961, pp. 407-413).

Mischa Titiev indicates something of the importance these associations could have in a succinct statement about one of the Northwest Coast tribes. "During the summer season," he writes, "the social organization of the Kwakiutl was based on ties of descent that sorted the people into clans. In the winter months, however, there prevailed an entirely different grouping, which depended on membership in secret societies. Individuals from each clan had a number of these societies from which to choose. . . ." (Titiev 1963, pp. 465-66.) It appears, in sum, that circumstances at times allowed advanced hunting and gathering peoples to settle in villages. Such early, preagricultural villages probably organized some ritual activities as common interest associations. Such sodalities would expectably have been important in social functions and rich in cultural associations.

Neolithic Villages

Villages, and with them sodalities, are unusual among Mesolithic peoples. Villages are, however, customary among cultivators. And when such villages are not integrated into complex political and economic systems, they seem characteristically to sponsor the elaboration of sodalities. Certainly, horticultural villagers in native North America, Oceania, and Africa evolved fascinating varieties of common interest associations. It seems reasonable to conclude that prehistoric horticultural villagers often did the same. If that is so, the emergence and spread of the Neolithic may be taken as a rough chronicle of the first widespread elaboration and diffusion of common interest associations. For those who like their dates in years, this yields a rough beginning date between 7,000 and 8,000 B.C., when a few agricultural communities first appeared in the Middle East, but when associations still were not common. (Rare, early Mesolithic villages could not have been more than a few thousand years earlier than this. Ertebølle is much later.)

These rough calculations would place the widespread growth and diffusion of early sodalities in the millennia after 7,000 B.C., when the Neolithic diffused from centers in the Middle East, Southeast Asia and Mesoamerica to major parts of the inhabited earth. In the process, older Mesolithic societies were eradicated, absorbed or displaced, until they remained only as a diminished minority in marginal areas. The process has had no clear end. It lasted into our era. Neolithic settlers were still moving onto uninhabited islands in Oceania as recently as circa A.D. 1000, when the Maori moved to New Zealand. Even within the last century, cultivators have pushed into residual Mesolithic enclaves in many places, including South Africa, for example, where the Bushmen have been driven off all but the forbidding Kalahari Desert by neighboring Bantu peoples. In the same decades, of course, both Mesolithic and Neolithic societies have been threatened, transformed, or destroyed by urban-industrial intrusions, so the situation now is quite complex. What is clear is that villages, and presumably sodalities, became widespread phenomena.

Long ago, Robert H. Lowie drew attention to the importance of associations where they occur. "Sex moieties, divisions on the basis of matrimonial status, social clubs, secret fraternities, all crisscross the bonds of the family and sib, creating new units of incalcuable significance for the individual's social existence" (Lowie 1947, p. 296). Lowie really meant it when he described their significance as incalculable. He could find no common characteristics beyond the fact that they all excluded nonmembers (Lowie 1947, p. 336). For a generation anthropologists shared this point of view. Research, as a result, was limited largely to acquiring more descriptions of specific cases and to attempting cautious historical reconstructions of a very limited sort.

Lowie himself provided a thorough description of Crow sodalities (Lowie 1935). He also compared the associations of numerous Indian tribes to hypothesize that at least on the Plains age societies were a local and late development out of simpler antecedents (Lowie 1947, p. 334). Others contributed studies of associations in other parts of the world, so that when Lowie wrote a new book on social organization a quarter of a century after his first one, he could draw on a greatly enlarged reservoir of descriptive reports. Yet even then, he could find no satisfactory way to generalize about the place of associations in social organization. "Since sodalities represent a congeries of diverse associations set off by negative rather than positive criteria, they defy logical classification," he concluded (Lowie 1948, p. 295).

Following the work of Lowie and the stimulus he gave to such studies, the effort to comprehend the character of associations has turned for some to an evolutionary perspective, which stresses the role of common interest associations in societies at a certain stage of development.

Elman Service, working in terms of a progressive sequence of band, tribe, chiefdom, primitive state, and archaic civilization, observes that sodalities have been reported for some bands, although it is rare; that they occur commonly at the tribal level; and above that level they are found in increasing variety. Above all, he sees sodalities as most significant at the tribal level. At that stage they are more numerous, larger, and more socially significant than among bands, where they are rare; yet they are not supplemented by other integrative institutions as in chiefdoms and states. Particularly in achieving some degree of pantribal solidarity, they may perform essential institutional functions (Service 1963, pp. xxi-xxiii).

Walter Goldschmidt, who also works in terms of an evolutionary model, was perhaps the first to insist that sodalities became increasingly important in that *middle range* of societies which more or less corresponds to the tribal level or the Neolithic Era. In particular, speaking of the surviving examples of societies in Melanesia, Africa, and North America, but referring as well to the noncultivating villagers of central California and the Northwest Pacific Coast, his attempt to generalize shows we have not gotten much beyond the work of Lowie in our comprehension of the role of sodalities in such communities.

There is always a magico-religious aspect to such groups. They are characterized by ritual induction or initiations, by secret rites and ceremonies, and by a system of mythological justification. Often they also have a power function, uniting the senior men, the adults, or some especially selected group against the women and children or all outsiders. Occasionally there are countervailing women's organizations. (Goldschmidt 1959, p. 156.)

The secret societies which occur in some communities have particularly intrigued many investigators, even though E.D. Chapple and C.S. Coon years ago argued that categorizing associations as secret was of little value. They argued that secrecy, defined as "the enforced isolation of the members of an institution during some or all periods of their interaction as members of the system," occurs to some extent in every institution, and is therefore not "diagnostic of associations." Families and nations also have secrets (Chapple and Coon 1942, pp. 442-43.) Even so, sodalities in some social systems—particularly in many of those of West Africa, Melanesia, and North America—do stand out for the extremes to which they emphasize, formalize, and build upon secrecy in carrying out their activities.

Kenneth Little, in a survey of West African examples, finds secret societies highly effective as guardians of tradition. Through them, the larger society may educate its young, train its warriors, regulate sexual conduct, perform religious rituals, and supervise political and economic affairs. Such associations may also provide important social services, including medical treatment, entertainment and recreation (Little 1949). Discussing the highly secretive Poro Society as it occurs among the Kpelle of Liberia, James L. Gibbs, Jr. particularly noted political functions. He describes judicial activities, for example. The fraternity could punish tribesmen for incest, arson, or other delict. Further, the group assumes administrative prerogatives. "Several bits of field data confirm the view," he concludes, "that political power and Poro power tend to be lodged in the hands of the same individuals, and it is not unlikely that chiefs utilize Poro mechanisms to underscore their political decisions. By 'putting the country under Poro oath' all of the men of a given area can, under penalty of Poro sanctions, be required to carry out a specific action or abstain from one...." (Gibbs 1965, pp. 219-21.)

The fact that other institutions normally maintain secrecy about some of their activities, and the fact that nonsecret associations may duplicate, in a general way, any of the functions achieved by a secret organization, does not diminish the significance secrecy has when it is explicitly built upon to turn sodalities into effective social agencies. However diverse in their particular functions, such associations share a distinguishing characteristic. "As a rule secrecy is employed for more effective control over nonmembers and the uninitiated or for more stringent maintenance of the internal solidarity of the group of individuals who have discovered or built up common interests" (Miller 1934, p. 621). To this extent, at least, a cross-cultural category of secret societies has value for comparative analysis.

In a similar way, age-sets (associations which generally group individuals by sex as well as by age) constitute a category with particular potentialities in social organization. In many African societies especially, age-sets have been found to have social and political functions that crosscut or complement the generally more pervasive functions of lineage and clan. Among the Nandi (Huntingford, 1960) and the Nuer (Evans-Pritchard 1940), men separated by lineage loyalties are united by age-set sentiments and commitments, an arrangement which tends to reduce factionalism in the tribe. Among the Nyakyusa, Monica Wilson found that age superseded kinship as the most important organizational principle. A new local community there is established when land is allocated to a group of young men and their wives. Since the villagers are diverse in their kin relationships, the initial bond of solidarity is membership in a single age grouping. In this way, age-mates create something sufficiently unique to merit the special term, age-villages (Wilson 1963).

Sodalities in the middle range of societal evolution, in short, have important social and cultural functions. Efforts to generalize about them, however, have not yet yielded very impressive results. We have not yet cracked the nut on which Lowie worked. The best we can do is to characterize them broadly and note regularities limited to particular parts of the world or to particular associational mechanisms such as secrecy or age alignment. Lowie did as much half a century ago.

Preindustrial States

The next period in the history of associations is one in which the place of this institution in social behavior was important, yet very different from what it had been. The centuries around 3,000 B.C. may be taken to approximate inauguration of this new phase. In Mesopotamia and Egypt at that time, the first Bronze Age cities were built. In subsequent millennia, early towns emerged in India, China, Mesoamerica, and Africa. With the passage of time, cities, nations, and empires appeared in various parts of the world. While some were growing to moments of greatness, others declined to extinction or had not yet begun their historic venture. With time, too, technological and political complexity progressed, so that early towns seem small and simple in later comparison.

The history of early cities and states is an historical maze. Yet many analysts encapsulate it as a single unit for sociocultural study, the period or the category of preindustrial cities or states (Sjoberg 1960). Among anthropologists, in spite of its ambiguities, the contrast of preindustrial with industrial, of traditional with modern, has been a widely accepted strategem of analysis (Foster 1953B, p. 163).

As we have seen, very few regularities have been defined for associations in societies of a Neolithic sort. Nearly none are proposed for those of the preindustrial urban world. We get merely descriptions: the *collegium* or *sodalitas* of Rome (Brinton 1930), the merchant association of Greece and Egypt, or the guild of the Middle Ages in Europe (Nicoló 1932). And even these provide only a distorted picture, since they usually say nothing of those great orphans of history, the peasantry and the proletariat. Where records survive, they generally are silent about sodalities in the higher classes. Only rarely do they give evidence that associations existed among plebeians and rustics.

What we do know of associations in preindustrial states is not quite what unexamined assumptions about steady evolutionary progress might lead one to expect (see Banton 1968, p. 358; Goldschmidt 1959, pp. 156-57). Even though voluntary associations were prominent in the Neolithic, and even though they have become prominent in recent, postindustrial societies, they were often restricted or absent in major parts of stratified, urban societies of the preindustrial sort. Put differently, between the crests of association development in Neolithic communities and modern industrial nations lies a trough of quiescence, when the importance of associations was comparatively reduced.

Paucity of the historical record allows one only to illustrate rather than systematically to sample the place of associations in traditional nations. We may note that in China merchants formed guilds. But the highest and lowest classes seem largely devoid of sodalities until nineteenth-century political chaos and incipient modernization led villagers to form shared interest associations on a scale unknown to them before.[3] Ancient Rome had more association activity than most preindustrial states. In addition to merchant guilds, many Romans belonged to the congregations of religious cults or to clublike groups. Peasants may have remained largely untouched by such movements, however. In Traditional Europe, guilds epitomized the potentialities of common interest groups. Clubs did appear, but they were late and matured as concomitants of emergent industrialization involving mainly the upper and middle classes. Peasants rarely formed voluntary associations of any kind (Anderson 1970 passim; Boak 1932; Brinton 1930, p. 574; Lowie 1948, pp. 295, 307, 312-13; Nicoló 1932, p. 206; Sjoberg 1960, pp. 187-96).

From such a sampling of the historical record, we illustrate a tentative generalization: in traditional civilizations from ancient Ur to recent Europe and China, sodalities were confined mainly to the merchant class. Peasants and the elite generally organized solely in terms of territory and kinship.

Perhaps because sodalities were prominent in Rome, which greatly influences our thinking about classic society; perhaps because merchant guilds, which greatly influence our thinking about the Middle Ages, seem typically to have enlivened European city life with their activities; and perhaps merely because the record so neglects peasant villages where sodalities were rare, one of the most intriguing questions about the history of voluntary associations is itself generally neglected. Why did the elaborate associational traditions of the Neolithic decline so thoroughly?

With the growth of states, sodalities in villages seem typically to have become extinct or not to have developed (Hamer 1967, pp. 89-91). As foci of political power, including a degree of pantribal influence, their very success in the Neolithic no doubt doomed them. The state imposed its own authority in their place. Other institutions took up surviving functions. The state itself regulated part of village life. Various kinds of family and village structures organized the rest (Wolf 1966, pp. 60-95; Foster 1965, pp. 301-2). In some areas, loose associations met special needs, as in formalized but usually impermanent or semipermanent harvesting associations found in many parts of the world. But peasants typically restricted their associational commitments to mutual aid. "There must be a limit," Wolf argues, in making such observations, "to the degree to which one's own resources can become committed to those of a neighbor, lest one be dragged down by his potential failure" (Wolf 1966, p. 80).

Consistent with his own observations, the mutual-aid clubs, parent-burial associations, sugar-making groups, irrigation societies, and crop-watching societies which Wolf refers to for Chinese villages must be regarded as exceptional rather than typical (Wolf 1966, p. 83; see note 3). They were probably the product in China, for the most part, of deterioration of the state apparatus, a partial return, in other words, toward a more pristine condition, even though the form such sodalities took may have reflected early industrial influence. In a similar way, the prominence of formal voluntary associations in colonial Bali (Geertz, 1959) was associated with freedom from heavy-handed state control. The island, in its remoteness, was a buffer against total erosion of the Neolithic condition. Certainly, however, where the state permits, where circumstances require, and where traditions encourage, sodality formation may take place among peasants (Hamer 1967, pp. 89-91). Villages in Spain and Latin America provide a cogent example, since they support religious brotherhoods of greater or lesser social significance (Foster 1953A). Many though not all villages in Tokugawa, Japan had sodalities in the form of age grades, shrine associations, and cooperative groups (Befu 1965, p. 30; Norbeck, 1962, pp. 74-75). Other examples could be cited.

The failure of sodalities normally to materialize within the ruling class is equally as impressive as their failure generally to survive or emerge in peasant villages. The reduced size of the elite population is undoubtedly the critical feature here as with simple bands of hunters. The ruling class in an agrarian nation is normally small enough to constitute a face-to-face society. Aristocrats typically coagulate into lineages, while the personal contacts of such individuals and their kinsmen provide all the necessary larger networks of social interaction. Sodalities would be superfluous. Where common interest does appear as a basis for union, it takes place as loose, more or less ephemeral groupings. The entourage of Eleanor of Aquitaine was no more, really, than a peripetetic cluster of courtiers (Kelly 1950, pp. 198-212, passim).

Preindustrial merchants seem led toward the creation of sodalities just as firmly as others seem led away from them (Sjoberg 1960, pp. 188-89). Their population size was not necessarily great (Sjoberg 1960, pp. 36-37). Mere density of population did not lead to their growth. Nor did they appear merely because kinship ties were too inchoate. In Europe family ties often were weak (Lopez 1952, pp. 268, 295-6). But in parts of Africa, guilds have replaced well-developed lineage structures among urban craftsmen (Lloyd 1953). Guilds seem, above all, a response to the need for those with a shared interest in a craft or occupation to unite for economic and political power (Sjoberg 1960, p. 190). Certainly the need for power was important in the growth of guilds in medieval Europe. While aristocrats controlled government in larger ways, merchant sodalities claimed smaller realms of commerce, small sovereignties within towns. Often they claimed the towns themselves, in which cases guild organization became town government (Carus-Wilson 1952, pp. 368-69, 373-74, 383-86; Jones 1952, pp. 510-18; Lopez 1952, p. 295; Mumford 1961, pp. 269-73; Painter 1951, pp. 79-84). In other parts of the world, too, merchant guilds seem more than all else a response to the need for power (Morse 1966, pp. 2-3; Miner 1965, pp. 53-60). Only through a heightened degree of self-government could merchants maintain the freedom of movement and of industry which was essential to their success, and guilds gave them that self-government (Painter 1951, pp. 71-73).

Preindustrial states, in brief, typically supported a considerable elaboration of associations within the merchant community. But among aristocrats and peasants the institution was rare. Merchants and artisans comprised only a small part of the state as a whole. Perhaps 90 percent of the total population of such nations had no personal involvement in voluntary associations of any kind.

Industrial Nations

Modern urban-industrial growth is a worldwide phenomenon, although it first took shape in Europe and North America. Where it took place in the West, it was correlated with a new, wider development of voluntary associations (Rose 1958, passim). As permitted by the government—and often the government outlawed or limited them (Rose 1958, passim)—associations proliferated at all levels of society. The new working class joined or imitated older artisans in establishing unions. The expanded elite, its rank swelled by industrialists and businessmen, founded clubs and action groups. Cooperative associations and other sodalities spread into villages. New involvement in urban-industrial society seemed to bring with it a new need to create institutions on an intermediate level, larger than the family, yet smaller than the state (Sills 1968, pp. 373-74). A new phase in the history of voluntary associations was inaugurated.

As a prominent feature of transformed voluntary associations, their mode of operation changed. Subsequent to the evolution of democratic and bureaucratic techniques in government, and related to it, sodalities have shifted to electoral and bureaucratic norms and procedures. This new quality of associations may be characterized as rational-legal (Anderson and Anderson 1965, pp. 9-12). A rational-legal association possesses written statutes clearly defining the membership, participant obligations, leadership roles and conditions of convocation. It normally possesses a legally recognized corporate identity. It is rational in the sense that, as a body, it is geared to efficiency in making decisions and taking action, particularly as leaders are—in principle at least—impartially chosen by election of the most qualified to take office. It is legal in the sense that compliance in decisions and actions is sanctioned by the impersonal force of law. In all these ways, a rational-legal association represents a new kind of sodality. As the industrial revolution spread throughout the world to towns and cities as well as into rural communities in urban hinterlands, new social forms spread too, including the new type of voluntary assocation. Rational-legal associations are now found in every part of the globe, especially in cities, but also in many rural areas (Sills 1959; Norbeck 1961, p. 312).

What place do rational-legal associations occupy in the scheme of things? David L. Sills has pointed out how difficult it is to decide in any complete way what the social and individual benefits of voluntary associations may be (Sills 1968, pp. 372-76). Here, as elsewhere, we fall very much short of our target as we look for regularities. Yet a few can be identified. They concern the capacity associations have to facilitate the transition of individuals and societies to participation in the modern world (see Smith 1966).

It should be stressed immediately that rational-legal associations may be established in a traditional community in advance of substantive incorporation of that community into the new international milieu. When that occurs, whether it is in cities or in villages, the new type of association apparently does not introduce significant change in the social organization of the adopters (Anderson and Anderson 1962, p. 161). Quite the contrary, the intrusive sodalities seem to adapt to traditional norms. To do this the association typically retains its formal structure based on written statutes, but functions informally in terms of traditional modes of interaction. This was true, for example, of some voluntary associations established as recently as the early 1960s in Hyderabad, a city in India which has only since then wrenched substantially away from preindustrial anachronisms (Anderson 1964, p. 180). It seems equally true of rational-legal associations established in Sicily in the last couple of decades (Levi 1958, pp. 180-87; LaPalombara 1957, p. 42).

It appears that modern associations not only do not in themselves introduce rational-legal modes of interaction to a traditional society, they may actually enhance the integrity of traditional social institutions. In numerous parts of Europe, voluntary associations are found to reinforce social stratification at the village level by restricting membership to individuals from a given stratum. Where this occurs, the practice symbolizes in a new way the persistence of customary strata. It also enhances the capacity of a socioeconomic stratum to function as a representative, action-taking body within the community (Anderson and Anderson 1965, pp. 287-89). Far from modernizing traditional communities, rational-legal associations by themselves seem to actually enhance the capacity of old communities to persist structurally intact.

Something similar may be said for cities. Voluntary associations may play a special role for migrants. Often they allow villagers to recreate in a distant, urban milieu something of the traditional society to which they were accustomed. Tribal associations in West Africa often function this way. Speaking of urbanization in that part of the world, Kenneth Little notes, " of all the societies organized by migrants, voluntary associations of fellow tribesmen are often the most common." He goes on to give an example. "Ibos in Lagos in the present day belong to 'meetings' which correspond roughly with the basic social units at home—village, village group, and clan" (Little 1965, p. 26). Migrants transplant, in this way, traditional institutions to foreign soil. While Claude Meillassoux finds the village association only very loosely organized in Bamako, a town in Mali, he does argue that such a group "is the prolongation into the city of village life and loyalties" (Meillassoux 1968, p. 78). The process is undoubtedly worldwide. Peasant Ukrainians who had migrated to towns and cities in France, for example, transplanted village customs as the activities of multipurpose associations in the host country (Anderson and Anderson 1962, pp. 162, 167-68). Michael Kenny found twentieth-century Spaniards in Mexico City organized into formal voluntary associations which apparently help expatriates maintain their "ethnic identity" (Kenny 1962, p. 174).

Michael Banton and David L. Sills each have stressed the social integrative functions of urban associations (Banton 1968, p. 361; Sills 1968, p. 373). Banton in particular found in Freetown, Sierra Leone, that such groups meet a need for social control. By rewarding approved behavior and withholding approval or punishing that which is not approved, they dampen immorality, delinquency, and crime (Banton 1957). An important function of voluntary associations in cities, in fact, is their capacity at times to maintain a stable base for traditionalists resident in a nontraditional milieu.

Where fundamental economic and demographic changes are occurring, on the other hand, the new modernity apparently gains momentum with the help of rational-legal associations. Sometimes the new associations seem founded to meet needs not obviously the responsibility of any older organization. Chapple and Coon see this as a dominant characteristic. "It must be remembered that, whatever the other characteristics of an association, it is always formed at the point of tangency of several institutions, or of subsystems within an institution" (Chapple and Coon 1942, p. 418). A parent-teacher association, to illustrate, joins individuals from the family with others from the school, each otherwise members of separate groups. In a comparable way, the Alaska Native Brotherhood may be said to unite clans and tribes in a new union in North America

(Drucker 1958, pp. 73-74, 103-107), and the Kenya African Union welded divergent tribes together in colonial East Africa (Leakey 1952, p. 93).

Although some associations do form on the tangents of established groupings, other bases for organization also occur. Under urban influence, the association may unite in ways not obviously related to older alignments. Edward Norbeck notes the growth of common interest groups in Japan to organize activities in villages in which real and fictive kinship had atrophied (Norbeck 1962, p. 81). In Bamako some associations group "on the sole basis of Western values: money, education, and status seeking." The older family class and tribal ties of Mali are ignored (Meillassoux 1968, p. 145).

Often associations are neither tangential to other groups nor independent of them, but rather reorganize or duplicate old institutions to give them a new rational-legal structure. In this way, traditional institutions remain viable in a changed society. The process may take the form of a reorganization of the old groups. S.D. Gamble reports that in eleven Chinese communities before 1933 the trend was for cooperative groups to evolve "from the informal to the formal and from the customary to the legal basis" (Gamble 1963, pp. 33-42). In India the modern success of the Ramakrishna Monastery is correlated with its formal reorganization as a rational-legal association consciously patterned on Western models. The old monastic structure was submerged in the new (Gambhirananda 1957). Some castes have done the same, coopting hereditary leaders into the new structure by electing them to newly defined offices.

In many places, a traditionally organized group persists along side of a new rational-legal association with substantially the same membership. Many castes retain a traditional structure, but add to it a new caste association, its officers sometimes vying with the hereditary leadership, sometimes cooperating with it (Anderson 1963). In France the capacity of the family to survive is enhanced by the effectiveness of family associations which supplement but certainly do not replace the traditional entities (Anderson and Anderson 1965, pp. 213-16). Tribes in East Africa organize for contemporary purposes in a similar way (Beidelman 1970. See also Banton 1956); so have secret societies in West Africa (Ruel 1964). According to Edward Norbeck, age grades in Japan have become youth associations in recent years (Norbeck 1953, pp. 376, 382). Kenneth Little reports that some clans in West Africa remain meaningful for migrants as modern clan associations are established in towns and cities. In the city, "a person can no longer go to a fellow clansman in the expectation of receiving help automatically in the way it was given in the past," Little observes. "The urban version of a clan, therefore, has a new hierarchy of officers and a new set of duties and privileges which are limited to registered members" (Little 1965, pp. 31-32). The establishment of rational-legal associations in cases like these apparently provides the means of adapting for modern success groups otherwise held together by traditional loyalties and obligations. It is a recurrent phenomenon which merits further study.

Part of the versatility of voluntary associations in urban-industrial circum-stances is the training function they have for individuals not yet accustomed to modern role-playing. It seems particularly true for individuals of tribal or peasant background. The Alaska Native Brotherhood socialized Indians to techniques necessary for success under American rule (Drucker 1958, pp. 17-18). Philip Drucker notes that "there seems to have been a deliberate attempt to create a large number of offices in order to give as many people as possible the opportunity of getting experience in the business of the organization" (Drucker 1958, pp. 23-24; see Banton 1956, p. 366). Similarly in parts of Africa, participation in voluntary associations trains individuals in skills they can apply more widely in city life (Hamer 1967, pp. 84-86; Little 1965, pp. 103-117). In some cases, the capacity of the association to train may be enhanced as it merges traditional with modern activities (Anderson 1966, p. 339). As Kenneth Little has observed, "by continuing such familiar norms as kinship, the provision of proper burial rites, etc., the associations make the innovations seem less strange. They build for the migrant a cultural bridge and in so doing they convey him from one kind of social universe to another" (Little 1965, p. 87).

The educational potentiality of voluntary associations must not be exagger-ated, however. In some cases, participation seems to follow rather than precede socialization of the individual to new norms. Perhaps in most cases, education only extends a process already underway, so that it constitutes a secondary, but not a primary training ground. Participation in Rotating Credit Associations in India, it has been argued, build on neither traditional nor modern norms, and fail therefore to teach villagers and urban migrants how to participate in commercial encounters, since traditional individuals unite in terms of older, noncommercial sanctions (Anderson 1966, p. 339). The social clubs of Bamaka, to give another example, seem capable of polishing an individual's fluency in French and his effectiveness in urban activities. But recruitment requires a high degree of polish and effectiveness in the first place, so that the training function is additive rather than fundamental (Meillassoux 1968, pp. 138-39). Many nineteenth-century Danish peasants got their first real lessons in modern involvement from joining a cooperative society. Yet is notable that the leaders of cooperative associations typically were already transformed as individuals through earlier education in folk high schools, through participation in religious revivals, and through involvement in political democracy (Rørdam 1965, p. 155). Associations, in short, may provide the primary educational experience for some individuals, but for a population as a whole they apparently require reinforcement from other institutions.

In urban-industrial nations, voluntary associations acquire new, highly impor-tant functions. They contribute to the stability of modern societies by providing social units intermediate between the individual and the community. They seem especially effective as institutions supportive of social change. Yet voluntary associations are vehicles of change, not motors of change. They function to adapt the social structure for modern requirements. They function to adapt individuals for modern participation. But they do not create a new social structure in a traditional society, and they do not socialize an individual when broader circumstances are not favorable. "Voluntary associations, therefore, seem like bubbles rising and disappearing on the surface of boiling water. It is from deeper sources that the people who stir them find their motivation, and it is at more signifcant levels that we must try to explain a society . . ." (Meillassoux 1968, p. 147).

Summary

From a survey of anthropological, historical, and sociological research, tentative generalizations about the history of formal voluntary associations can be made. The studies reviewed generally offer qualitative rather than quantitative assessments. They are good or adequate for many parts of the contemporary world, but are inadequate and incomplete for historical periods.

Early men, dependent upon hunting and gathering, and organized into simple bands, did not normally establish FVOs (formal voluntary organizations or voluntary associations). A few exceptions have been noted. (Strength and direction of relationship: strong; consistency: very high.)

Late in the history of man, when he became a food producer and thus entered the Neolithic stage, FVOs became well developed. Generalizations are still not wholly satisfactory, although FVOs have been found to serve as integrating mechanisms for the society as a whole, as institutions for socialization of the young, and as moral arbiters. (Strength and direction of relationship: moderate; consistency: high.)

With the emergence in recent millennia of preindustrial complex societies in which urban and rural as well as class differences are prominent, the place of FVOs in the social structure changed. They became relatively unimportant for villagers and the dominant elite. In contrast, however, they were important for members of the burgher class. (Strength and direction: moderate; consistency: medium.)

In modern or modernizing nations in which urbanization and industrialism are significant, FVOs tend to become prevalent again. Norms of membership participation changed, however, to become rational-legal in character. Rational-legal associations may be established in traditional village communities, but in themselves, they do not introduce new norms for social interaction. On the contrary, they may actually enhance the viability of the traditional social order. Similarly in cities, they may allow members to maintain traditional norms in a modern urban context. (Strength and direction: very strong; consistency: strong.)

Where fundamental economic and demographic changes are occurring, however, FVOs facilitate adjustment. They are capable of uniting people in ways different from those of traditional institutions. They become mechanisms for adapting traditional kinds of groups for viability in modern circumstances, either as older groups redefine themselves as rational-legal associations, or as the membership establishes coexisting rational-legal associations. FVOs also facilitate modern adjustment by serving as training institutions for mobile individuals. (Strength and direction: strong; consistency: very high.)

Notes

1. For a summary of earlier speculation on the history of voluntary associations, see Lowie 1948, pp. 309-312. For a brief statement on the principles of evolutionary reconstruction, see Service 1962, pp. 3-10, or Service 1963, pp. xvi-xx.

2. For comparative analysis, a very broad definition of voluntary association is required. In this essay, the term "voluntary associations" and its synonyms, including the term "sodality," are taken to refer to formally constituted groups bound primarily by ties of shared interest rather than kinship or coresidence (see Lowie 1948, p. 14; Sills 1968, pp. 362-63; Anderson 1964, pp. 175-76).

3. As concerns the upper class, Cheng Ch'eng-K'un stresses the extent to which the large family, more typical of the gentry than of the peasantry, "was self-contained, self-disciplined, self-perpetuating, and self-sufficient. It fulfilled almost all the functions of an organized society. . . ." (Cheng 1953, p. 85.) With families of this sort, the gentry had little need to establish sodalities. This assumption is borne out in accounts of gentry life, which are notable for not attaching importance to associations (see Yee 1963; Fei 1953).

As concerns the peasantry, Daniel H. Kulp, II describes several kinds of sodality found in South Chinese villages (Kulp 1953, pp. 119-122). Only the Parent Burial Association is said by him to be old, otherwise antiquity is not indicated. It is notable that twentieth-century traditional villages in both the south and the north have been described, in at least four instances, with no indication that voluntary associations were present or more than a rather insignificant part of the social structure (Fei 1946; Hsu 1949; Osgood 1963; Yang 1945).

For a description of merchant associations see Morse 1966. For a view less polemic than mine of voluntary associations in China, see Freedman 1958, pp. 92-95. Note also, Gamble 1963, pp. 33-42.

References

Anderson, Robert T.
1963 "Preliminary Report on the Associational Redefinition of Castes in Hyderabad-Secunderabad." KROEBER ANTHROPOLOGICAL SOCIETY PAPERS, no. 29: 25-42.

1964 "Voluntary Associations in Hyderabad." ANTHROPOLOGICAL QUAR-
TERLY 37, no. 4: 175-190.

1966 "Rotating Credit Associations in India." ECONOMIC DEVELOPMENT
AND CULTURAL CHANGE 14, no. 3: 334-339.

1970 TRADITIONAL EUROPE: A STUDY IN ANTHROPOLOGY AND
HISTORY. Belmont, California: Wadsworth Publishing Co.

Anderson, Robert T. and Barbara Gallatin Anderson

1962 "Voluntary Associations Among Ukrainians in France." ANTHRO-
POLOGICAL QUARTERLY 35, no. 4: 158-168.

1965 BUS STOP FOR PARIS: THE TRANSFORMATION OF A FRENCH
VILLAGE. New York: Doubleday.

Banton, Michael

1956 "Adaptation and Integration in the Social System of Temne Immigrants
in Freetown." AFRICA 26, no. 4: 354-367.

1957 WEST AFRICAN CITY: A STUDY OF TRIBAL LIFE IN FREETOWN.
London: Oxford University Press.

1968 "Voluntary Associations. I. Anthropological Aspects." In INTERNA-
TIONAL ENCYCLOPEDIA OF THE SOCIAL SCIENCES, edited by
David L. Sills, vol. 16. New York: Macmillan and Free Press.

Befu, Harumi

1965 "Village Autonomy and Articulation with the State: The Case of
Tokugawa Japan." JOURNAL OF ASIAN STUDIES 25, no. 1: 19-32.

Beidelman, Thomas O.

1970 "Umwano and Ukaguru Students' Association: Two Tribalistic Move-
ments in a Tanganyika Chiefdom." John Middleton, ed., BLACK
AFRICA: ITS PEOPLES AND THEIR CULTURES TODAY. New York:
Macmillan.

Boak, A.E.R.

1932 "Late Roman and Byzantine Guilds." ENCYCLOPEDIA OF THE
SOCIAL SCIENCES, Edwin R. Seligman, editor in chief, vol. 7. London:
Macmillan.

Brinton, Crane

1930 "Clubs." ENCYCLOPEDIA OF THE SOCIAL SCIENCES, Edwin R.
Seligman, editor in chief, vol. 3. London: Macmillan.

Carus-Wilson, Eleanora

1952 "The Woolen Industry." THE CAMBRIDGE ECONOMIC HISTORY OF
EUROPE, edited by M. Postan and E.E. Rich, vol. II. Cambridge:
Cambridge University Press.

Chapple, Eliot Dismore and Carleton Stevens Coon

1942 PRINCIPLES OF ANTHROPOLOGY. New York: Henry Holt and Co.

Cheng Ch'eng-k'un

1953 "Familism the Foundation of Chinese Social Organization." Irwin T.
Sanders, et al., eds., SOCIETIES AROUND THE WORLD, vol. 2, New
York: Dryden Press. (First Published, 1944.)

Driver, Harold E.
1961   INDIANS OF NORTH AMERICA. Chicago & London: University of
       Chicago Press.
Drucker, Philip
1958   THE NATIVE BROTHERHOODS: MODERN INTERTRIBAL ORGAN-
       IZATIONS ON THE NORTHWEST COAST. Bulletin 168. Smithsonian
       Institution. Bureau of American Ethnology. Washington, D.C.: Govern-
       ment Printing Office.
Elkin, A.P.
1964   THE AUSTRALIAN ABORIGINES. Anchor Books. Garden City, New
       York: Doubleday and Co. (Originally published, 1938.)
Evans-Pritchard, E.E.
1940   THE NUER: A DESCRIPTION OF THE MODES OF LIVELIHOOD
       AND POLITICAL INSTITUTIONS OF A NILOTIC PEOPLE. Oxford:
       Clarendon Press.
Fei Hsiao-t'ung
1946   PEASANT LIFE IN CHINA: A FIELD STUDY OF COUNTRY LIFE IN
       THE YANGTZE VALLEY. New York: Oxford University Press.

1953   CHINA'S GENTRY: ESSAYS ON RURAL-URBAN RELATIONS. Chi-
       cago & London: University of Chicago Press.
Foster, George M.
1953a "Cofradia and Compadrazgo in Spain and Spanish America." SOUTH-
       WESTERN JOURNAL OF ANTHROPOLOGY 9, no. 1: 1-28.
1953b "What is Folk Culture?" AMERICAN ANTHROPOLOGIST 55, no. 2:
       159-171.
1965   "Peasant Society and the Image of the Limited Good." AMERICAN
       ANTHROPOLOGIST 67, no. 2: 293-315.
Freedman, Maurice
1958   LINEAGE ORGANIZATION IN SOUTHEASTERN CHINA. London
       School of Economics Monographs on Social Anthropology, no. 18.
       London: Athlone Press.
Gambhirananda, Swami
1957   HISTORY OF THE RAMAKRISHNA MATH AND MISSION. Calcutta:
       Advaita Ashrama.
Gamble, S.D.
1963   NORTH CHINA VILLAGES: SOCIAL, POLITICAL AND ECONOMIC
       ACTIVITIES BEFORE 1933. Berkeley, University of California Press.
Geertz, Clifford
1959   "Form and Variation in Balinese Village Structure." AMERICAN AN-
       THROPOLOGIST 61, no. 6: 991-1000.
Gibbs, James L., Jr.
1965   "The Kpelle of Liberia." In PEOPLES OF AFRICA. Edited by James L.
       Gibbs, Jr. New York: Holt, Rinehart and Winston, Inc.

Goldschmidt, Walter
1959   MAN'S WAY: A PREFACE TO THE UNDERSTANDING OF HUMAN SOCIETY. New York: Henry Holt and Co.

Hamer, John H.
1967   "Voluntary Associations as Structures of Change among the Sidamo of Southwestern Ethiopia." ANTHROPOLOGICAL QUARTERLY 40, no. 2: 73-91.

Hsu, Francis L.K.
1949   UNDER THE ANCESTORS' SHADOW: CHINESE CULTURE AND PERSONALITY. London: Routledge and Kegan Paul.

Huntingford, G.W.B.
1960   "Nandi Age-Sets." Simon and Phoebe Ottenberg, eds., CULTURES AND SOCIETIES OF AFRICA, New York: Random House. (First published, 1953.)

Jones, Gwilym Peredur
1952   "Building in Stone in Medieval Western Europe." THE CAMBRIDGE ECONOMIC HISTORY OF EUROPE edited by M. Postan and E.E. Rich, vol. II. Cambridge: Cambridge University Press.

Kelly, Amy
1950   ELEANOR OF AQUITAINE AND THE FOUR KINGS. Vintage Books. New York: Random House.

Kenny, Michael
1962   "Twentieth Century Spain Expatriates in Mexico: An Urban Sub-Culture." ANTHROPOLOGICAL QUARTERLY 35, no. 4: 169-180.

Kulp, Daniel H., II.
1953   "Village Associations." SOCIETIES AROUND THE WORLD, vol. 2, edited by Irwin T. Sanders, et al., New York: Dryden Press. (First published, 1925.)

LaPalombara, Joseph
1957   THE ITALIAN LABOR MOVEMENT: PROBLEMS AND PROSPECTS. Ithaca: Cornell University Press.

Leakey, L.S.B.
1952   MAU MAU AND THE KIKUYU. London: Methuen and Company.

Levi, Carlo
1958   WORDS ARE STONES. IMPRESSIONS OF SICILY. Angus Davidson, tr. New York: Farrar, Straus and Co.

Little, Kenneth
1949   "The Role of the Secret Society in Cultural Specialization." AMERICAN ANTHROPOLOGIST 51, no. 2: 199-212.

1965   WEST AFRICAN URBANIZATION: A STUDY OF VOLUNTARY ASSOCIATIONS IN SOCIAL CHANGE. London: Cambridge University Press.

Lloyd, Peter C.
1953   "Craft Organizations in Yoruba Towns." AFRICA 23, no. 1: 30-44.
Lopez, Robert B.
1952   "The Trade of Medieval Europe: The South." THE CAMBRIDGE
        ECONOMIC HISTORY OF EUROPE, edited by M. Postan and E.E.
        Rich, vol. II. Cambridge: Cambridge University Press.
Lowie, Robert H.
1935   THE CROW INDIANS. New York: Farrar and Rinehart, Inc.
1947   PRIMITIVE SOCIETY, New York: Liveright Publishing Corporation.
        (First published, 1920.)
1948   SOCIAL ORGANIZATION. New York: Rinehart and Co.
Meillassoux, Claude
1968   URBANIZATION OF AN AFRICAN COMMUNITY: VOLUNTARY
        ASSOCIATIONS IN BAMAKO. Seattle and London: University of
        Washington Press.
Miller, Nathan
1934   "Secret Societies." ENCYCLOPEDIA OF THE SOCIAL SCIENCES, vol.
        13. London: Macmillan.
Miner, Horace
1965   THE PRIMITIVE CITY OF TIMBUCTOO. Rev. ed. Anchor Book. New
        York: Doubleday. (First published, 1953.)
Morse, Hosea Ballou
1966   THE GUILDS OF CHINA, WITH AN ACCOUNT OF THE GUILD
        MERCHANT OR CO-HONG OF CANTON. Taipei: Ch'eng-Wen Publish-
        ing Co. (First published, 1909.)
Mumford, Lewis
1961   THE CITY IN HISTORY: ITS ORIGINS, ITS TRANSFORMATION,
        AND ITS PROSPECTS. New York: Harcourt, Brace and World.
Nicoló, Mariano San
1932   "Guilds in Antiquity." ENCYCLOPEDIA OF THE SOCIAL SCIENCES,
        Edwin R. Seligman, editor in chief, vol. 7. London: Macmillan.
Norbeck, Edward
1953   "Age-Grading in Japan." AMERICAN ANTHROPOLOGIST 55:
        373-384.
1961   "Cultural Change and Continuity in Northeastern Japan." AMERICAN
        ANTHROPOLOGIST 63, no. 2, 1: 297-321.
1962   "Common-Interest Associations in Rural Japan." In JAPANESE CUL-
        TURE: ITS DEVELOPMENT AND CHARACTERISTICS. Edited by
        Robert J. Smith and Richard K. Beardsley. Viking Fund Publications in
        Anthropology, no. 34.
Osgood, Cornelius
1963   VILLAGE LIFE IN OLD CHINA: A COMMUNITY STUDY OF KAO
        YAO YÜNNAN. New York: Ronald Press.
Painter, Sidney
1951   MEDIEVAL SOCIETY. Ithaca, New York: Cornell University Press.

Rose, Arnold M.
1958   THE INSTITUTIONS OF ADVANCED SOCIETIES. Minneapolis: University of Minnesota Press.

Ruel, M.J.
1964   "The Modern Adaptation of Associations among the Banyang of the West Cameroon." SOUTHWESTERN JOURNAL OF ANTHROPOLOGY 20, no. 1: 1-14.

Rørdam, Thomas
1965   THE DANISH FOLK HIGH SCHOOLS. Sigurd Mammen, tr. Danish Information Handbooks. Copenhagen: Det Danske Selskab.

Service, Elman R.
1962   PRIMITIVE SOCIAL ORGANIZATION: AN EVOLUTIONARY PERSPECTIVE. Studies in Anthropology. New York: Random House.

1963   PROFILES IN ETHNOLOGY. New York: Harper and Row.

Sills, David L.
1959   "Voluntary Associations: Instruments and Objects of Change." HUMAN ORGANIZATION 18, no. 1: 17-21.

Sills, David L.
1968   "Voluntary Associations. II. Sociological Aspects." In INTERNATIONAL ENCYCLOPEDIA OF THE SOCIAL SCIENCES, edited by David L. Sills, vol. 16. New York: Macmillan and Free Press.

Sjoberg, Gideon
1960   THE PREINDUSTRIAL CITY, PAST AND PRESENT. Glencoe, Illinois: The Free Press.

Smith, David Horton
1966   "The Importance of Formal Voluntary Organizations for Society," SOCIOLOGY AND SOCIAL RESEARCH 50, no. 4: 483-494.

Titiev, Mischa
1963   THE SCIENCE OF MAN. Rev. ed. New York: Holt, Rinehart and Winston.

Wilson, Monica
1963   GOOD COMPANY. A STUDY OF NYAKYUSA AGE-VILLAGES. Boston: Beacon Press. (First published, 1951.)

Wolf, Eric R.
1966   PEASANTS. Foundations of Modern Anthropology Series. Englewood Cliffs, New Jersey: Prentice-Hall.

Yang, Martin C.
1945   A CHINESE VILLAGE: TAITOU, SHANTUNG PROVINCE. New York: Columbia University Press.

Yee, Chiang
1963   A CHINESE CHILDHOOD. New York: W.W. Norton and Co.

2

Voluntary Associations in Ancient Societies

Jack Ross

In this chapter, attention is directed to four ancient societies, each of which took state form. In order to explore the relationship of voluntary associations and society, with the factor of "state" held constant, states will be selected that vary in major ways. The four here used may be characterized, with some simplification, as having a single major feature which, when examined in conjunction with the common element of statehood, provides a source of insight into the nature of voluntary associations. The four are China, the familism state; India, the caste-state; Rome, the military-bureaucratic state; and Greece, the city-state.

China: The Familism State

To presume to make general statements of any accuracy about a subject as vast as the social life of China seems at the outset to be absurd. However, most scholars are agreed that there has been a remarkable continuity to Chinese society and that in spite of the succession of dynasties and the impact of invaders, the core features of Chinese life survived with very little change until very recently.

This consistency applies to associational life as well, down to the first half of the twentieth century, and even contemporary communes bear some resemblance to earlier foundations. The primary forms of voluntary association, now and a thousand years ago, are concerned with matters which are not easily handled by families or clan associations, such as crop-watching, credit assurance, harvesting, and theatrical performances, among others.

Unlike contemporary Western societies, voluntary associations in China do not become proportionately more numerous as the status hierarchy is ascended. Voluntary associations are mainly an activity of lower strata. How does such a striking difference from modern societies come about?[1]

Outside of the nobility and a small merchant stratum in coastal cities, the main component of the upper stratum[2] was the literati in ancient China. The literati was composed of scholars who had passed a series of state examinations. All state officials were chosen from the certified literati, but many who passed the examinations were not appointed to office. The unappointed literati

29

sometimes found employment as tutors, and they are mentioned as secretaries of village associations.

The most crucial explanation of the absence of upper stratum voluntary associations is found in the character of the literati, who were not only the most prevalent upper stratum members, but whose ideals and practices were decisive determinants of values of others of the stratum, as well as of imperial policy.

The scholar prided himself in purely individual accomplishment. The knowledge he sought was always of the past. In spite of the extreme difficulty of the examinations (those who failed sometimes committed suicide), knowledge was not as important as other virtues: propriety, etiquette, poise, elegant expression, and piety toward authority. The Confucian scholar sought to become a paragon of indifference, a model of involuted charisma. The religious ideal was acceptance of the world, not mastery of it. Neither thrift nor strategic expenditure was proper. In sum, a motive for collective action was lacking.

Confucian ethics stipulated rank ordering of obligations. These duties are to master, father, husband, older brother, and friend. In effect, these obligations tended to bring about "rejection of other than purely *personal* ties among family members, and students as companions" (Weber 1951, p. 209). In the everyday life of peasants, however, the practical obligation to neighbors was added to the five classical obligations, and this was the basis among villagers for formation of mutual aid associations which united people other than kin.

One might well look at the practical as well as the ideational impossibility of a voluntary association of Confucian literati. How, after all, could the Confucian ever get through a committee meeting or business session when his overwhelming commitment was to elegance of expression, ritual perfection, and indifference to the problematic? Success for the Confucian depended on fate, not world mastery.

The state religious cult was typically orthodox and Confucian, while Taoism and Buddhism were heterodox. The typical tension between the palace courtier groups (eunuchs, the harem) and the officials (Confucian scholars) often resulted in intrigues with the heterodox religions and their spokesmen. The Confucians usually won, and the religious sects[3] only rarely became the basis of formation of true voluntary associations.

National, and later international, secret societies have been known in China for many centuries. In general they are religiously heterodox. Some have been associations of bandits. The best known military movements or revolutions in modern times originated in secret societies: the Boxers (Fist for Protection Society, or Fists for Righteous Protection), the Kuomintang, and even the Communist Party (Daroul 1965, pp. 208-219). Because the secret associations were usually opposed to the state cult and membership was dangerous, they exerted strong control over their members. There seems to be no reliable information about their sources of membership, but the clan seems to be most likely. Under circumstances of conflict with government, it is unlikely that strict voluntarism develops; under circumstances favorable to open membership, voluntarism may exist.

The significance of the Chinese secret society cannot easily be overstated. It is the basis for the development of modern guerrilla warfare in Southeast Asia, and a strong force in political, military, social and economic affairs wherever Chinese are found. It has been a force in American life as well, for not a small part of American xenophobia (the "Yellow Peril," etc.) of the first part of the present century was based on fear of the Chinese Tong or secret society.

Filial piety and patrimonial government produced extremely effective authority. The gap between the lowest order of officials and the people ranked below them was extreme. Officials were an independent stratum with little orientation to localism. This was fixed by use of the prebendial system in which offices were administered for their profitability to the administrator. The state left the villages alone except for the corvee (labor draft) and taxes. The state cult of the emperors was of minor importance to villagers, who worshipped their many gods in a congeries of local temples.

This sharp barrier between strata left room for the emergence of a variety of associational forms among lower strata. Villages sometimes were composed of plural clans, and there were strangers. Under such circumstances, voluntary associations sometimes arose. Harvest associations were more than temporary work groups, and can be called voluntary associations.

Gamble (1963, pp. 32-34) describes associations (of degrees of voluntarism) in Shansi, Honan, Shantung, and Hopei as they existed before 1933. Some of them were of ancient origin. He delineates two main types, the *hui* ("meeting" or "association") and *she* ("god of earth" and "land"). Here is Gamble's (1963, p. 32) compact description of the variety and concentration of organizations.

In the Peiping area there were the Green Crop association (*ch'ing-miao Hui*) and the Public Association, the United Association, the Public Welfare Association, and the Public Discussion Association.

I-po Hui, the "Common Ground Association," or *Kung K'an I-po Hui*, the "Co-operative Crop-Watching Association," was the most prevalent type of village association in Shantung.

Some Shansi villages called their group the Field Patrolling Association, or simply the Crop Association. Religious associations took their names from the particular god worshipped or the temple with which they were connected.

Gamble examined a large number of village associations and concluded that they could be grouped into three types, varying from the purely social and traditional, to the later, more nearly political type. The "general association" took care of all interests of a village (Gamble 1963, p. 35). It was a group of leaders, selected on the basis of ability or rotation among families. Gamble's (1963, p. 36) second type is the "specific association," of which "some were purely religious, related to temple worship or temple maintenance, watching, canal repair, or granaries."

Gamble's (1963, p. 36) third type is called "compound." "The compound association consisted of an over-all association with semi-independent minor organizations operating under it. The minor units generally were organized on a territorial or clan basis."

The associations described by Gamble had many kinds of membership criteria. Some religious associations were divided on a street basis. Some were divided between tenants and landowners. Some villages were divided into districts and had general associations in each area. Some *she* were named after the dates of the dramas which they presented.

We have kept Gamble's term "association" in all of the foregoing. He does not take up the issue of voluntarism, but his evidence suggests a variation in degree of independent choice. A large amount of voluntarism would exist in the case of the dramatic and the crop-watching associations, while the general village association represented the assumption of obligations on the basis of inherited identity. The entire example of Chinese village associations is significant for the study of voluntary associations because it illustrates vividly the inadequacy of the concept of voluntarism as it is typically used in modern sociology. The issue is really not whether a particular person acts voluntarily, but that Chinese society drew a line between strata in such a way that the entire lower category was permitted to follow traditions as it wished. Until more cases of a similar nature have been presented, no attempt can be made to sort out the nuances of difference between voluntarism and prudence.

Conditions favorable to development of associations and voluntary associations are typical in cities, because of the elaboration of vocational roles and the emergence of a merchant class which has much to gain by organization. The ancient Chinese city, however, differed from the occidental city in that it was bureaucratically administered by the imperial government, and was not the primary locus of citizenship. There was no sworn association of burghers, or a commune, which could be the model for further associational growth.

Gilds did develop in China. They were usually local. They were similar to European gilds in that they set standards, controlled apprenticeship and developed internal administration based on religion. However, their place in government differed from that of the European gilds and they were different from the voluntary associations out of which the European gilds emerged. Their power was sometimes great, and like the heterodox religions, represented a force with which the emperors had to contend. Of particular interest is the gild of bankers, which asserted control over currency.

Under feudal conditions peasants grouped themselves around a feudal lord for protection. In return they owed him taxes and services. This sometimes resulted in a "joint liability association," a form of guaranteed mutual aid and required savings organization (Weber 1951, p. 65). The organization bears comparison to the English *frith*, a mutual security organization, and similar organizations in other societies, and is the direct antecedent of the revolving credit association of the later Orient. The later forms are certainly voluntary associations. It should be noted, however, that the clan association was usually the most decisive source of guaranteed performance, financial and otherwise.[4]

India: The Caste State

There were few voluntary associations in ancient India. In any examination of social life in India, all explanations must be structured about the operation of the caste system. The relative lack of voluntary associations is no exception. Since local voluntary associations are face-to-face organizations, so far as their group aspect is concerned, hypothetical cases would immediately be concerned with the fact that interaction across caste bounds is defiling, to a degree depending on the specific caste relationships. Of course there might be voluntary associations within a caste which by itself would not prevent association formation: indeed the caste association itself, or the *panchayat* (ruling council) of village or regional subcaste were such organizations, and the gild in its most frequent form was usually narrowly organized along caste lines.[5] The actual restrictiveness of caste then was not the way in which it limited relations of caste members—this merely limited possibilities. We may use as a clue Max Weber's statement that caste in its "whole spirit" inhibited the growth of capitalism (Weber 1958, p. 112). As Weber elsewhere phrased it, "the castes excluded every solidarity and every politically powerful fraternization of the citizenry and of the trades" (Weber 1958, p. 38). Let us turn then to the several elements of this "whole spirit," with attention to the kinds of reasons for formation of voluntary associations which have been identified so far.

Dharma (ritual duty) proved to be an operative restriction, with its extreme stipulation of actions of individuals appropriate to each caste or subcaste. Dharma was interpreted by caste councils or associations, but in the long run, brahmanical interpretation (i.e., an upper caste decision) was decisive. Compared to the relation to the Chinese literati, there was no vast gap between villagers and upper strata: Brahamanic interpretation was institutionalized throughout. Dharma, in effect, limited actions of all sorts, while *karma* (fate in the life cycle) made it plain that opportunity came from more favorable rebirth or fate after death, not from action oriented to change in this world. Thus even where voluntary organizations existed, they were always expressions of the same fatalistic attitude about the limits of human action.

The occupational gild and the occupational subcaste operated differently as to control of fraternization: it was permitted through the gild and restricted by the caste. Thus the gild provided for the needed relationships with consumers of products across caste lines, and nondefiling interaction with other subcaste workers in the workshop.[6]

The Indian gild was far less voluntary than the occidental gild, where free choice of master was theoretically possible. The gild was a comprehensive organization of workers of a common subcaste, and it had extreme powers over its hereditary members.

The sect also provided some social life transcending caste lines, though even here it was restricted or segmented. The sects, however, inhibited voluntary association development, because they were divided into monks (leaders) and others, and strong discipline imposed on the rank and file inhibited congregationalism. The *guru* was a personal spiritual leader, not the shepherd of his flock, and this was true of Brahmans generally. Even if the sect could be interpreted as a voluntary association, its total effect was small. Weber (1958, p. 326) estimates the total public membership in all sects at no more than 5 percent.

The panchayat was a body of decision-makers. Its similarity to the Chinese village association (hui) is notable. Both governed village affairs in a traditional nonpolitical manner, with recourse to a governmental agent (a *patee* or head-man in India, Confucian official in China). Both were composed of elder clan members or representatives. But here the resemblance ends: the decisive articulation of the Chinese was "vertical" (i.e., to the clan, its ancestors and present superiors); of the panchayat, the "horizontal" relation of the caste. "Horizontal" relations for the panchayat were possible but limited by dharma— for the Chinese the affairs of similarly ranked peasants were open to collectivization by some means, and the means taken was often associational, in degrees of voluntarism. The Hindu generally had no such latitude.

Scholars (e.g., Opler, 1955; Srinivas 1960, and many contributors to his volume) warn of generalizations about India's villages, since each tends to be dominated by a single subcaste, and thus are specialists in a certain occupation with its related dharma. It is therefore even more remarkable that few or no voluntary associations are found to cope with the diversity. Caste permeates all.

In our analysis of China it was found that the heterodox religions provided the basis for formation of sects and secret societies. What was the situation in India? Unlike China with its single official cult, India was tolerant of numerous cults and sects. India was only erratically an empire. Through much of its history it was a grouping of princedoms, constantly at war and under no single ruler. The unified kingdom of the Buddhist Ashoka was an exception. Cults and sects were integrated into the caste system and used variants of the same cultural materials of all Hindus. In this sense Hinduism was never a religion, but a culture which easily absorbed religious systems. Heterodoxy was not subversive in India: it might cause conflicts and groupings of people, but it usually drove no one underground or into the formation of separate religions. Thus Christianity found little resistance when it was introduced: it became merely another part of Hinduism.

A second source (chronologically the earliest) of heterogeneity and possible associationalism was tribalism. Hinduism, with its caste system, emerged from contact of outsiders with primitive people. Tribes typically merged with the caste system by becoming whole subcaste or by fragmenting and becoming guest peoples, to be absorbed at the level of each occupation. The former has left its traces in tribal names of subcastes and is most easily traced. Tribes did not lead to voluntary association formation, since their integration was accomplished directly into the caste system.

Certain subcastes seem to have been readily transformed into secret societies. The Thugs are the best known (Daraul 1965, pp. 159-170). Unlike the Chinese secret societies which were extensions of familism, the Thugs kept their identity, they were mainly a subcaste association and not a voluntary association with accessible membership.

Voluntary Associations in Athens and Hellenism

Athens in the ancient classical era was a beehive of voluntary association activity. Voluntary associations were the major mode of collective activity in religion, leisure and recreation, education, economics, and politics. The rare man who was not a member of some club was remarkable for his nonmembership. Even slaves had their own voluntary associations.

An unbiased synoptic view of Athenian life, however, must bring a reserved evaluation. Athenian justice favored the wealthy in spite of the activities of voluntary associations—in fact, because of them in many cases. Athenian social clubs were fragmented and particularistic, and in their pursuit of group interests promoted disunity and disintegration. After a description of the major types of voluntary associations, attention will be directed to examination of the causes of these characteristics.

The *thiasi* and *erani* were perhaps the earliest forms of Greek voluntary association. The thiasi was an organization for religious purposes, and may be the outgrowth of tribal totemic associations. The thiasi may be viewed as a kind of erani or "benefit club" (St. John 1971, p. 75). The mutual benefit theme bears comparison to the Chinese limited liability voluntary association, a type of risk-sharing organization which is encountered again and again as various societies are examined.

There were several membership bases for the erani (which shall serve as a generic name henceforth), each related to some common identity. "Sometimes the citizens of a whole Demos, or borough, formed themselves into a club, or ship's crew, or an eating society, or persons having a right to the same burial-ground, or the partners in a mercantile expedition" (St. John 1971, p. 76).

Although the declared goal of each erani might differ, all erani were similar in structure and operation. Members had an agreement as to mutual liability in relation to their declared purpose, supported by the law of Solon. There was usually a convivial aspect, involving feasting and pleasurable gatherings. They provided some means for sharing the cost of a sacrifice to a patron divinity. Erani typically involved a monthly subscription which was legally enforceable, and from this fund provided for loans and charity. They usually had a president who was also treasurer. They might also rotate meetings among homes of members, in which case the host would be the chairman.

Hetaeri is the name given to erani in politics. Usage varies in available sources and it is not possible to determine whether, in any particular case, an erani was taking on political functions, or whether an hetaeri was organized solely for political reasons. As the revolution of 411 B.C. approached, the latter seems to have been more prevalent. Calhoun's judgment is that "it was by no means unusual for political clubs to have social features, and also that clubs which existed primarily for social purposes would upon occasion aid their members in the courts or take part in politics" (Calhoun 1970, p. 26).

The term *hetaeri* may be translated as "congeniality." Hetaeri were also known as "conspiracies." The implication was apparently that friendship created a bond of loyalty between friends which was expedient for political purposes.

The erani mode of institutionalization of voluntarism was found in other parts of Greek life as well. The "gymnasium" was the basic educational organization. It is an error, however, to refer to it simply as a school, as we now understand the term. Our understanding of Greek education will be more accurate if we see the modern school as a kind of narrow abstraction of the gymnasium. The best mental picture of the gymnasium for moderns is the image of the community center, a comprehensive local organization for a variety of voluntary educational, social and cultural activities. Rostovtzeff (1953, p. 1065) is perhaps accurate when he speaks of "the prosperity and striking development of the gymnasia, and of the associations connected therewith, in all Greek cities of Asia Minor."

As with other Greek organizations, the gilds appear to have begun with a religious orientation (San Nicolo 1948, p. 205). *Emporoi* were gilds of traders, and *naukleroi* were gilds of shipowners. After the fifth century B.C., there were "organizations not only of merchants, shipowners, and navigators, but also of artisans and craftsmen in definite unions, more and more clearly differentiated according to profession" (San Nicolo 1948, p. 205).[7] In their earlier stage the gilds were very much like thiasi—later they became more exclusively rational in their orientation to purely economic issues. But it is clear that the same ethical orientation to mutual obligation underlay the entirety.

Now that the major types of ancient Greek voluntary associations have been described, let us turn to analysis of their limitations.

When any collective phenomenon occurs repeatedly in a society under similar conditions we may infer the existence of a social institution. An institution may be defined as a "standardized solution to a collective problem" (Martindale 1960, p. 260). We may then seek an explanation of the occurrence of voluntary associations by reference to the repeated problems to which the organizations addressed themselves, and by patterns these collective responses took.

To deal fully with the implications of the previous paragraph would call for a book-length study. But without too much distortion, some generalizations may be made. Greek democracy was a great experiment in government along lines for which there was little precedent. From our vantage point, with many later examples, some of its problems seem obvious.

First, in order for there to be an associational, rather than an individual or kin response to problems,[8] there needs to be some authoritative guarantee that individuals may organize without undue interference. The law of Solon provided for this freedom of association; in fact, there was an entire section devoted to associational law. Wherever voluntary associations flourish, such a guarantee, legal or traditional, will be found, and conversely, wherever tyranny and dictatorship are found, voluntary associations contrary to that form of rule are suppressed or were not present when tyranny arose.

This principle of freedom of association may be stated in a number of ways, and the division between legal and traditional guarantees may vary, but the elements are always the same: within the confines of the voluntary organization, people are permitted to regulate behavior in their own way, provided that compliance does not exceed certain limits; the organization may undertake any legal purpose within defined categories; the organization assumes defined liability for its acts in relation to nonmembers.[9] In Athenian voluntary associations neither law nor custom provided adequate restrictions or regulations, and the organizations became powerful before the law could be altered. Athenian democracy closed its experiment before it was done: Socrates, Plato, and Aristotle were too late. Hetaeri became vehicles of privilege. They became accustomed to bribing officials, fixing juries, tampering with elections. Certain of them became specialists in sharp practices in advocacy, in the absence of a profession of advocate, with its voluntary associations and a code of ethics. Corrupt practices of the hetaeri of the wealthy were unchecked by laws which might have limited their depredations.[10] In short, freedom of association was out of balance with obligations of responsibility.

The second issue is somewhat related to the first. It concerns the fact that Athenian (and all Greek) voluntary associations remained small. They had no idea of plural organizations in structures which in some way matched the entire society; they acted solely in their own interests and not for the entire society. This is all the more surprising when we realize the advantages to be gained from combinations. Nevertheless, only when great crises seemed imminent were coalitions of organizations attempted, and then only temporarily. The reasons are hard to trace. Among them must be the prevalence throughout of an important ethic of mutual personal obligation as a foremost reason for collective action. In addition, the clubs acted as protection for individuals against other clubs or individuals, so that the clubs were constantly pitted against each other on matters of personal litigation.

Third, Athenian government was structured in such a way that there was a high level of direct participation by large assemblies. Democracy overwhelmed republicanism. The possible good effects of representative action was usurped by the hetaeri. The usurpation, however, resulted in action by the hetaeri in their own interest and governed by their own internal ethics, and not by rules of the governing assembly. Thus the hetaeri could and did vote as a bloc in assemblies, and their oath of mutual obligation frequently superseded their public responsibility.

The Athenian society had three civic ranks: citizens, free aliens or guests, and slaves who were either public (war captives) or private. As commerce grew and wars continued, the numbers of noncitizens grew. Yet nowhere in the Hellenic world was there any provision for absorption of guest peoples into citizenship.[11] Although noncitizens were allowed to form their own clubs, there were distinct limitations on them, particularly regarding restriction of the right to own property. Even though slaves might, in principle, sue their owners, the effectiveness of the hetaeri made the privilege irrelevant (though juries frequently favored the poor). Furthermore, the stratum barriers were so impenetrable that clubs did not effectively integrate strata, in spite of a superficial equalitarianism among Greeks everywhere.

Because it was easy to form small voluntary associations, metics (guest people) everywhere tended to make their voluntary associations their home away from home—an island of a foreign culture. But under the circumstances of slow communication by sea and difficult terrain which separated Greek cities themselves, voluntary associations did not form leagues or even federations which might have helped provide a functional integration of societies.[12] This functional integration was not even approximated, and the integration provided by the Romans was mostly normative and not functional until much later.[13]

For an institution to persist it is necessary that the population in considerable numbers be effectively exposed to similar definitions of situations and accept similar actions in response. In addition to the principle in law of freedom of association which was mentioned above, there needs to be socialization to germane values. This was provided in several ways in Athens. Classical Athens had a number of clubs for youth, which resembled those of adults. The gymnasium provided for coordination and role-learning. And gymnasia developed alumni organizations to carry on the old traditions. The voluntary gilds of the early era undoubtedly provided for induction through apprenticeship. Socialization to voluntary association life was a fully developed part of Athenian society.

Voluntary Associations in the Roman Military-Bureaucratic State

Many types of voluntary associations known to classical Athens were present in republican Rome: the gild, the mutual benefit organization, and the social club.

Some of the similarity was due to the diffusion of Hellenism; some was due to the similarity of problems to which voluntary associations were a similar collective response. But the nature of Roman society later, under the Empire, did not permit full development of voluntary associations, and this tendency is most marked in the absence of political clubs as an instrument of change.

As in the case of Greece, a brief description of each main type of voluntary association will be followed by an explanation, couched in terms of the institutional processes to which the organizations were related.

Waltzing (1895), whose four-volume work on Roman occupational organizations is the source of much of the material which is used here, provides a useful classification of "corporations"[14] (1895, I, p. 33). He notes that all of them were more or less religious, but had in addition certain dominant characteristics which can be distinguished as political, amusement, and professional. Some were solely religious, however, and these may be divided into official and semiofficial, that is, private religious organizations with free selection of cultic gods but under official charter or leadership. The official cultic organizations were of ancient origin, and in time came to be associated with leading patrician families. Membership in these cults was opened to strangers and then to the public, and the bases of membership was common profession or residential area. The semiofficial cult was an expansion of this principle, and became the broad base for organization of voluntary associations. As Waltzing puts it (1895, I, p. 42), the semiofficial or private cultic organizations "had another goal, often more important, a professional, political or funeral goal" (translation supplied). Political collegia were suppressed under the Empire, but the others remained.

Roman legend ascribes the origin of professional associations or corporations (*collegia opificum*) to the ancient King Numa (San Nicolo 1948, p. 206). He is said to have founded gilds of "carpenters, dyers, shoemakers, tanners, workers in copper and gold, flute players, and potters" (Abbott 1965, p. 216).[15] It is doubtful, however, if trade gilds (*collegia fabrorum*) existed in any significant number until the Empire—the period of time for this study (San Nicolo 1948, p. 206). The collegia, as the generic form under the *lex collegia*, or law of organizations, manifested themselves in a variety of applications, all of which were continuously scrutinized by government and frequently, especially under the *lex Julia*, put to governmental use as part of the bargain for their existence.

Collegia for the purpose of trade and navigation apparently emerged early, as was the case in Greece, and varied from the temporary partnership for a venture to a fully developed permanent association. Conquest, dominance, and tribute were always significant, and hence a true merchant capitalism did not become decisive, nor did merchants often become middle class or wealthy. This is not to deny the existence of trade, but only to establish its relative unimportance in Roman values.

Virtually every craft was represented in Rome. Evidence of the concentrated location of specific occupations is preserved in street names and shop signs.

Many tombstones preserve the record of a man's occupation and of his affiliations. Abbott (1965, p. 217) says there were eighty different trades which were organized into gilds in Rome in the Empire period, including unskilled laborers such as porters, and more skilled trades such as physicians and goldsmiths. Certain specialized trades were found, typical of very large cities, such as *pastillarii* (pastilemakers), *scabillarii* (castanet players), checkerboard makers, perfumers, hay dealers, and sculptors. There was a different issue involved perhaps in the formation of collegia of women senators or of bridesmaids. The *schola* were collegia of students. Some collegia reflect the uniqueness of Rome's preoccupation with spectacles and violence: there were gilds of actors, dancers, jugglers, and even of gladiators.[16] There were gilds of various lower military ranks and of veterans, not only in Rome but in many foreign garrison settlements, and these organizations were sometimes powerful locally (Waltzing, 1895, I, p. 51).

The type of collegia which Waltzing (1895, I, p. 51) called "cercles d' amusement" were organizations with typical kinds of collegial features which became prominent at the height of Roman indulgence in luxury. Some of them had names which indicate their purposes: the ball players, the late drinkers, the pilferors and the sluggards. They seem, in general, to be "degenerate" forms of the old religious cults in which the feasting and convivial aspect had become exclusive of the religious.

Youth Collegia were modeled after adult ones. They usually had an adult curator and official scrutiny. Some, like adult counterparts, were pressed into municipal service.

The municipal gild was present in Roman cities throughout the Empire, and it performed numerous official functions, such as that of municipal fire department. As was the case with other kinds of collegia, state service was demanded as part of the price of existence, and as time wore on, this became more and more onerous. Voluntary association was never an unqualified right of free association. And as central rule became more despotic in the later years of the Empire, the voluntary aspect of the collegia was progressively restricted. Near the end of the Empire, gilds became monopolistic, children were required to enter the occupations of their parents, and the latitude for decision by members was slight.

Rome was a city with many foreign residents. As in Athens, foreigners were allowed to form limited voluntary organizations. In particular the cult was allowed to flourish and, like the development of the semiofficial religious collegia of Romans, became the source of gilds in which ethnicity or origin was the criterion of joining. Among the leading cults in early Rome were those of the Greeks, Syrians, and Egyptians. Jews were also represented, and during the Empire, Christian collegia developed under the regulated indulgence of the *lex Julia*. The letters of Paul to the Romans as brotherhoods testifies to at least a prototypical collegium of Roman Christians.

The practice of calling all the aforementioned organizations "gilds" is well established in the available literature on the era. It should be recalled, however, that the names that the Romans themselves gave to the cultic organizations was *sodalitas*, and to the others the generic term *collegia* plus some auxiliary descriptive term. The use of "gild" (more often "guild" in earlier work) is due to the European origin of most of the writers. The error of these writers is that they look at history in natural reverse chronological sequence, instead of seeing the ancient society as its members saw it. The collegium was a way of organizing which was common to Roman culture, just as the erani were to Hellenic Greek culture. The collegium was an institutional way of dealing with problems in an uncertain world, and the organization was formed by a small group of people who knew each other or had some reason to share a venture or interest. As in Greece, they were rarely large and their interrelationships did not create a collective force of any significance. Occupation was a frequent source of common identity and common problems, but not the only source, and so the essential basis of membership of gilds was not simply common occupation but community and common interests.

Abbott (1965, p. 221) makes the point emphatically when he describes how Roman gilds differed from modern unions or medieval gilds. "They [Roman gilds] made no attempt to raise wages, to improve working conditions, to limit the number of apprentices, to develop skill and artistic taste in the craft, or to better the social or political position of the labourer." Like the erani, the gild members gathered for conviviality, to deal with bereavement and burial costs, to share feasts and temple expenses. The purpose of the gild is succinctly stated in an epitaph of one member. "He bequethed to his guild, the rag-dealers, a thousand sesterces, from the income of which each year, on the festaval of Parentalia, not less than twelve men shall dine at his tomb" (Abbott 1965, p. 222).

The institutionalization of the collegia is also seen in the common features of internal structure. There was usually a stipulated yearly fee, and rules covering default. The insurance features or death benefits were stipulated, as well as the manner of payment. Funds were invested and the interest was used for collective or private benefit. Interest rates, however, were often drastically manipulated (e.g., doubled or halved) by the Emperor for fiscal purposes, and thus the collegia were economically at the mercy of outside forces in spite of their attempt to meet problems of insecurity and crisis. Each collegium had a standard set of officers which resembled Roman governmental posts, such as quaestor, curator, praetor, and aedile. One cannot escape the feeling of irony here: the plebes were playing at government which they never really shared, while the patricians governed through the military, the bureaucracy, bread, and circuses.

With so many features in common, it might be presumed that Roman and Greek voluntary associations played a similar part in society. Yet we have seen that the differences were great. Let us attempt to present a somewhat more systematic explanation of the differences.

First, the conditions for the full development of the idea of freedom of association were missing in both. In Greece, as explained above, there were insufficient laws or customs to regulate the political and judicial excesses of voluntary associations. Among the Romans, there were no hetaeri, nor any voluntary associations sufficiently free from state domination or control to develop into effective political forces.

Second, two economic features of Roman life seem prominent in limitation of the development of power through associations. Though both Greece and Rome had slaves, slavery was more pervasive and important in the Roman economy and household. The existence of competitive slave labor limits the ability of free labor to further its lot by restriction of apprenticeship, control of sales, and production. In addition, imported goods and booty from the vast Roman Empire diluted the significance of craftsmen and hence their gilds in Rome itself.

Third, the Roman stratification system limited social mobility through trade and skill. The Roman estate system awarded highest rank to the endogamous stratum of Senators, followed by knights, and commoners. While there was considerable mobility through wealth, it typically was the result of individual political administrative and military talent, and not through capitalistic enterprise in which organized associations were prominent.

Political ambitions were channeled through purely individual means, such as clientage, plots, group conspiracy and even assassination, as well as legal sequences of office. Social institutions which might support public associational means for influence of government were absent. In their place was a fanatical pride in individual merit. This individual pride, manifest in conspicuous consumption, sybartic luxury and display, was extreme in Rome. The power of the wealthy was enormous. This wealth was often used for public benefit. However, a man's prestige was measured by his retinue and display of wealth. This retinue was secured through the patron/client relationship which tended to exclude the organization of people to gain advantage as a collectivity. Client advantage in relation to knights or Senators was an individual, not a collective gain. Clientage, a major occupation of freedmen, was a servile and crafty role in which flattery, ingratiation and demeaning service was developed to a master's art. Nevertheless, the rewards were usually limited. The client might gain a place at the patron's table, get a few old clothes, or an occasional gift. Since the patron gained prestige by the size of his retinue, he considered the economics and personal relationships of the system rather carefully. The patron gained standing by grumbling to his friends about how many pests he had hovering about him, all the while encouraging them as much as possible.

The patricians in their turn had a similar relationship to those who ranked above them. The emperor's court was the apex of the hierarchy. Favor at court was the surest way to wealth, and thus cultivation of a courtly manner became a preoccupation. The knightly partron of the third estate clinets attempted to ingratiate himself to the senators, who waited in their own time on the emperor or others with high office.

In this system, talented but socially despised people, usually freedmen or their offspring, were very useful, since they could accumulate wealth but could not legally aspire to the citizen's normal sequence of offices or privileges. The wealthy freedman, not the parvenu merchant or wealthy Jew as in medieval courts, was the ace-in-the-hole of the emperor in trouble with his aristocrats or in financial difficulties elsewhere.[17]

The individualism of Romans regarding wealth and power was also related to the custom of small family size among the upper estates and instrumental-legal rather than traditional inheritance. A woman might want to have one child or sometimes two, but scions were not the best heirs. Wedding salutations did not include a wish for many sons. The reason was that an elderly bachelor could attract many more clients than a man with scions, and he might use manipulation of his will (altered many times a year to keep clients on their toes) as a means of gaining a clientage. Some elderly men even took special medicines which purported to make them look pale and unhealthy so they might attract more sychophants. And of course for every scheming bachelor there were scheming clients. There was even one group of clients who specialized in seeking out and poisoning rich bachelors.

In sum, the Roman attitude toward social advantage was that of an exclusively individual "vertical" arrangement in which the ethics of mutuality and sharing would seem very foreign. This does not exclude, of course, voluntary associations for other reasons.

The Roman bath was an institution which might seemingly become the matrix of voluntary associations. Baths were popular gathering places, and in this regard bear some comparison to the Greek gymnasium. The bath was a public institution, and at the same time was a place of service to male vanity. Though social contacts were frequent, we have found no record of a formal connection of the bath with voluntary associations.

The patronage system of Rome had a public as well as a private aspect. The wealthy made large gifts for public purposes, and supported construction of streets, city walls, and even at times footed the bill for the army. "Bread and circuses" was not just a euphemism either. Grain distribution at public expense was routine, and privately endowed circuses with the most barbaric sort of entertainment for the masses were common.

In short, there was no intent to encourage and support the thorough growth of a pluralistic society of self-sufficient and educated citizens pursuing interests which could have democracy as a result. Rome was a mass society with patrician rule, and every attempt was made to keep it that way. Under such circumstances, the policy of keeping voluntary associations active, but controlled and oriented to limited public service can be seen as a policy of shrewd Roman statecraft, and not as a basic commitment to citizen's rights or participatory democracy.

With the emphasis on prestige in interpersonal relationships and on extreme dominance, it seems strange to find voluntary associations at all, especially in the lower strata. Yet the two principles of organization—horizontal or associational, and vertical or hierarchical—were found continuously. With the tension that this created, we might expect either law which clarifies the relationships between the two systems, or forms of social life where both principles obtain. Both existed. The *lex collegia* has been mentioned already. In the gild system is found the *arte* which Privite-Orton (1929, p. 237) sees as a kind of gild commune or community of gilds, with governance by masters and consuls who represent the vertical principle. But it seems evident that the arte never became a powerful force in Roman life.

Summary

Voluntary associations were present in three of four ancient states: China, Greece, and Rome. They were not significant in India, although some did exist (depending partly on the strictness of one's definition of voluntary association). The fullest development occurred in ancient Greece.

The presence of voluntary associations was found to be related to certain types of government. Where powerful central government was the means of control, voluntary associations were absent or permitted only strictly controlled local development. Voluntary associations were not generally found in the stratum which constituted the court.

Development of voluntary associations was seen to be closely related to the value systems of the society. Where individual prestige and power were honored, voluntary associations were subdued. Where collectivism was honored, voluntary associations were more frequent.

Societies seem to have institutionalized ways of organizing voluntary associations to deal with typical problems. These voluntary institutions result in generic names: the Chinese *hui*; the Greek *erani*; the Roman *collegia*. Once the institution is established, it may be activated in relation to other problems which arise. In India the caste system did not allow active development of such an institution, though the *panchayat* or council, a traditional local government organization of a quasi-voluntary character, frequently handled similar problems.

The structure and procedures of the basic kind of voluntary associations of each of the kinds of society are strikingly alike, and consistent within each society. The common elements include some basic cash payment (or sometimes payment in kind) associated with stipulated individual and collective benefits, rules covering other obligations, and the administration of default. Roles within the organization were typically consistent within each society, but varied between societies: the Romans tended to have three or four officers, the Greeks a simple, single officer system, and the Chinese sometimes pressed local scholars into service as secretaries.

The principle of freedom of association took legal form in Greece and Rome, while the Chinese were merely indulgent or permissive about voluntary associations. In no case was freedom of association as fully developed as under late Anglo-Saxon law or in the United States.

Voluntary associations, when they existed to any significant degree in the three ancient societies we have examined, were closely related to the system of stratification. Only among the Greeks were voluntary associations found throughout society and probably more frequently among higher ranked strata. The court system and small patrician or aristocratic stratum made no place for voluntary associations. Only in ancient Greek society were voluntary associations effective political instrumentalities or vehicles for personal ascendancy.

Notes

1. Since the issue of a precise definition of voluntary association has not yet been taken up, a statement like this is open to misinterpretation. If such organizations as gilds are included among voluntary associations, the empirical statement would need to be modified, since merchant gilds might be interpreted as upper strata. Even if this kind of association were included, the statement still stands. The voluntarism of gilds depends on the specific gild—some prove to be more voluntary than others, depending mostly on the issue of hereditary apprenticeship. Oriental gilds in general are more often hereditary than their occidental counterparts.

2. The word "class" will be reserved for a ranked category sharing a common economic position. Although the emperor had much wealth, wealth itself was never the sole basis of rank, and certainly not among scholars.

3. De Groot enumerated fifty-six sects (Weber 1951, p. 219).

4. Weber (1951, p. 91) gives "club association" as the translation of *hui*, and says "the club thrived in all spheres of life, especially in credit relations." Whether this means that the *hui* was to be found among merchants or above the lower strata cannot be determined from this statement. If so, then our earlier statement about the prevalence of lower stratum voluntary associations needs modification, though it would still be true. A similar confusion results from the work of Vinacke (1948, p. 219-221), who calls virtually all Chinese associations gilds, and does not distinguish the voluntary from the nonvoluntary.

5. Either the past or present tense could be used here. India, like China, changed little up to the middle of this century. The past tense is selected for consistency.

6. India offers a fascinating opportunity for application of social psychological insights. The restrictions of caste presented a constant necessity for definition of the situation by means of reading clues about the identity of parties to interaction. In the case presented above, the definition of the interaction permitted across caste lines is expanded by creation of a social

establishment, or enclosure, with a shared social definition of expected behavior. This explains much of the confusion about India that many outsiders share: if we take the formal definition of Indian life at face value, it seems obvious that social life in work and play would be virtually impossible. But Indians have rules about not using rules that deal with most situations, and life is possible after all.

7. Tarn (1966, p. 94) notes that "the professional trade guild was practically unknown to Hellenism, unless in Egypt; true guilds only evolved under the Roman Empire. . . ." This seems to be a comment in which "true" refers to the formal and exclusive character of the closed liturgical and monopolistic association.

8. Tarn (1966, p. 93) notes the appearance of Greek family associations around 200 B.C.

9. A complete statement of freedom of association would be very complex. We have not attempted to deal with the difference between an association and a legal corporation.

10. Tarn (1966, p. 88) says that "before 300 the old system of trying cases by a jury composed of a large body of citizens was fast breaking down, as it deserved; it was about the worst legal system ever invented, for the juries' decisions were habitually influenced by politics, mass passion, and prejudice." Further evidence of the lack of institutions is provided by the contrast with later judicial practice, in which external judicial commissions tried cases as visitors—a principle suggesting the medieval Italian *potesta*, or the guest city manager.

11. The start of honorary citizenship is noted in the third century, B.C. (Tarn 1966, p. 84) and became common under the Romans. Isopolity, or categorical citizenship of another city, began about the same time.

12. Tarn (1966, p. 44) sums up the later Hellenic period when he writes that the club "became so much the standard model that the most diverse forms of activity—the philosophic schools, the Museum at Alexandria, . . . the Old Boys from this or that Gymnasium—all adopted the same form of organization."

13. Dramatic and festive associations with branches in several cities began to appear after the Alexandrian conquests ca. 280 B.C. (Tarn 1966, p. 114).

14. The term "corporations" was frequently used in nineteenth-century scholarship as a generic word for all forms of association, both legally "uncorporated" or not. Waltzing is close to modern legal usage here, since Roman collegia were usually approved by the Senate or later by consuls. They were not, however, incorporated as a legal person.

15. Medieval gilds, which had considerable political power, found it necessary to establish an actual ceremonial rank, and an inner circle or oligarchy of organizations. Roman gilds, which had less power, established only a myth about their origins, and the *arte* or commune of gilds had little power.

16. With this kind of competition, it's no wonder the Christians had to get organized.

17. The Roman system bears comparison to the Chinese, which it resembles

more than the Greek, at least so far as the form of government is concerned. The function of the Chinese eunuch and the Roman freedman or slave was similar, insofar as their utility arose from their deviant identity. The minority ethnic group member in modern government functions to deflect criticism of minority power blocs, which is quite a different matter.

References

Abbott, Frank Frost
1965 THE COMMON PEOPLE OF ANCIENT ROME. New York: Bilbo and Tannen.
Banton, Michael
1968 "Voluntary Associations: Anthropological Aspects." David L. Sills, editor, INTERNATIONAL ENCYCLOPEDIA OF THE SOCIAL SCIENCES, vol. 16. New York: The Macmillan Company and the Free Press.
Calhoun, George Miller
1970 ATHENIAN CLUBS IN POLITICS AND LITIGATION. Austin, Texas: University of Texas Press.
Daraul, Arkon
1965 SECRET SOCIETIES. London: Tandem.
Gamble, Sidney D.
1963 NORTH CHINA VILLAGES: SOCIAL, POLITICAL, AND ECONOMIC ACTIVITIES BEFORE 1933. Berkeley and Los Angeles: University of California Press.
Martindale, Don
1960 AMERICAN SOCIETY. Princeton, N.J.: D. Van Nostrand.
Opler, Morris Edward
1955 Forward, in Dube, S.C., Indian Village London: Routledge and Kegan Paul.
Previté-Orton, C.W.
1929 "The Italian Cities till c. 1200." In THE CAMBRIDGE MEDIEVAL HISTORY, vol. 5. Edited by J.R. Tanner, et al, Cambridge: at the University Press.
Rostovtzeff, M.
1953 THE SOCIAL AND ECONOMIC HISTORY OF THE HELLENISTIC WORLD, vol. 2. Oxford: at the Clarendon Press.
San Nicoló, Mariano
1948 "Guilds in antiquity." Edwin R.A. Seligman, editor, ENCYCLOPEDIA OF THE SOCIAL SCIENCES, vol. 7. London: Macmillan.
Srinivas, M.N.
1960 INDIA'S VILLAGES, revised edition. New York: Asia Publishing House.
St. John, J.A.
1971 THE HISTORY OF THE MANNERS AND CUSTOMS OF ANCIENT GREECE vol. 3, Port Washington, N.Y.: Kennikot Press.

Tarn, Sir William
1966 HELLENISTIC CIVILISATION, third edition. London: Methuen.

Vinacke, Harold M.
1948 "Chinese Guilds." Edwin R.A. Seligman, editor, ENCYCLOPEDIA OF THE SOCIAL SCIENCES, vol. 7. London: Macmillan.

Waltzing, Jean Pierre
1895 ETUDE HISTORIQUE SUR LES CORPORATIONES PROFESSION-ELLES CHEZ LES ROMAINS DESPUIS LES ORIGINES JUSQUE LA CHUTE DE L'EMPIRE D'OCCIDENT, 4 vols. Louvain: Paters.

Weber, Max
1951 THE RELIGION OF CHINA. Hans H. Gerth, editor and translator. Glencoe, Illinois: The Free Press.

Weber, Max
1958 THE RELIGION OF INDIA. Hans H. Gerth and Don Martindale, editors and translators. Glencoe, Illinois: The Free Press.

3

Modernization and the Emergence of Volunteer Organizations

David Horton Smith

In this chapter we shall sketch briefly some of the major factors underlying variations in the prevalence rates of formal volunteer organizations among sociohistorical contexts differing in modernization levels and among social systems in general. The focus here is on formal volunteer organizations[1] (hereafter abbreviated as "FVOs") as units and on individual memberships only insofar as they are indices of the prevalence of FVOs. The root antecedent or causal factor examined will be the analytical type of society involved along a continuum of modernization. The transition, analytical or chronological, from primitive to peasant to industrial society appears to produce, or at least is correlated with, the growth of formal organizations and contingent roles, including FVOs as a subtype. Many social observers and sociologists have noted this transition, implicitly or explicitly, for the past 100 years or so. For instance, Henry Sumner Maine wrote of a transition from status to contract society, Durkheim of mechanical and organic solidarity, Cooley of primary and (inferentially) secondary groups, MacIver of communal and associational relations, Sorokin of familistic and contractual relations, Linton of ascribed and achieved roles, Toennies of *Gemeinschaft* and *Gesellschaft* relations, and so forth for the present generation of sociologists such as Parsons, Loomis, and others.

All of these authors have noted that the growth of modern industrial society entails the growth of a type of relationship that may be termed "contingent" as opposed to "ascriptive." FVOs and the relationships they involve are by definition contingent, and so also are formal work organizations and formal coercive organizations, of course. Thus, although few of these authors may have mentioned FVOs explicitly, they have all implicitly remarked on their growth by dealing with the broader category of contingent relationships (and contingent groups) and more especially formal contingent relationships. But what of the empirical evidence?

Happily, there is some survey data that may serve to support this sort of impressionistic analysis. We refer to Almond and Verba's study, THE CIVIC CULTURE (1963), and Lerner's study, THE PASSING OF TRADITIONAL SOCIETY (1958). The data of Almond and Verba are far superior to those of Lerner, being national probability samples of approximately 1000 cases each for

This chapter is a somewhat revised version of a paper by the same title printed in the INTERNATIONAL JOURNAL OF COMPARATIVE SOCIOLOGY, June 1972.

five countries (though the Mexican sample includes only urban respondents). Lerner's quota samples consist mainly of urban persons with about 275 to 300 cases for each of six countries. This means that Lerner's data is very likely an overestimate of FVO participation for the countries in his sample, since urban FVO participation may be expected to be higher than rural participation in these countries.

In addition to FVO membership data from these two studies, data on an additional series of variables for these countries is available from various published statistical sources. Banks and Textor (1963) have performed a valuable service in their book A CROSS-POLITY SURVEY by classifying all the countries in the world in terms of a standard set of important political and sociological variables, partly on the basis of the published statistics and partly on the basis of subjective ratings (utilizing published social, economic, political, historical, and other works). Let us not try to pass judgment on these ratings beyond saying that the ones based on published statistics are probably fairly reliable, but not too much so, while the purely subjective ratings are subject to all the methodological criticisms of any such judgments done by a single person, however well-informed. Nevertheless, both these sets of data (FVO membership and cross-polity data) are independent of each other and, more importantly, were gathered with aims independent of the present analysis.

In reviewing the data in Table 3-1 on some eleven countries ranging from highly underdeveloped (near the peasant society end of the dimension) to highly industrialized societies (the United States, Britain, West Germany), the first thing of importance to note is that our impressions of increasing FVO membership with increasing economic and industrial development are borne out almost perfectly: FVO membership figures range from a high of 57 percent of the adult population in the United States to a low of 18 percent of the (largely urban) sample for Turkey. Further, the table indicates that the ordering by economic development status and the percentage of the population in agricultural pursuits is broadly the same, as one would expect, thus generally validating the more subjective economic development status rating.

The only real exception to the pattern is Egypt. This anomaly may perhaps be explained by the fact that the FVO membership figure is inflated for Egypt (as well as Greece, Jordan, Lebanon, Syria, Turkey) owing to oversampling the presumably higher participating urban respondents, who constituted about 75 percent of the interviews vs. about 28 percent of the population as a whole. This inflation works against rather than for our postulated relationship between industrialization and FVO membership prevalence. Thus since subjects in all of the Middle Eastern countries in Lerner's sample were chosen similarly as regards rural vs. urban residence (25 percent vs. 75 percent), all of these countries in actuality should have substantially lower percentages of membership, making confirmation of the postulated relationship even clearer. The rank order may shift somewhat if better data is obtained, but the overall pattern will probably not change very much.

Table 3-1

FVO Membership by Economic Development Status and Agricultural Population

Country	Percentage of Sample Belonging to One or More FVOs[a]	Economic Development Rating[b]	Agricultural Population[c]
United States	57	Developed	Low
United Kingdom	47	Developed	Low
West Germany	44	Developed	Low
Egypt	32	Underdeveloped	High
Italy	30	Developed	Low
Greece	26	Intermediate	Medium
Mexico	25	Intermediate	Medium
Jordan	21	Underdeveloped	Medium
Lebanon	20	Underdeveloped	Medium
Syria	19	Underdeveloped	High
Turkey	18	Underdeveloped	High

[a]Figures for United States, United Kingdom, West Germany, Italy, and Mexico are from Almond and Verba (1963, p. 302). Figures for the other countries are our calculations from the original data cards of Lerner's study, obtained from his office at the Massachusetts Institute of Technology, Cambridge, Massachusetts. Thanks are due Prof. Lerner for his help.

[b]Ratings for all countries are from Banks and Textor (1963), Finished Characteristics Tables 41 and 42.

[c]Ratings for all countries are from Banks and Textor (1963), Finished Characteristics Tables 30 and 31.

In order to extend the above line of analysis we may use a rating by Banks and Textor (1963) of what they call "interest articulation by associational groups,"[2] actually an index of the degree of pressure group activity of FVOs in each country considered. Comparing interest articulation by associational groups with the actual prevalence (membership) of FVOs in the eleven countries for which some survey data is available, Table 3-2 indicates that the relationship between the two measures is quite close. Of the first five countries with higher FVO membership rates in the survey data, all but Egypt (deviant again) were rated "significant" on interest articulation, while for the second six countries with lower FVO membership rates, all were rated as having less than significant interest articulation.

On the basis of the above demonstrated relationship, then, let us take Banks and Textor's rating of interest articulation as a rough measure of FVO prevalence for all countries. Using this measure we may again examine the relationship of FVO prevalence to analytical type of society, using as indicators of societal type a number of measures of modernization. Table 3-3 presents the relevant results, indicating that our postulated relationship is highly confirmed:

Table 3-2

Survey-Reported FVO Membership by Rated Interest Articulation of Associational Groups

Country	Percentage of Sample Belonging to One or More FVOs[a]	Rated Interest Articulation of Associational Groups[b]
United States	57	Significant
United Kingdom	47	Significant
West Germany	44	Significant
Egypt	32	Not Significant
Italy	30	Significant
Greece	26	Not Significant
Mexico	25	Not Significant
Jordan	21	Not Significant
Lebanon	20	Not Significant
Syria	19	Not Significant
Turkey	18	Not Significant

[a]See note a, Table 3-1.

[b]Ratings for all countries are from Banks and Textor (1963).
Finished Characteristics Table 115, collapsed to two categories for present purposes.

FVO prevalence is much more likely to be "significant" or "moderate" in the industrialized countries, characterized by high urbanization, medium or low agricultural population, high or very high per capita Gross National Product, an economic development rating of "developed" or "intermediate," higher literacy, and higher percentage of labor force working in industry. Conversely, FVO prevalence as measured by the interest articulation rating is much more likely to be "limited" or "negligible" in the more peasantlike countries, having scores at the opposite ends of the urbanization, agricultural population, GNP, development status, literacy, and industrial work force measures.

As an additional attempt to determine the relationship between modernization measures and FVO prevalence, a multiple regression analysis was performed using simultaneously all six modernization variables in Table 3-3 to predict interest articulation by associational groups. The resulting regression equation produces a multiple correlation of 0.86, accounting for about 74 percent of the variance in interest articulation by associational groups for the approximately 100 countries involved. This is a very substantial result indeed, indicating that the present measure of FVO prevalence is much more strongly associated with measures of modernization (especially, percentage of the population not working in agriculture, economic development status of the country, level of literacy, and percentage of the working age population employed in industry) than with

Table 3-3

Rated Interest Articulation of Associational Groups by Measures of Analytical Type of Society (Modernization)[a]

Measures of Analytical Type of Society	Rated Interest Articulation of Associational Groups:	
	Number of Societies Significant/Moderate	Number of Societies Limited/Negligible
Urbanization		
High	31	23 $N = 102$
		$\chi^2 = 36.9$[b]
Low	0	48 $P < 0.001$
Agricultural Population		
Medium or less	31	24 $N_2 = 109$
		$\chi^2 = 36.5$
High	1	53 $P < 0.001$
Per Capita Gross National Product		
High or very high	28	12 $N = 111$
		$\chi^2 = 48.6$
Medium or less	4	67 $P < 0.001$
Economic Development Status		
Developed or intermediate	26	9 $N = 108$
		$\chi^2 = 52.5$
Underdeveloped or very underdeveloped	4	69 $P < 0.001$
Literacy		
High	29	22 $N = 105$
		$\chi^2 = 33.1$
Low	2	52 $P < 0.001$
Percentage of Working Population in Industry		
High	24	9 $N = 65$
		$\chi^2 = 19.2$
Low	5	27 $P < 0.001$

[a]All ratings in this table except percentage working population in industry are taken from Banks and Textor (1963), Finished Characteristic Table 116, relationships with Finished Characteristics 29, 30, 35, 42, and 45. The rating of percentage of working population in industry is taken from Russet et al. (1964), p. 185f., dichotomizing at the median of the reported distribution. The total number of countries in the world at the time of compiling the ratings was about 115 and varies owing to ambiguous or unascertainable cases.

[b]The chi-square ("χ^2") calculations were all performed on the fourfold contingency tables here reported, and hence have one degree of freedom involved. In every case the statistic is significant at far less than the 0.001 level of probability ("$P < 0.001$").

any other kinds of variables (since only 26 percent of the variance is left to be accounted for by any other kinds of variables).

There is one important kind of methodological criticism that could be leveled at the foregoing results with reasonable justification: In spite of our quite successful attempt to validate the interest articulation measure against actual survey data for several countries, it is still possible that there was a significant amount of "modernization bias" involved in the interest articulation ratings. That is, the rater(s) may well have tended to give higher interest articulation ratings to modern countries than to traditional ones, even where the actual descriptions of FVO activities in the coding sources for various countries were nearly identical. Such a bias would tend to inflate the observed relationship between modernization measures and FVO prevalence.

The only way to eliminate such biases is to use more objective measures of FVO prevalence, such as the survey data already reviewed. As a further attempt to provide such "objective" data on FVO prevalence, relatively recent data on union membership for most of the countries in the world can be examined (U.S. Department of Labor, 1964). These data admittedly have many flaws, and their "objectivity" is indeed quite questionable, especially for the less developed countries where the membership figure is likely to be more of an estimate than a figure derived from carefully kept records. Still, the biases involved should be more random and noncumulative than the biases involved in the interest articulation measure. This follows from the fact that the union membership figures, insofar as they are estimates (hence subjective ratings), came from a large number of different persons, each one representing a different country and having had a great deal of experience with union activities in that country. The interest articulation measure, on the other hand, is likely to reflect the cumulative and nonrandom biases of one or two individuals, both working without deep and extensive personal experience of FVO phenomena in nearly all of the countries involved. Hence, the union membership data are at least more objective and less susceptible to any systematic modernization bias than is true of the interest articulation rating.

A major drawback of using union membership as an index of FVO prevalence, however, is the fact that such an index is very narrow, representing only one of many important types of FVOs potentially present in every country. Further, many will even challenge whether unions are FVOs at all. In terms of the definition of FVOs being used here (see note 1), unions do qualify as FVOs—even when membership is semicompulsory or compulsory for people in a certain occupation or work organization—since most participants in unions are volunteers, not being directly remunerated for their participation in the union. (In fact, people pay dues to belong to unions, rather than being paid themselves to participate.)

Recognizing, then, that union membership is an imperfect measure of FVO prevalence for various reasons, it will still be worthwhile to examine union prevalence data as possible additional corroboration for the postulated relationship between modernization and FVO prevalence. Since union membership is strongly related to population and size of the labor force across countries, and since we are primarily interested in union membership as an indicator of the prevalence of FVOs, we formed an index of union prevalence by dividing a country's reported union membership by the number of persons in the labor force in that country. In this way our resulting index is the proportion of the labor force in each country who belong to unions.

Before examining the association between our union prevalence index and various modernization measures, let us note in passing that the union prevalence index and the interest articulation rating are significantly correlated (Pearsonian $r = 0.33$, $P < 0.01$), although the magnitude of the association is only low-moderate.

When we compute a multiple regression equation predicting the union prevalence index, the six modernization variables of Table 3-3 combine to yield a multiple correlation of 0.63, accounting for about 40 percent of the variance in union prevalence. While not as strong a relationship as we get using the interest articulation measure as a measure of FVO prevalence, the present results are still quite strong and significant, lending substantial additional support to the postulated relationship between modernization and FVO prevalence. The strongest independent predictors of union prevalence (judging from the sizes of the Beta weights in the regression equation) appear to be (1) the percentage employed in industry out of the total working age population, and (2) the level of economic development of the country.

A third, independently derived and quite objective measure of FVO prevalence is the number of international nongovernmental organizations (abbreviated as "INGOs") to which a country (or some persons or organizations within the country) belongs. Derived from information in the YEARBOOK OF INTERNATIONAL ORGANIZATIONS (Tew, 1966) this index of INGOs correlates positively and significantly with the two previous FVO prevalence measures we have considered: $r = 0.84$ with interest articulation by associational groups and $r = 0.32$ with the union prevalence index. Hence, all three measures seem to be dealing with different aspects of the same underlying theme, although the INGOs index and interest articulation measure are by far most strongly related. The virtue of the INGO index is its great objectivity—countries either are or are not formal members of each of the nearly 2 thousand existing INGOs, and the listings in the YEARBOOK may reasonably be taken as definitive. But the INGO index does have a major defect: Although the index includes all types of FVOs as far as goals are concerned, the precise relationship between the INGO index and the true prevalence of FVOs of all types within countries is not known. It seems quite reasonable, however, to assume that the relationship is a positive and at least moderately strong one, in view of the strong association of the INGO index with the independently derived interest articulation measure. Also our assumption seems likely on theoretical grounds, since "external" FVO activity can be viewed as an extension of the "internal" FVO activity of a country.

When we compute, once again, a regression equation between the six measures of modernization and our third dependent FVO prevalence measure (the INGO index), a multiple correlation of 0.82 results, accounting for 68 percent of the variance of INGOs among countries. Of the six predictors, economic development status and percentage of nonagricultural population are most strongly and significantly associated in a positive direction with the INGO index. Hence, these results lend further strong confirmation to the postulated association between FVO prevalence and societal modernization.

We have now demonstrated at least the likelihood that FVO prevalence is positively associated with modernization, and the development from a primitive or peasant society into a modern industrial society. Yet we have not seen so far any evidence of an "FVO revolution" as one moves from one analytical type of society to another. Presumably, such a "revolution" would involve some sort of extremely rapid growth of FVOs as modernization indices increase beyond certain levels. One might expect to find, for instance, that FVO prevalence is some sort of power function of a society's level of modernization (e.g., growing as the square of some set of modernization indices). An examination of some of the present data, however, gives little indication of the presence of an exponential curve of any sort. Using the number of INGOs per country as the best measure of FVO prevalence we have available, FVO prevalence was plotted against percentage of the labor force working in agriculture as a good modernization index. There was in this scatter plot (not reproduced here for reasons of space) some tendency for the FVO prevalence index to rise somewhat more rapidly as the percentage of the labor force working in agriculture dropped below 50 percent. Yet there were a number of exceptions that fall far off the "ideal" exponential curve that might otherwise have been drawn through the data points. When all data points were "smoothed" by taking a moving average of the number of INGOs for countries in each 5 percent interval of labor force in agriculture, the resulting smoothed curve was nearly a straight line.

Hence, no significant evidence was found for an exponential growth of INGOs as modernization increases. A similar result was obtained when the percentage of the labor force belonging to unions was plotted against the percentage of the labor force working in industry. Therefore, insofar as there is in any sense an "FVO revolution" as modernization increases, it is probably a matter of the speed with which modernization takes place. If modernization takes place slowly in a given society, FVO prevalence will probably grow slowly also, in fairly direct proprotion to the level of modernization. On the other hand, if modernization takes place very rapidly in a society (an "industrial revolution" or "urban revolution" occurring, for instance, over the space of several decades rather than centuries), FVO prevalence will probably also grow very rapidly and will be seen as an "FVO revolution," as part of a general "organizational revolution."

The next question that arises is, "Why does FVO prevalence seem to be directly related (perhaps as a linear additive function) to modernization?" Even to ask this question is to affirm that the obvious superficial explanation is inadequate—it is not sufficient by way of explanation to state that urbanization, industrialization, educational up-grading, etc. are the causes. Surely these processes play a central role, but a fully adequate explanation must show in detail what aspects of these very broad modernization processes are direct and essential determinants of FVO prevalence, and what aspects are peripheral and causally unimportant concomitants. The remainder of this chapter attempts to suggest an explanatory scheme that is more nearly adequate than the obvious one.

The Explanatory Scheme Proposed

There are, it has been argued, three main analytical criteria for the existence and definition of groups, in addition to the trivial criterion of two or more individuals being involved. First of all, there can be no group or organization if there is no intercommunication among the set of individuals being considered. Second, there can be no group if there is no shared goal or set of goals among these individuals. Third, there can be no group if there is no shared collectivity orientation or sense of group identity.[3]

If we are correct in delineating these as the main criterial elements of all groups, then any theory of group formation and decay may specify the growth and decline of these elements as a major part of its explanatory apparatus. We intend to do just this in our model of FVO prevalence. Modernization, or changes in analytical level of society from primitive to peasant to industrial, will be related to changes in the intercommunication network, goal differentiation, and collective action orientation within these types of societies, and these differences in turn will be used to explain differences in FVO prevalence in primitive, peasant, and industrial societies.

In simplest form the model states that the prevalence rate (number in existence at a given point in time) of FVOs in a society (or social system) is an additive function of three characteristics of the society: The nature of its intercommunication network, the nature of its goal differentiation, and the nature of its collective action orientation. Consider now the set of individuals forming a society within which we are trying to predict or explain the FVO prevalence. How does the model specifically require that we assess this society?

First of all, we must assess its intercommunication structure or the degree to which it forms a true intercommunication network. An intercommunication network is defined as a set of individuals each of whom may be seen as communicating within a specified time period with every other individual in the set, if enough intermediary communication links are traced. As the term will be used here, an intercommunication network is often more of an assumption than a proven fact about a set of individuals, though its presence could easily be established empirically. Let us assume, then, that the society considered is in an intercommunication network.

There are at least three crucial aspects of an intercommunication network for present purposes: its per capita internal volume,[4] its connectivity, and its permanence. The per capita internal volume of an intercommunication network may be defined as the ratio of the total number of intercommunications initiated and received by members of the network to the total number of individuals comprising the network. This ratio gives a rough measure of the relative frequency of communication activity occurring among the members of the network at a given point in time or during a given period of time. The connectivity of the network refers to the average extent to which each individual intercommunicates with a large range of other individuals in the network as opposed to intercommunicating merely with a small circle of close friends or relatives. The greater the connectivity of the network, the fewer the number of communication links (person-person intercommunication relationships) necessary to reach any individual in the network starting from any other individual. The permanence of the network refers, of course, to the average duration of the intercommunication relationships occuring among the members of the network.

The general proposition of the FVO prevalence model, then, is as follows with regard to the nature of the intercommunication network: FVO prevalence will be generally higher for greater per capita internal volume, connectivity, and permanence of a communication network.[5] The argument is that FVOs are groups, and that the incidence-prevalence rates of all types of groups tend to be increased by high levels on the three aspects of an intercommunication network here distinguished. The latter is at the very least true at the extremes: By definition, no group of any kind is possible when there is zero per capita internal volume of intercommunication, zero connectivity, and zero permanence. Most will also agree that being at the high end of the scale on all of these dimensions is associated with a high degree of group formation. Basically, however, this must be considered an empirical postulate of the model and hence subject to subsequent testing.

Where the aspects of the communication network considered above represented basically formal aspects of the network, the extent of interest and goal differentiation represent a basic content aspect of the network. For a group to exist there must be shared goals among the members; for many groups to exist within a communication network there must be a variety of goals, each one shared distributively within various subsets of individuals of the network. If all the members of the network shared exactly the same goals, we would expect to find not many groups but one group within the network. At the opposite extreme, however, it is theoretically possible for a communication network to be characterized by too much goal differentiation, so that there is not enough consensus among subsets of individuals to permit the formation of any groups.

But such an extreme case is rare in practice, and hence the model holds as a first approximation that FVO prevalence will be higher for greater interest and goal differentiation of a communication network.

The third major type of independent variable of the model may be termed the collective action orientation of the members of a communication network. The model holds that FVO prevalence will be greater for increases in at least four important elements of collective action orientation: (1) the degree of permission of collectivities by the larger social system, (2) the degree of instigation of collectivities within the communication network, (3) the average resources for collective action of individuals of the network, and (4) the net payoffs for collective action to individuals of the network.

In the case of FVOs, the degree of permission of collectivities by the larger social system refers to the extent to which the enacted and customary laws and the informal norms and practices of the society or social system permit the formation of FVOs, both as a general type of group and for various specific purposes. In short, permission here refers to freedom of association. Instigation of collectivities refers here to the extent to which specific individuals ("organizers"), already existing groups of organizations, and widespread social attitudes directly tend to instigate the formation of FVOs in general and/or specific FVO types in particular. The resources for collective action[6] includes persons' facilitative cognitions (perceptions, beliefs), motivations, affections (sentiments, feelings), their facilitative capacities and skills, the time available to them, and the financial and material resources they have available. The payoffs of collectivity formation are the objective gains and losses of FVO formation (and membership) for the potential members. The net payoffs are what an FVO can do that the individuals alone or informally organized could not do, together with the disadvantages such collective action incurs for its participants.

In summary then, the model holds that there will be a greater prevalence of FVOs in societies (or intercommunications networks) characterized (1) by greater per capita internal volume, permanence, and connectivity of intercommunication networks, (2) by greater differentiation of goals and interests, and (3) by greater permission, instigation, resources, and payoffs for FVOs.[7]

The Sociohistorical Contexts

For the sake of exposition let us focus on more or less autonomous societies as the basic unit of inquiry. We shall define a society as an ascriptive social group of a basically political nature, in which the ascriptive criteria of membership are birth and/or territorial residence, and where the group involved represents the largest set of persons for a given territory possessing shared expectations about the legitimate use of ultimate force (i.e., execution, ostracism, restitution, etc.) among themselves.

Following a now increasingly standard practice, we shall consider societies as classifiable into three broad analytical types. First of all there are "primitive societies" (folk, preliterate, precivilized societies), societies characterized by small size; (relative) isolation from the political, economic, and cultural influence of other societies; homogeneity and a strong sense of intimacy and group solidarity; illiteracy or preliteracy (lack of a developed written language); lack of infrequency of full-time non-food-producing specialists; predominance of kinship relations; prevalence of close, personal relationships to the exclusion of more "secondary" relationships (Kroeber 1948, pp. 281 ff.; Redfield 1953, Chap. 1).

The second type of society may be called "peasant" society (literate preindustrial society, medieval society, underdeveloped society), and is characterized by the presence of large sized (e.g., 5 thousand and more persons) settlements (cities, urban areas), the institution of tribute or taxation with resulting central accumulation of capital, monumental public works, the art of writing (literacy, of at least some fraction of the population), the beginning of empirical science and mathematics, full-time technical specialists (in non-food-producing occupations), developed economic institutions (beginnings of a market economy) making possible a greatly expanded foreign trade, a privileged ruling class, religious specialists, and developed governmental institutions as indicated by full-time government leaders and administrators (according to Childe 1950).

Whereas primitive society is made up almost completely of rural food-producing specialists (subsistence food collectors, hunters, fishermen, herdsmen and farmers), peasant society is made up of rural food-producing specialists plus a large number of non-food-producing, full-time specialists supported by food the first group produces. Most of the full-time non-food-producing specialists reside in urban centers or cities, thus constituting the second major element of peasant society. Peasant society is thus distinguished from primitive society not so much by the existence of peasants as by the existence of city people.

The third type of society may be termed "modern" or "industrial" society. As the latter name suggests, this type of society is distinguished from peasant society primarily by its possession of a more developed industrial technology (e.g., factories using power driven machinery), with its correspondingly greater division of labor and occupational specialization and an elaborate market economy. In addition, industrial society is characterized in general by increased levels of literacy and institutionalized mass education, by the decreasing importance of extended kinship ties, by increasing secularization, rationalism and the importance of science, by increasing urbanization, and by increased interrelations with other societies.

As usual, there are clear polar cases fitting each of these three societal types, and there are many marginal cases whose classification is arbitrary. Modernization as a process is viewed as change from primitive toward peasant society or from peasant toward modern industrial society. Since our purpose is heuristic, we shall fit the cases examined to the three Procrustean beds outlined above.

Applying the Model to Analytic Sociohistorical Contexts

Primitive Society

Now we shall try to show how the general variation in FVO prevalence rates according to analytical type of society, suggested by the first section of this paper, can be explained in terms of our model. First of all, consider primitive society as a broad analytic type. The prevalence rate for nearly all types of FVOs in primitive society is generally low.[8] The model would explain this fact in the following manner. Although the per capital internal volume, stability, and connectivity of the communication network of a primitive society are fairly high (when small, isolated single tribes are considered), there is very little differentiation of interests and goals, owing to the only rudimentary occupational specialization and to the lack of differential experiences and socialization in any marked degree. In a primitive society a man's goals and values are generally the same as those of his father (parents and relatives) and also of his neighbor. Exposure to innovations (new ideas, new interests, objects, and experiences) and to variations in custom is low. Where it increases significantly, we may expect to find a corresponding increase in FVO formation. (The well-known "cargo cults" formed by certain primitive tribes in oceania are examples.)

In addition, primitive societies tend predominantly to lack development of the various aspects of the collective action orientation crucial to FVO prevalence. The freedom to form FVOs is limited by the strength of traditional (generally ascriptive) modes of group formation. Once formed, a new FVO may well tend to be viewed as a group of deviates at a very basic moral level (no matter how innocuous the FVO's goals), leading to the application of strong negative sanctions by the other members of the society either to ostracize or abolish the FVO entirely.

The level of instigation of FVOs is very low because on the one hand there are no (or few) existing FVOs or individuals within the society who are interested in extending FVOs to new subsets of the population, and on the other hand there are few individuals or organizations from outside the society who are interested in coming in to instigate FVO formation, since a primitive society in the ideal-typical case is isolated, by definition, and generally has little of value to offer outsiders. A fairly common exception to the latter point in contemporary times is the case where missionaries of various (usually Christian) churches from outside the primitive society come into it and have some (usually small) success in establishing a new religious FVO (a branch of the mother church) in that society. Similarly, national governments often try to establish FVOs (e.g., cooperatives) among folk societies living within their territory.

The resources for collective action are also quite low in primitive society. To pick just two examples from the realm of beliefs and values, primitive peoples in general tend to be low in their sense of competence (mastery, efficacy) and low in their trust of others (especially where not closely related by kinship), yet both of these are generally facilitative of FVO prevalence. Also important may be the fact that primitive peoples, because of their economic inefficiency, have to spend much of their time in primary productive activities with little resulting accumulation of capital or consumables. As a result, they have little leisure time and a minimal leisure class (within which FVOs tend to arise first).

Probably the most important resource for collective action orientation that is missing from primitive society is a set of general attitudes toward and beliefs about formal organizations. Primitive men are not much familiar with the concept of contingent formal organizations. They neither know how to form such organizations nor consider them useful or efficacious. All the more do they lack positive attitudes towards specific types of FVOs and their goals and programs.

Finally, primitive societies tend to be so small and homogeneous that the potential gains of FVO formation are negligible. Social relations are already highly structured by kinship, sex, and age, so that there is little to be gained from either inclusive or exclusive social FVOs. Similarly, the attainment of most instrumental goals is already taken care of by institutionalized forms, so that the addition of instrumental FVOs is largely unnecessary. For all of the above reasons, then, the model would predict low FVO prevalence rates in primitive society.[9]

Peasant Society

Now let us turn to peasant societies. Peasant societies grow up as a result of gradually increasing agricultural efficiency and political centralization leading to the "urban revolution." The range from the most ancient peasant societies and kingdoms to present-day underdeveloped countries is a very great one in terms of societal characteristics, yet they do all manifest a certain structural similarity. One aspect of this similarity is the tendency to have a significant, but in absolute terms a low, prevalence of FVOs of nearly all types, though they may have at times a fairly high prevalence of some particular FVO type (e.g., gilds). The model explains this on the basis of the following factors. First, peasant society maintains a high degree of stability and moderate per capita internal volume of the total intercommunication network, but the connectivity is much lower than in primitive society, owing to the much larger size of the overall society and the absence of rapid modern communication and transportation. Thus, peasant society generally represents a large number of rather primitive villages and rural areas brought together with a few large urban areas into a very loosely intercommunicating network.

The lower connectivity, however, is offset by the second factor—much greater division of labor and consequent differentiation of goals and interests in peasant society vs. primitive society. Although agricultural and other primary production pursuits remain predominant (e.g., for 50 to 90 percent of the population), a significant proportion of the population now becomes involved in a variety of secondary occupations (crafts, handicraft manufacturing, mining) and tertiary occupations (service-political, religious, and other specialists). When this begins to happen, especially in urban areas, large numbers of people no longer have so much in common with the other subsets of people in the society. Yet they have much in common with that subset of people in the society having the same occupation as themselves. Two other factors concomitant with the rise of peasant societies are the growth of writing, records, and a learned "high culture" on the one hand, and the great increases in geographical mobility and intercommunication among various societies that take place, on the other hand. These two developments contribute further to the differentiation of goals and interests in the society: The growth of writing permits the accumulation of an ever-increasing cultural base of knowledge so important for the invention (or discovery) of further knowledge and interests. The increased communication with other societies permits the diffusion of new ideas, beliefs, values, goals, and the like from outside the given society.

Third, peasant society also tends to be much higher than primitive society on the various dimensions of collective action orientation. The freedom to form FVOs may be legally curtailed in certain specific cases and for certain periods of time, but on the whole, permission is increased in urban areas, especially on the customary or informal (as opposed to legal) level, by the much greater size of settlements and correspondingly greater anonymity in these urban areas. Rural areas show little change relative to primitive societies in this particular aspect. In fact, rural areas in peasant societies tend to show little change relative to primitive societies right across the board for the dimensions we are now considering. Thus the key to the greater FVO formation in peasant society lies in the changes taking place in urban areas (or more correctly, the very formation and development of urban areas as differentiated from rural areas).[10]

There is also in peasant society a substantial increase in the instigation of FVOs relative to primitive society. This fact is closely related to increases in the diffusion of ideas that we noted above. Good examples here are the various religious sects such as Christianity and Islam that arose in one peasant society as FVOs and spread by diffusion to other societies, generally carried by "outside instigators" or organizers. On a smaller scale there is a certain amount of instigation of other types of FVOs by the nobility and wealthy bourgeoisie individuals. Examples are early private schools, political cabals, secret societies, men's clubs, learned discussion groups, courtly "salons," and various semiformal and formal voluntary social-recreational organizations.

With regard to resources for collective action, here too there is an increase in the level of peasant society (because of the presence of cities) compared with primitive societies. Especially marked here is the increase in leisure time and the growth of a leisure class as a result of the increased agricultural efficiency and the accumulation of wealth through centralized taxation and trade. Time that does not have to be spent in full-time primary productive occupations is more available for FVO participation, among other pursuits. There is probably also a certain increase in the sense of trust and competence among at least the higher classes of urban peasant society, further facilitating the growth of FVOs for social and instrumental purposes.

Finally, there are in peasant society, as opposed to primitive society, many potential gains to be made from the formation of FVOs of certain types. Most important are the gains to be made from the organization of members of the same type of urban occupation into an FVO of some sort (e.g., gilds). Such an FVO permits its members a great many benefits of mutual aid (e.g., death benefits) and protection of the occupational group as a whole in the market (e.g., fixing standard prices for services, controlling admission to the occupations, etc.). The benefits of organizing students into a school with one or more tutors for all students were also essentially economic, in this case for the parents, who saved money by each paying only part of the salary of one general tutor, rather than each having to pay for a private tutor. The gains to be made from early political and religious FVOs were essentially ones of increased strength or power of the "cause," however, rather than economic ones.

Even more importantly, as time goes by there tends to develop in peasant society a generally favorable attitude toward the gains to be made from creating contingent formal organizations in pursuit of any purpose. Though this attitude is and has been of quite limited extent in peasant societies, nevertheless it is extremely significant where present. Thus FVOs, as one type of contingent formal organization, have enjoyed a significant stimulation in peasant societies, relative to primitive societies, through the growth of this broader concept of the potential gains to be reaped from formal organization in general, and an incipient knowledge of how to form them and how they work. Primitive societies are so permeated with the concept of kin-based groups that they seldom achieve this knowledge of contingent groups.

For all of these reasons, then, the model would predict or explain a greater prevalence rate of FVOs in peasant societies than in primitive ones. The connectivity of the communication network is lower in peasant society, but this is far more than offset by the greater goal differentiation and collective action orientation in peasant societies. We should reiterate, however, that the main differences between primitive and peasant societies occur in urban areas, which are absent in primitive and present in peasant societies. The actual percentage of FVO members in the society as a whole, or the number of FVOs per capita, or other indices will usually not show great overall differences between the two types of societies, although the rates for peasant society will be consistently higher.

Industrial Society

Now let us turn to an examination of industrial society. The striking data here are that the industrial revolution has brought with it, after a time lag of some 100 years or so, an "organizational revolution" in modern society (see Boulding 1953). Whereas the "urban revolution," passing from primitive to peasant society, brought only small increases in FVO prevalence rates (extremely significant when the base rate is zero), the industrial revolution has generally brought much greater increases in FVO prevalence rates. Why?

The answers are, we believe, clear. First, although the permanence of communication networks in industrial society is somewhat reduced by high rates of geographic mobility, this decrease in permanence is offset by a correspondingly great increase in the connectivity of the total network, owing to modern mechanized transportation and electronic communication devices. Further, the negative effect of high mobility rates is softened by the growth of an attitude that long acquaintance is unncessary for establishing close personal relations and by the ability to carry on relations at a distance by telephone and mail. Besides, although the general spatial mobility rate is high, the average length of time in the same community or urban area is not so low in an absolute sense (i.e., it is not less than two years), so that there can be much mobility as measured by rates of changing of housing per year for the population without really destroying the stability of communication networks.

Finally, with increasing urbanization the majority of the population have types of urban occupations that involve frequent intercommunication and live in high density urban agglomerations that facilitate such intercommunication, as contrasted with having rural agricultural occupations and residential patterns that are more frequently solitary or relatively isolated. The peasant farmer in the field or the primitive hunter in the forest may go all day without communicating with a single soul; the modern urban office or factory worker can scarcely do so. The result of this is an increase in the per capita internal volume of communications in industrial as opposed to peasant or primitive society.

Overall, then, industrial society is characterized by a communication network at least as developed as that of peasant society, and probably more so, though perhaps not reaching the level of intercommunication present in small, primitive societies. Most important is the fact that the size of the active intercommunication network is very great in industrial society, making it more likely that diverse sets of individuals with similar interests will make contact among themselves and thus lay the base for FVO formation.

Second, in the degree of differentiation of interests and goals we find vast increases as we pass from peasant to industrial society. This differentiation follows from the great increases in occupational specialization, in urbanization, and in exposure to a variety of experiences, values, beliefs, and ideas through the joint operation of mass education and the mass media of communication (TV, radio, newspapers, magazines, etc.). Each of these influences has played its part in providing modern industrial man with a range of choices among alternative goals and interests undreamt of in peasant societies, let alone primitive society. And each of these multifarious interests can and does, somewhere, serve as the focal purpose of some FVO—or perhaps a thousand or ten thousand FVOs.

Where peasant society differed from primitive society mainly in respect to the small part of the population residing in urban areas of the former, industrial society differs from peasant society (at least as a polar case) in both urban and rural areas: In industrial society not only are urban residents more "modern" (i.e., characterized by much greater interest differentiation, etc.) than urban residents in peasant society, and not only is the percentage of urban residents much greater than in peasant society (e.g., 50 to 80 or 90 percent, as opposed to 10 to 49 percent), but even the rural residents of industrial society (including most of the farmers and their families) tend to be "modern" men as compared with the rural residents of peasant society. This means that the fertile ground for the growth of FVOs is extended from a small (urban) percentage of the population of peasant society to essentially the total population of industrial society. The extension is made even greater still by virtue of the "emancipation" of women and the prolonged adolescent period of children in modern industrial society. Only rarely did women and children form or participate in FVOs in primitive and peasant societies, while in industrial societies there is a large amount of FVO activity among women and children. The increase owing to FVO participation by women and children may account by itself for much of the general increase in FVO participation in industrial society.[11]

Third, this expanded participation of rural people, women, and children is partly a consequence of greater differentiation of goals and interests within these groups, but partly also a result of increased collective action orientation in these groups as well as in the male, adult urbanites. After initial periods of suppressive legislation, most modern industrial societies have permitted the formation of a wide variety of FVOs. In the case of labor unions, early laws, for example made them illegal "conspiracies" in both the United States and Britain, while more recent laws at least permit unions and may even require union membership of workers in a unionized industry or company—the case of "closed-shop" unionism (see Gregory 1958; Sultan 1958).

In the United States as elsewhere there is a long history of constitutional law dealing with freedom of association, not only with regard to unions but also dealing with religious, political, and other types of FVOs (Fellman 1963; Rice 1962). Robert Horn (1956, p. 18) has summarized the principal generalizations growing out of this body of law in the United States: Individuals have the right to form and join associations so long as such activities do not infringe upon the rights of others or threaten serious injury to the society as a whole or its political institutions. Further, the government may foster associations when the public interest suggests it and the government may even require private persons to enter into legal relations with associations when appropriate.

The high overall level of legal permissiveness of the FVOs in the United States, however, lies more in the application of these principles than simply in their existence. A similar set of principles might, for instance, summarize the general situation in a modern industrial totalitarian society. The big difference would be in the application there of a broad range of restrictions and control of FVOs and their activities in the name of a greatly expanded version of the public welfare and general good of the country.[12]

At the level of custom and informal norms, permission of FVOs in industrial society throughout all sectors of the population is generally much greater than in peasant society. To form an FVO of most any sort in (nontotalitarian) industrial society scarcely draws a raised eyebrow, let alone more severe informal sanctions or ostracism as might occur in peasant or especially primitive society. More important than this passive permission, however, is the great amount of active instigation of FVOs in industrial society, relative to peasant society (or primitive society). This is most clearly the case with all of the "instrumental" types of FVOs (economic, political, educational, religious, scientific, health, and welfare FVOs, etc.), rather than with social and recreational FVOs.

Labor unions and cooperatives have their professional organizers (or instigators, in our terminology) that try to stimulate new FVOs in areas and with people as yet unclaimed by such FVOs;[13] so do political parties and religious groups (e.g., "missionaries"). The other instrumental FVOs are more likely to depend on nonprofessional (i.e., "volunteer") organizers, but may at times have professional ones. Not only do the larger (e.g., national or federated) FVOs of various types mount expansion programs and put organizers into the field, but governments may play a big hand in FVO instigation in certain cases. In the totalitarian countries the government is far and away the single paramount organizer of FVOs (e.g., the Hitler Youth in Nazi Germany, or the mass organizations of Communist China (Chao 1952).

With respect to the resources for collective action orientation, industrial society also shows important increases in all areas. The facilitative values and beliefs, such as trust and competence (mastery), generally show an increase in industrial versus peasant society, as do the various abstract conceptual and verbal skills also contributory to the formation and functioning of FVOs. In the matter of leisure time, things became worse for the bulk of the population before they became better: The industrial revolution and the (steam-powered) factories it brought consumed fourteen hours per day or even more of workers' time. It is only since about 1850 in the United States that there have been real reductions in working hours for manufacturing and mining workers, and more recently for agricultural workers (Wilensky 1961).

Perhaps more important than simple reduction in working hours has been the increased differentiation between working time and leisure time. Where in primitive and peasant (especially rural) society work and play were often run together, modern industrial society has clearly distinguished FVOs as groupings of people pursuing common nonwork leisure interests. It is also relevant to recall here the great increases in the leisure time available to women and youth (especially adolescents) in modern society, as mechanized household conveniences permit women to devote much less of their time to household tasks (see Bacon 1942) and as the rising age of first full-time entry into the labor force provides youth with extra "idle" years (considering that schooling takes up less of their time than a full-time job would). As mentioned earlier, however, changes in attitudes toward and held by women and children are probably more significant in their greater FVO participation than is sheer free time.

The so-called emancipation of women in modern industrial society has meant that women have been granted (under pressure) a new independence not found in peasant or primitive society as a rule. This independence of attitude coupled with available leisure time permits the formation of FVOs catering to women's special interests, where prior FVOs were almost exclusively male or centered around male interests. With increasing entry into the labor force and increasing education, women in industrial society come to have both the desire and opportunity to form and maintain a variety of FVOs.

The trend away from older, authoritarian child-rearing practices and toward more democratic, independence-promoting practices in industrial societies has contributed to a similar "emancipation of children." With increased education and prolonged adolescence, modern youth have more desire and opportunity to form their own FVOs also. This reflects both the admission by adults that youth are persons with independent rights and interests, and the growth of youth's own desire to form and join FVOs specializing in the pursuit of youth's goals. Part of this process, of course, is a result of the imitation of the adult forms of social organization (e.g., FVOs) by youth desiring to prove they are adults.

Finally, in industrial society the net payoffs or perceived gains of collective FVO action relative to disadvantages are much greater than in peasant society. For totalitarian societies, mass FVOs controlled and run by the government are a major means of control of the masses and maintenance of the elite in power. For more democratic societies, FVOs tend to form and represent the influences of a broad range of competing interests. In this situation, each set and social category of people tends to become at least partially aware of the advantages of formal organization to make itself heard and to further its interests. And the way to further a collective interest, it has become clear and accepted, is to form an organization of some kind—to gather voices, votes, and dollars and pour on the collective pressure. Marx was one of the first to note this explicitly a century ago. This technique is most useful for the "instrumental" types of FVOs. FVOs more nearly social and recreational in purpose have as their major collective gain the fellowship of like-minded souls, and to some extent the exclusion of presumed "alien" souls. But this perceived gain of fellowship can be very great indeed in our contemporary industrial society that breaks older ascriptive ties and breeds anonymity with its huge metropolitan complexes and with its high geographic mobility.

For all of these reasons, then, our model would predict (or explain) the greatly increased FVO prevalence rates in industrial as contrasted with peasant society. The resulting large increases in FVO prevalence, however, are a "revolution" only insofar as there are very large and/or very rapid changes in a society's modernity indices. If the magnitude and pace of modernization (and its concomitant elements relevant to FVO prevalence) are small and slow, the changes in FVO prevalence will tend to be correspondingly small according to the present model.

The value of the proposed model for future research lies in its capacity to make differential predictions of FVO prevalence when the gross levels of modernity of two or more societies (or other social systems) appear roughly identical. In addition, the present model permits differential prediction of FVO prevalence at lower social system levels (e.g., regions, cities, neighborhoods) where "modernization" indices are decreasingly available or applicable.

Summary

Some survey and judgmental rating data have been adduced to lend significant support to the postulated increases in FVO prevalence with increasing modernization, examining data for the contemporary nations of the world. Rejecting a simple explanation of this increase in terms of urbanization, industrialization, etc., we have presented a model purporting to account for the differential prevalence of formal voluntary organizations among societies or, by extension, among smaller social systems. The basic independent variables are communication network development, degree of goal differentiation, and degree of collective action orientation development. These variables and their components are used to explain the increase in FVO prevalence from primitive to peasant to industrial societies. The basic predictions of the model can and should be tested on appropriate data (both cross-sectional and longitudinal) gathered from the various societies of the world, as well as being tested with data from various lower social system levels within various societies.[14]

Notes

1. For the purposes of the present discussion formal volunteer organizations are defined as formal organizations, the majority of whose members are neither paid for participation (as in formal work organizations) nor physically coerced into such participation (as in formal coercive organizations). Participation in formal volunteer organizations may be normatively induced or even demanded in some degree, but such organizations are still volunteer by definition so long as physical coercion is not used or threatened. The organizations or groups of

interest here are formal ones rather than informal ones, meaning they have a proper name, formal criteria of membership, explicit leadership roles, explicit goals, regular meetings, etc. (The distinction among volunteer, work, and coercive formal organizations derives from Etzioni's distinction among normative, utilitarian, and coercive organizations (see Etzioni 1961, Chaps. 1, 2, 3).

2. Finished Characteristic Table 116.

3. The principal exceptions to these criteria are formal coercive organizations such as prisons, where only the elite or controlling higher participants have these three characteristics. The inmates or lower participants in such cases may not form true groups. Their organization "membership" is thus determined solely on a coercive basis (see Smith 1967; Smith 1972).

4. Related measures, such as net per capita external volume of communication, or total communications volume, may be important for other problems, especially when dealing with international (or intersystem) relations.

5. When more empirical data is available and the model has been appropriately tested, we will be able to assign differential weights to these three factors for the prediction of the prevalence of various types of FVOs or other groups in various types of situations. For the present, however, let us just assume that each of the elements and subelements of the model are to be weighted equally in any summary prediction, lacking other information.

6. A more detailed exposition of psychological resources for collective action may be found in Smith, 1966.

7. We should mention, just for the sake of completeness, that a more refined theory would present separate analytic and mathematic functions for incidence and prevalence rates, and would assign powers and constants to an equation containing the above-mentioned variables. The present model has a long way to go before reaching these stages.

8. For the present this must be taken largely as an impression. There have been no empirical studies of general FVO prevalence in primitive societies, but Simmons (1945) provides some data on one particular type of FVO—the so-called secret society. In this work Simmons rated 71 primitive societies from all parts of the world on a series of 234 variables. One of these variables was the presence of secret societies. Unfortunately, the term "secret society" is not defined by Simmons nor are the rating criteria explicitly stated. Hence Simmons' rating may be an overestimate of the number of FVOs in primitive society, since his rating includes ascriptive organizations as well as contingent (or achieved status) organizations—true FVOs. In addition, we have no way of knowing what proportion of all types of primitive FVOs fall into Simmons' secret society category, although we may expect that a large proportion were so included because of the generality with which the category is used.

In spite of these deficiencies, however, it is interesting to note that out of the 71 societies treated in a total of 336 anthropological sources, only 39 societies can be coded for the presence-absence of secret societies on the basis of definite mentions in the source material. If we can trust the professional thoroughness of anthropologists, we might assume that, at the very least, formal social groups that are present in a culture always are mentioned in their reports on that culture. Then we can argue that only about 27 percent of the 71 randomly selected primitive societies show moderate or marked elaboration of secret societies, the other 73 percent showing slight elaboration (about 4 percent), mentioned absence of this culture trait (about 25 percent), or no mention of the trait (the remaining 44 percent). If secret societies represent a substantial proportion of the FVOs that exist in primitive society, and there is reason to believe this is true, then we must conclude that the overall prevalence of FVOs in primitive societies is rather low, according to Simmons' data.

Anderson (Chapter 1 of this volume) has indicated that FVOs occur fairly frequently in Neolithic forms of primitive society, though largely absent from earlier forms. However, this conclusion and the ethnographic studies and comparative summaries on which it was based do not permit any numerical estimates of FVO prevalence, merely broad trends.

9. Confirming the conclusion of Anderson (Chapter 1 of this volume), Simmons' data (1945) on secret societies indicate that what FVOs (actually, secret societies) there are in primitive societies are more frequent in stable agricultural societies than in roving hunting-fishing-gathering societies. The author's calculations made on Simmons' data produced a chi-square for this relationship significant at less than the 0.10 level of probability, for one degree of freedom. This result also is predicted by the model, principally by the fact that agricultural societies are more economically efficient and allow somewhat more accumulation of food supplies (though still only at a low absolute level). Hence more resulting leisure time and a rudimentary leisure class, or at least secondary and tertiary occupational specialists, tend to develop. Out of the increased leisure time and the increase in the division of labor come an increased size of the population that the society can support, a consequent increase in differentiation of goals and interests, and an increase of the probability of FVOs.

10. If this formulation is correct, the model also enables us to explain why FVOs should be formed historically first in urban areas.

11. Gabriel Almond and Sidney Verba (1963, p. 303) state that the national differences in the number of individuals participating in voluntary associations in their five countries (the U.S.A., U.K., West Germany, Italy and Mexico) "can be largely explained by differences in the proportion of women who report such membership." Moreover, the two less developed and more peasant-like societies (Italy and Mexico) had significantly lower female FVO membership rates than the three more developed industrial societies (an average of 17 percent female membership in the lower two versus an average of 34 percent in the upper three—Germany, Great Britain, and the U.S.A.). All of this data is from (nearly) representative random samples of the adult population of the countries involved.

12. Although we shall not consider them explicitly, modern industrial

totalitarian regimes, such as Russia and its satellites, usually have a large amount of FVO activity. The main differences from nontotalitarian regimes lie in (a) the restricted range of types of organizations (with principal concentration in political, educational, and economic areas), and (b) the presence of government control and government programs of activity in nearly all types of FVOs.

13. Kolb (1959, p. 141) reports for instance, that a study of 351 voluntary groups in five rural counties showed that about 90 percent were stimulated by some influence from outside the local community.

14. Research currently being performed by the author will attempt to assess more adequately the relevance of the present model to explaining FVO prevalence variations across a variety of social system levels—countries, states, cities and towns, primitive tribes. The present chapter is intended to present the problem and a suggested explanatory scheme, not to test that scheme in detail.

References

Almond, Gabriel and Sidney Verba
1963 THE CIVIC CULTURE. Princeton, N.J.: Princeton University Press.
Bacon, Elizabeth M.
1942 "The Growth of Household Conveniences in the United States from 1865 to 1900." Cambridge, Mass.: unpublished Ph.D. thesis, Radcliffe College.
Banks, Arthur S., and Robert B. Textor
1963 A CROSS-POLITY SURVEY. Cambridge, Mass.: Massachusetts Institute of Technology Press.
Boulding, Kenneth
1953 THE ORGANIZATIONAL REVOLUTION. New York: Harper and Bros.
Chao, K.C.
1952 THE MASS ORGANIZATIONS IN COMMUNIST CHINA. Cambridge, Mass.: Harvard University Press.
Childe, V. Gordon
1950 "The Urban Revolution." TOWN PLANNING REVIEW 21: 3-17.
Etzioni, Amitai
1961 A COMPARATIVE ANALYSIS OF COMPLEX ORGANIZATIONS. New York: The Free Press of Glencoe, Macmillan.
Fellman, David
1963 THE CONSTITUTIONAL RIGHT OF ASSOCIATION. Chicago, Ill.: University of Chicago Press.
Gregory, Charles O.
1958 LABOR AND THE LAW, 2nd ed. New York: Norton.
Horn, Robert
1956 GROUPS AND THE CONSTITUTIONS. Stanford, Calif.: Stanford University Press.

Kolb, John H.
1959 EMERGING RURAL COMMUNITIES. Madison, Wisc.: University of Wisconsin Press.

Kroeber, A.L.
1948 ANTHROPOLOGY. New York: Harcourt, Brace.

Lerner, Daniel
1958 THE PASSING OF TRADITIONAL SOCIETY. Glencoe, Ill.: The Free Press.

Redfield, Robert
1953 THE PRIMITIVE WORLD AND ITS TRANSFORMATIONS. Ithaca, New York: Cornell University Press.

Rice, Charles E.
1962 FREEDOM OF ASSOCIATION. New York: New York University Press.

Russett, Bruce M., Alker, H.R., Deutsch, K.W., and Lasswell, H.D.
1964 WORLD HANDBOOK OF POLITICAL AND SOCIAL INDICATORS. New Haven, Conn.: Yale University Press.

Smith, David Horton
1966 "A Psychological Model of Individual Participation in Formal Voluntary Organizations: Application to Some Chilean Data." AMERICAN JOURNAL OF SOCIOLOGY 72: 249-66.
1967 "A Parsimonious Definition of 'Group': Toward Conceptual Clarity and Scientific Utility." SOCIOLOGICAL INQUIRY 37: 141-67.
1972 "Organizational Boundaries and Organization Affiliates." SOCIOLOGY AND SOCIAL RESEARCH 56: 494-512.

Simmons, Leo
1945 THE ROLE OF THE AGED IN PRIMITIVE SOCIETY. New Haven, Conn.: Yale University Press.

Sultan, Paul
1958 RIGHT TO WORK LAWS: A STUDY IN CONFLICT. Los Angeles: University of California at Los Angeles, Institute of Industrial Relations.

Tew, Eyvend S., ed.
1966 YEARBOOK OF INTERNATIONAL ORGANIZATIONS 1966-67. Brussels, Belgium: Union of International Associations.

U.S. Department of Labor
1964 DIRECTORY OF LABOR ORGANIZATIONS. EUROPE, vols. 1 and 2. WESTERN HEMISPHERE, vols. 1 and 2. AFRICA, vol. 1. ASIA-AUSTRALIA, vols. 1 and 2.

Wilensky, Harold L.
1961 "The Uneven Distribution of Leisure: The Impact of Economic Growth on 'Free Time.' "SOCIAL PROBLEMS 9: 32-56.

4

Formal Volunteer Organization Prevalence Among Nations

Burt R. Baldwin

The basic problem for this chapter centers around the topic of formal volunteer organization (FVO) prevalence. The primary question to be answered is why does the number of FVOs differ among various nations of the world, even after controlling for differences in population size? Why do FVOs grow and flourish in one type of society but fail to do so in another? Before getting into a discussion of the factors considered to be relevant for explaining differences in FVO prevalence rates, it will be helpful to discuss briefly the meaning of the term "FVO prevalence" and how it is related to the sphere of voluntary action in general.

Distribution of Voluntary Action

It is usually the case that persons interested in describing the distribution of voluntary action within a society deal solely with individuals belonging to formal volunteer organizations. That is, attention is focused upon the number of people who belong to and participate in FVOs. The problem of FVO prevalence, however, focuses upon the distribution of the types of setting within which voluntary action occurs. Figure 4-1 depicts the three basic types of settings within which such action occurs.

The basic dimension underlying Figure 4-1 is the degree of organizational structure present in the different social settings. In the personal setting, organizational structure is at a minimum, if present at all. Here voluntary action is often a result of interpersonal encounters and may be manifested in what can be referred to as "helping behavior." Stopping to aid someone who has had an accident, encouraging someone to continue his education, giving a panhandler a quarter, etc., are examples of this type of voluntary action.

In the informal group setting, voluntary action is engaged in by a number of

An earlier version of this chapter formed part of the author's Ph.D. dissertation, entitled THE PREVALENCE OF FORMAL VOLUNTEER ORGANIZATIONS: AN ANALYSIS ON THE INTERNATIONAL LEVEL (Dept. of Sociology, Boston College, 1971). A still earlier version was presented to the 1970 American Sociological Association Annual Meetings at the "Seminar Session on Voluntary Action Research: Steps Toward Synthesis," organized by David Horton Smith and Burt R. Baldwin.

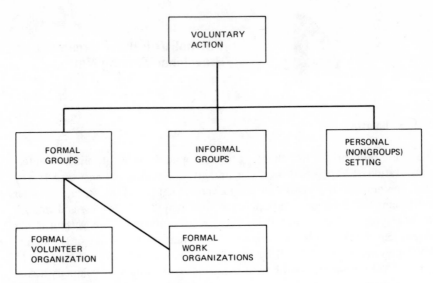

Figure 4-1. Analytic Types of Setting of Voluntary Action. Source: Adapted from David Horton Smith, Richard D. Reddy, and Burt R. Baldwin, "Types of Voluntary Action: A Definitional Essay," in David Horton Smith et al., eds. (1972).

individuals acting in concert. However, this action usually occurs only for a short period of time and is usually not engaged in with any regularity. An informal game of touch football, participating in a demonstration, or a group of housewives getting together for a morning cup of coffee and gossip are typical of voluntary action occurring on this level.

It is at the level of the formal organization where our attention will be focused in this chapter. Most formal organizations can be classified as being either work organizations or volunteer organizations. The basic difference between the two are that in work organizations, one participates primarily as a result of economic motivations, whereas in the volunteer organization one participates primarily as a result of motivations based upon the anticipation of psychic benefits. However, voluntary action can and often does occur within formal work organizations.

In some societies the government goes to great lengths to encourage high-level performance in formal work organizations by trying to inject psychic benefit factors into the work situation. In the USSR during the initial stages of industrialization there was an attempt by the government to identify work with devotion to the motherland. One did not work just to make money, but to advance the nation. The Stakhanovites, a corps of elite workers, were highly motivated by noneconomic factors and were often used to encourage other workers to develop the same ideological fervor. Although it is difficult to determine how much of this type of work was motivated either by personally held values, or governmental compulsion, it is perhaps a good example of voluntary action occurring within the formal work organization setting.

Participation in the Peace Corps or VISTA is an example of quasi-work roles usually laden with high degrees of voluntary action. Although there are economic payoffs, there are also usually a large number of psychic benefits derived from "working" in such organizations.

We are most interested here in voluntary action that occurs in the formal volunteer organization. Although not all of the behavior engaged in by members of FVOs acting in terms of their capacity as FVO members can be considered voluntary, a large proportion of it usually is. A full discussion of the nature of formal volunteer organizations may be found in Smith, et al., eds., 1972 (Chapter 10). Roughly speaking, FVOs are voluntary associations or formalized groups of persons most of whom are participating as members out of the expectation of psychic and social benefits, rather than because of coercion or the expectation of direct, high probability economic rewards.

FVO Prevalence and Voluntary Action

The problem of FVO prevalence must be considered as a specific concern of the more general problem of the distribution of voluntary action. Voluntary action can occur in different types of social settings, including personal, informal group, and formal work group settings, as well as in FVOs. Given one society, the basic prevalence question is, how is voluntary action distributed among these various settings. Given several societies, the basic question can include the question of why in some societies voluntary action occurs predominantly within the confines of FVOs, whereas in other societies it occurs predominantly within the confines of formal work organizations. Thus it can be seen that societies may differ drastically with respect to the number of FVOs present per capita, but they may be quite similar with respect to the amount of per capita voluntary action, by virtue of voluntary action being carried out in non-FVO settings.

Given this relation of FVO prevalence to the area of voluntary action in general, let us now consider two specific problems related to comparing FVO prevalence across various countries. The first problem is that of the "multi-functionality" of organizations. The number and types of functions performed by a typical British Co-op dramatizes this problem.

It would not be misleading to view many British Co-ops as nearly total communities. Almost all of the consumption needs of the members were met by various types of Co-op shops. Aside from providing "hard" consumer items, the typical Co-op also provided its members with educational opportunities through scholarships for members' children and by maintaining newsrooms furnished with daily and monthly newspapers and magazines. As one old-time Co-op member put it, the Co-op could "feed, clothe, shelter (by providing a mortgage for house purchase) and in the end, bury us." (Ostergaard and Halsey 1968, 138.)

It could well be the case that a handful of British Co-ops provided the same functions that many hundreds of separate organizations would be engaged in doing in some other country.

In a country where large multifunction types of FVOs tend to develop, FVO prevalence rates will be very low when contrasted to a country where specific-function types of FVOs tend to develop, other things equal. It may well be that the amount of voluntary action per capita occurring within these settings is the same, but a large FVO prevalence rate difference would be encountered.

Another problem which tends to confound the comparability of FVO prevalence rates is that the number of FVOs and participation in them can be significantly influenced by governmental action. Hajda has provided a good example of this phenomenon:

The Czechoslovak Boy Scout organization was established in 1910. It grew slowly but constantly and reached 150,000 members in the summer of 1940. The German Nazi occupation government dissolved the Boy Scouts in October, 1940. The organization was re-established after the end of the Second World War, in May, 1945, and by the summer of 1948 had a membership of 200,000. The organization was dissolved again by the Czechoslovak Communists (who took over in February, 1948) sometime in 1949. The recent brief period of liberalization brought again the re-establishment of the Boy Scouts in February, 1968. The organization grew to 240,000 members by the end of the summer, 1970, when it was dissolved by the pro-Soviet regime in September of that year.[i]

Depending upon when one measured the extent of FVO prevalence in Czechoslovakia, a "high" or "low" rate could be expected. In other words, a change in a nation's FVO prevalence rate can occur almost overnight as a result of governmental suppression. It is interesting to note that in the case of Czechoslovakia the Boy Scout movement reappeared after every period of governmental suppression came to an end. Thus the implication that there are or were consistent underlying factors influencing the development of FVOs but that their "natural" influence or working out was thwarted by governmental action. The fact that FVOs reappeared many times could be interpreted to mean that certain basic structural factors were not changed by governmental intervention.

The problem of multifunction FVOs and governmental interference with the development of and participation in FVOs can make the comparison of prevalence rates difficult. The amount of voluntary action occurring in FVOs could be the same in societies having either many specific FVO types, or a few multifunction FVOs. Also, were it not for the sole factor of government intervention, some societies would likely have a much higher FVO prevalence rate than they actually do (Rose 1954). These considerations must be kept in mind when dealing with problems of FVO prevalence over time and on a cross-national basis.

Factors Affecting National FVO Prevalence

Particular studies directed toward understanding the problem of FVO prevalence are very limited in number. Hence, much of the literature reviewed in this chapter will only indirectly refer to this basic problem. This literature may be broken into three major analytical categories (although we shall treat them together): (1) studies dealing with the factors leading to the development and proliferation of formal organizations, regardless of their specific type; (2) studies dealing with the factors leading to the development of representative democracies as contrasted with other types of political systems (of central concern to most studies in this second category are the concept of pluralism and the notion of competing interest groups which are, by and large, formal volunteer organizations); and (3) a few studies dealing specifically with the problem of FVO prevalence. With these considerations in mind, let us move to the task at hand.

Modernization

Etzioni has pointed out that "earlier societies had some organizations but modern society is a society of organizations" (Etzioni 1964, p. 104). Indeed, during the past seventy-five years many countries have undergone a series of changes resulting in what Boulding has dubbed "the Organizational Revolution" (Boulding 1953). Studies of this "revolution" or of modernization, as some prefer to call it, are basically studies of the development of large numbers of various sized formal organizations and the impact or effects they have on both the individual and society.

Not only do formal organizations increase in numbers but they assume augmented significance in the lives of actors in modernizing societies. The sheer fact that so much time is spent within formal organizations provides a rough index to this fact. Beyond that, however, it can be noted that formal organizations provide citizens of a modern society with his income, his security—both financial and in terms of social control—much of his recreation, and so on. Thus, when the citizens of modern societies confront new dilemmas, the main thrust of their response is to create new formal organizations. (Friedland 1969, p. 68.)

According to this statement by Friedland, formal organizations have become central to the operation of modern societies. What has led to this ascendency of the formal organization?

In a very real sense, the models of society developed by Durkheim, Tönnies, Weber, Redfield, and other sociologists and anthropologists of the nineteenth and early twentieth century were all concerned with the factors and processes involved in what are currently called studies of modernization. For Durkheim "modernization" was a transition to societies integrated in an organic, rather than a mechanical, manner. For Tönnies, it was the transformation from societies integrated in terms of the principles of *Gemeinschaft* to those of *Gesellschaft*. Weber saw the basic transition taking place in terms of a change from traditional to rational principles of organization. In other words, all of these men dealt with the fact that the basic forms of social organization, particularly those characterizing Western societies, were undergoing substantial changes.

There are several major factors related to or comprising the process of modernization. Chief among these are industrialization, urbanization, bureaucratization, an increase in education and literacy, and the development of the mass media. Our task will be to analyze several of these factors of modernization from the standpoint of FVO prevalence. The factors comprising the modernization process are themselves complexly interrelated. In order to facilitate their coverage we will first discuss each one separately and later attempt to show how they are related to one another. Again, all of this will be done from the perspective of FVO prevalence.

Industrialization. If one point were to be selected as the beginning of the process of modernization, most students of this topic would select that period in a country's history when it started to industrialize significantly. As Etzioni states it:

Industrialization presages major changes in all societal sectors. A rise in educational standards and achievements, the spread of political consciousness, secularization, the rapid growth of science, the decline of the family, an increase in social mobility; all are associated with industrialization. We refer to all these related changes as modernization. (Etzioni 1964, p. 105.)

Stinchcombe, another student of modernization and the development of organizations, essentially agrees with Etzioni's comment on the impact of industrialization upon the structure of a society. According to him, "the speed of industrial advance is an indicator of the organization-forming capacity of a population" (Stinchcombe 1965, p. 151). Thus the general proposition is tendered that as a country becomes more industrialized, so also does it develop a large number of formal organizations of all kinds.

Rose (1954 p. 103) has commented on the effects of industrialization on the development of FVOs as distinct from other types of formal organizations. He argues that prior to the industrial revolution, the community, the church and the extended family were capable of fulfilling almost all of the individual's social and psychological needs. However, with industrialization, the impact of these "institutions" was weakened. Although the deterioration of the influence of the community, the church and the extended family was everywhere concomitant with industrialization, the reaction of people to these changes differed from country to country. "In the United States and several other Western countries it largely took the form of forming associations."

Smith (Chapter 3 of this volume), also addressing himself specifically to the development of FVOs, maintains that:

If modernization takes place slowly in a given society, FVO prevalence will probably grow slowly also, in fairly direct proportion to the level of modernization. On the other hand, if modernization takes place very rapidly (an "industrial revolution" or "urban revolution" occurring, for instance, over the space of several decades rather than centuries), FVO prevalence will probably also grow very rapidly and will be seen as an "FVO revolution," as a part of a general "organizational revolution."

Smith also maintains that industrialization plays a key role in modernization. Thus Etzioni, Stinchcombe, Rose, and Smith all agree that industrialization is a primary factor influencing the development of formal organizations. However, there is an important difference between these students of the development of organizations and modernization.

Etzioni's and Stinchcombe's remarks deal with formal organizations as a whole; that is, they have not specifically differentiated between FVOs and other types of formal organizations. Smith and Rose do, however, make this distinction, addressing themselves specifically to the problem of FVO prevalence. Smith's position relates to FVOs what Etzioni and Stinchcombe have related to all formal organizations, that is, their propensity to increase as a direct result of modernization. Rose, on the other hand, points out that, with respect to FVOs, this is not necessarily the case. It is possible for a country to undergo the process of modernization but not develop a meaningful number of FVOs.

Not all modern countries have a high number of FVOs, Rose argues. Indeed, he went to great lengths to point out why France, a Western industrialized nation, had developed relatively few FVOs. The question thus must be posed of whether industrialization leads to the development of all types of formal organizations including FVOs, or whether there are certain selective mechanisms in operation which inhibit the development of FVOs in some countries, even though these countries are as industrialized as other countries which also have a large number of FVOs per capita. This question will be more thoroughly discussed when we get to the section on cultural contexts.

Let us now turn to some empirical findings between levels of industrialization and the development of formal organizations.

Lipset (1959), has presented some findings which, at least tangentially, support the hypothesis that as industrialization increases, so also does the development of formal volunteer organizations. Although Lipset was concerned specifically with the development of democratic regimes, he included within his definition of democracy the development of interest groups, many different types of which can be considered FVOs (ibid., p. 71).

Lipset found that the percentage of employed males in agriculture (one measure of industrialization) "was 21 in the 'more democratic' European countries, and 41 in the 'less democratic,' 52 percent in the 'less dictatorial' Latin American countries, and 67 in the 'more dictatorial' " (ibid., p. 78). The other measurement of industrialization used by Lipset—per capita commercially produced energy being used in the country—also resulted in "equally large" differences. Thus the more industrialized countries are also more likely to have democratic rather than nondemocratic political institutions.

Smith (Chapter 3 in this volume), found that the more modernized societies of the world today tend to have a relatively higher FVO prevalence rate, as indicated by both qualitative and quantitative measures. Also, of the various measures Smith used to indicate the level of a country's modernization, those referring specifically to industrialization—percentage of agricultural population, economic development status, and percentage of population in industry—were consistently the "best" predictors of variation in FVO prevalence rates across different societies.

Several other students of modernization have commented on the relationship between industrialization and the development of formal organizations and/or democratic forms of government (Lerner 1958; Horowitz 1967; Breese 1966; Stinchcombe 1965). However, some have presented industrialization and urbanization as one complex whole, rather than analyzing them as separate factors. Therefore, before their works are referred to, let us first discuss the factor of urbanization separately and then combine it with a discussion of urbanization-industrialization.

Urbanization. Urbanization has been related to a multitude of social phenomena. Our task will be to evaluate urbanization only insofar as it affects the organization-forming tendencies of a society. Wirth points out the fact that in large urban populations, which are made up primarily of strangers, somewhat rigid social restrictions for governing the interaction between these strangers must be developed. As he puts it: "The close living together and working together of individuals who have no sentimental and emotional ties fosters a spirit of competition, aggrandizement, and mutual exploitation. Formal controls are instituted to counteract irresponsibility and potential disorder" (Wirth 1964, p. 68). Without some adherence to predictable routines, a large compact society would scarcely be able to maintain itself. The need for "formal controls" to regulate behavior in large urban areas functions, as pointed out by Stinchcombe, to facilitate the development of formal organizations.

According to Durkheim, there is no room for debate about the effects of the concentration of populations upon the social organizations of a society. "Civilization is itself the necessary consequence of the changes which are produced in the volume and density of societies. If science, art and economic activity develop, it is in accordance with a necessity imposed upon men" (Durkheim 1964, p. 336).

Davis, relying heavily on the works of Durkheim and Wirth, explicitly states the connection between urbanization—as defined by the size and density of a population—and the development of FVOs. He points out that in urban areas, people with similar characteristics tend to form voluntary organizations to realize their common goals. Even primary groups tend to become more voluntary and specialized in the urban setting, as can be seen in patterns of courtship, marriage, parenthood and even in the formation of friendships. "Thus the number of group memberships per capita is extremely high in the urban population, and these are divided among a bewildering variety of cliques, clubs, nationalities, and neighborhoods having relatively little to do with one another except in an economic sense." (Davis 1948, p. 334.) Let us now turn to the consideration of some empirical studies to see how urbanization has been found to be related to the development of FVOs.

Returning to Lipset's study on "Some Social Requisites for Democracy," it can be seen that urbanization is correlated in a positive direction with the development of democratic countries. Lipset used three measures of urbanization: the percentage of the population in: (1) places of 20,000 or more, (2) communities of 100,000 or more, and (3) standard metropolitan areas (1968, p. 78). He concludes that "on all three of these indices of urbanization, the more democratic countries score higher than the less democratic, for both of the political culture areas under investigation" (ibid.). Thus a political system characterized by the development and competition of interest groups (FVOs) is more likely to be found in highly urbanized countries as contrasted to less urbanized countries.

Smith (Chapter 3 in this volume), relied upon a single measure of urbanization composed of the percentage of the population in cities of 20,000 or more and in cities of 100,000 or more (Banks and Textor 1963, p. 60). He found that the more urbanized countries tend also to have more formal volunteer organizations per capita.

Ashford (1961) collected data on seven "politically significant" and nationally organized groups in Morocco. Information on the local chapters of these national organizations was gathered from 304 different geographic locations which were classified as being "Urban," "Advanced Rural," or "Retarded Rural." One of his major findings was that "there is indisputably a higher level of group development in the more advanced social settings" (p. 324). He goes on to state that "for all but two of the groups the percentage of occurrence in the urban setting is 80 or higher. In fact it appears likely that group activity in the larger Moroccan cities is very similar to that in more advanced societies as a whole" (ibid.). Thus, Ashford's findings affirm the general contention that as the degree of urbanization increases so also does the prevalence of volunteer organizations.

Rate of Urbanization. We have pointed out that urbanization has been found to be positively related to the development of FVOs. However, one factor which can confound this relationship is the rate at which urbanization is taking place. As Kornhauser (1959, p. 173) has pointed out, "if urbanization proceeds at a very rapid rate, especially in its earlier stages, it is likely to involve the uprooting of large numbers of people and the failure of associations to emerge."

Inkeles, in a vein similar to Kornhauser maintains that when growth is very rapid, a city may not be able to deal adequately with the strains placed upon it. Large slum areas may develop around the periphery of the city "in which people are in the city but not of it, cut off from many of the benefits and from the modernizing influence of urban life." (Inkeles 1968, p. 367.) This appears particularly to be the case in many Latin American and Asian cities which have recently experienced large increases in their populations (Hauser 1958, 1961; Breese 1966; Fava 1968).

Stinchcombe (1965, p. 151), approaching the effects of the rate of urbanization on the formation of organizations from the opposite tack, is in substantial agreement with these statements. According to him, "urbanization, particularly when it is slow enough to allow routines of urban living to develop without being revamped by new waves of rustics, has the same effect of facilitating organization formation as literacy does, i.e., a positive effect." Thus, in discussing the effects of urbanization across different societies, one must pay close attention to the rate at which this urbanization is taking place.

It should be noted that, in contrast to industrialization and overall urbanization, no empirical testing has been carried out on the relationship between the rate of urbanization and the formation of organizations. Our confidence in this relationship must therefore be more tentative than it is with respect to industrialization and overall urbanization, at least until some empirical verification is provided.

Education and Literacy. From the perspective of the individual, an increase in education and literacy is perhaps the most important factor leading to his transition from a traditional or peasant orientation to a "modern" orientation. According to Inkeles, there is little disagreement that education ranks first in terms of "affecting the degree of modernization of individuals" (1968, p. 367). The six-nation study of BECOMING MODERN by Inkeles and Smith (1973) confirms this empirically. Lerner, concentrating on the concept of literacy, points out that "literacy becomes the sociological pivot in the activation of psychic mobility, the publicly shared skill which builds man's varied daily round into a consistent participant life style" (1958, p. 64). Lipset, also referring to the individual level, states that education is the most important factor in differentiating people who indicate democratic orientations from those who do not (1959, p. 79).

Turning to the perspective of the organization rather than the individual, Stinchcombe argues that with increases in literacy and education, people are exposed to more alternatives of action in a number of different areas. Interaction with strangers over long distances becomes feasible. Records of transactions can be kept thereby making the future more predictable. "In short, literacy and schooling raise practically every variable which increases the staying power of new organizations." (Stinchcombe 1965, 151.) As can be seen, Stinchcombe has related education to many of the modernization factors discussed in this chapter. However, it is itself an important independent factor in this process.

Deutsch (1961) and Kamerschen (1968) have argued that the effects of education and literacy are most likely not continuous in nature; that is, there appears to be a threshhold effect. Deutsch, commenting on the effects of literacy on the birth rate (which itself has been shown to be intricately related to the modernization process), points out that it is only when literacy rates reach the 80 percent level or higher that a "conspicuous" decrease in the birth rate is to be found.

Kamerschen similarly argues that the effects of literacy on socioeconomic development is generally in a positive direction until it reaches a certain level, and then literacy becomes either "indiscriminating" or works in the opposite direction. Thus the effects of education and literacy (as we have seen with the effects of urbanization) on the development of organizations are complex and must not be over simplified. However, it appears in general that an increase in education and literacy will improve the likelihood of more formal organizations also developing.

Again, empirical verification of the effects of literacy thresholds on the development of organizations has not been provided so our acceptance of this relationship must be more or less tentative for the time being. However, the empirical data of Smith's study (Chapter 3 in this volume) are clearly supportive of the positive impact of literacy levels on the prevalence of FVOs in the countries of the contemporary world.

Mass Media Development. One of the major factors believed by many to be intricately involved in the modernization process is the development of the mass media. The basic contention here is that the mass media allows for the dissemination of information, ideas, and concepts which can, if adopted by the population, result in a change in their attitudes toward existing institutions and allow either for their change and/or the development of entirely new ones. As Schramm has stated it: "Whatever the grand patterns of communication growth may be, it is clear that the development of modern communications goes along with the development of other modern institutions" (1967, p. 8).

Tocqueville (1961, pp. 134-37), writing in the early nineteenth century, was perhaps the first to point out the relationship between aspects of mass media development (in this instance, newspapers) and the prevalence of formal volunteer organizations. It was his contention that it was the large number of locally based newspapers, reporting on a variety of matters, which acted as a stimulus to help develop a large number of FVOs in the United States early in its history. Newspapers thus played a catalytic role in bringing people of like interest or persuasion together.

Smith (Chapter 3 in this volume) makes the development of mass media and other aspects of a communication/transportation network a crucial element in his theory of FVO prevalence. He argues that one of the very reasons why industrialization, urbanization, and other structural aspects of modernization result in higher FVO prevalence is that they increase the development of a communication/transportation network, which in turn directly increases FVO prevalence.

Smith (1968, pp. 47-51) has presented some preliminary findings which tend to verify the independent impact of mass media. Smith's study deals with the problem of FVO prevalence in eight Massachusetts cities and towns. After gathering certain information on all of the cities and towns in Massachusetts, he selected four high FVO prevalence towns and four low FVO prevalence towns to study. The towns selected were matched by pairs on median income, and size of the population. One part of the study involved an intensive analysis of the newspapers published in the eight towns. Smith concludes that

high FVO prevalence towns have a markedly higher number of local newspapers pages published per week than do low FVO prevalence towns. The magnitude of these differences is due principally to the fact that in three of the four high FVO towns there are daily local newspapers, while *none* of the low FVO towns have daily local newspapers. Thus, one extremely simple way to distinguish high FVO prevalence towns from low FVO prevalence towns is to find out the number of newspaper pages published per week in or for the town. . . . (p. 48.)

Turning our attention to the international level, Lerner (1958), has argued that media participation is one of the basic characteristics of the modern or empathic man, "for rising media participation tends to raise participation in all sectors of the social system" (p. 62). The development of the mass media occurs after industrialization, urbanization, and advances in literacy and education have gotten underway. However, once the mass media have begun to develop, they can operate to facilitate further the development of the first three factors of modernization, just mentioned. That there is a high correlation between mass media participation or development and other factors of modernization has been pointed out by Lerner (1958, p. 62-63), and by Schramm (1967).

With respect to the development of FVOs, the mass media can function to make people aware of others who have similar interests and who thus may benefit one another by engaging in an organized activity of one type or another.

Law and the Legal System. Hoselitz and Moore, speaking of the development of FVOs in general point out that "obviously, a major conditioning factor is the legal code—i.e., whether freedom of association is broadly interpreted or virtually nonexistent" (1963, p. 350). The previously cited example of the development of the Boy Scouts in Czechoslovakia illustrates this point well, for with each intance of change in governmental control came specific legal changes which served to suppress the development and functioning of this organization, as well as, presumably, many other different types of FVOs. Rose (1954, pp. 101-125) has gone to some lengths to indicate how the government of France, by means of laws and their enforcement, was able to successfully inhibit the development of a large number of FVOs.

In many countries, particularly those located in the West, the governments usually permit a fairly large scope of freedom of association and rarely interfere with the activities of FVOs as long as they do not violate certain basic legal and political limits. Thus, by means of laws and the legal system, governments can encourage, discourage, or be relatively neutral toward the development and functioning of FVOs. Consideration of the factors which lead governments to take different positions toward the development of FVOs will be discussed in another section. For now the point is that governments, in large part, determine laws and how they are to be enforced and in so doing influence whether or not certain types of social organizations tend to develop or not.

Let us now switch our attention from the control of legal systems by governments to some of the characteristics of laws and legal systems in general which can influence the development of FVOs. Galanter, studying the effects of the development of a modern legal system (hierarchy of courts with codified law and rationalized indigenous law) in India points out that "the modern legal system may be viewed as an important unifying element" (1968, p. 76). He argues that an all-India legal culture has developed and that its major source of strength is the growing number of lawyers who share a common perspective and orientation toward future goals. These lawyers, spread throughout India, play "important roles in devising new organizational forms for forwarding local interests (e.g., caste associations, political parties, economic interest groups)." (ibid.)

Two things are of major importance in Galanter's comments on the development of India's legal system: (1) a new role—the nationally oriented lawyer—is developing, and, one "unanticipated" consequence of the development of this role is the involvement of these lawyers in the formation of local organizations, many of which appear to be FVOs, and (2) the development of these organizations is challenging the domination of local affairs by religious and traditional authority groups.

Tocqueville (1961, pp. 319-20) and Rose (1954, pp. 101-102) have both argued that local autonomy is crucial for the development of a large number of FVOs. However, to be effective for the development of these organizations, this local autonomy must not be based upon elite domination and noninvolvement by the masses. Without a relatively open system of participation, local autonomy can have no significance for the development of FVOs. The development of a national legal structure which challenges the arbitrariness of domination by traditional elites is thus an important factor in the process leading to the development of formal volunteer organizations.

Given the existence of a national legal system, Evan and Schwartz (1964, pp. 270-271) point out three ways in which its functioning may encourage or inhibit the development of formal organizations, particularly FVOs. (1) Through the granting of charters, licenses, franchises, etc., the legal status of formal organizations is defined by the law. (2) By passing "enabling" legislation, new organizations may be formed. For example, the expansion of American trade unions was due in large part to the passage of the National Labor Relations Act. (3) Laws can modify the functioning of existing organizations as was the result of the passage of "right to work" laws in a number of states.

With respect to formal volunteer organizations particularly, it appears that many of them arise or develop in order to help provide for either the implementation or the blocking of a new law or series of laws. For example, the civil rights movement of the 1960s saw the development of organizations trying both to impede the movement (the White Citizens' Council and others) or to help it by implementing newly and previously enacted legislation. CORE, SNCC, and the SCLC are just a few of the major organizations which developed and in turn helped to define and structure the civil rights movement.

In many instances legislation is, for all practical purposes, sponsored by various FVOs in attempts to achieve some of their major goals. If passed, other organizations (as Evan and Schwartz point out) may develop in order to protect their interests as they see them. Thus the nature of a society's legal system and the changes brought about by its everyday operation act to influence the development of all types of organizations.

In view of these kinds of considerations, Smith (Chapter 3 in this volume) argues that the "permission of collectivities" as well as the "instigation of collectivities" are crucial factors affecting FVO prevalence in any territorial unit. Law and the legal system are important examples of how government can permit or even foster FVO development.

The studies reviewed in this section have been inductive and argumentative rather than empirical. Thus some comparative empirical verification is needed to increase our confidence in the effects of laws and the legal system on the development of organizations, especially FVOs.

Social Heterogeneity. An important factor which may have a very definite influence on the number of FVOs which develop within a society is the extent to which basic "social cleavages" exist. By this is meant to what extent are there significantly different racial, ethnic, religious, and social-class differences within a society. The greater the number of population groupings "produced" by differentiations based on these factors, the greater the likelihood that, other things being equal, a larger number of FVOs will develop than in situations where the population is relatively homogeneous.

Minnis (1953) has provided evidence that religious, ethnic, racial, and social class differences do operate to produce a greater proliferation of FVOs in a city than would be the case if those differences either did not exist or were very minimal. Minnis studied all formally organized women's organizations in New Haven having memberships made up of persons above the age of eighteen. She found that racial, religious, ethnic, and social prestige differences were all of importance in determining membership in various women's organizations. (The relative importance of these factors was the same as the order in which they have been listed.) To illustrate her findings she states that there are no less than "seven Junior Leagues in New Haven—Junior League of New Haven (Protestant), Catholic Junior League, Junior Community League (black), B'nai B'rith Junior League (Jewish), Swedish Junior League, Italian Junior League, and Polish Junior League" (p. 53). It is quite likely that if the population of New Haven had been basically homogeneous, there would have been but one Junior League.

LaPalombara, in studying Italian interest groups, has provided evidence which essentially substantiates the findings by Minnis on the effects of basic social cleavages on the proliferation of formal volunteer organizations. Speaking of the development of several political subcultures in Italy, the major ones being identified with "Catholicism; a secular middle class; and a modernizing and innovating class," LaPalombara argues that within each of these subcultures, identical types of organizations have tended to develop. "It is not uncommon, for example, to find Communist, Catholic, Socialist, Liberal, Republican and Neo-Fascist rough equivalents of the American League of Women Voters." (1965, p. 152.) Also, within one particular subculture, one may find the same phenomena occurring but with the breaks being made on social class or liberal versus conservative differences.

Stinchcombe (1965, p. 153) and Almond and Powell (1966, p. 79) point out that in some societies there are large-scale "organization forming" organizations, such as the Catholic Church or the Communist Party. Although these organizations may or may not be formal volunteer organizations, part of their operation includes the formation of FVOs of various types. It appears, also, that these organization-forming organizations tend to reflect basic social cleavages within the society. Thus the greater the number of these basic cleavages, the greater the potential for the development of a large number of FVOs, other things being equal.

In terms of Smith's theory (see the preceding chapter) social heterogeneity is an example of the broader analytical category he calls "goal differentiation"—a major factor in FVO prevalence. Goal differentiation is also indicated, however, by structural differentiation of other kinds (e.g., occupational specialization) and by cultural differentiation as fostered by increased education, etc.

Organizational Density and Collectivity Experience. Friedland was quoted earlier as saying that "when the citizens of modern societies confront new dilemmas, the main thrust of their response is to create new formal organizations" (1969, p. 68). Stated somewhat differently, the more experience people have in meeting environmental and social changes by means of forming formal organizations, the greater the likelihood that as "new" changes occur, they will be met in the same manner. The presence of this phenomenon of generalizing organizational experience to new situations has led Stinchcombe to claim that "the level of organizational experience of a population is a main determinant of their capacity to form new organizations" (1965, p. 152). We thus have a feedback situation where the increased development of formal organizations is in part due to the prior level of development of these organizations.

Given a large number of formal organizations, it appears that the manner in which any given one pursues its goals becomes increasingly dependent upon the activity of the other organizations. Thus Terryberry argues that "other formal organizations are increasingly the important components in the environment of any formal organization" (1967, p. 591-592).

In Smith's theory (Chapter 3 in this volume), the present kind of organizational density/collective experience factor falls into the broader category of "resources for collective action." In particular, the collective attitudes toward, and experiences with, FVOs that characterize a population are seen to have an important positive impact on territorial FVO prevalence. Other "resources for collective action" include higher intelligence, certain personality traits, more free time, etc., according to Smith's model.

Political Revolution. The role of political revolution in the development of formal volunteer organizations is to be found in the process, of the removal of constraints on a social system. This allows for the development of new institutional structures (Stinchcombe, 1965, p. 152). Morse (1969), in an essay entitled "Becoming vs. Being Modern: An Essay on Institutional Change and Economic Development," points out that significant changes in institutions come about only as a result of revolutionary action. Evolutionary processes do account for a certain amount of change but "only the overt use of noninstitutionalized power can dislodge institutionalized power and bring about basic change." (p. 322.) The revolution Morse speaks of does not have to involve violence, but it must occur if substantial changes are to occur in the basic institutional make-up of a society.

The development of a large number of organizations represents a basic change in a nation's social structure. What Morse is arguing is that for some countries, primarily non-Western, underdeveloped countries, a revolution is needed (which can be either violent or nonviolent), if what he calls modernization is to occur. He does not deal specifically with the development of FVOs. It could well be, however, that FVOs are one of the major ways of "filling the interstices among the new formal organizations."

Martindale in discussing the development of communities as defined in a very broad sense (Parsons' total social system), extends the historical scope of the present discussion on the role of revolution. He points out that "to form new communities men must first transform their old ones. Revolutionary upheavals are discernible in the formative periods of all of the historically significant communities" (1964, p. 86).

Smith's theory (Chapter 3 in this volume) views political revolution as having an important impact on FVO prevalence insofar as it results in such basic changes as greater development of the communication/transportation network, increased goal differentiation (e.g., less suppression of alternative values and goals), or increased collective action orientation (e.g., increased permission and instigation of FVOs, less suppression of FVOs, etc.). Where political revolutions do not bring about such changes (e.g., where there is merely a change in who is running the country, not in how it is run), no increases or decreases in FVO prevalence are predicted by Smith's theory, other things equal.

Integrating the Factors of Modernization

In the preceding section we have presented several factors felt to be closely associated with the development of formal organizations and especially FVOs. For the most part, these factors were presented separately with only a few comments being made on how they were interrelated. This section will deal specifically with the problem of the interrelation of these factors as seen from the perspective of organizational prevalence in general and FVO prevalence in particular. In order to carry out this task, we will present two differing orientations used for explaining the particular configuration which a social structure may have at one point in time: the convergence model and the historical specificity model.

Convergence Model

The convergence model is based upon the notion that, given certain inputs into a social system, certain consequences will generally occur, cultural differences notwithstanding. Karsh and Cole (1968, pp. 46-47), state the convergence hypothesis as follows: "the relations which define industrial work tend to inevitably take on the same characteristics regardless of the setting and regardless of the pace and structure of industrialization along the way...." After referring to the "logic of industrialism," Karsh and Cole go on to state that it "inevitably leads to a convergence which cuts through and undermines 'tradition' irrespective of the main features of culture, history and values with which the industrializing society began." In other words, if one knows that a nation has begun to industrialize, and that this process is likely to continue, then one can state that certain consequences are bound to follow.

Further, Deutsch (1961, p. 495), Cutright (1963, p. 255), Lipset (1959, p. 80), and Lerner (1958, p. 63) argue that industrialization forms a systemic cluster with related variables such as urbanization, literary-education, media participation, and so forth. Multiple regression results computed by Lerner (1958, p. 63) generally confirm this.

Without committing ourselves to a definite convergence position, there can be little doubt that given the facts of industrializations, other basic changes are almost certain to follow. However, the question every convergionist must ask himself is: just what are the limits of this inevitability? In other words, when will cultural constraints and specific historical consideration act to alter the course of development set off by industrialization? With respect to the basic problem of this chapter, will industrialization, if carried far enough, automatically 'cause' the development of a large number of FVOs per capita, as some students of modernization have maintained, or are the development of FVOs not to be considered a part of the "systemic whole" which has been under consideration? In order to respond to this question, we must first clarify the distinction between the development of all types of formal organizations as opposed to FVOs in particular. We must also see how general the convergence approach is. This will be done by comparing developed to under- or undeveloped countries with respect to the basic factors of modernization.

There are few students of formal organizations who would disagree with the claim that as societies become more modern, so also do they rely more upon rational forms of social organization, as contrasted to ones based upon tradition or charismatic allegiance. In other words, as Friedland (1969), Etzioni (1964), Stinchcombe (1965), and others have argued, modern society is a society of formal organizations, be they bureaucratic or nonbureaucratic in nature.

In reviewing the literature in the area of general organizational prevalence, it was found that FVOs were generally lumped together with all other types of formal organizations, thus implying that there were no major differences in the factors affecting organizational prevalence in terms of specific type of organization (Little 1965; Fava 1968, p. 273; Bollens and Schmandt 1970, p. 402). Bollens and Schmandt, for example, in discussing the social organization related to urbanization, point out that one of them is the "creation of numerous formal or voluntary associations corresponding to the occupational, professional, social, political, and religious interests of the citizen body" (1970), p. 402). Thus, with modernization, we have not only the development of formal organizations in general, but formal volunteer organizations in particular.

Smith (in the preceding chapter) has presented a very explicit argument contending that FVOs do indeed develop along with all other types of formal organizations. He points out that "the transition, analytical or chronological, from primitive to peasant to industrial society appears to produce, or at least is correlated with, the growth of formal organizations and contingent roles, including FVOs as a subtype." After referring to several nineteenth century and early twentieth century sociologists, Smith goes on to say that:

All of these authors have noted that the growth of modern industrial society entails the growth of a type of relationship that may be termed "contingent" as opposed to "ascriptive." FVOs and the relationships they invoke are by definition contingent, and so also are formal work organizations and formal coercive organizations, of course. Thus, although few of these authors may have mentioned FVOs explicitly, they have all implicitly remarked on their growth by dealing with the broader category of contingent relationships (and contingent groups) and more especially formal contingent relations.

Smith thus maintains that one should definitely expect to find FVOs developing along with other types of formal organizations.

Karsh and Cole (1968, p. 47) have maintained that as a result of convergence, social relations in industrializing countries tend to become universalistic and based on contract or the Weberian notion of formal rationality. This is another way of saying that social relations are more and more carried out within the confines of organizations which are primarily formal in nature. Thus if the contention is accurate that FVOs do develop along with the development of all types of formal organizations, those upholding the convergence model would maintain that given the conditions of industrialization in any society, the increased development of FVOs is only a matter of time.

It is at this point where those persons arguing from the perspective of historical specificity exhibit basic disagreement with the convergionists. Before pursuing the substance of this disagreement, let us briefly review the historical perspective.

Historical Specificity Model

The historical specificity model is, at least on the surface, diametrically opposed to the convergence model in terms of explaining the relations which come to hold between the various factors of modernization. Mills (1959) has clearly stated the two basic principles underlying this model: (1) "The image of any society is an historically specific image," and (2) within any particular society. "various mechanisms of change come to some specific kind of intersection. These mechanisms, which Karl Mannheim—following John Stuart Mill—called 'principia media,' are the very mechanisms that the social scientist, concerned with social structure, wishes to grasp" (Mills 1959, p. 149).

Much of Weber's work was based upon the notion of historical specificity. At one point, Lipset (1959, p. 103) quotes him as saying that "the spread of Western cultural and capitalist economy did not, *ipso facto*, guarantee that Russia would also acquire the liberties which had accompanied their emergence in European history.... European liberty had been born in unique, perhaps unrepeatable, circumstances at a time when the intellectual and material conditions for it were exceptionally propitious." Weber's statement was selected not only because it is a good statement of the historical specificity position, but also because it provides a substantive link between this type of model and the convergence model.

The basic point which unites the two models is the realization that there are indeed some relative consistent relations between certain basic structural elements. Neither the person arguing for the convergence model nor the one arguing for the historical specificity model would expect to find a highly industrialized and urbanized society to have a highly illiterate population, or one in which the mass media are absent or poorly developed. These basic elements are, as several scholars have maintained, part of a systemic whole.

The area of contention between the two models is that much of what the convergionists claim to result, *ipso facto*, as a consequence of the development and interplay of the primary factors of modernization, is not accepted by the persons upholding the historical specificity model. Thus, with respect to our problem of FVO prevalence, we have the convergionists arguing that given industrialization it is only a matter of time before FVOs develop, whereas the person arguing from the perspective of historical specificity maintains that whether or not FVOs develop depends, no doubt, upon industrialization and the related basic factors of modernization, but that these factors are not *sufficient* for their development. What is important is how these factors of modernization are related to other elements in a society's social structure or culture, and how they are all changing relative to one another.

In order to clarify the major differences between these two perspectives, let us all too briefly contrast some highlights which the course of modernization has taken in the West as opposed to non-Western countries.

Fava (1968, p. 73) has posed the question of "whether industrialization 'requires' social organization on the Western order?" Also, as Breese (1966, p. 9) points out, "The contrast between the familiar Western Urbanization and the urbanization occurring in these newly developing areas is likely to be so strong that a familiarity with the Western pattern is grossly inadequate preparation for comprehending the full gamut of the urban society in newly modernizing countries."

Hah and Schneider (1968), after reviewing several studies of modernization, point out that one of three major criticisms is that all of the studies "assume that development in the new nations will follow familiar U.S. patterns of modernization."

In many underdeveloped countries, urbanization is occurring at a much faster rate than is industrialization (Hauser 1958, p. 9; Browning 1967, p. 74). As a result the urban areas often contain 'peasant villages,' 'cocoon neighborhoods' or 'barriadas' wherein social organization is basically an extension of the rural village or tribe (Beyer 1967, p. 200). Where ties with village or tribe are loose or broken, kinship ties often predominate. The following description by Aldous of a new type of family organization developing in Lagos is an excellent example of the adaptation of an already strong social institution to changes being brought about by urbanization.

Many extended families in Lagos are very complex, performing a number of functions in a manner more similar to a formal organization than to a kinship unit. Some families hold monthly meetings where the affairs of the members are discussed and joint decisions made on a number of activities in various areas. Frequent celebrations focussing around births, deaths, naming ceremonies, marriages, etc. are held by members of the family. These and other activities led Aldous to conclude that the extended family, "as a group, . . . often took on the form and character of a voluntary association." (Aldous 1962, p. 9.) It appears, then, that unlike developments in the West where it has often been maintained that urbanization has led to the breakup of the extended family, urbanization in Lagos has led to a situation where the extended family has become more formalized and of increased social importance.

The argument has been advanced that, given enough time, the effects of industrialization and urbanization will be the same in non-Western countries as they have been in the West. Obviously, this criticism cannot, in many instances, be answered one way or the other. Abegglen, however, in his study of the Japanese factory system, points out several basic differences between the factory system which has come to prevail in Japan and that which evolved out of industrialization in the West. He argues that one should not view Japan's development as being at a midpoint and that it will eventually conform to the pattern of industrialization characteristic of Western nations. As he states the argument, it is not sufficient "to say that since Japan's industrialization is relatively recent these divergencies from the pattern as seen and set forth in the West will in time mend themselves and fit harmoniously into one of these several categories without conflict or with few conflicting elements." (Abegglen 1958, p. 290.)

It is thus apparent that the effects of industrialization, urbanization, and so forth, will be mediated by the characteristics of the social structure and culture within which they are taking place. In other words, structural and cultural factors act to limit the possible outcomes of industrialization, urbanization, and so on. Some structures may be conducive to the development of many FVOs per capita whereas others may inhibit their development and growth.

Eisenstadt (1966, p. 146) has succinctly stated this basic criticism of the convergence hypothesis. He argues that the conventional indicators of modernization basically reveal only the extent to which traditional, self-contained societies have become weakened or disintegrated. "They do not in themselves indicate the extent to which a new, viable, modern society capable of . . . continuous growth may develop, or exactly what kind of society will develop, what its exact institutional contours will be."

Convergence and Specificity Models:
The Middle Ground

Our discussion of the convergence and historical specificity models leads us to the general conclusion that both have some merit in helping to understand the development of formal volunteer organizations within society. It appears as if FVOs are "borderline" cases existing at some distance from the basic structural changes involved with industrialization. However, if certain cultural and historical factors are favorable, industrialization can almost invariably lead to the development of a large number of FVOs per capita. The basic task for understanding differences in prevalence rates is thus to comprehend the interaction of cultural and historical factors with the core factors of modernization. Neither taken by themselves can be sufficient for understanding these differences.

Note

1. Personal correspondence from Prof. Jan Hajda, dated October 20, 1970.

References

Abegglen, James C.
1958 THE JAPANESE FACTORY: ASPECTS OF ITS SOCIAL ORGANIZA-
TION. New York: The Free Press.
Aldous, Joan
1962 "Urbanization, The Extended Family, and Kinship Ties in West Africa."
SOCIAL FORCES 61: 6-12.
Almond, Gabriel, and G. Bingham Powell, Jr.
1966 COMPARATIVE POLITICS: A DEVELOPMENTAL APPROACH. Boston: Little Brown and Co.
Almond, Gabriel, and James Vernon
1960 THE POLITICS OF THE DEVELOPING AREAS. Princeton: Princeton
University Press.
Apter, David E.
1966 THE POLITICS OF MODERNIZATION. Chicago: The University of
Chicago Press.

Ashford, Douglas E.
1961 "Patterns of Group Development in a New Nation: Morocco." AMER-
ICAN POLITICAL SCIENCE REVIEW 55: 321-32.
Bennett, John W.
1968 "Tradition, Modernity, and Communalism in Japan's Modernization."
JOURNAL OF SOCIAL ISSUES 24: 25-43.
Beyer, Glenn H. (ed.)
1967 THE URBAN EXPLOSION IN LATIN AMERICA: A CONTINENT IN
PROCESS OF MODERNIZATION. Ithaca, New York: Cornell University
Press.
Blankensten, George I.
1959 "Political Groups in Latin America." AMERICAN POLITICAL SCIENCE
REVIEW 53: 106-127.
Bollens, John C. and H.J. Schmandt
1970 THE METROPOLIS: ITS PEOPLE, POLITICS, AND ECONOMIC LIFE.
New York: Harper and Row.
Boulding, Kenneth
1953 THE ORGANIZATIONAL REVOLUTION. New York: Harper and Row.
Breese, Gerald
1966 URBANIZATION IN NEWLY DEVELOPING COUNTRIES. Englewood
Cliffs, New Jersey: Prentice Hall, Inc.
Browning, H.L.
1967 "Urbanization and Modernization in Latin America: The Demographic
Perspective." In THE URBAN EXPLOSION IN LATIN AMERICA: A
CONTINENT IN PROCESS OF MODERNIZATION. Glenn Beyer, ed.
Ithaca, New York. Cornell University Press.
Cattel, Raymond
1949 "The Dimension of Culture Patterns of Factorization of National Charac-
ters." JOURNAL OF ABNORMAL AND SOCIAL PSYCHOLOGY 44:
443-69.
Cutright, Phillips
1963 "National Political Development: Measurement and Analysis." AMER-
ICAN SOCIOLOGICAL REVIEW, 28: 253-64.
Davis, Kingsley
1948 HUMAN SOCIETY. New York: Macmillan Co.
Deutsch, Karl W.
1961 "Social Mobilization and Political Development." AMERICAN POLITI-
CAL SCIENCE REVIEW 55: 493-514.
Dore, R.P.
1965 "On the Possibility and Desirability of a Theory of Modernization in
Asia." INTERNATIONAL CONFERENCE ON PROBLEMS OF MOD-
ERNIZATION IN ASIA. Seoul, Korea. Korea University Press.
Durkheim, Emile
1964 THE DIVISION OF LABOR IN SOCIETY. George Simpson (trans.). New
York: The Free Press.

Eisenstadt, S.N.
1961 ESSAYS ON SOCIOLOGICAL ASPECTS OF POLITICAL AND ECO-
NOMIC DEVELOPMENT. The Hague: Mouton and Co.
1966 MODERNIZATION: PROTEST AND CHANGE, Englewood Cliffs, New
Jersey: Prentice Hall, Inc.

Etzioni, Amitai
1964 MODERN ORGANIZATIONS. Englewood Cliffs, New Jersey: Prentice
Hall, Inc.

Evan, William M. and Mildred A. Schwartz
1964 "Law and the Emergence of Formal Organizations." SOCIOLOGY AND
SOCIAL RESEARCH 48: 270-80.

Fava, Sylvia Fleiss (ed.)
1968 URBANISM IN WORLD PERSPECTIVE: A READER. New York:
Thomas Y. Crowell.

Friedland, William H.
1968 "Traditionalism and Modernization: Movements and Ideologies." JOUR-
NAL OF SOCIAL ISSUES 24: 9-23.
1969 "A Sociological Approach to Modernization." In MODERNIZATION BY
DESIGN. Chandler Morse, et al. (eds.). Ithaca, New York: Cornell
University Press.

Galanter, Marc
1968 "The Development of Traditional Law in Modern India." JOURNAL OF
SOCIAL ISSUES 24: 65-91

Gerth, Hans and C. Wright Mills
1964 CHARACTER AND SOCIAL STRUCTURE: THE PSYCHOLOGY OF
SOCIAL INSTITUTIONS. New York. Harcourt, Brace and World.

Goode, William J.
1963 WORLD REVOLUTION AND FAMILY PATTERNS. New York: The
Free Press.

Hah, Chong-Do, and Jeanne Schneider
1968 "A Critique of Current Studies on Political Development and Modernization." SOCIAL RESEARCH 35: 130-58.

Hauser, Philip M. (ed.)
1958 URBANIZATION IN ASIA AND THE FAR EAST. Calcutta: UNESCO.
1961 URBANIZATION IN LATIN AMERICA. New York: International Documents Service.

Himmelstrand, Ulf and F. Olu Okedjii
1968 "Social Structure and Motivational Tuning in Social and Economic
Development." JOURNAL OF SOCIAL ISSUES 24: 25-42.

Hing, Yong Cheng
1968 "The Emergence and Spread of the Ombudsman Institution," ANNALS
OF THE AMERICAN ACADEMY OF POLITICAL AND SOCIAL SCI-
ENCE 377: 20-30.

Horowitz, Irving L.

1967 "Electoral Politics, Urbanization and Social Development in Latin America." in THE URBAN EXPLOSION IN LATIN AMERICA: A CONTINENT IN PROCESS OF MODERNIZATION. Glenn Beryer, (ed.). Ithaca, New York: Cornell University Press.

Hoselitz, Bert F.

1964 "Advanced and Underdeveloped Countries: A Study in Development Contrasts." In THE TRANSFER OF INSTITUTIONS. William B. Hamilton, (ed.). Durham, North Carolina: Duke University Press.

Hoselitz, Bert F. and Wilbert E. Moore (eds.)

1963 INDUSTRIALIZATION AND SOCIAL CHANGE. The Hague: Mouton.

Inkeles, Alex

1968 "The Modernization of Man." In URBANISM IN WORLD PERSPECTIVE: A READER. Sylvia Fava (ed.). New York: Thomas Y. Crowell.

Inkeles, Alex and David Horton Smith

1973 BECOMING MODERN. Boston: Little Brown and Co. (in press).

Kamerschen, David R.

1968 "Literacy and Socio-Economic Development." RURAL SOCIOLOGY 33: 175-88.

Karsh, Bernard and Robert E. Cole

1968 "Industrialization and the Convergence Hypothesis: Some Aspects of Contemporary Japan." JOURNAL OF SOCIAL ISSUES 24: 45-64.

Knott, James E., Jr.

1962 FREEDOM OF ASSOCIATION: A STUDY OF THE ROLE OF INTERNATIONAL NON-GOVERNMENTAL ORGANIZATIONS IN THE DEVELOPMENT PROCESS OF EMERGING COUNTRIES. Brussels: Union of International Associations.

Kornhauser, William

1959 THE POLITICS OF MASS SOCIETY, Glencoe, Illinois: The Free Press.

LaPalombara, Joseph

1965 "The Utility and Limitations of Interest Group Theory in Non-American Situations." JOURNAL OF POLITICS 22: 29-49.

Lerner, Daniel

1958 THE PASSING OF TRADITIONAL SOCIETY. Glencoe, Illinois: The Free Press.

Lipset, Seymour Martin

1959 "Some Social Requisites of Democracy: Economic Development and Political Legitimacy." AMERICAN POLITICAL SCIENCE REVIEW 53: 69-105.

Little, Kenneth

1965 WEST AFRICAN URBANIZATION: A STUDY OF VOLUNTARY ASSOCIATIONS IN SOCIAL CHANGE. New York: Cambridge University Press.

Lowry, Ritchie P.
1965 WHO'S RUNNING THIS TOWN? New York: Harper and Row.
Macura, Milos
1961 "The Influence of the Definition of the Urban Place on the Size of the Urban Population." In URBAN RESEARCH METHODS. Jack Gibbs (ed.). New York: D. Van Nostrand.
Martindale, Don
1964 "The Formation and Destruction of Communities." In EXPLORATIONS IN SOCIAL CHANGE. George K. Zollschan and Walter Hirsch (eds.). New York: Houghton-Mifflin Co.
Mills, C. Wright
1959 THE SOCIOLOGICAL IMAGINATION. New York: Oxford University Press.
Minnis, Mhyra S.
1953 "Cleavage in Women's Organizations." AMERICAN SOCIOLOGICAL REVIEW 18: 47-53.
Morse, Chandler
1969 "Becoming versus Being Modern: An Essay on Institutional Change and Economic Development." In MODERNIZATION BY DESIGN. Morse Chandler, et al. (eds.). Ithaca, New York: Cornell University Press.
Neuman, Franz
1966 BEHEMOTH: THE STRUCTURE AND PRACTICE OF NATIONAL SOCIALISM, 1933-1944. New York: Harper Torchbooks.
Nisbet, Robert A.
1969 SOCIAL CHANGE AND HISTORY: ASPECTS OF THE WESTERN THEORY OF DEVELOPMENT. New York: Oxford University Press.
Ostergaard, G.N. and A.H. Halsey
1968 "Power in Cooperatives." In STUDIES IN BRITISH SOCIETY. J.A. Banks (ed.). New York: Thomas Y. Crowell.
Rose, Arnold M.
1954 THEORY AND METHODS IN THE SOCIAL SCIENCES. Minneapolis: University of Minnesota Press.
Rudolph, Loyd I. and Susanne Hoeber Rudolph
1968 "The Political Modernization of an Indian Feudal Order: An Analysis of Rajput Adaptation in Rajasthan." JOURNAL OF SOCIAL ISSUES 24: 93-128.
Saric, M.
1963 "Birth and Development of Political Parties and Political Movement in Black Africa." NASA STVARNOST 10: 371-78.
Schramm, Wilbur and W. Lee Ruggels
1967 "How Mass Media Systems Grow." In COMMUNICATION AND CHANGE IN THE DEVELOPING COUNTRIES. Daniel Lerner and William Schramm (eds.). Honolulu: East-West Center Press.

Shannon, Lyle W.
1959 "Socio-economic Development and Political Status." SOCIAL PROB-
LEMS 7: 157-69.
Smith, David Horton
1968 "Second Progress Report on Massachusetts FVO Prevalence Study."
Unpublished manuscript. Boston: Institute of Human Sciences, Boston
College.
Smith, David Horton, Richard D. Reddy, and Burt R. Baldwin, (eds.).
1972 VOLUNTARY ACTION RESEARCH: 1972 (Lexington, Mass.: Lexing-
ton Books, D.C. Heath and Co.)
Starbuck, William H.
1965. "Organization Growth and Development." In HANDBOOK OF ORGANI-
ZATIONS. James March (ed.). Chicago. Rand McNally Co. 451-533.
Stinchcombe, Arthur L.
1965 "Social Structure and Organizations." In HANDBOOK OF ORGANIZA-
TIONS. James March (ed.). Chicago. Rand McNally Co. 142-93.
Sussman, Marvin B.
1956 "The Calorie Collector: A Study of Spontaneous Group Formation,
Collapse, and Reconstruction." SOCIAL FORCES 34: 351-56.
Terryberry, S.
1967 "The Evolution of Organizational Environments." ADMINISTRATIVE
SCIENCE QUARTERLY 12: 590-613.
Tocqueville, Alexis de
1961 DEMOCRACY IN AMERICA, vol. 2. New York: Schocken Books.
Vyver, Frank T. de
1964 "The Transplantation of Trade Unionism to British Africa." In THE
TRANSFER OF INSTITUTIONS. William B. Hamilton, (ed.). Durham,
North Carolina: Duke University Press.
Weber, Max
1947 THE THEORY OF SOCIAL AND ECONOMIC ORGANIZATION. A.M.
Henderson and Talcott Parsons (trans.). New York: The Free Press.
1958 THE CITY. Don Martindale and Gertrude Neuwirth (trans., eds.). Glen-
coe, Illinois: The Free Press.
Wheeler, Harvey
1968 DEMOCRACY IN A REVOLUTIONARY ERA: THE POLITICAL
ORDER TODAY. N.Y.: Frederick A. Praeger.
Wirth, Louis
1964 "Urbanism as a Way of Life," in ON CITIES AND SOCIAL CHANGE:
Selected Papers. Albert J. Reiss, Jr., (ed.) Chicago: The Univ. of Chicago
Press.

5

The Growth of International Nongovernmental Organization in the Twentieth Century

Kjell Skjelsbaek

Introduction

Transnational interactions have been defined as "the movement of tangible or intangible items across state boundaries when at least one actor is not an agent of a government or an intergovernmental organization" (Nye and Keohane 1972, p. xii). Correspondingly, transnational organizations can be defined as transnational interactions institutionalized. There may be several reasons why participants in transnational interactions may find it convenient to found a permanent organization and to endow it with a certain amount of authority to coordinate their interaction. First of all, the intensity of a particular kind of interaction may rise to such a level that more personnel and other resources are needed to regulate and facilitate the process. The most economical way of responding to this need may be to establish a joint secretariat. Second, although the intensity of exchanges between each pair of interacting entities may be constant, the number of participants may increase. This process results in a problem of coordination and the need for a coordinating agent in the form of, for example, an international body. To put it slightly differently, institutionalization tends to follow multilateralization. Third, although neither of the above conditions may obtain, an organization may be founded to achieve fast action in emergencies requiring joint operation. Finally, an organization, and in particular its officers, may serve as mediator and arbitrator in situations of conflict and competition between interacting members. Such activities are, for example, promoted by the Inter-American Commercial Arbitration Commission.

The relative importance of these and other possible causes of the institutionalization of transnational interactions is hard to assess, but the impressive increase in many kinds of transnational interactions since World War II has in fact been paralleled by a considerable increase in the number of transational organizations.[1] Today there are probably somewhere between 2,500 and 3,000 transnational, nonprofit organizations in the world; the exact number depends on which definition of transnational organization one prefers. If profitmaking organizations, that is, multinational business enterprises, are included, the figures

This chapter was originally published in Joseph S. Nye, Jr. and Robert O. Keohane, eds. TRANSNATIONAL RELATIONS AND WORLD POLITICS 1972. Reprinted by permission of Harvard University Press. Copyright 1971 by The President and Fellows of Harvard College.

will be much higher, but I have left them out (they are discussed elsewhere).[2] Some of the nonprofit organizations with which I am concerned, for example, the International Red Cross, are well known to the public and to students of international relations. Others are seldom mentioned in mass media but have a recognized standing in the world of international organizations and have occasionally caught the attention of scholars. Most of the organizations are, however, rather inconspicuous; some of them perform important functions for their members and the societies they represent, while others are of moderate significance even to them.

Transnational organizations operate in a variety of fields. Organizations concerned with commerce, industry, health, medicine, and natural science are particularly numerous. But there are also organizations in the areas of sports, religion, international relations, art, economics and finance, agriculture, education and technology among others.[3] Some examples of transnational organizations will indicate the range of their activities: Among the more important organizations are the International Air Transport Association (IATA), the International Olympic Committee (IOC), the World Council of Churches (WCC), the International Commission of Jurists (ICJ), and the World Federation of Trade Unions (WFTU).[4]

For an organization to be "transnational" two minimal requirements must be met: At least two different countries must be represented in the organization and one of the representatives must not be an agent of a government. In practice it would probably be wise to specify that at least one-half of the members of the multilateral organization should not act in a governmental capacity. In either case, however, the criteria for a transnational organization should emphasize membership composition.

The empirical part of this essay is based on data collected by the Union of International Associations (UIA) and by myself on the basis of UIA definitions of various kinds of organizations.[5] Unfortunately, the UIA uses a legalistic criterion to distinguish between intergovernmental organizations (IGOs) and international nongovernmental organizations (NGOs). This criterion defines IGOs as organizations established by intergovernmental treaty, as specified in a United Nations Economic and Social Council (ECOSOC) resolution of 1950, regardless of the character of their membership.[6] Most but not all IGOs include only governmental members, and in practice many NGOs have both governmental and nongovernmental members. Thus the UIA's list of NGOs is somewhat different from and generally more restrictive than a list of transnational organizations compiled according to the membership criteria suggested earlier.[7] I have altered the UIA definition in one way by excluding approximately 250 business and professional groups within the European Economic Community (EEC) and the European Free Trade Association (EFTA). These organizations are officially recognized as international interest groups by either the EEC or EFTA and cooperate with these IGOs but are still often merely subcommittees of larger European NGOs and should therefore not be counted twice.[8]

Most of my aggregate data has been drawn from UIA publications, particularly from the tenth (1964-65) edition of the YEARBOOK OF INTERNATIONAL ORGANIZATIONS, and has been coded and put on punch cards.[9] I have also collected my own data on the basis of a questionnaire which was mailed to the secretaries-general of all IGOs and NGOs in 1967.[10]

The Development of the NGO World

The NGO world is growing and changing in many ways. New organizations are added and old ones disappear. New countries become represented and others see their relative share of influence reduced. New functions are performed, new procedures adopted, and more channels of information established. Internal structures of organizations are reformed. These changes affect the importance of NGOs in the world. It is hard to form a conclusive opinion about the role they are playing today and harder still to predict their future significance. For both purposes, however, knowledge of the past development of the NGO world puts us in a better position for analysis and evaluation.

Development means changes in certain dimensions. Particularly important for the assessment of the strength and size of the NGO world are the following dimensions:

1. Domain of the NGO world—the number of units or NGOs in the global system.
2. Number of national representations—the number of countries that have individual citizens, national organizations, and/or governmental agencies affiliated with an NGO.
3. Scope and intensity of NGO activity—the number of functions which an NGO performs (scope) at certain rates (intensity).
4. Interconnection of the NGO world—the degree of cooperation between NGOs. The more NGOs cooperate with each other instead of fighting or remaining isolated, the more effective they presumably are in performing their functions and upholding their independence vis-à-vis IGOs and nation-states.

Increases in one or more of these dimensions are defined as growth. Two more dimensions are included, however, because they seem to be politically significant:

5. Distribution of NGOs by field of activity—the distinction between those organizations concerned with, for example, sports and those mainly concerned with influencing the international political situation.

6. Distribution of NGOs across countries—the variation in peacemaking potential between NGOs limited in their membership and activities to one region of the world and those NGOs whose membership and activities are evenly distributed.

The theoretical justification for these two dimensions is elaborated in subsequent parts of this essay.

These six dimensions are treated individually. The validity of their empirical indicators often leaves much to be desired because data on more satisfactory variables simply does not exist.

The first dimension, the domain of the NGO world, is by far the easiest to operationalize. The variable used is the number of independent organizations. The first NGO—the Rosicrucian Order—is said to fit the UIA definition since 1694 which makes it a unique phenomenon for nearly one and one-half centuries.[11] Figure 5-1 shows the number of NGOs founded during each five-year period since 1850. The most striking characteristic of the trajectory is the general upward trend interrupted by two very marked dips at the time of the world wars. Unfortunately, it has not been possible to calculate the net increases for the periods before 1950, but in all probability they were negative imme-

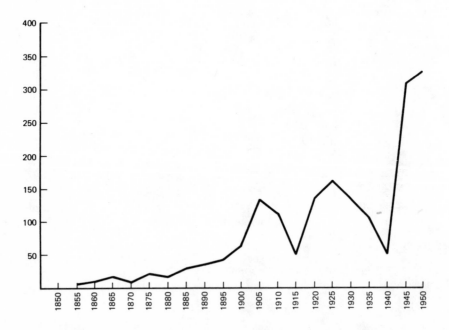

Figure 5-1. Number of NGOs Founded per Five-Year Period, 1850-1954. Source: Speeckaert 1957, p. 1.

diately before and during the wars as in the case of IGOs (Skjelsbaek 1970a, Chap. 4, p. 7). Grave international conflicts apparently curtail the formation of NGOs.[12]

Reliable biennial data for the years 1954-68 makes it possible to calculate mean percentage increases in different periods (see Table 5-1). Although mergers and splits do take place in the NGO world, there are more of the former than of the latter. The high growth rates in Table 5-1 can therefore not be attributed to a relatively high number of splinter groups.

Table 5-1
Active NGOs, 1954-68

Year	Number of NGOs	Percentage Increase
1954	1,012	–
1956	975	−3.7
1958	1,060	8.8
1960	1,255	18.4
1962	1,324	5.5
1964	1,470	11.0
1966	1,685	14.6
1968	1,899	12.7
Mean increase per annum, 1954-68		4.7
Mean increase per annum, 1962-68		6.2

Source: YEARBOOK OF INTERNATIONAL ORGANIZATIONS (5th-12th eds.; Brussels: Union of International Associations, 1955-69).

The second dimension of the NGO world is the number of national representations. The figures for this variable, presented in Table 5-2, indicate a steady increase in the number of national representations which means that NGOs on the average now involve more countries than in previous years. This is partially due to the increasing number of states in the world, but this is probably not the entire explanation.[13] The increase is not due, however, to any increased percentage of universal organizations. In fact, the proportion of regional organizations increased until at least 1962. This is shown in Table 5-3.[14]

The scope of an NGO is defined as the number of functions an NGO performs. Since it is unclear how a "function" should be defined, it is impossible to operationalize this concept. NGO programs now appear to be more encompassing and diversified than before. Probably more important is the fact that new organizations formed every year engage in new activities hitherto not taken up at the international level. In spite of the importance of this dimension, however, an attempt at empirical verification of the hypothesized expansion of scope must be temporarily postponed.

108

Table 5-2
National Representations in NGOs, 1951-66

Year	Mean	Standard Deviation	N	No Information
1951	21.0	–	583	240
1956	22.3	–	897	76
1964	23.7	19.9	1,458	12
1966	25.7	–	1,416	269

Sources: "La Participation des états aux organisations internationales," INTERNATIONAL ASSOCIATIONS, October 1957 (9th Year, no. 10), Tables 2 and 3, pp. 708-709; YEARBOOK OF INTERNATIONAL ORGANIZATIONS (10th ed.; Brussels: Union of International Associations, 1965).

Table 5-3
Distribution of Regional NGOs, 1954-62

Continent	Percentage by year			
	1954	1956	1960	1962
Europe	55.1	60.7	65.0	61.1
Americas	33.5	28.0	24.6	25.5
Africa	6.3	4.8	4.6	7.0
Asia	5.1	6.5	5.7	6.4
Sum	100.0	100.0	99.9	100.0
N	158	186	280	298
Percentage of all NGOs	13.9	18.2	24.2	25.0

Source: E.S. Tew, "Représentations nationales dans les organisations internationales," INTERNATIONAL ASSOCIATIONS, November 1963 (15th Year, no. 11), Tables K and L, pp. 694-95.

Intensity of activity can be measured by numbers of paid staff members and budgets. About one-third of all NGOs in 1964 had no paid staffs; they were administered by elected secretaries on a voluntary basis. Another one-third of the NGOs had staffs of one to three persons. The average for all organizations, however, was nine which indicates that a few large NGOs have more staff personnel than all the others together. Unfortunately, dispersion measures cannot be computed for other years, but the means are given in Table 5-4 together with the corresponding mean size of budgets. It is clear that no trend toward larger mean size of staff or budget is evident for NGOs.[15]

There is no comparative data over time on relationships between NGOs or the degree of interconnection between them, but this dimension of growth is

Table 5-4
Budget and Paid Staff of NGOs, 1954-64

Year	Budget			Paid Staff		
	Mean[a]	N	Percentage Response	Mean[a]	N	Percentage Response
1954	710	327	32	–	–	–
1958	610	477	45	12.5	478	45
1960	587	521	42	8.3	491	39
1964	629	417	28	9.0	615	42

Sources: "Un Réseau inextricable?" INTERNATIONAL ASSOCIATIONS, October 1958 (10th Year, No. 10), tabulation and Table 3, pp. 682-83; E.S. Tew, "The Organizational World," INTERNATIONAL ASSOCIATIONS, December 1960 (12th Year, no. 12), Tables 3 and 4, pp. 734-35; YEARBOOK OF INTERNATIONAL ORGANIZATIONS (10th ed., 1965).

[a]In thousands of US $.

nevertheless so important that it deserves brief discussion. The increasing number of organizations in various fields of activity probably leads to a need for coordination which in turn may beget new "super-NGOs" as coordinating mechanisms.[16] My hypothesis, therefore, is that interaction between NGOs and between NGOs and other actors is increasing. The base from which this increase would take place is fairly substantial: In 1964 about one-third of all NGOs reported some kind of formal relationship with two or more other NGOs, and a slightly smaller fraction had formal relationships with IGOs in the form, for example, of consultative status.[17]

The fifth dimension, the distribution of NGOs by field of activity, is roughly measured by the data presented in Table 5-5. IGOs are also included in these figures, but since they comprise only about 10 percent of the total, they constitute only a minor problem. Many of the organizations founded in these three time periods no longer exist, but the death rate is claimed to be approximately equal in the largest categories (Speeckaert 1957, p. xiv). A more important problem is the difficulty of defining and classifying the various fields of activity. Because one man, G.P. Speeckaert, has done the classification, the consistency is relatively high, although he has not entirely escaped the problems posed by organizations working in several fields.

Despite all of these reservations some of the changes indicated in Table 5-5 are large enough to be considered significant. Most notable is the category of economic and financial organizations. They constituted 12.5 percent of the number of organizations founded in the period after World War II compared with only 3.3 percent before 1914. Commercial and industrial organizations show a similar, although less marked, pattern. It is remarkable, however, that the relative number of pure science organizations is diminishing. Scientists seem to have organized internationally at an early period, and much of the expansion and diversification in the postwar period must have taken place within the existing organizations. Applied science, however, is an area with an increasing number of international organizations.[18]

Table 5-5
International Organizations Founded, 1693-1954

Field of Activity	Percentage by Year		
	1693-1914	1915-1944	1945-1954
General, press, documentation	6.3	3.5	5.6
Philosophy, ethics, peace	7.1	5.0	4.0
Religion	5.3	3.8	2.9
Social science	1.8	1.2	2.1
Economics, political economy, finance	3.3	9.5	12.5
Labor	8.6	3.0	5.2
Law, administration	10.0	9.2	8.6
Relief, education, youth and women's movements	8.6	11.6	12.1
Commerce, industry	5.7	8.3	9.2
Philology, languages	5.5	2.0	.9
Pure science	10.6	6.5	4.9
Medicine, health	9.4	10.5	9.6
Engineering, technology	2.9	4.1	4.6
Agriculture, domestic science	4.9	5.1	6.0
Transport	2.0	4.5	4.5
Art	2.0	5.6	4.7
Sports	5.1	5.0	1.7
Literature	0	1.2	.2
Geography, history	.8	.9	.7
Sum	99.9	100.5	100.0
N	509	666	803

Source: Speeckaert, 1957, p. xiii.

Note: About 400 organizations, for which the foundation date is missing, are not included in the table. Most of them are not in existence today. See "The Development of the International Structure," NGO BULLETIN, July 1952 (4th Year, nos. 6-7), p. 247.

A more valid indicator than the number of organizations founded is the total number of organizations active at various points in time. Very reliable data is now available for NGOs alone for the period 1964-68. Relative distribution by field of activity appears to be quite stable, but the long-run trends mentioned earlier are clearly discernible (Skjelsbaek 1970a, Chap. 4, p. 25; 1970b, vol. 2, pp. 90-136).

I hypothesize that the relative number of NGOs has been growing precisely in those areas that are most politically relevant and in which national governments are likely to be most active. If this is so, the consequences may be far-reaching. Governments may respond to NGO expansion in several ways: by curbing NGO activities by establishing an IGO; by trying to influence their respective states in the relevant NGOs; or by trying to nationalize the particular types of activity. Conversely, the composition of the membership of NGOs may be such that it not only brings different national nongovernmental groups together but also facilitates contacts between governmental and nongovernmental sectors. At least some of the European agricultural organizations seem to have this potential. In short, all kinds of bargains can be struck.

The final dimension to be discussed is that distribution of NGOs across countries.[19] It goes almost without saying that the particular configuration of organizations across countries to a large extent determines the culture of the NGO world and its acceptance in various national societies. To simplify this analysis I divided the 219 countries in the world in 1969 into eight categories or regions on the basis of economic and political similarity rather than territorial contiguity or geographical proximity.[20] The eight regions are:

1. Northwest—North America and Western Europe plus Australia, Cyprus, Israel, Japan, New Zealand, and the Republic of South Africa. This label obviously refers to political, not geographical, position.
2. Latin America—all countries in the Western Hemisphere except the United States and Canada.
3. Arab World—all members of the League of Arab States plus Iran and the Arab ministates.
4. Western Asia—all other Asian states not ruled by Communist parties.
5. Communist Asia—the Democratic People's Republic of Korea (North Korea), the Democratic Republic of Vietnam (North Vietnam), the Mongolian People's Republic, and the People's Republic of China (Communist China).
6. Eastern Europe—the Communist-ruled states in Europe.
7. Black Africa—all non-Arab countries in Africa not under colonial rule or ruled by white elites in 1969.
8. Other—all other nation-states and territories.

Two of these regions, the Northwest and Eastern Europe, are "developed," and two regions, Eastern Europe and Communist Asia, consist exclusively of Communist countries.

Since the Northwest has a disproportionate share of involvement in international organizations in general and in NGOs in particular, three subregions will be looked at separately: North America, Canada, and the United States; northern Europe, the members of the Nordic Council; the EEC group, the six members of the European Economic Community. This classification is not very different from others derived by empirical methods.[21]

Table 5-6
National Representations in NGOs, 1951-66

Region	Percentage by Year					
	1951	1956	1960	1962	1964	1966
Northwest	66.2	63.5	58.3	57.8	54.5	53.5
Latin America	15.5	17.2	16.4	15.9	16.5	16.6
Arab world	3.5	5.4	4.8	5.2	5.2	5.3
Western Asia	6.6	6.7	8.5	7.4	7.7	8.3
Communist Asia	.1	.4	.3	.3	.5	.5
Eastern Europe	7.9	6.6	7.5	7.7	8.0	7.9
Black Africa	.2	.3	3.5	4.8	6.7	6.8
Other	0	0	.9	1.0	.9	1.1
Sum	100.0	100.1	100.2	100.1	100.0	100.1
N	12,249	20,027	24,144	28,827	34,486	36,341
Number of NGOs	583	897	–	–	1,458	1,416
Missing data	240	76	–	–	12	269
North America	6.0	5.2	4.6	4.6	4.5	4.3
North Europe	12.2	11.3	10.2	10.0	9.3	9.4
EEC group	20.9	20.0	18.9	18.4	17.0	16.4

Source: As for Table 2 plus "Ninety-Seven Sovereign States and the International Non-Governmental Organizations," NGO BULLETIN, May 1952 (4th Year, no. 5), Table 1, p. 215.

Table 5-6 shows the distribution of national representations in NGOs, regional and universal, across the various regions. I have not corrected for the different number of countries or for population size in each region, but it is still quite clear that the Northwest is much overrepresented. At the opposite extreme is Communist Asia. This region is virtually excluded from the NGO world.[22] The Latin American share of the total is probably closest to what may be considered "just," taking into account the number of countries and the size of the population in this region. All the other regions are more or less underrepresented, especially Western Asia. There has been an important decrease in the percentage of representations of the Northwest during the past fifteen years, however, and the shares of the subregions have been reduced in roughly the same proportion. The other regions are, by and large, stable. Black Africa is the significant exception. The remarkable influx of African representatives into NGOs is of course partly due to the liberation of former colonies.[23] There are far more ties between African countries and the NGO world now than in the beginning of the 1950s.

The number of national representations is only one indicator of a country's involvement in international organizations. Other indicators are the number of officers of the particular nationality, headquarters and secondary offices located on its territory, the number of international meetings held there, presumably administered by the local NGO branch, and financial contributions. Data exists for several of these variables at different points in time. In all cases the trend is roughly similar to that of the number of national representations. The percentage of the Northwest has diminished and the share of Black Africa has increased. But the differences between the variables are more interesting than the similarities. For this comparison it is sufficient to look only at the Northwest (Table 5-7). Two conclusions can be drawn from the data. First, the higher the level in the organizational structure at which involvement takes place, the larger is the percentage of Northwest representation. Second, the higher the organizational level, the more slowly the percentage of Northwest representation diminishes. Although there is a visible development in the direction of a more egalitarian distribution of involvements in NGOs, there are still gross biases particularly with respect to the decision-making nuclei of the organizations. The NGO world will experience strains when less developed countries become more conscious of this and when and if Communist countries want to become more active participants.[24]

To summarize, although the available data is not as complete and valid as one

Table 5-7
Role of the Northwest in International Organizations, 1951-68

Indicator	Percentage by Year								
	1951	1954	1956	1958	1960	1962	1964	1966	1968
Site of publication	—	93.3	—	—	91.3	—	—	—·	—
Site of headquarters[a]	93.2	93.2	—	92.0	—	90.8	89.4	88.7	87.1
Officers	—	—	—	—	88.4	—	—	—	—
International meetings[a]	87.0	83.3	83.3	84.3	77.5	76.8	78.6	75.5	—
Site of secondary offices[a]	—	—	—	76.6	—	68.9	64.4	58.9	57.5
Representations	66.2	—	63.5	—	58.3	57.8	54.5	53.5	—

Sources: As for Table 6 plus "Répartition par matières et par pays des publications périodiques des ONG internationales," NGO BULLETIN, December 1953 (5th Year, no. 12), pp. 505-507; and the following articles in INTERNATIONAL ASSOCIATIONS: Geneviève Devillé, "Les Réunions internationales en 1958," June 1959 (11th Year, no. 6), Table 4, pp. 444-45; Eliane Dolo-André, "International Periodicals," October 1959 (11th Year, no. 10), pp. 704-710; Geneviève Devillé, "Le Développement géographique de la coopération internationale," December 1962 (12th Year, no. 12), pp. 799-803; "The Leaders of International Organisations and Their Nationality," May 1967 (19th Year, no. 5), pp. 354-355; "Geographical Distribution of International Meetings 1956-1966," February 1968 (20th Year, no. 2), pp. 92-93; and Kjell Skjelsbaek, "Location of Headquarters of International Organizations (1960-1968)," January 1970 (22nd Year, no. 1), pp. 36-37.
[a]Figures for IGOs and NGOs combined.

might wish, a reasonably clear picture of different trends of development has emerged. The number of NGOs has annually grown at a rate of about 6 percent. Most NGOs have small secretariats and, if the pattern of the past can be extended into the future, little prospect of enlarging them. On the other hand, a majority of NGOs has added new national branches and is likely to continue to do so. Over the past 100 years relatively more NGOs have tended to operate in fields that are also of great concern to national governments, for example, economics, finance, commerce, industry, and technology. There is a clearly diminishing concentration of NGO involvement in capitalist, developed countries and a rising number of NGO involvements in African countries. Because this is partly explained in terms of decolonization, changes in this dimension will be relatively smaller in the immediate future.

Some Causes of the Development of NGOs

The causes of these trends are complex, and the following discussion does not pretend to provide definitive answers to the questions that inevitably arise. It is rather an attempt to formulate some relevant hypotheses.

A glance at Table 5-6 immediately suggests that two characteristics of national societies are particularly conducive to participation in NGOs: (1) a high degree of technological and economic development and (2) a pluralistic ideology. In general it appears that the more economically developed a country is, the more involved it will be in NGOs.[25] Whether the average degree of pluralistic ideology has increased over time is harder to assess although suggestive evidence is available to confirm a relationship between this variable and NGO membership also.[26]

Economically developed, pluralistic societies are clearly more likely to have a multitude of national interest groups than are less developed, less pluralistic societies. In addition, these societies are also more likely to have interest groups that will expand transnationally. As economic and technological development proceeds, specialization ensues with the result that some categories of persons, groups, or industries are no longer large enough to constitute functional communities that can satisfy their members' needs. Functional communities are hardly less important to people now than earlier, and, if they cannot be organized satisfactorily on the national level, the logical procedure, particularly with relatively decreasing communication and transportation costs, is to make them transnational. The shortage of personnel is naturally first experienced in small and medium-size countries which, other things being equal, should be more involved in transnational organizations.[27]

If the development of the NGO world is to a large extent the result of economic and technological development, there is good reason to believe that the number of NGOs will increase in the years ahead—assuming that the international system is not marked by increased tension or revived nationalism. With a modest growth rate of 5 percent per year from 1968, there will be 9,049 NGOs in the world in the year 2000. The correlation with economic and technological development also makes it likely that more countries will participate actively in such organizations as they reach a higher stage of development. Japan's participation in NGOs, for example, has increased despite the obstacles of language and distance: In 1964 it ranked sixteenth with representation in 611 NGOs. Thus the mean number of national representations will increase in the future as it has done in the past, although not as fast as in the past because the artificial effect of decolonization will be absent. After some years there will be a ceiling effect because many NGOs need not, and should not, be universal. Many problems are local and can be dealt with effectively by limited-membership organizations.[28]

If my hypothesis about the transnational consequences of specialization is correct, it partly explains why many NGOs are so small. Although most leaders of organizations wish to increase their domains, many organizations will expand only within certain limits determined by the number of persons having the same special interests. However, a large number of organizations, such as political parties, trade unions, and religious organizations, are based on widespread interests. Their potential domain is large indeed, and these mass-support organizations will generally continue to grow in proportion to the improvement of communications and economic conditions. The two types of NGOs have different capabilities: The first kind is based on expertise; the second kind has influence by leading and representing large segments of the public in various societies.

Different levels of economic and technological development may also explain different distributions of involvement across various fields of activity. The impression derived from Table 5-5 is that relatively more NGOs have recently been established in fields closely connected with politics—finance, industry, and technological development—than in less political areas. It is in exactly these fields that the most developed states were most active.[29]

NGO Increase and the Analysis of International Relations

The state-centered view of world affairs, the interstate model which still enjoys so much popularity in the study of international relations, has now become too simplistic as a result of new developments in the global system, particularly since World War II. The interstate model is especially unfit for projections and predictions about the future. Another model is proposed that I regard as more realistic but also far more complex.

There are two reasons why the interstate model is inadequate. First, the above analysis shows that nation-states are not the only actors on the world scene. Some NGOs probably have more power and influence in their respective fields than some of the smaller nation-states. The same applies to several IGOs and undoubtedly to many multinational business enterprises which have more employees and a larger production output than most countries.[30]

The crucial question for our analysis, however, is whether these organizations are so dependent on the consensus of governments for their operation that they merely carry out common governmental policies or whether they formulate and pursue policies of their own, sometimes even in opposition to governments. Only to the extent that they formulate and pursue independent policies are they independent actors in world affairs.[31]

Independence from governmental control may be denoted as "extranational-ism." Extranationalism differs from transnationalism, which is defined in terms of activities across state borders by nongovernmental actors, and supranational-ism, which implies that organizations have some formal authority over govern-ments as in the case of the Commission of the European Communities. Extranational actors may have *de facto* authority in fields governments seldom regulate themselves, for example, the execution of research programs. They may also have a say in matters in which governments are involved but that are to a certain extent beyond governmental competence and control. IATA actions against certain governments in connection with airplane hijacking are a case in point. The IATA has sometimes effectively put pressure on governments for release of a plane, but it has been less successful with the semigovernmental, semi-international Arab guerrilla organizations.

The second reason for the inadequacy of the interstate model of world affairs is connected with the first. States are not like ships that have unified structures of command and can pursue only one course of action at a time. States are not necessarily unified: One group may engage in transnational processes and organizations to thwart actions of other groups, for example, the government. Thus political parties with similar views frequently discuss common policies and problems in their respective NGOs; multinational business enterprises may have interests that run counter to the wishes of governments and other groups in the countries in which they operate. Functionally similar groups in different societies may therefore organize themselves to change the policies of govern-ments; conversely, governments may ally to change the actions of transnational organizations. This can be done directly by issuing orders to the secretariats in the case of IGOs and indirectly by gaining control over the national branches of NGOs. Transnational organizations are not just another category of social actors on the world scene: They permeate the old ones, nation-states, and vice versa.

An alternative model of the global system should therefore inlcude IGOs, NGOs, and multinational business enterprises as well as nation-states.[32] Figure 5-2 directs our attention toward relations between various types of actors, as well as between states, IGOs, NGOs, and multinational enterprises. Cell 3, for example, represents policies of states toward NGOs; cell 9 indicates the converse

	NATION-STATE	IGO	NGO	MULTINATIONAL BUSINESS ENTERPRISE	
NATION-STATE	1	5	9	13	150
IGO	2	6	10	14	250
NGO	3	7	11	15	2500
MULTINATIONAL BUSINESS ENTERPRISE	4	8	12	16	1000

Figure 5-2. Proposed Model of the Global System. Note: The figures outside the matrix have been approximated.

relationship. This is not the place to discuss all the cells in the matrix, but each one of them may be the point of departure for research projects and policy recommendations. In the case of IGO-NGO relationships, for example, there is a notable asymmetry on both a quantitative and qualitative level. Quantitatively, the relationship is asymmetric because a limited number of IGOs have connections with a very large number of NGOs, while each of these NGOs only has official connections with from one to six or seven IGOs. Qualitatively, some NGOs feel that they trade information and expertise for the dubious prestige of being on a list of selected consultants.[33] Focusing on another set of relationships—that between IGOs and multinational business enterprises—it has been suggested that one way to finance IGOs would be to permit them to tax such enterprises on the ground that these organizations benefit from the general peace and prosperity of the international level at which they operate (see Galtung, 1969a, pp. 23-4; Modelski, 1968, pp. 64-79).

Two factors make the model more complex than the relatively simple matrix in Figure 5-2 may indicate. In the first place, there are numerous overlapping memberships in the system. A given individual is the citizen of a state which is member of several IGOs. He may simultaneously, however, be a member of a trade union that belongs to one or more NGOs, and he may work in a plant that is part of a multinational business enterprise. Second, NGOs themselves are often linked in superorganizations as discussed earlier. Thus the predominantly horizontal perspective presented should be supplemented by a vertical perspective encompassing the connections between individuals at the bottom and super-NGOs at the top. This also cannot be illustrated in a two-dimensional presentation.

The suggested model is now very complex and comprises an almost infinite number of relationships. No researcher can possibly study all of them simultaneously, but by using the total model as his point of departure, he will be more aware of the apsects he excludes from consideration when he singles out certain categories of relationships for closer scrutiny. Moreover, he may find that the same general theories are applicable in the most different parts of the model. Finally, he will be more conscious of the many possible future paths of development of the global social structure. The proposed model seems to be more useful than the old interstate model for people interested in "social engineering" at the world level.

Consequences of NGO Development for Peace

The possible consequences of the development of the NGO world for peace cannot be analyzed unless some criteria of "a peaceful world" have been laid down. They can hardly be specified without running into an ideological discussion. I consider two conditions essential to a state of peace: (1) the substitution of positive relationships and interactions for violence or potential violence and (2) the absence of exploitation so that interacting parties benefit about equally from their relationship.[34]

A variety of arguments has been offered over the past few decades to show that international organizations, including NGOs, contribute to the prevention of war or the threat of war. For example, it is argued that positive interactions may take place within the organizations; that functional organizations may perform such useful functions that governments are reluctant to launch conflicts for fear of disrupting them; and that functional cooperation may "spill over" into other areas where force is more likely to be used, that is, into areas of "high politics."[35] This study provides no data that bears directly on these arguments.

Another argument in favor of NGOs is that they contribute to the blurring of regional as well as national boundaries. In my opinion, however, exclusive regional integration and the substitution of interregional conflict for international conflict is no improvement at all since larger units can engage in larger wars. Numerous NGOs and several functional IGOs recruit members and operate according to functional needs, disregarding ideological and political barriers.[36] If all international organizations did that and there were many of them, the world would be an intricate web of overlapping memberships and affiliations. Japanese, for example, would sit together with Chinese for regulation of fisheries, with Americans to organize radio satellite systems, and with Indians for the advancement of Buddhism. Adversaries and competitors in one connection would be allies and collaborators in another. If the argument holds for IGOs, it should be truer still for NGOs since most governments permit their citizens to have contacts that they do not for political reasons maintain themselves.[37]

The data indicates, however, that about one-fourth of all NGOs do not fit the ideal description but declare themselves as regional organizations. On the other hand, many of them do not take their self-imposed limitations very seriously, and cluster and factor analysis of NGO comemberships in regional, local, and universal organizations reveal regional tendencies but no sharp borders.

It is particularly interesting that a systematic, pairwise analysis of NGO representations of the divided countries of the world—the Germanies, Chinas, Koreas, and Vietnams—showed that in each case there were *more* comemberships between them than expected on the basis of each country's total number of comemberships. IGO comemberships, however, were almost nonexistent. Most extreme was the relationship between the two Germanies: In 1964 the Federal Republic of Germany (West Germany) was represented in 93 percent of the NGOs in which the German Democratic Republic (East Germany) was represented. It is not known to what extent these channels are used for positive interaction between national delegations, but they are at least potentially important.

Although it is difficult to construct a simple measure of the degree to which NGO relations are affected by regional and/or political borders, some figures on NGO comemberships in Europe will at least shed some more light on this.[38] The following tabulation presents the normed mean number of NGO comemberships between and within political blocs in Europe in 1964. The figures in parentheses are the number of pairs.

	West	Neutral	East
West	161 (156)	(104)	(91)
Neutral	116	74 (56)	(56)
East	71	55	65 (42)

The countries were classified according to their military alliances with the United States and the Union of Soviet Socialist Republics. The figures are normed so that the mean number of memberships over all pairs equals 100; thus scores over 100 indicate more comemberships than the average, and scores under 100 indicate fewer comemberships. It is remarkable that the score is lower for intra-East pairs (65) than for East-West pairs (71). This means that East European countries generally have more NGO contacts with Western states than with each other.

This data is only suggestive; for further confirmation one must look at the kinds of organizations in which interblock contacts take place. One study of the NGOs in which both the Soviet Union and the United States are represented reports that these organizations are mainly concerned with high-consensus issues. In addition, they have a lower level of activity and a less centralized decision-making structure than other NGOs (Kriesberg, 1968, p. 479). If this holds generally for interbloc organizations, the score of 71 for the East-West relationships may be misleadingly high. Nevertheless, NGOs are less affected by the alliance structure than are interactions like international trade, airline connections, and diplomatic exchanges.[39]

The second criterion for peace is that all interacting parties should benefit about equally from their relationship. One actor should not be able to exploit another. At first sight participation in NGOs has little to do with exploitation. However, if one looks at all NGOs—what I loosely have called the NGO world—instead of each separate organization, the picture is quite different. As shown above less developed countries partake much less in NGOs than do developed countries, and they are especially poorly represented in the central organs of these organizations. Thus the distribution of NGOs does not contribute much to the reduction of unequal opportunities in the global system. Furthermore, if a high density of NGO comemberships with a group of national societies results in a higher degree of integration between them which, in turn, leads to more power for that group, then NGOs at present contribute to the consolidation and improvement of the already dominant group of countries in the world, the Northwest. However, within that region they probably favor small and medium-size countries most. As a consequence the evaluation of NGOs as a peace-and justice-producing factor depends very much on whether one has a global or more limited perspective.[40] It also depends on whether one takes into consideration the activities of NGOs and not only their distribution. Some of them undoubtedly do a good job of improving conditions in less developed countries regardless of the Northwest bias of their membership composition. But these organizations are nevertheless open to the suspicion of neocolonialism.

The only real solution to this problem lies in the establishment by less developed countries of their own organizations whenever possible and their collaboration with the rest of the NGO world through these organizations. This will admittedly be a difficult task considering the relative absence of the two factors which have been so conducive to the formation of NGOs in other parts of the world—a highly developed technology and economy and some kind of pluralistic ideology. Although I would hope not, such organizations may be met by skepticism and resentment from people with vested interests in existing organizations. On the contrary, I hope that the proposed arrangement will serve two purposes: (1) to give less developed countries an opportunity to establish and run NGOs according to their own ideologies and needs and (2) to link developed and less developed countries to each other in a more symmetric way than is the case now, particularly in order to solve problems common to both groups.

Whether or not this happens, it is clear that the institutionalization of transnational interactions in nongovernmental organizations is continuing apace and that in a variety of ways it may be an important factor in future patterns of world politics. Students of international relations as well as policy-makers must come to understand this new phenomenon clearly to ensure that it promotes peace to the greatest possible extent.

Notes

1. Much statistical information on transnational interaction has been collected and utilized by Angell (1969).

2. See the essays by Louis T. Wells, Jr., and Raymond Vernon in Nye and Keohane (1972). For an effort to list and classify multinational business enterprises see A.J.N. Judge (1968-69).

3. See the YEARBOOK OF INTERNATIONAL ORGANIZATIONS, p. 13. Characteristics of organizations and processes in some of the particular fields are discussed by the authors in parts II and III of Nye and Keohane (1972).

4. The functions of the IATA are interestingly described by Robert L. Thornton in Nye and Keohane (1972); the essay by Robert W. Cox in that volume deals with problems of international trade unions.

5. The Union of International Associations in Brussels is itself an interesting transnational actor. It was founded in 1907 to serve as a documentation center on international governmental and nongovernmental organizations, their activities and meetings. The UIA also works to promote research in the same field and to publicize studies. I have found its publications very useful and appreciate the time spent by its staff in consultation with me.

6. "Any international organization which is not established by inter-governmental agreement shall be considered as a non-governmental organization. . . . " ECOSOC Resolution 288 (X), February 27, 1950.

7. There are several additional differences between the lists that can be briefly mentioned. The UIA excludes bilateral organizations, of which there appear to be few, organizations in which one national delegation is completely dominant through the budget or by means of the voting arrangements, and ephemeral organizations established to organize a single international meeting. It also excludes organizations without a formal structure. Moreover, universities, colleges, churches, and religious missions fall outside the scope of the UIA. On the other hand, the UIA definition includes some organizations that are formally subunits of others if they act relatively independently and elect their own officers. Thus eleven international trade union secretariats of the WFTU as well as the WFTU itself are included. Profit-making organizations are, or course, excluded.

8. EEC business and professional groups have been studied by Jean Meynaud (1967) and Dusan Sidjanski (1969).

9. None of the tables from UIA publications appears in its original form since I have split and regrouped the data.

10. The representative quality of the returned questionnaires turned out to be very high; see Skjelsbaek (1970a, Chapter 3).

11. The traditional history of the Rosicrucian Order began in Egypt about 1500 B.C. It is an educational and fraternal order whose teachings present a system of metaphysical and physical philosophy to help the individual utilize his natural talents to better advantage. There are about 100,000 members in 53 countries. See the YEARBOOK OF INTERNATIONAL ORGANIZATIONS, pp. 976-77; and Speeckaert (1957, p. 1).

12. It could be argued that the causal relationship operates in reverse, i.e., that NGOs make up an integrative subsystem of world society and that, if the integrative subsystem weakens, conflicts will erupt. In my mind there is an interplay between the two factors, but interstate conflicts still have more effect on NGOs than the other way around. However, this may well be changed in the future as the NGO world expands. For an interesting theoretical justification of this kind of thinking see Paul Smoker (1967).

13. Sixty-one percent of the organizations surveyed expected to gain new national branches in the future in spite of the small likelihood of a corresponding increase in the number of nation-states and territories.

14. The organizations were classified as regional on the basis of their names. I have tried this procedure myself and found it very difficult. There is a basic confusion about the term region. The UIA does not distinguish between region and continent, which makes it hard to place Arab organizations or NGOs with members from Western Europe and North America only. Moreover, the name of an organization may be misleading, and it may have one or two members from other regions. Israel, for example, is represented in some European organizations. The blurred lines between regions may be annoying to the researcher, but they may be functional for other purposes. See the discussion about the peace relevance of NGOs in the last section of this chapter.

15. Staff and budget indicators are, of course, closely related—the gamma correlation equals 0.88. Missing data represents a difficult problem since many organizations, particularly the smaller ones, are loath to report the size of their staffs and budgets. But since these are probably the same organizations every year, the general trends shown may be reliable even though the particular means may be incorrect.

16. Descriptions of several "super-NGOs" are found in Lador-Lederer, (1962, p. 66). According to a recent count there are almost 100 superorganizations consisting partly or exclusively of other NGOs; see A.J.N. Judge (1969).

17. For details see Skjelsbaek, 1970a, Chap. 3, p. 13. Negative relationships are formalized neither in the NGO world nor in the nation-state world; see ibid., appendix B, p. 1, for a discussion of negative alliances. Negative, or at least competitive, relationships may exist between NGOs of different ideological

color. The most clear-cut ideological divisions are probably found between trade unions; see Cox, in Nye and Keohane (1972).

18. The mean number of national representations is different for the different categories of organizations. In general the means are lowest in those areas that are most relevant for politics. Commercial NGOs have, for example, about fifteen representations on an average which is half the mean number of countries represented in sports organizations.

19. The term "country" is used here instead of state because many units that ordinarily do not classify as independent states may have representatives in NGOs, e.g., Hong Kong.

20. The classification was based on the PRIO list of countries and territories obtainable from the International Peace Research Institute. See also Gleditsch (1968); and Skjelsbaek, (1970a, appendix L, pp. 1-3). The complete distribution of countries in regions is found in ibid., appendix A, pp. 1-2.

21. To my knowledge the most thorough effort to define regions empirically has been done by Bruce M. Russett (1967). One of Russett's variables is comemberships in IGOs. I have done a similar factor analysis with NGO comemberships, and the differences from Russett's findings were small indeed.

22. Cluster and factor analysis bring out the four countries as a very distinct and isolated group. It is interesting to note that the National Liberation Front (NLF) of the Republic of Vietnam (South Vietnam), which probably would have clustered with the same countries had the organization been considered a separate political entity by the UIA, was represented in eleven NGOs in 1966. Some of these belonged to the international "establishment" and had consultative relations with the UN specialized agencies. A general evaluation of revolutionary organizations as transnational actors is found in J. Bowyer Bell's essay in Nye and Keohane (1972). The number of NGOs with world revolution as their primary concern seems to be very low.

23. Corresponding IGO figures show an increase from 1.5 percent in 1956 to 18.0 percent in 1966 for Black Africa; see Skjelsbaek, 1970a, Chap. 4, p. 3.

24. There are already signs of skepticism expressed by delegates from less developed countries within ECOSOC. The Soviet delegation, too, has several times criticized "infringement of national sovereignty" by, for example, Western-dominated civil rights NGOs. See Campbell, 1969, p. 37.

25. Pearson's correlation between an index of economic development and the number of representations in NGOs was 0.64 in 1964; See Skjelsbaek (1970a, Chap. 5, p. 26).

26. The hypothesis can be tested by comparing countries equally developed economically but with different degrees of pluralism. An approximate method may serve as an illustration. Suppose that the countries of the Northwest are generally more pluralistic than the countries of Eastern Europe but about equally developed economically. Then the mean number of national representations in NGOs should be higher in the former region, which indeed it is:

	Mean number of NGO representations	Mean degree of economic development	Mean size of population
Eastern Europe (7 countries)	322	.758	42.7
Northwest (21 countries)	763	1.096	22.7

In calculating the mean degree of economic development, the mean for all countries in the world weighted by their population is zero. The average deviation is one. This tabulation also suggests that the size of population (presented in millions) may be a factor of importance, and it probably is in an intricate way.

27. A list of countries ranked according to the number of NGOs in which they are represented gives a good indication of this, but, after dividing by the size of their population, the tendency stands out much more clearly. The six countries that have most NGO representations per million inhabitants are: Israel, Norway, Switzerland, Denmark, Finland, and New Zealand. Countries with less than one million people have been excluded.

28. In addition, there may be many regional NGOs with members exclusively from nation-states that are in the process of forming a political union. The best example is the high number of business and professional groups within the EEC. I have reserved the term "local international organization" for bodies that intentionally limit their domain geographically but not in accordance with the borders of a prospective political union. The Mediterranean Social Sciences Research Council (MSSRC), for example, is a local NGO.

29. Most organizations in these fields were not only more "developed" in their membership composition but also more Western on the East-West political dimension; see Skjelsbaek (1970a, Chap. 5, p. 20).

30. Only seventeen countries have gross national products greater than the annual output of General Motors Corporation; see Galloway (1970, Table 2, p. 511).

31. I do not mean primarily "high politics." Most of these organizations operate in other fields and their possible influence on "high politics" is mainly indirect but not, a priori, negligible.

32. Many of the ideas in this section are the result of several seminar discussions directed by Johan Galtung at the International Peace Research Institute.

33. Conversely, some IGOs may feel that NGOs are too afraid of losing their independence to be willing to participate in joint programs.

34. The second dimension may also be denoted as social justice or equality. It is included in the definition of peace because the lack of such qualities in the international system frequently has the same consequences as do wars—spiritual

and physical destruction of human beings. Since 1945 more people have probably died from malnutrition and lack of medical care than in military battles. Since exploitation typically takes place in an egalitarian social structure, the net result is often referred to as structural violence. Revolutionaries are often willing to use personal or direct violence to end structural violence, while people that profit from such a structure may claim that they can prevent violence in the traditional sense of that term through their control of the system. The Pax Romana is the classic example of this kind of a situation. In my opinion nothing is gained by trading one kind of violence for another if the change does not result in fewer degraded and lost human lives. For a discussion of these problems see Schmid (1968); Galtung (1969b) and Galtung and Høivik (1970).

35. The "spillover" hypothesis has been seriously contested lately in a number of articles in the JOURNAL OF COMMON MARKET STUDIES. See, for example: Stanley Hoffmann, "European Process at Atlantic Cross-purposes," February 1965 (Vol. 3, No. 2), pp. 85-101; Karl Kaiser, "The U.S. and the EEC in the Atlantic System: The Problem of Theory," June 1967 (Vol. 5, No. 4), pp. 388-425; Ernst B. Haas, "THE UNITING OF EUROPE and the Uniting of Latin America," ibid., pp. 315-343; Paul Taylor, "The Concept of Community and the European Integration Process," December 1968 (Vol. 7, No. 2), pp. 83-101; and Andrew Wilson Green, "Review Article: Mitrany Reread with the Help of Haas and Sewell," September 1969 (Vol. 8, No. 1), pp. 50-69.

36. Cf., Mitrany (1966). When Mitrany introduced this kind of argument, he was thinking of functional IGOs. A counterargument is that such a world structure for many purposes will be ineffective and give rise to serious problems of coordination. Some states will be involved in some functional agencies while others will not and may even be supporting competing ones. Agencies in related functional fields may quarrel over the lines between their respective areas of responsibility.

37. The multilateral setting of international organizations forces national delegations to have direct and indirect contacts with representatives from countries they ordinarily avoid interaction with, but sometimes exclusions and withdrawals take place. Several attempts to exclude countries from IGOs are well known. My own data gives reason to believe that such cases are very rare in NGOs.

38. Europe was chosen because the continent is relatively homogeneous in terms of economic and technological development, the distances are short, and the East-West conflict is the only overriding, political conflict dimension. An extended discussion is found in Skjelsbaek, 1970a, Chap. 5, pp. 31-34.

39. The comparisons were made by means of chi-squares calculated on the basis of matrices corresponding to the tabulation on p. 440. The difference between NGOs and IGOs in this respect is negligible. A very interesting general study of NGOs as a means of East-West interaction has been done by Paul Smoker (1965).

40. On the other hand, in less developed regions there seems to be a closer coupling between general rank and amount of involvement in NGOs. The single best indicator of general rank, in my mind, is gross national product. However, the hypothesis about regional differences with regard to this relationship has not been carefully tested.

References

Angell, Robert Cooley
1969   PEACE ON THE MARCH: TRANSNATIONAL PARTICIPATION. New York: Van Nostrand Reinhold Co.
Campbell, Persia
1969   "United Nations Report: Do NGOs Have a Role?" INTERNATIONAL DEVELOPMENT REVIEW 11, no. 3: 34-39.
Galloway, Jonathan F.
1970   "Worldwide Corporations and International Integration: The Case of INTELSTAT." INTERNATIONAL ORGANIZATION 24, no. 3: 503-519.
Galtung, Johan
1969a "Non-Territorial Actors and the Problem of Peace." Revision of a paper delivered at the World Order Models Conference, Northfield, Massachusetts, June 18-24.
1969b "Violence, Peace, and Peace Research." JOURNAL OF PEACE RESEARCH, 6, no. 3: 167-92.
Galtung, Johan and Høivik, Tord
1970   "Structural and Direct Violence: A Note on Operationalization." Mimeo. Oslo: International Peace Research Institute.
Gleditsch, Nils Petter
1968   "The Structure of the International Airline Network." Oslo: Magister's Thesis, Univ. of Oslo.
Judge, A.J.N.
1968-69 "Multinational Business Enterprises." In YEARBOOK OF INTERNATIONAL ORGANIZATIONS. 12th ed. Edited by Eyvind S. Tew, Brussels: Union of International Associations.
1969   "International NGO Groupings" INTERNATIONAL ASSOCIATIONS 21, no. 2: 89-92.
Lador-Lederer, J.J.
1962   INTERNATIONAL NON-GOVERNMENTAL ORGANIZATIONS AND ECONOMIC ENTITIES: A STUDY IN AUTONOMOUS ORGANIZATION AND "IUS GENTIUM." Leiden: A.W. Sijthoff.
Kriesberg, Louis
1968   "U.S. and U.S.S.R. Participation in International Non-Governmental

Organizations." In SOCIAL PROCESSES IN INTERNATIONAL RELA-
TIONS: A READER. Edited by Louis Kriesberg. New York: John Wiley
& Sons.

Meynaud, Jean
1967   GROUPES DE PRESSION ET COOPÉRATION EUROPÉENNE. Paris:
Centre d'études des relations internationales.

Mitrany, David
1966   A WORKING PEACE SYSTEM: AN ARGUMENT FOR THE FUNC-
TIONAL DEVELOPMENT OF INTERNATIONAL ORGANIZATION.
Chicago: Quadrangle Books.

Modelski, G.
1968   "The Corporation in World Society." In THE YEARBOOK OF WORLD
AFFAIRS. 1968. London: Stevens & Sons.

Nye, Joseph S., Jr., and Robert O. Keohane
1972   TRANS NATIONAL RELATIONS AND WORLD POLITICS. Cambridge: Harvard University Press.

Rosenberg, Adrea
1967   "International Interaction and the Taxonomy of International Organizations." INTERNATIONAL ASSOCIATIONS 19, no. 11: 721-29.

Russett, Bruce M.
1967   INTERNATIONAL REGIONS AND THE INTERNATIONAL SYSTEM:
A STUDY IN POLITICAL ECOLOGY. Chicago: Rand McNally.

Schmid, Herman
1968   "Peace Research and Politics." JOURNAL OF PEACE RESEARCH 6,
no. 3: 167-92.

Sidjanski, Dusan
1969   LES GROUPES DE PRESSION DANS LA COMMUNAUTÉ EURO-
PÉENNE. 2 vols. Montreal: Université de Montreal.

Skjelsbaek, Kjell
1970a   "Peace and the Systems of International Organizations." Oslo: Magister's
Thesis, Univ. of Oslo.
1970b   "Development of the Systems of International Organizations: A Dia-
chronic Study." PROCEEDINGS OF THE INTERNATIONAL PEACE
RESEARCH ASSOCIATION THIRD GENERAL CONFERENCE. IPRA
Studies in Peace Research. 3 vols. Assen, the Netherlands: Royal Van
Gorcum.

Smoker, Paul
1965   "A Preliminary Empirical Study of an International Integrative Subsystem." INTERNATIONAL ASSOCIATIONS 17, no. 11: 638-46.
1967   "Nation State Escalation and International Integration." JOURNAL OF
PEACE RESEARCH 4, no. 1: 61-75.

Speeckaert, G.P.
1957   THE 1,978 INTERNATIONAL ORGANIZATIONS FOUNDED SINCE
THE CONGRESS OF VIENNA: A CHRONOLOGICAL LIST Brussels:
Union of International Associations.

6

Trends in U.S. Collegiate Voluntary Associations in the Twentieth Century

Virgil Peterson

Introduction

In Chapter 11 of this volume, Theodore points out the paucity of our information about collegiate voluntary associations. The campus unrest of the past decade stimulated many studies of students. But these studies, by highlighting protest groups, left other associations even more shadowy than before. The neglect of other associations constitutes a serious gap in our understanding of student life.

To narrow that gap represents the first reason for this chapter. Traditional examinations of academic life have concentrated on the cognitive experiences of the classroom. Research inspired by campus unrest has focused on protest. Student voluntary associations, other than protest groups, have been generally ignored.

A second reason for examining U.S. collegiate voluntary associations is that the proportion of our society with college experience is rising dramatically. During this century the ratio of college students per 100 of total population has risen from 0.31- (1900) to 3.51 (fall, 1969)—see U.S. Bureau of the Census, 1971, p. 68, table 90. Or, looked at in another way, only 18 percent of all workers currently in mid-career attended college. That this percentage will increase considerably is indicated by a 1970 Life Insurance Institute study which predicted that by 1980, "80% of all new workers will have attended but not necessarily graduated from college." (see Cook 1972). The amount and kinds of collegiate organizational experience this large influx of college educated members of our society have had may cause significant social changes.

A third reason is that much of the maturation which occurs during college years results not from the academic program, but from nonacademic experiences. As Marjory Lozoff (1969, p. 257) observes:

Often membership in an affiliation group, or, conversely, inability to become part of a group, have meaningful effects on this process [of the social development of adolescents].

A final reason for studying collegiate associations is that an analysis of the kinds of organizations which students join may help us anticipate their future commitments and associational choices. We know that the college-educated, in

129

later life, join organizations more frequently than the non-college-educated (see Payne, Payne and Reddy, 1972). Further, Wright and Hyman (1958) have shown that joiners manifest more interest and are more active in public affairs than those who do not join voluntary associations.

The organizations which students choose in college may predict the voluntary action choices they make in adult life, and may have an important bearing on the degree of citizen participation in public affairs in this country. The student who chooses a fraternity may be more likely in adult life to select the Masonic Lodge than an *ad hoc* commmittee for school betterment or environmental improvement. Conversely the student who chooses to work as a tutor in a ghetto may be more likely to engage in voluntary action for the "Big Brother" program or the American Civil Liberties Union than to isolate himself in a country club.

Method and Data

Several different sources of data were used in performing the present study, ranging from original primary data to previously published material. These sources were as follows:

1. Six editions of the ENCYCLOPEDIA OF ASSOCIATIONS published from 1959 to 1972. These editions list Greek letter societies—social, professional, and honorary, and include information on membership.
2. A mail survey of 139 Greek letter collegiate professional and honorary societies (the total listing of all such associations in 1970 edition of the ENCYCLOPEDIA OF ASSOCIATIONS). Each of these organizations was asked to provide membership data for each decade from 1900 to 1960 and each year from 1960 to the present. Fifty-two organizations responded of which thirty-seven provided usable data. Only two of the organizations had data going back to 1900. Many had no data earlier than their current mailing list. Others had only sketchy data available. All that was not continuous was rejected. Fifty-seven percent of those with memberships of over 100,000 provided usable data. The returned data represent about half of the total membership in honorary and professional Greek letter organizations.
3. In addition to the mail survey, queries went to the heads of national organizations of the Interfraternity Council, the National Pan Hellenic Council, the YMCA and YWCA, Young Americans for Freedom, Northern Student Movement, the National Student Volunteer Program, and other non-Greek letter organizations with student affiliations.
4. Finally, the literature of student movements was examined. The most severe limitation to generalizing on the basis of the above data is that local organizations with no national affiliations are only slightly represented. Of

the above sources, only the National Student Volunteer Program provides data on local organizations though these typically constitute a majority of recognized student groups.

Some Definitions: Expressive and Instrumental
Voluntary Associations

Gordon and Babchuk (1959, p. 27) write that the expressive voluntary organization

provides the framework for immediate and continuing gratification to the individual, [exemplified in colleges by social fraternities and clubs, usually local, with special interests such as chess, astronomy, outings, etc.]. These groups perform a function primarily for the individual participants through activities confined and self-contained within the organization itself. More specifically, they provide the opportunity for carrying on activities, such as recreation, of direct interest to the participant or help to provide satisfactions of personal fellowship. Also included in this category are honorific or status conferring organizations. [On campus, Phi Beta Kappa and other honoraries best exemplify these.] This type of organization has been designated as expressive. In the main, the orientation of the group is not to the attainment of a goal anticipated for the future, but to the organized flow of gratifications in the present.

The instrumental voluntary organization, on the other hand, orients itself to

activities which take place outside the organization. It seeks to maintain a condition or to bring about change which transcends its immediate membership. (Ibid., p. 28.)

. . . .

Certain groups do not exist primarily to furnish activities for members as an end in itself, but serve as social influence organizations designed to create some normative condition or change. Such groups exist in order to attain goals that lie outside of the organizations themselves. (Ibid., p. 25.)

Jacoby and Babchuk (1963, p. 464) state that the instrumental-expressive dimension incorporates three elements:

1. The degree to which the activities of the organizations are designed to provide gratification either immediately or at a later time.
2. The degree to which the activities are oriented to and confined within the group or to persons outside of the group.
3. The degree to which the activities of the organizations are ends in themselves or represent means to external ends.

Applying this typology to the U.S. collegiate voluntary groups dealt with here results in the following two categories: (1) expressive groups—Greek letter honoraries and professional fraternities and social fraternities; and (2) instrumental groups—student volunteer groups dedicated to service or advocacy in the area of social problems and groups intending to influence the political or social scene.

Trend Data on U.S. Collegiate Voluntary Associations

Expressive Organizations

A principal finding of this research is that in the 1960s expressive organizations (Greek letter honoraries and professional fraternities, social fraternities and sororities) have not kept pace with the growth in enrollment in U.S. colleges and universities. Furthermore, the evidence suggests a trend toward corresponding increases in affiliation with instrumental organizations (service and political groups), as we shall see in the next section.

Table 6-1 shows the growth trends in professional and honorary Greek letter fraternities from 1900 to 1970 and compares that growth with percentage increases in college enrollment. Honoraries and professional fraternities experienced rapid growth during the first decades of the century. That growth roughly parallels the surge in the founding of Greek-letter organizations shown in Table 6-2.

Social fraternities begin earlier and peak earlier (1910-20) than professional and honorary fraternities (1920-30). But both had passed their founding surge by 1930. Subsequent growth was to occur, not in new organizations, but in numbers of chapters and chapter membership.

The founding of collegiate Greek-letter societies reflects the general growth of fraternal and sororal orders in America. Schmidt and Babchuk (Chapter 7 in this volume) state that "most fraternal and sororal orders were organized in the latter half of the 19th and first quarter of the 20th century. . . . By 1920, the United States had approximately 800 different secret orders with 30 million members in this country. . . ."

The membership growth rate for collegiate honoraries and professional fraternities declines steadily during the entire period 1900-1970, except for the 1960s, when there was a huge increase in the numbers of students enrolled in college. During this decade, the membership growth rate falls behind the percentage increase in total enrollment in higher education, although there is continuing absolute growth in numbers of memberships.

Table 6-3 presents the total membership listed for all organizations classified as Greek-letter professional and honorary societies in six editions of the ENCYCLOPEDIA OF ASSOCIATIONS.

These data confirm the pattern discernible in Table 6-2 based on the mail survey. The watershed date is, again, 1960, after which percentage increases

Table 6-1

Membership Trends in Selected Honorary and Professional Societies, 1900-1970[a]

Date	Number of Organizations Reporting (Both Years)	Membership Total at End of Decade	Increase in Membership[b]	Percentage Increase in Membership	Percentage Increase in Higher Education Enrollment[c]
1900-10	2	4,026	3,317	467.8	49.5
1910-20	6	16,990	12,964	322.0	68.3
1920-30	10	68,345	51,355	302.3	84.1
1930-40	17	158,003	89,658	131.2	35.7
1940-50	20	343,341	185,338	117.3	52.7
1950-60	26	614,705	271,364	79.0	57.0
1960-70	31	1,280,845	520,521	68.3	121.1

[a]This table is based on a mail survey of the Greek letter professional and honorary societies listed in the 1970 edition of ENCYCLOPEDIA OF ASSOCIATIONS. The societies reported in this table represent the following disciplines:

Chemistry	(1)
Commerce, Business	(4)
Dentistry	(2)
Economics	(1)
Education	(4)
Engineering	(3)
Forensics	(1)
History	(1)
Journalism	(2)
Language, Literature	(1)
Library Science	(1)
Mathematics	(1)
Music	(3)
Pharmacy	(3)
Radio, Television	(1)
Political Science	(1)
Psychology	(1)

[b]The increase was computed on the basis of those organizations reporting for both years, not simply on the basis of membership totals at the end of each decade as reported in the third column.

[c]Computed from figures given by the U.S. Bureau of the Census, DIGEST OF EDUCATIONAL STATISTICS (Washington, D.C.: U.S. Government Printing Office, 1971), p. 68. Beginning in 1950, the enrollment data are for total degree-credit opening fall enrollment; previously, the data are for resident, degree-credit students enrolled at higher institutions during the entire year (and, therefore, some students are counted more than once if they transferred to another institution during the academic year.) Beginning in 1960, enrollment figures include both resident and extension degree-credit students; previously, data did not include extension students. The data for 1966, 1967 and 1971 are estimates by the U.S. Department of Health, Education and Welfare.

Table 6-2
Founding Dates for Greek Letter Societies: Social, Professional, and Honorary

Decade	Social	Professional and Honorary	Total
1770s	1[a]	0	1
....	0	0	0
1820s	3	0	3
1830s	3	0	3
1840s	8	0	8
1850s	7	0	7
1860s	8	1	9
1870s	7	2	9
1880s	2	9	11
1890s	13	12	25
1900s	17	32	49
1910s	23	36	59
1920s	8	51	59
1930s	2	8	10
1940s	0	9	9
1950s	1	1	2
1960s	0	1	1
Totals	103	162	265

Source: ENCYCLOPEDIA OF ASSOCIATIONS, 1970 edition.

[a]Phi Beta Kappa is listed here as a social fraternity. BAIRD'S MANUAL states: "Phi Beta Kappa had all the characteristics of the present-day fraternity." He lists secrecy, ritual, grip, motto, badge, etc. and adds, "It was formed for social and literary purposes and held regular and frequent meetings." However, after about fifty years it became "and since has remained a scholarly honor society." John Robson, ed. BAIRD'S MANUAL OF AMERICAN COLLEGE FRATERNITIES. (Manasha, Wisconsin: George Banta Company, 1963), p. 7.

in this form of associational membership fall behind percentage increases in total enrollment in higher education.

Data on growth of social fraternities do not permit exact comparisons with enrollment increases in higher education. However, the data in Table 6-4 indicate roughly that social fraternities exceeded or approximately kept pace with increases in college enrollment until about 1960. During the 1960s, their percentage growth has been substantially less than percentage growth in total enrollment.

Data for social sororities was unavailable from the National Pan Hellenic Council, but the BULLETIN of the Interfraternity Conference Research and Advisory Council (1972) reports a National Pan Hellenic Conference study showing a 48.5 percent increase in total members for the 1961-71 period. Social fraternities during that period increased 38.9 percent. Total enrollment in higher education increased 117 percent.

Table 6-3

Membership Trends: Collegiate Professional and Honorary Societies

Year	Total Membership	Increase in Membership	Percentage Increase in Membership	Percentage Increase in Total Enrollment in Higher Education[a]
1958	1,705,920	n.a.	n.a.	n.a.
1960	2,009,384	303,464	17.8	11.0
1963	2,326,917	317,533	15.8	25.7
1967	2,555,518	228,601	9.8	42.2
1969	2,906,820	351,302	13.8	17.8
1971	3,056,068	149,248	5.1	12.0
Totals		1,350,148	79.1	159.9
			(Increase: 1958-71)	(Increase: 1958-71)

Source: ENCYCLOPEDIA OF ASSOCIATIONS (Detroit, Michigan: Gale Research Co., 1959, 1962, 1964, 1968, 1970, 1972.) Organizations were not included if their data were discontinuous or if they had clearly changed their counting procedures during the series, e.g., Kappa Delta Pi lists 142,000 members in the 1959 edition. In subsequent editions membership never exceeds 55,000. The higher education enrollment figures come from the source noted in Table 6-1, note C.

[a]Compared to the prior year's figure listed in this table—e.g., 1960 is compared with 1958.

Table 6-4

Membership Trends: Collegiate Social Fraternities

Period	Membership Total at End of Period[d]	Percentage Change in Membership	Percentage Change in Higher Education Enrollment[e]
1900-10[a]	256,797[a]	96.1	49.5
1910-20[b]	371,633[b]	44.7	68.3
1920-29[c]	800,094[c]	142.1	84.1
1929-48	1,103,178	37.7	37.8
1948-60	1,809,542	63.0	64.1
1960-70	2,402,322	32.8	121.1

[a]Actually represents the period 1898-1912 for fraternity membership and the roughly corresponding period 1899-1909 for higher education enrollment.

[b]Actually represents 1912-20 for membership and 1909-19 for enrollment.

[c]Actually represents 1920-29 for membership and 1919-29 for enrollment.

[d]Data come from a question put annually to member fraternities: "What is your total living membership?" National Interfraternity Conference, Indianapolis, Indiana (personal communication.)

[e]Data come from U.S. Census. See note C to Table 6-1.

Data from the ENCYCLOPEDIA OF ASSOCIATIONS for the period 1958 to 1971 confirm the foregoing trends. Though not reported fully here for reasons of space, these data show percentage increases in social fraternities and sororities gradually falling behind percentage increases in total enrollment in higher education for comparable two or three year periods (with the exception of a minor reversal in the 1967-69 period). And over the whole thirteen-year period, social fraternities and sororities grew only 74.6 percent as contrasted with a growth in enrollment of 159.9 percent for the same period. These figures were computed by aggregating the data on all Greek-letter voluntary associations listed as social fraternities and sororities listed in the 1959-72 editions of the ENCYCLOPEDIA.

From all of the data presented in the present section on U.S. collegiate expressive voluntary associations, a few simple conclusions emerge regarding trends. Most of these groups were founded in the late nineteenth and early twentieth centuries. They have been growing steadily in absolute size of membership since their founding. However, when these membership data are compared with the corresponding changes in total enrollment in U.S. higher education a different picture emerges. We find that both the honorary/professional fraternities and the social fraternities and sororities are showing a marked decline in their appeal to college students as a kind of voluntary activity. This decline in relative appeal is fairly steady from about 1930 (where we have data available), but it becomes most noticeable after 1960. During the decade of the sixties, collegiate expressive voluntary associations finally began falling behind enrollment increases in higher education in general.

A projection of the trends observed in the present data suggests that the growth in absolute numbers of members of these kinds of voluntary associations will eventually decline also, perhaps in the next decade or two. At that time, these groups will shift from growing more slowly to not growing at all—in fact, to actually declining numbers. As the next chapter indicates, this actual decline in memberships has already begun in adult fraternal associations. This absolute decline in numbers of members will occur before too many decades in spite of continuing increases in enrollments in higher education. Nevertheless, it will be a long time before collegiate expressive voluntary associations of the traditional Greek-letter variety fade from the scene entirely, judging from the data reviewed here.

We have looked at two different kinds of expressive collegiate voluntary groups—the honorary/professional fraternity and the social fraternity or sorority. Careful examination of our trend data leads to the conclusion that the relative decline in social fraternities and sororities is slightly (about 5 percent) more marked than the relative decline in honorary/professional fraternities. This may be due partly to the fact that the latter have somewhat greater relevance to instrumental goals, although still being essentially expressive. Honorary/professional fraternities award membership on the basis of achievement, by and large, rather than primarily on the basis of social and interpersonal considerations. Still, honorary/professional fraternities seldom *do* anything much. This puts them in a relatively poor growth position in contemporary American society, as contrasted with collegiate instrumental organizations now to be discussed.

Instrumental Organizations

Data on instrumental collegiate voluntary organizations are more elusive, but two categories are fruitful—student volunteer service organizations and political groups. Let us first examine data for the 1960s and then go back in time to present what is available for earlier periods.

Political groups, particularly protest groups, have been by far the most conspicuous during the past ten years. But service groups are larger in terms of man-hours of involvement. Members of service groups typically spend three hours per week on a volunteer service project, perhaps 75 to 100 hours over a school year. By contrast, to be counted as a participant in a protest group—in a student "strike for peace," for example—one need only stay away from a class, an act of a few minutes or hours.

Service Organizations. Table 6-5 presents data pieced together to give some indication of the student service volunteer movement. Data on student service groups is somewhat sketchy, incomplete and inconsistent. But that which is available (see Table 6-5 below) provides clear evidence of a strong student service volunteer movement growing in the late 1960s and early 1970s. In spite of this large and rapid growth, however, the student service volunteer movement still has a long way to go before it can match the sheer number of members of social and honorary fraternities.

Since little has been written about these student volunteer programs, a brief history is appropriate here. Though student service projects have existed in the past, frequently associated with campus YWCAs and YMCAs, the character and thrust of the current college student service volunteer movement begins in the early 1960s when students emerged from the apathetic lifestyle of the 1950s. The Supreme Court decision on desegregation in May 1954, and President Eisenhower's use of federal troops in Arkansas in 1957 confirmed the sense of certain societal wrongs. The lunch counter sit-ins, begun by black students in February 1960, and President Kennedy's announcement of the Peace Corps in March 1961, dramatized the view that young people had a role in social change.

The Northern Student Movement, founded in 1961, consisted of college students helping blacks. Tutoring was a typical undertaking, but NSM also sponsored citizenship and leadership training workshops and voter registration. Many of the students who went south to register voters in the Student Nonviolent Coordinating Committee (SNCC) project of 1961 and the Council of

Table 6-5

Colleges and Universities with Service-Oriented Volunteer Programs and Numbers of Participating Students

Year	1963	1965	1967	1969	1971	1972
Number of Colleges and Universities	65[a]		1000[c]	1263+[d,e]	1672[f]	1800[f]
Number of Students		4,000[b]	200,000[c]	250,000[e]		400,000[f]

[a]The number of campuses with students active in the Northern Student Movement, an organization which, at its peak of activity, had seven city projects and affiliated groups "involved in tutorial and other efforts for ghetto residents." Cited in Theodore, Chapter 11 in this volume.

[b]Estimation of the number of college students involved in volunteer work across the country. Source: "100,000 Hours a Week—Volunteers in Service to Youth and Families." New York, National Federation of Settlements and Neighborhood Centers, 1965.

[c]Estimation of the number of campuses with tutorial programs oriented toward helping economically disadvantaged children and the number of college students serving as tutors. Source: James S. Noce, "Research and Evaluation of Tutorial Programs," Tutorial Assistance Center, U.S. National Student Association, Washington, D.C., 1967.

[d]Estimation of the percentage of colleges and universities with organized student volunteer programs and the number of participating students. Source: "Campus Activists Reflect Social Concerns Through Volunteer Programs," TEACHING TOPICS, 19, no. 1, 1970.

[e]Number of U.S. colleges and universities in total obtained from source C to Table 6-1 (1971).

[f]Result of unpublished surveys conducted by the National Student Volunteer Program. Source: National Student Volunteer Program, Washington, D.C.

Federated Organizations (COFO) project of 1963, returned to their campuses and became organizers of local projects geared to the amelioration of social problems.

In 1965 the National Student Association obtained an Office of Economic Opportunity grant to establish the Tutorial Assistance Center. In 1967 Michigan State University established an office with a full-time coordinator of volunteer programs. The arrival of the Nixon administration heralded a new look at voluntarism and the establishment of the National Program for Voluntary Action with George Romney as its chairman. One of the results was the establishment of the National Student Volunteer Program, an office with the mission of finding ways to contribute to the quantity and quality of student volunteer efforts.

This decade of activity reveals the tremendous potential of youthful energy and idealism. Also, the student impulse toward service converges with the goals of educational reformers who urge the importance of experience in the educational process and who stress the affective or emotional domain.

Political Groups. The major political parties do not have a separate category for campus groups. Young Democrats and Young Republicans include everyone of their party's affiliation under mid-thirties—college and noncollege. The Young Americans for Freedom (YAF) claims to be the largest, college-based political organization. It began in the early sixties and has since been active particularly in political campaigns and in defending American involvement in Vietnam. Table 6-6 presents membership data its headquarters supplied. It indicates fairly steady growth through the early 1960s, with a flattening and actual decline in recent years.

Table 6-6
Membership in Young Americans for Freedom

Year	Total Membership	Increase over Two-Year Period	Percentage Increase over Two-Year Period
1960	150	...	...
1962	8,000	7,850	5233%
1964	40,000	32,000	400%
1966	50,000	10,000	25%
1968	55,000	5,000	10%
1970	65,000	10,000	18%
1972	58,000	(−7,000)	(−11%)

Source: Headquarters, Young Americans for Freedom, Washington, D.C., 1972. (Personal communication.)

Students for a Democratic Society (SDS) is closest to a left-wing equivalent of YAF. The 1972 edition of the ENCYCLOPEDIA OF ASSOCIATIONS lists SDS as fragmented and underground. No address is available. There is, therefore, no official source for membership data. Theodore (Chapter 11 of this volume) summarizes the data on SDS membership as follows:

Califano (1970) places the total membership of Students for a Democratic Society . . . at about 5,000-7,500 in 1969, with the ability to arouse about 70,000 sympathetic colleagues during a period of campus crisis. Blumenthal (1967) states that SDS grew from 1,200 members and 30 chapters in 1965 to more than 6,000 members and 227 chapters in 1967.

Lipset (1971, pp. 74-75) refers to surveys which he believes overestimate SDS membership. He gives the example of one prepared for CBS News by Daniel Yankelovich Associates which places SDS membership in 1969 at 4 percent of the total student body. This would mean 280,000 members. Yet, SDS in 1969 claimed a dues-paying membership of only 7,000. Thus estimates vary, although SDS clearly grew during the 1960s.

Richard Peterson (1968, p. 39) wrote—based upon data compiled from a survey of deans in May 1968—that "the number of colleges reporting student Left groups (these would mainly be SDS chapters) has almost doubled, from 26 percent in 1965 to 46 percent in 1968." Yet despite this increase, "the student movement is still a minority phenomenon. 'Members' of the student Left amount to something on the order of two percent of the national student population [about 128,000]. An additional eight to ten percent are strongly sympathetic with the 'movement for social change' and are capable of temporary activation depending on the issues. And the numbers of activist students, while not increasing spectacularly, are nevertheless rising steadily."

To move from those whom Peterson classifies as "members" to those who are capable of "temporary activation," is to skate on even thinner ice. Lipset (1971, p. 45) presents data drawn from Harris surveys in 1965, 1969 and 1970 indicating a substantial increase in the numbers of students who registered their protest of the war in group activity. There were 60 percent of the students reporting participation in demonstrations in 1970, a steady increase being shown from the 29 percent in 1965 and 40 percent in 1969. Similar results were found for picketing, which rose from 18 percent in 1965 to 29 percent in 1970 (though the increase was clearly smaller and less steady—18 percent picketed in 1969 as well as in 1965).

These figures become more significant if the general increase in numbers of college students is also taken into account. Based upon college enrollments of 5.5 million (1965), 7.5 million (1969), and 7.9 million (1970), there was an increase from 1,595,000 to 4,740,000 students (1965-70) involved in demonstrations, and a corresponding increase from 990,000 to 2,291,000 students involved in picketing.

The estimates of students who identify themselves with the radical left are considerably more modest than the figures of those who have protested the war. Peterson's 2 percent agrees closely with the Harris Poll, spring 1968, counting "between 1 and 2 percent" or about 100,000 (Lipset and Altbach 1969, p. xvii). Lipset and Altbach (ibid.) note that the percentage of students working in political campaigns or in the area of civil rights during 1964-65 was 17 percent (Harris Poll) and during 1967-68 was 20 percent (Gallup Poll).

These data are consistent in suggesting that the trend toward increasing involvement in volunteer service organizations has a parallel in another form of instrumental voluntary organization—political groups.

For the forties and fifties, data on instrumental associations are nearly nonexistent. The forties was a time of preoccupation with the Second World War and the fifties, a time of apathy and political quiescence.

To move back to the thirties, however, is to discover a time which is, in many ways, similar to the sixties. Antiwar feeling was strong and socialism and communism held an appeal comparable to the less ideological Left of the sixties. A convenient bench mark for measuring the activism of the thirties against that of the sixties is the student strike against war in 1935. Hal Draper (1967, p. 170), a participant in the student movement of the thirties, writes that

In 1934 . . . the two radical student organizations [National Student League and Student League for Industrial Democracy] launched what seemed to many at first a rather wild idea, but which turned out to be the most important single action of the movement: a 'Student Strike Against War.'

On April 13, 1934, the date set to commemorate the entrance of the United States into the First World War students were asked to attend their scheduled 11 o'clock classes and leave with as many students as they could persuade to join them.

Despite pressure from administrations about 25,000 students participated in 1934 and the following year the strike drew about 150,000 students according to Draper (1967, p. 171). Lipset (1971, p. 179) sets the figure at about 185,000.

Taking Draper's figure (the more conservative), 13.2 percent of the college students in 1935 participated in that one event. No single student demonstration of the sixties achieved that level of involvement.

Lipset (1971, p. 179) provides further documentation of the scope of leftist affiliations:

The American Student Union, formed in 1935, as a coalition of Socialists, Communists, and liberals, was to report twenty thousand members out of a student population of over one million, clearly proportionately much more than has ever been claimed by all the radical student groups in the hectic 1960s.

Lipset (1971, p. 185) describes the unpublished detailed report of a survey done by FORTUNE in 1936. Twenty-four percent of the students surveyed picked "socialism" as a term which "suggests ideas toward which you feel sympathetic." The figure for "communism" is 6 percent; "conservatism," 15 percent; and "liberalism," 45 percent.

FORTUNE estimated the politically active and concerned at a maximum of from 5 to 10 percent (that estimates of radicalism usually ran higher FORTUNE attributed to the strong leftist orientation of college newspapers.) Lipset (ibid.) comments on the similarities between the thirties and the sixties which shared a "cycle of concern for political reform . . . [in which] college athletic and fraternity type social events lost appeal in favor of a more positive concern for relevance in courses."

The commonalities between the thirties and the sixties and the contrast they represent to the intervening decades make cyclical theories enticing. David Riesman (1971), noting the decline in activism and radical expression during 1970-71 academic year speculated that we may be entering a new phase in the "recurrent cycles of activism and withdrawal."

The data gathered here do not *generally* suggest the existence of recurrent cyclical patterns in collegiate voluntary associations. Such patterns may exist in *instrumental* associations, especially those which are political, but our data suggest a forty to fifty year decline in interest in expressive fraternal (social and honorary) organizations, rather than a thirty-year cycle.

Conclusions

The principal conclusions which may be drawn from these data are as follows:

1. For expressive collegiate voluntary organizations 1960 is a watershed. Prior to that date, fraternities grew more rapidly than the student body (honorary and professional fraternities) or increased at approximately an equal rate (social fraternities). Now they are growing much more slowly than the college population.
2. Instrumental student voluntary associations and collective protest activity, geared to the relief or dramatization of social problems show a dramatic increase during the sixties. Both off-campus service and off-campus advocacy are included here. Yet these activities do not match the numbers of expressive organizations.
3. Instrumental student voluntary groups and activities with political goals show patterns of growth for the sixties which closely resemble the thirties and contrast sharply with the two intervening decades.

What significance does the apparent shift in relative emphasis from expressive to instrumental voluntary associations among college students have for the future? The findings of this investigation suggest that social issue and social problem concerns of students will increase. These values may well affect increasingly the career choices students make after they have left college.

For example, the National Center for Voluntary Action recently gave 119 awards to groups and individuals who have given outstanding volunteer service. Among those cited was James P. Hertig who, as a student at Case Western Reserve, organized professional assistance to 100 inner-city minority businesses in Cleveland. Mr. Hertig, now an executive for Xerox Corporation, has formed the Xerox Community Activities Program in Cleveland (no author, 1972).

A poll conducted in 1969 revealed that 13 percent of all adults had already contributed to their communities by serving with groups concerned about such community problems as housing, juvenile delinquency, and the shortage of recreational facilities. Sixty percent said they were willing so to serve. Typically respondents were willing to give four hours per week (U.S. News and World Report, 1971, p. 15).

Students of the sixties and seventies, if their collegiate choices anticipate their adult behavior, will greatly enlarge that already vast pool of citizens willing to volunteer their time and talent to the melioration of our social problems through both service and advocacy voluntary associations. Put another way, future decades are likely to see a marked increase in socially concerned voluntary action as the college students of the sixties follow up on their school experiences in the larger societal context.

References

Cook, David T.
1972 "For the Young, a Job Isn't Everything." THE CHRISTIAN SCIENCE MONITOR, July 6.
Draper, Hal
1967 "The Student Movement in the Thirties: A Political History." In AS WE SAW THE THIRTIES edited by Rita J. Simm. Urbana, Ill.: University of Illinois Press.
Gale Research Company
1959, 1962
1964, 1968 ENCYCLOPEDIA OF ASSOCIATIONS. Detroit, Mich.: Gale Re-
1970, 1971, search Co.
1972
Gordon, C. Wayne, and Nicholas Babchuk
1959 "A Typology of Voluntary Associations" AMERICAN SOCIOLOGICAL REVIEW 24, No. 1: 22-29.
Jacoby, Arthur P. and Nicholas Babchuk
1963 "Instrumental and Expressive Voluntary Associations" SOCIOLOGY AND SOCIAL RESEARCH 47: 461-471.
Lipset, S.M.
1971 REBELLION IN THE UNIVERSITY. Boston: Little, Brown.
Lipset, S.M., and Philip G. Altbach
1969 STUDENTS IN REVOLT. Boston: Houghton-Mifflin.
Lozoff, Marjorie M.
1969 "Residential Groups and Individual Development." In NO TIME FOR YOUTH. Edited by Joseph Katz et al. San Francisco: Jossey Bass.
Payne, Raymond, Barbara Pittard Payne, and Richard D. Reddy
1972 "Social Background and Role Determinants of Individual Participation in Organized Voluntary Action." In VOLUNTARY ACTION RESEARCH: 1972. Edited by D.H. Smith et al. Lexington, Mass.: Lexington Books, D.C. Heath and Co.
Peterson, Richard E.
1968 THE SCOPE OF ORGANIZED STUDENT PROTEST IN 1967-68. Princeton, N.J.: Educational Testing Service.

Riesman, David
1971 Commencement Address, Univ. of Pennsylvania, Spring 1971. Cited in Lipset 1971, p. 195.
U.S. Bureau of the Census
1971 DIGEST OF EDUCATIONAL STATISTICS. Washington, D.C.: U.S. Government Printing Office, 1971.
U.S. News and World Report
1971 PEOPLE HELPING PEOPLE. Washington, D.C.: U.S. News and World Report.
Wright, Charles R., and Herbert H. Hyman
1958 "Voluntary Association Memberships of American Adults: Evidence from National Sample Surveys." AMERICAN SOCIOLOGICAL REVIEW 23 (June): 284-94.
No author given
1972 "Top Honors Taken by Brown, Rhode Island and Ohio Universities." NSVP NEWS 1 (April): pp. 2-3.

7

Trends in U.S. Fraternal Associations in the Twentieth Century

Alvin Schmidt and Nicholas Babchuk

A majority of adult Americans are affiliated with voluntary associations.[1] It is becoming apparent, moreover, that the number who affiliate is increasing and probably will continue to increase in the future.

The number of those belonging to fraternal associations is substantial, upward of 20 million. Of these, the groups having the largest memberships include the Benevolent Protective Order of the Elks with 1.5 million members, the Loyal Order of Moose with 1.125 million members, the Independent Order of Odd Fellows with 365 thousand members, and the Fraternal Order of Eagles with about 850 thousand members. But the largest, most conspicuous, and undoubtedly most important fraternal order is the Masons; they claim a membership of approximately 4 million. However, despite their numbers and ubiquity as organizations, fraternal orders appear to be in serious trouble. With one or two exceptions, particularly the Elks and Eagles, such groups are not only finding it difficult to recruit new members but to retain the members they have. The young seem reluctant to affiliate with fraternal orders; for many, such groups appear to be an anachronism. Fraternal groups certainly play a less important role in the community and for their members individually than they did ·in the past.

In the present inquiry, we will historically examine a number of fraternal organizations. Our main interest will center on factors which account for the decreasing importance of fraternal groups (e.g., societal complexity, impersonality, anonymity, etc.) though we will, at the same time, seek to provide insight into why some groups such as the Elks and Eagles are not only holding their own but thriving. Undoubtedly, change from a rural and small-town society to a complex industrial one has had a particularly important impact on fraternal groups. But apart from urbanization and industrialization, the decreased vitality of many fraternal orders is probably due to their present-day intractable orientation toward change.

At an earlier time in their history, groups such as the Masons were quite amenable to modifying their rules and ritual to fit the times. But their recent history shows them to be dogmatic and unchanging about their ritual. They

This chapter was originally published under the title "Formal Voluntary Groups and Change Over Time: A Study of Fraternal Associations," in the JOURNAL OF VOLUNTARY ACTION RESEARCH 1, No. 1 (1972): 46-55.

have, increasingly, subscribed to a principle of goal displacement or a phenomenon whereby instrumental values that once made a group viable become terminal values or values to be cherished for their own sake. When this happens, groups such as the Masons apparently may find it difficult to survive; they have not remained attuned with the times. Conversely, groups such as the Elks which have been growing and becoming more viable have engaged in goal succession, or the process of adjusting the organization to fit more closely with different demands made in a changing society.

The main thesis in this paper will be that voluntary fraternal groups which engage in goal succession are more likely to remain viable, while those which engage in goal displacement tend toward atrophy. This thesis will be explored within a historical context in which fraternal groups have functioned.

The Prevalence of Fraternal Orders

Modern fraternal orders came into being in England in A.D. 1717. Their evolution into orders as we know them today occurred when Freemasonry changed from an "operative" to a "speculative" organization. Operative Freemasons consisted literally of practicing stonemasons dedicated to the welfare of men engaged in building stone-made edifices. When Freemasonry changed from an "operative" order to a "speculative" one, it shifted to incorporating mostly nonstonemasons as members, devoted to building character rather than edifices. Less than two decades (ca. 1730) after the reorganization of Freemasonry in England, Masonry made its appearance in the United States.

Most fraternal and sororal orders were organized in the latter half of the nineteenth and the first quarter of the twentieth century. To illustrate, the Independent Order of Odd Fellows came into existence in 1821; the Order of the Eastern Star was formed in 1857; Knights of Pythias in 1864; the Benevolent and Protective Order of Elks in 1868; the Loyal Order of Moose in 1888; the Fraternal Order of Eagles in 1898; the Fraternal Order of Orioles in 1901; the Order of Owls in 1904; and the Pythian Sisterhood and the Pythian Sisters merged in 1907. Numerous other orders could be included. By 1920, the United States had approximately 800 different secret orders with 30 million members in this country (Merz 1927). "Lodges [in the United States] multiply by thousands, new ones every day. Redmen, Woodmen, Klansmen, Icemen, Elks, Moose, Eagles, Beagles, Bears" (Merz 1920, p. 328). Another observer noted: "We have more secret societies than any other country. . . ." (Gerould 1923, p. 593.) A vast majority of the lodge groups that came into existence in America were not foreign in origin (Merz 1927, p. 330), as was the case with Freemasonry.

But while a majority of fraternal groups were American in origin, most modeled themselves after the Masons and were greatly influenced by Masonic practices.[2] The secret oath(s), initiation rites, hand grips and even the name "lodge" that many orders adopted stem from Freemasonry, originally a British group.

Many of the rites and ceremonies adopted by indigenous American lodges were assumed by nonlodge groups such as college fraternities, scholastic honorary societies and labor unions. For example, the Knights of Labor originally was a secret organization that utilized many features of speculative Freemasonry (Stevens 1907, pp. 389-92) and, with respect to college Greek societies, Stevens notes that "some of the better known college fraternities give unmistakable evidence . . . of having rummaged in the bureau drawers of Free-masonry, Odd Fellowship, Forestry, the Templars, Knights of Malta, and other 'orders' for ritualistic finery" (1907, p. 346). Indeed, Vorhees (1945) shows that Phi Beta Kappa (organized in 1776 at the College of William and Mary) initially employed Masonic ritual to a considerable degree.

Functions of Fraternal Orders

The fact that by the 1920s there were hundreds of different secret lodge groups having millions of members in the United States prompts the question: What factors helped produce the phenomenon that Gist (1940) called "one of the major patterns of American civilization"? Some light can be shed on this question by focusing on several social functions that fraternal orders provided in the past.

Social Integration [3]

The phenomenal growth of fraternal organizations during the latter part of the nineteenth and early part of the twentieth century parallels another unique phenomenon during the same period of American history: the tidal waves of immigration to the United States. The immigrants left behind them, not only their homeland, but also a way of life. Coming to America destroyed many of their "habitual patterns of action and thought" (Handlin 1961, p. 12) and also resulted in the loss of their sense of community.

To be sure, the immigrants could never really reconstruct the community as they had experienced it. They were, however, able to devise some substitutes for the lost sense of community through association in the form of newly-created fraternal, religious, and cultural organizations. These organizations provided many benefits that the community had provided for them in their country of origin (Handlin 1961, p. 15).

In lodges, immigrants were able to meet relatively like-minded people with whom they could feel "at home," at least in spirit. Lodges also aided in integrating the newcomers socially by exposing them to American values such as democracy and separation of church and state (two values highly cherished by American fraternal groups). Moreover, the acceptance of these values (and others) was undoubtedly facilitated by the fact that lodge meetings frequently were conducted in the immigrants' native language. (Even when meetings were conducted in English, members had the opportunity to communicate with others in their native tongue.) For instance, in 1868 the Knights of Pythias (the national organization) had a German ritual committee, and, in Pennsylvania, German was spoken at many meetings of this order. Provision was also made for use of the Bohemian language in Iowa (JOURNAL OF PROCEEDINGS, KNIGHTS OF PYTHIAS, 1868-1878, volumes I and II). The same could be said about the language practices that occurred among the Odd Fellows and Redmen (Handlin 1959, p. 156).

Social Prestige

Simmel (1906) and Wedgewood (1930), respectively, in their articles, "The Sociology of Secrecy and of Secret Societies" and "The Nature and Functions of Secret Societies," maintained that by belonging to secret orders people gained in social prestige simply because it was felt that members knew something that nonmembers did not.

Whether the reasons cited by Simmel and Wedgewood were important, or whether other factors played a more important role in providing American fraternal orders with relatively high social prestige, is open to debate. What is not debatable, however, is that membership in lodges at one time provided high social status. This was not only borne out by large memberships in such groups but by the desire of many to become affiliated with them; this is manifest in remarks made by many astute observers of the American scene.

Max Weber, while visiting the United States in 1904, saw lodges as "typical vehicles of social ascent into the circle of entrepreneurial middle class" (1946, p. 308). Warner, in his community study of Jonesville, also refers to the relatively high social status that lodges once possessed. However, at the time of his study (late 1940s) he noted that lodges were "no longer a means of meeting important men of the community, and membership [was] no longer a mark of esteem" (1949, p. 120).

Apart from the social prestige that fraternal orders provided, they also, at one time, were useful means whereby one could enhance or improve his business or occupational standing. This fact was noted by Weber when speaking about men joining lodges. He remarked: "One could observe that business opportunities were often decisively influenced by such legitimation" (1946, p. 308). More recently, Dalton voiced the same sentiment through a skilled workman in his study of employees in four firms. This workman observed, "Promotion comes by being a Mason. . . . Hell, all bosses are Masons." Similarly, a foreman in one of these firms said: "Nearly all the big boys are in the Yacht Club, and damn near all of 'em are Masons. You can't get a good job without being a Mason. . . ." And another employee remarked: "There's no promotion system whatever. Seniority, knowledge, or ability don't count. . . . I was once asked to join the Masons, and it was hinted that there'd be a good job in it for me" (1959, pp. 152, 154, 155).[4]

Benevolency

Together with providing social integration and social prestige, many lodges also provided a third function; benevolency—either in the form of a mutual aid, charity, or insurance. Harger quotes a widow saying: " 'The members of the lodge came here two at a time and stayed with him [her husband] every night; they brought me and the children things we needed, and they have paid me two thousand dollars, every cent I have in the world, and which will give me a little start to make a home for the children. I am glad he belonged to the lodge' " (1906, p. 490). Harger notes that by 1906 fraternal insurance included about one-third of all insurance policies written in the United States "at a cost not one twentieth of that necessary in the management of old-line companies" (ibid.).

The Benevolent and Protective Order of Elks came into being as a group of fun-loving, beer-drinking actors and to provide welfare for their unfortunate colleagues in the theatrical profession (Fehrenbach 1967). Hence the word "Benevolent" in the organization's name. In 1913 the Loyal Order of Moose established in Mooseheart, Illinois, a home and school for children of deceased Moose members and, in 1922 established "Moosehaven," a home for aged members and their wives in Florida ("History of Mooseheart"; "Information on Moosehaven," mimeographs). According to Whalen (1966, p. 53), Freemasonry operates children and old folks homes in thirty-one states for the immediate kin of Masons in good standing. The Independent Order of Odd Fellows, sometimes known as "poor man's Masonry," also maintains a chain of homes for orphans and the aged.

Although some lodges, like the Masons and the Odd Fellows, never did sell insurance to their members, they all furnished some form of charity or mutual aid. This undoubtedly attracted many people to lodgery, particularly since no federal social security program was in existence during the late 1800s and early 1900s.

Religion

In studying the history of fraternal orders in this country, one notes that for many Americans lodges provide a religious function through rituals, prayers, and moral teachings. Blumenthal, in SMALL TOWN STUFF, suggested that for some Masons "the ritual is virtually a religious practice. . . . Some of the Masons openly state that Masonry is their 'substitute for going to church' " (1932, p. 267). A Masonic writer supports this observation by showing that, for many new settlers, Masonry rather than the church furnished religious solace (Denslow 1925).

That lodgery served a religious function for many (and probably still does for some) becomes especially apparent when one notes that, to this day, nearly all fraternal groups furnish their regular meeting room with an altar, upon which a Bible is usually placed. Moreover, all lodges require a prospective candidate to profess a belief in a deity. For instance, the Elks say: "No person shall be accepted as a member of this Order unless he be . . . a believer in God" (CONSTITUTION AND STATUTES, 1968-1969, p. 70). In addition, well-known lodge authorities often assert that their respective order is religious: "Every Masonic lodge is a temple of religion" (Pike 1881, p. 213). Joseph Fort Newton, a Masonic official, wrote a book, THE RELIGION OF MASONRY (1927). The Eagles maintain that they inculcate "the universal Fatherhood of God" (RITUALS OF THE FRATERNAL ORDER OF EAGLES, 1949, p. 76). And as recent as 1963 the Odd Fellows issued a statement saying: "Free and extensive use of the Holy Scriptures is made in much of the secret work of the Order and in the lectures" (Quoted in Whalen 1966, p. 124).

Fraternal Orders Today

Fraternal organizations of today are distinguished from those in the past in two important respects. First, they are fewer in number. Second, with rare exceptions, they are consistently losing members. Many secret societies that were listed in Stevens' CYCLOPEDIA OF FRATERNITIES (1907) are no longer in existence today. Some went out of existence for economic reasons; on occasion they could not meet the demands of their insured members, who frequently were promised various insurance policies (death, accident, sickness, disability benefits and even free services of a family physician) for an incredibly low fee (Merz 1927). Others became extinct due to irreconcilable schisms within the group produced by accusations levied against members who reportedly violated ancient traditions of a given lodge (ibid.).

The loss in membership, especially in recent years, is occurring on both the national and state level.[5] The Odd Fellows had 559,455 members nationally in 1958, but in 1967 they had 364,483 (a loss of 34.8 percent in one decade). In the state of Nebraska the loss is even more pronounced; in 1958 there were 10,754 Odd Fellows as compared to 5,987 by 1968 (a decline of 44.2 percent). Nationally, the Knights of Pythias sustained a drop in membership from 232,248 in 1957 to 191,017 members by 1966 (a decrease of 17.7 percent). The Pythians in Nebraska had 1,243 knights in 1958, but by 1966 their number had decreased to 970 (a loss of 21.9 percent).

The Masons, who have not only served as a model for many lodge groups, but commanded greater social prestige than most lodges, have also experienced the loss of members. On the national level their roster declined from 4,104,003 in 1960 to 3,862,161 by 1969, (a decrease of 5.8 percent). The Iowa Masons suffered even a greater loss recently. In 1959 they listed 93,594 members, but by 1968 the number was down to 83,728 (a decline of 10.5 percent). Losses similar to these are reported by nearly all fraternal organizations. A conspicuous exception is the Elks, whose membership continues to increase each year. In 1959 the Elks had 1,214,163 members and by 1968 there were 1,452,187 (an increase of 19.6 percent).

It is difficult to determine precisely when the widespread decline in the membership of fraternal orders began. The Lynds (1929), in their study of Muncie, Indiana, noted that a decline in lodge attendance was taking place and that members saw little value in fraternal ritual. Warner, in DEMOCRACY IN JONESVILLE, noted that belonging to the lodge was no longer a mark of esteem (1949, p. 120). Similarly, Hughes (1943, p. 127) wrote that fraternal groups "are becoming *passé* in the United States."

Apparently the lodges are no longer satisfying the need for social prestige, social integration, welfare, and religion that they once did, at least not to the same degree. Let us consider why this may have occurred.

Urbanization

The vitality of fraternal orders in the past not only provided certain payoffs or benefits for members, but furnished the given benefits in ways that were particularly meaningful to individuals in a developing industrial society.[6] The lodge frequently served as "the social focus of many a town" (Harger 1906, p. 488). But in today's urban society "the importance of fraternal organizations appears to be in inverse ratio to the size of the city" (Smith 1946, p. 131). Thus, with increasing urbanism, accompanied by the decline of small towns, the lodges have become less important.

Anonymity

One factor which is linked to the decline in lodgery is urbanism and the anonymity which accompanies it. Traditionally the United States has laid great emphasis on the value of equality, which logically does not support an emphasis on the differences inherent in ritual and ceremony (though pomp and ceremony might have been a drawing card for recruiting members in an earlier period). It was particularly in the small town, where practically no one was a stranger, that lodge ritual and ceremony meant most. Fraternal members could impress fellow townsmen that, by belonging to certain groups, they were different and distinctive. Merz expressed this eloquently:

It is characteristic of secret orders that the names they bear are high-spirited and resounding, on a plain above the routine affairs of daily living. The Shriners are not simply Shriners; they are members of the Ancient Arabic Order of Nobles of the Mystic Shrine. . . . No secretary is a secretary in this world of dreams come true; he is a Thrice Illustrious Scribe. No treasurer; he is an August Keeper of the Strong-Box. . . . Lodge night for the Shriners brings out the fezes. Lodge night for the Odd Fellows, when the Third Encampment meets, brings out the purple gowns, the yellow belts, the miters and the breastplates (1927, pp. 332-33).

The feeling of exclusiveness was further reinforced by the belief that lodge members possessed secrets that the "profane" (nonmembers) were not privileged to know.

Our discussion earlier regarding the relatively high social status lodges once enjoyed is, of course, peculiar to a time when the United States was essentially a small-town society. Today, with increasing anonymity in the urban environment, pomp and ceremony, apparently, have become less meaningful. (After all, what does it mean to impress strangers, if, indeed, one can impress them at all?).

Secularization

Another factor which seems to have affected the vitality of secret societies is secularization. As with anonymity, secularization accompanies urbanism (Cox 1965). Before showing how secularization relates to the decline of most fraternal groups, it might be useful to consider two different treatments of this concept. First, secularization in the light of Yinger's formulation is viewed as a process "in which traditional religious symbols and forms have lost force and appeal" (1957, p. 119). More recently the concept of secularization has been viewed in the sense of "fun" or the "swinging life." This latter view is Klapp's (1969, p. 181-210), who uses the concept in the context of "secular cult." Earlier it was noted that for many persons the lodge with its ritual, prayers, and moral teachings served a religious function. Undoubtedly the lodge still serves this function for some members. But in general, that situation has changed. For example, the ritual (the traditional method whereby religious and moral values are stressed) of fraternal groups not only does not attract new members but fails to impress those who are members.

Some groups (the Masons for instance) have been very reluctant about recognizing problems associated with lodge ritual, but recently the Masons have been conceding that there is "an increasing tendency among some brethren and Lodges to abridge the ceremonies by curtailing and sometimes by omitting parts of our beautiful and impressive ritual" (Doe 1966, p. 493). Perhaps more in tune with the present times, Block notes: "How many of us are coming to know more about 'the bidding of two spades' than we are about the conferring of the Ritual?" (1958, p. 470).

Secularization and the loss of religious meaning relative to lodge ritual is increasingly evident; it is also evident in the current search for meaning in the nonritualistic and the nonsacred areas of life. Klapp expresses this latter position as follows: " 'fun' is becoming a new focal point of mass interest and the playboy has risen as a hero of the ideal of 'living it up,' the 'swinging life.' For more and more people, with puritanism declining, he stands as a model, not of how to *waste* one's life, but of how to live it *more fully*" ([sic] , 1969, p. 183).

Several fraternal groups have read the "signs-of-the times" and have sought to accommodate themselves to present reality. To illustrate, the Elks, who once had secret hand grips, aprons, blindfolds, and passwords (borrowed from Freemasonry), have not only discarded most of their original ritual (Fehrenbach 1967), but are also providing their members with the "fun" and entertainment that Klapp speaks about. Unlike most lodges, the Elks are experiencing consistent membership increases. The Eagles are also changing. They write: "In line with modern needs and up-to-date procedures, the colorful regalia trappings of yesterday are no longer" ([sic] Quoted in Whalen 1966, p. 22). And even more recently, the Knights of Pythias (SUPREME LODGE PROCEEDINGS, 1968) have "softened" their stand regarding ritual with the hope of reviving a decline in membership.

Organizational Change

Our discussion of the history of fraternal orders reveals that they prospered in the past; this was due, in part, to goal succession. To illustrate, the Elks, as noted earlier, changed from an actors' organization to a broader, benevolent orientation; later in its existence it jettisoned most of its religiously oriented ritual to remain in harmony with the times. Presently this organization is largely a club-type group, continues to change, and has proven to be quite successful as an organization.

A parallel can be drawn between the Elks and Freemasons, particularly in the early history of Freemasonry. This latter group changed from an instrumental to an expressive association; it modified its ritual and expanded the base from which it could draw members and shifted its orientation from nominal-Christian to a non-Christian (diestic) group. In the United States, the Freemasons also increased the number of degrees that could be achieved, made the grand lodge a state rather than a national organization, and modified its structure in other ways. The Odd Fellows, the Knights of Pythias, the Pythian Sisters, and other fraternal and sororal groups also introduced changes and expanded their organizational objectives in their early history.

In effect the succession of goals was a beneficial factor in the growth and prosperity of most American fraternal orders. By contrast, virtually no goal succession is apparent for most orders today. In fact, many orders have engaged, instead, in "goal displacement,"[7] or a process whereby "instrumental values which at one time made it possible for the groups to fulfill their objectives become a terminal value" or values in themselves (Merton 1940, p. 563).

Increasingly, many lodges have refused to modify their traditional ritualistic practices. Unlike the Elks and Eagles, they are unwilling to change their secret oath(s), ritual, and other outmoded customs. Indeed the Masons, are even unwilling to hear any discussion relative to the ritual because for them the ritual has become an "ancient landmark"—a rule for behavior that can never be changed (Mackey 1967, p. 19; Robbins 1966, p. 609). The Masons even refuse to go, part way, in the direction of becoming more of a social club or "fun" oriented group, even at the cost of losing many members.

The literature on nonfraternal groups suggests that an important factor for organizational viability and well-being, whether instrumental or expressive, is the process of "goal succession." To illustrate, the National Foundation for Infantile Paralysis (March of Dimes) effectively transformed itself from a single to a multipurpose organization and has prospered. Or to take another case, the Patrons of Husbandry (the Grange) initially was a social and fraternal group. Some time after its formation it became involved in operating cooperative stores, manufacturing, and even in banking and insurance (Buck 1913). Taking on new objectives apparently revived the Grange from an early disappointing start (Taylor 1953, pp. 124-27) into a successful organization. Today, the Grange continues to change by placing a strong emphasis on education. Zakuta (1964) shows that the Cooperative Commonwealth Federation (a political party) gained members and general overall strength after engaging in goal succession.

Summary and Conclusion

Fraternal societies are no longer the vehicles of social integration they once were. The values of social prestige that lodges once possessed in a predominantly rural society have become less significant and many of the benevolent functions that these organizations once provided have been preempted by governmental programs. Furthermore they have lost their religious aura.

Given this situation, fraternal lodges are faced with one of two alternatives, namely, to engage in organizational change, or to resist change at the cost of losing members. One or two orders have opted for the former choice with apparent success; most groups, however, have not.

The future of fraternal organizations, we believe, will largely depend on whether they are willing to change. If they do, they might be able to reestablish the viability they once possessed.

Notes

1. This statement is supported by data in practically every study utilizing a probability design directly concerned with voluntary-group membership. See, for example: Axelrod 1956; Babchuk and Booth 1969; Scott 1957. An exception is a study by Wright and Hyman 1958: Their figures, however, are questionable as discussed by Rose 1965, pp. 395-98.

2. The fact that Freemasonry served as a model for numerous other American lodge groups is evident not only from reading respective rituals, but also supported by authorities. For instance, Acker refers to Masonry as "the mother of lodges" (1959, p. 14); Hannah calls organizations patterned after Freemasonry as "quasi-Masonic" (1955, p. 214).

3. Babchuk and Edwards (1965, p. 149) note: "The concept of social integration is extremely complex. With respect to voluntary associations an implicit definition considers the amount and quality of personal ties between members in relation to the objectives of the groups. . . . On the other hand, voluntary associations may be integrative with regard to cultural standards or with regard to norms, the exchange of meanings, or services essential to the well being and survival of the society." They have reference to Landecker's (1951) four types of integration.

4. Lodges, especially Freemasonry, have not formally sanctioned joining their fellowship for personal gain. Mackey, a renowned Masonic authority says an applicant desiring to become a Mason (1967, p. 52) "must be uninfluenced by mercenary motives [sic]."

5. Membership statistics are cited from either annual proceedings or periodical publications of the respective fraternal groups.

6. Our reference to urbanization does not intend to imply that this process refers only to the city. It obviously also has affected small towns and rural areas, as Vidich and Bensman (1958) have shown.

7. Blau (1955) sees the displacement of goals as the reverse of goal succession.

References

Acker, Julius W.
1959 STRANGE ALTARS. St. Louis: Concordia Publishing House.
Axelrod, Morris
1956 "Urban structures and social participation." AMERICAN SOCIOLOGICAL REVIEW 21 (February): 13-18.
Babchuk, Nicholas and Alan Booth
1969 "Voluntary association membership: A longitudinal analysis." AMERICAN SOCIOLOGICAL REVIEW 34 (February): 31-45.

Babchuk, Nicholas and John N. Edwards
1965 "Voluntary associations and the integration hypothesis." SOCIOLOGI-
CAL INQUIRY 35 (Spring): 149-62.

Blau, Peter M.
1955 THE DYNAMICS OF BUREAUCRACY. Chicago: The University of
Chicago Press.

Blau, Peter M. and Richard W. Scott
1962 FORMAL ORGANIZATION: A COMPARATIVE APPROACH. San Francisco: Chandler Publishing Co.

Block, Louis
1958 "Whither Masonry?" GRAND LODGE BULLETIN. Iowa. 59 (May):
469-70.

Blumenthal, Albert
1932 SMALL TOWN STUFF. Chicago: University of Chicago Press.

Buck, Solon Justus
1913 THE GRANGER MOVEMENT. Lincoln: University of Nebraska Press.

Cox, Harvey
1965 THE SECULAR CITY. New York: The Macmillan Company.

Dalton, Melville
1959 MEN WHO MANAGE. New York: John Wiley and Sons.

Darrah, Delmar Duane
1967 HISTORY AND EVOLUTION OF FREEMASONRY. Chicago: The
Charles T. Powner Company.

Denslow, Ray Vaughn
1925 TERRITORIAL MASONRY. Kingsport, Tennessee: Southern Publishers,
Inc.

Doe, Thomas Edward
1966 "Masonry Adequate to the New Age." GRAND LODGE BULLETIN.
Iowa. 67 (September): 492-93.

Fehrenbach, T.R.
1967 ELKDOM U.S.A. Published by the Benevolent and Protective Order of
Elks.

Gerould, Katharine Fullerton
1923 "Ritual and Regalia." ATLANTIC MONTHLY 132: 592-97.

Gist, Noel
1940 "Secret Societies: A Cultural Study of Fraternalism in the United States."
UNIVERSITY OF MISSOURI STUDIES 15: 9-176.

Handlin, Oscar
1959 BOSTON'S IMMIGRANTS. Cambridge: Harvard University Press.
1961 "Immigration in American Life: A Reappraisal." In IMMIGRATION AND
AMERICAN HISTORY. Edited by Henry Steele Commager. Minneapolis:
University of Minnesota Press.

Hannah, Walton
1955 DARKNESS VISIBLE. London: Augustine Press.

Harger, Charles Moreau
1906 "The Lodge." ATLANTIC MONTHLY 97: 488-94.

Hughes, Everett C.
1943 FRENCH CANADA IN TRANSITION. Chicago: University of Chicago Press.

Klapp, Orrin E.
1969 COLLECTIVE SEARCH FOR IDENTITY. New York: Holt, Rinehart and Winston.

Landecker, Warner S.
1951 "Types of integration and their measurement." AMERICAN JOURNAL OF SOCIOLOGY 56 (January): 332-40.

Lynd, Robert S. and Helen Merrell Lynd
1929 MIDDLETOWN. New York: Harcourt, Brace and Company.

Mackey, Albert G.
1967 JURISPRUDENCE OF FREEMASONRY. Chicago: The Charles T. Powner Company.

Merton, Robert
1940 "Bureaucratic Structure and Personality." SOCIAL FORCES 18 (May): 560-68.

Merz, Charles
1920 "Halt! Who Comes There?" THE NEW REPUBLIC 35 (August 15): 327-28.
1927 "Sweet Land of Secrecy." HARPER'S MONTHLY MAGAZINE 154: 329-34.

Newton, Joseph Fort
1927 THE RELIGION OF MASONRY. Richmond, Virginia: Macoy Publishing and Masonic Supply Company.

Pike, Albert
1881 MORALS AND DOGMA OF THE ANCIENT AND ACCEPTED SCOTTISH RITE OF FREEMASONRY. Charleston, South Carolina: Supreme Council, Southern Jurisdiction of the United States.

Robbins, Joseph
1966 "Annual Oration (1869)." GRAND LODGE BULLETIN. Iowa. 67: 603-610.

Rose, Arnold M.
1965 SOCIOLOGY. 2nd. Ed., rev. New York: Knopf, 395-98.

Scott, John C.
1957 "Membership and Participation in Voluntary Associations." AMERICAN SOCIOLOGICAL REVIEW 20 (June): 315-26.

Simmel, Georg
1906 "The Sociology of Secrecy and of Secret Societies." AMERICAN JOURNAL OF SOCIOLOGY 11 (January): 441-98.

Smith, Dwight C.

1946 "The Church and Organized Fraternalism." In THE CHURCH AND ORGANIZED MOVEMENTS, II. Edited by Randolphs, Crump, and Miler. New York: Harper and Brothers.

Stevens, Albert C.

1907 THE CYCLOPAEDIA OF FRATERNITIES. New York: E.B. Treat & Co.

Taylor, Carl C.

1953 THE FARMERS' MOVEMENTS, 1620-1920. NEW YORK: AMERICAN BOOKS.

Vidich, Arthur J. and Joseph Bensman

1960 SMALL TOWN IN MASS SOCIETY. Garden City, New York: Anchor Books.

Vorhees, Oscar M.

1945 THE HISTORY OF PHI BETA KAPPA. New York: Crown Publishers.

Warner, W. Lloyd

1949 DEMOCRACY IN JONESVILLE. New York: Harper and Row, Publishers.

Weber, Max

1946 "The Protestant Sects and the Spirit of Capitalism." In FROM MAX WEBER. Edited by H.H. Gerth and C. Wright Mills. New York: Oxford University Press.

Wedgewood, Camilla H.

1930 "The Nature and Functions of Secret Societies." OCEANIA. 1 (July): 129-45.

Whalen, William J.

1966 HANDBOOK OF SECRET ORGANIZATIONS. Milwaukee: The Bruce Publishing Company.

Wright, Charles R. and Herbert H. Hyman

1958 "Voluntary Association Memberships of American Adults: Evidence from National Surveys." AMERICAN SOCIOLOGICAL REVIEW 23 (June): 315-26.

Yinger, Milton J.

1957 RELIGION, SOCIETY AND THE INDIVIDUAL. New York: The Macmillan Company.

Zakuta, Leo

1964 A PROTEST MOVEMENT BECALMED: A STUDY OF CHANGE IN THE CCF. Toronto: University of Toronto Press.

Special Publications

1968-69 The Benevolent and Protective Order of Elks. CONSTITUTION AND STATUTES.

1968   SUPREME LODGE PROCEEDINGS.

n.d.   HISTORY OF MOOSEHEART, mimeographed by the Loyal Order of Moose.

n.d.   INFORMATION ON MOOSEHAVEN, mimeographed by the Loyal Order of Moose.

1868-78 Knights of Pythias. JOURNAL OF PROCEEDINGS, I and II.

1949   RITUALS OF THE FRATERNAL ORDER OF EAGLES.

Part Two
The Impact of Voluntary Action

Introduction to Part Two

David Horton Smith

The theme of Part Two of this volume is the impact and effectiveness of voluntary action, especially collective or organized voluntary action. As with Part One, we make no claims of covering the topic comprehensively here. Our aim is again to introduce the reader to the problem of impact/effectiveness at a number of different system levels and from a number of different perspectives. Like the basic theme of Part One, the present theme is also both extremely basic to voluntary action research and at the same time relatively little understood. The literature directly concerned with the impact of voluntary action is very sparse, except in a few specialized areas. Comprehensive, systematic, comparative empirical studies are very rare. Case studies, often of a retrospective rather than a longitudinal sort, are the rule. And the majority of attention has been focused at the level of impact of particular voluntary organizations, with little attention to the many other levels at which impact can be evaluated.

As a result, we are more interested here in helping to expand the future study of voluntary action impacts than we are hopeful of reaching very many broadly valid conclusions from masses of relevant research. Nevertheless, we are convinced that the present kind of endeavor is crucial to the progress of voluntary action research as a field of scholarly inquiry. The present series of volumes (VOLUNTARY ACTION RESEARCH: 1972, 1973, etc.) can do as much to stimulate research by pointing out the gaps in prior research as it can in attempting to review, summarize, and synthesize that research.

To accomplish such an end, however, it is necessary to find or create some sort of theoretical model, schema, or perspective that permits linking otherwise disparate pieces of research and even reviews of research areas into some kind of larger whole. In requesting chapters to be written for Part Two, we had a rough kind of theoretical schema in mind. We were interested in having reviews of research and thinking regarding the impact of voluntary action that touched on several different system levels where voluntary action can take place. By *system level* we mean the level of individual or social system aggregation on which interest is focused for analytical purposes.

In Part Two, we have included chapters reviewing aspects of the impact of voluntary action at the following system levels: the impact on the individual, the impact for the individual on higher social system levels, the impact of specific kinds of voluntary organizations or groups, the impact of coalitions among voluntary groups and other forms of interorganizational relationships, the impact of social movements (as ideologically related clusters of voluntary groups and institutions), and the impact of the voluntary sector as a whole on society.

In Chapter 8, Smith and Reddy look at the impact of voluntary organization participation upon the volunteer. Since the individual volunteer is at the root of voluntary action, it seems to make sense to begin Part Two with a consideration of what we know about how voluntary action affects the volunteer. Not surprisingly, to anyone who is familiar with the general dearth of social science knowledge about the effects of various kinds of experiences on people over time (i.e., with actual longitudinal data rather than simply inferences from cross-sectional data), there is not a great deal of directly relevant research on how voluntary action participation affects the volunteer. Evidence from related research areas (e.g., adult socialization research, learning research in general) together with the relatively small amount of voluntary action research directly relevant indicate that, by and large, individual volunteer participation *can* have a significant impact, although in many cases it probably does not—owing to weak involvement, short terms of exposure, and voluntary organizations that are often not particularly distinctive social environments. Nevertheless, the potential is there, and in some organizations the impact on the volunteer can be tremendous—"life-changing." There is food for thought here for those voluntary organizations that would like to have more impact on their members, since the characteristics of some voluntary groups that do have a powerful impact are fairly well delineated.

In Chapter 9, Warner turns the perspective around from Chapter 8. Instead of asking what the voluntary organization does to the individual, he asks what the organization does for the individual. Specifically, he attempts to help us understand better how and to what extent voluntary associations can effectively permit individuals to become involved in policy-making and administration. This is a crucial question for democracy in any society. If voluntary associations only permit individuals to become involved in service roles, but never policy roles in society, then voluntarism becomes an instrument of political suppression and tyranny, by defusing or diverting popular criticism and dissent. Participatory democracy is a mockery if it means no more than voting for leaders every few years. Voting like this takes place in most effective dictatorships—as "window dressing" and as a gesture. But real participatory democracy, whatever the nature of general political processes and ideologies in a society, must involve a pluralism of voluntary associations that are able to represent effectively a variety of individual interests.

Taking the case of contemporary America and utilizing natural resource voluntary organizations as an example (though he might as well have chosen any other subarea of voluntarism, or all of voluntarism), Warner discusses the various ways in which voluntary associations inadequately represent individual interests and why this is the case. Insofar as this is true in an advanced and modern industrial nation like the United States, where voluntary action is very prevalent (see Chapters 3 and 4 of this volume), voluntary associations are likely to represent individual interests even less adequately in developing or lesser developed countries where the sheer amount and variety of voluntary action is less. This does not mean that voluntary associations cannot effectively represent individual interests in policy-making and administration. Rather, it suggests that we have a long way to go before reaching an optimal level of participatory democracy and individual interest representation, even where voluntary action is presently flourishing as in the case of natural resource organizations.

From a consideration of how voluntary associations mediate individual participation in policy-making, we might have turned to a similar consideration of how they mediate individual participation in service, recreation, worship, protest, economics, etc. Being limited in space here, however, we must turn instead to another level of the impact of voluntary associations and voluntary action—the impact of specific kinds of voluntary groups upon their surrounding physical and social environment, community, and society. This is, of course, the kind of "impact" of voluntary action that most people think of when the impact/effectiveness question is raised.

The question here is basically a simple one: What impact do environmental voluntary associations, for instance, have on the quality of the biophysical environment and on the attitudes, beliefs, and actions of people at large that are relevant to the quality of that environment? This same kind of organizational impact question can be asked for any subarea of voluntarism. In the available space for Part Two we could only represent two important kinds of voluntary groups/voluntary action at this system level of impact. Rather than focusing on some fairly traditional areas of voluntarism, we chose instead to examine the activities and impact of two kinds of instrumental voluntary activity that have been of increasing importance in the past decade or so in the United States—student activism and citizen participation in federal programs.

In Chapter 10, Spiegel makes a careful and extensive review of what is known about citizen participation in federal programs in the United States. Naturally, this review must be in some ways "out-of-date" the minute it is written, let alone after spending a year or more in the editorial and publication process. These kinds of citizen involvement in the policy-making, administration, and implementation of federal programs are always in flux, as well as being highly variable across types of programs and areas of the country. Only a continual or periodic monitoring of voluntary action in society as a whole can begin to do justice to the complexity here (see Smith 1972).

Yet the conclusions of Spiegel's review, in the main, are likely to stand unchanged for several years to come, perhaps longer, unless some of the basic political dilemmas and issues he raises are faced squarely and dealt with. Federal administrators have a powerful vested interest in working out all manner of evasions of the letter and spirit of congressional "citizen participation" legislation. Similarly, most officials at state, county, and city government levels have little desire to share their power with organized citizen groups in implementing federal programs, whether they be matters of new roads, urban redevelopment, or health care systems. In view of these facts of political life in contemporary

America, effective citizen participation in federal programs in the United States is generally likely to remain more of a pious hope (or cynical game) than a reality aimed at articulating citizen needs and interests with those programs.

Spiegel concludes, roughly speaking, that there is a great deal more rhetoric and administrative regulations regarding citizen participation now than there was in past decades. But at the highest policy levels, citizen participation is viewed primarily as a gesture to be kept under control, so as not to disrupt (or markedly change) current municipal and federal program management. As a result, there is great variation from federal program to program and from one specific locality to another in how effective and meaningful citizen participation is. His review of the literature permits Spiegel to go on to specify some of the conditions of effective citizen participation. But in the end he leaves us with a warning regarding the possibility that citizen participation in federal programs may become (or may already have become in certain areas) a kind of "friendly fascism." Insofar as this occurs, the impact of such citizen participation will be to hinder rather than to promote adequate social change to meet the needs of all the people.

In the next chapter, 11, Theodore examines the role of college student voluntary participation as a catalyst for change. She takes as her major foci of interest the voluntary action of college students in two main settings—campus political activism and volunteer mental health service roles. Her review of the literature makes it clear that the primary scholarly attention given to such voluntary activities has been focused on the nature of the voluntary action and its impact on the individual participant. Although there have been numerous public statements and a Presidential Commission recognizing the importance of student voluntary action, adequate empirical data on the impact of this kind of voluntary action on the larger community and society are lacking. Nevertheless, anecdotal and fragmentary evidence suggest that, indeed, college student voluntary action can be a catalyst for social as well as personal change.

Having given some attention to the impact of certain kinds of voluntary groups as groups, we turn next to the level of interorganizational relationships. In Chapter 12, Klonglan, Yep, Mulford, and Dillman present a very general review of the literature on the nature and impact of interorganizational relations. Since this area of research is a very new one in the social sciences and even in the subfield of organizational research, it is not surprising that there is next to nothing that deals specifically with voluntary organizations per se. Yet voluntary organizations are often part of a larger network of social service agencies, public and private, that are involved in some kind of cooperative activities aimed at common goals. Therefore, nearly all of what the authors of Chapter 12 have to say has relevance to cooperative relations among voluntary organizations.

There is explicit consideration of what research has shown to be the impact of interorganizational relations, in spite of the fact that most research on the topic has viewed these relationships as an outcome rather than as a determinant.

What research there is suggests both internal effects of interorganizational relationships upon the cooperating organizations themselves, as well as a heightened potentiality for mobilizing community resources to meet common goals. Then a large portion of the chapter is devoted to presenting a model for describing interorganizational relations and a series of planning stages that are important to the formation of such cooperative relationships and coalitions. More than most other chapters in this volume, Chapter 12 presents something of a "how-to-do-it" manual, based on an extensive review of the literature and careful theoretical synthesis. The reader who is otherwise likely to be bothered by the lack of emphasis on voluntary associations per se in this chapter is urged to suspend judgment on its relevance to voluntary action until he/she has read it. The implications of this chapter are especially important given the relative lack of cooperation toward common goals among voluntary associations in American society (see Smith and Dixon 1973).

From the level of explicit coalitions and other cooperative relationships among specific voluntary groups, we move next to the level of social movements. At this higher social system level, we become concerned with the impact of whole sets of voluntary groups, organizations, institutions, and related collective behavior that are bound together by some overarching value premise and ideology. We are no longer talking about a strictly defined formal coalition here but instead refer to a very loose "tide" of voluntary organizations and groups all flowing more or less in the same direction. The great political and religious movements of history are the best examples here—Buddhism, Islam, Christianity, democracy, communism, etc.

A thorough review of the impact of all the major social movements in history, even in American history, is far beyond the scope of Part Two of this volume. Therefore, we have tried simply to include a single example of the impact of a social movement on the larger society. In Chapter 13, Landsberger discusses labor and peasant movements as sources of voluntary organizations and instruments of class mobility. His careful analysis views both peasant and labor movements as part of the larger analytical category of low status movements.

Landsberger sees such low status movements as growing out of an increasing "gap" between aspirations and reality, brought on by various possible factors. The degree of ideological egalitarianism present in a society and the attention of rising middle-class people and intellectuals to low status people are particularly important. Yet the success or impact of low status movements seems to be primarily dependent upon the strength of the resistance to such movements, rather than on the strength of the organizations formed to foster them.

These movements can be most effective where factory owners, landowners, middle classes, and especially the national government are willing to support the right of low status people to organize effectively to further their own interests in a society where most of the chances are stacked against them. In the most extreme cases, low status movements are able to topple a government or whole political system and/or to bring about a major redistribution of wealth in society. The result is a kind of total class mobility on an absolute scale. Peasants and workers may still be lowest on the prestige hierarchy in relative terms, but their net real wealth and income on an absolute scale are much increased. However, Landsberger is not very optimistic about the future of low status movements in the world today, for reasons he explains at length.

In Chapter 14, Smith discusses the impact of voluntary action from the perspective of a still higher social system level—the impact of the voluntary sector as a whole on society. When we get to this level of abstraction and aggregation, national boundaries and distinctions become increasingly hard to maintain analytically. To discuss the impact of the voluntary sector on American society, for instance, inevitably leads to a discussion of the impact of the voluntary sector transnationally on total human society—in the past, present, and future. Because there has been practically no research on this level of impact of voluntarism, the discussion must be largely theoretical and speculative. A major aim of this chapter is to interest other scholars in working on empirical research to test the hypotheses suggested.

The kinds of social system and individual system impacts that voluntary action can have are by no means exhausted by the range of impacts that we have been able to treat in Part Two of this volume. Yet, as with Part One, we have tried very hard at least to sketch out some of the broad outlines of this field of voluntary action research, and to provide examples of what might be done more extensively in the future by others. We will have succeeded in our endeavor if we have stimulated the reader to consider a wider range of possible impacts of voluntarism than he/she might otherwise have been inclined to contemplate.

References

Smith, David Horton
1972 "Future Trends in Research on Voluntary Action," INTERNATIONAL ASSOCIATIONS 24: 397-400.
Smith, David Horton, and John Dixon
1973 "Management, Governance and Voluntary Groups." In CHALLENGE TO LEADERSHIP: MANAGEMENT IN A CHANGING WORLD. Edited by Charles Darling and Theodore Smith, New York: Macmillan.

8

The Impact of Voluntary Action Upon the Volunteer/Participant

David Horton Smith and Richard D. Reddy

In the previous annual volume of this series (VOLUNTARY ACTION RE-SEARCH: 1972), the several chapters of Part Two gave systematic attention to the determinants of individual participation in organized voluntary action. Those reviews of the literature told us what prior research had to say about how people got into voluntary groups in the first place. The present chapter, by contrast, attempts to review what is known about how voluntary groups affect an individual once he or she joins and begins to participate in the group. We are thus concerned with the effects, influences, or impacts that membership and participation have—how these group-related experiences change a person from what he was prior to entry into the group.

What constitutes an impact? Impacts by definition are effects not causes. While the reasons (or causes) for the effect may be multiple, the impact is the presumed result of these impinging influences. We ordinarily equate impacts on the individual with changes—in actions, attitudes, personality traits, beliefs, skills, perspectives, and so forth. Nevertheless, taking a dynamic and interactive perspective, where a number of conflicting forces may be operating, the maintenance of an attitude, trait, skill, belief, or perspective can also be seen as the result, effect, or impact of those forces.

It is important to note that voluntary associations or programs normally have impacts beyond their influence on their current members. Their activities and perspectives may influence former members, eligible nonmembers, the community as a whole, or even wider realms. While the full scope of potential impacts deserves careful attention and study (see subsequent chapters), we are focusing here on the impact of associations and programs on their members.

To be interested in a voluntary organization's impact on its participants is not the same as having an interest in the organization's effectiveness. An organization's effectiveness is usually measured in terms of its ability to achieve its major goals. The focus of these goals is often external to the organization, rather than internal or on its own members. Most commonly we expect voluntary organizations either to serve the public directly or serve those elements of the public at large which need or can use the services and/or products they offer. The organization's ability to "deliver" or produce for those who are not the primary participants, for those who are not members, is likely to be the central evaluative criterion of performance and effectiveness.

On the other hand, the primary focus of activity for some voluntary associations may be on the members of the association itself. For these associations, the effect that the association has on its members may be its major goal and hence the major criterion of the organization's effectiveness. If an organization aims primarily at influencing its own members and if its members seek especially to be influenced or changed in and through the organization, the best measure of its overall effectiveness will be the extent to which the organization is able to achieve those internal aims.

Thus, Common Cause, a citizen lobbying group, would be judged effective as an organization if the bills it supports (or at least some of those bills) become law. This success might well please Common Cause's members, but it need not necessarily change them or have another sort of major impact on them as persons. On the other hand, a Weight Watchers club is effective to the degree that its own members are able to change themselves (i.e., weigh less) and to maintain that changed state.

Methodologically, impact studies present major problems in design, control, and analysis. In order to adequately assess the impact of an experience or series of experiences, especially when these experiences are multifaceted, longitudinal studies that include a substantial number of relevant variables are necessary. To date these studies have been generally lacking in social science, particularly with real (i.e., nonexperimental) groups. While these studies would be complex, the questions surrounding the assessment of impact are themselves difficult and complex.

A number of problems arise in the assessment of impacts. Four problems are especially worthy of note here. First, the person in everyday life experiences a welter of influences, some that serve to change him or aspects of his life, some that serve to maintain characteristics or tendencies or processes that already exist. At any given conscious moment an individual lives in a complex present, structuring, interpreting, and evaluating consciously, subconsciously, and unconsciously that present in terms of a multifaceted and multidimensional past and a variety of possible futures.

Even the newborn child is not a *tabula rasa*, having experienced and been increasingly influenced by aspects of his environment since the first stirrings of life. Each of these experiences is a part of the individual's "total life experience" during that time period. Each experience is only partially independent of many of the others, and many experiences are highly related and interactive. It is often quite difficult to separate out the impact of a given experience from the impacts of other life experiences.

Second, when our focus turns toward a given voluntary association or program and its members, we find that experiential inputs are rarely homogeneous or monolithic in their effects. Most commonly we find a heterogeneity of experience within a given context or organization setting, some persons being affected in one way, some affected in another, some in yet another, and so forth.

Third, virtually all studies of impact on individuals are analyzed and reported in terms of the average tendency within a group—showing the overall amount and direction of change for the group as a whole. While this summarizing approach is valuable in showing group trends, this group level of analysis may obscure the actual impacts on given individuals. Summarizing on the group level usually leaves us without knowledge of how many persons in the group actually experienced an impact, how many persons changed, and how much they changed in one direction or the other.

Fourth, we generally lack measures possessing high levels of reliability and validity for longitudinal measurement. We are generally unaware of what aspects of our indicators and scales are most subject to change or variation over short and longer periods of time and those that are not.

Impacts in General

Before turning to impacts in voluntary action settings, let us first explore the question, "What are the major sources of and settings for impacts on individuals as discussed in the literature of social science?"

Extreme Environments and Total Institutions

Darley (1938) postulated an expected continuum of stability (or imperviousness to change) for attitudes. Those attitudes recently arrived at in regard to objects of remote connection to oneself tend to be least stable, and those traits and characteristics which involve intimate self-evaluations are most stable and most difficult to modify.

Kelly (1955) estimated the long-range consistency of five domains of variables, measuring 38 variables for 116 spouses on two occasions twenty years apart. Highest consistency rates were found for values (48 percent) and for vocational interests (45 percent), both of which presumably were relatively well formed and thus less subject to change. Various self-ratings (31 percent) and characteristics such as self-confidence, sociability and others (30 percent) were found subject to more change. Attitudes (8 percent) showed least stability over the twenty years.

However, as Bloom (1964) indicates in his classic work, STABILITY AND CHANGE IN HUMAN CHARACTERISTICS, it is difficult to measure adequately stability and change over time. There are numerous methodological problems, such as overcoming unevenness of scales, providing more room for change at all points on a scale, creating more nearly equal intervals, etc. Also, over time, the meaning and rates of change of items may differ. Further, self-reported personality measures may be susceptible to conscious and unconscious distortion. Thus caution is necessary in evaluating Kelly's data, or that of any other long-term study of personal change.

According to Bloom, only some human characteristics are rather stable, while others change very rapidly over time. Stable characteristics are either nonreversible or only partially reversible. They either have an underlying structure of their own or are based on underlying patterns of personality, habits, and motivation. Although a stable characteristic will not itself change, the modes of expression of such a characteristic may constantly change. Also, Bloom sees stable characteristics as being supported by relatively constant cultural norms and values. He finds that personal growth and development are not in equal units per unit of time. That is, personal growth, development, and change may be slow at some periods of one's life and very rapid in others. Ordinarily, periods of rapid change take place early in the life cycle.

However, normally stable characteristics may be subject to change in "extreme environments," such as in concentration camps, prisons, brainwashing, and so forth. Other situations such as psychotherapy and exposure to other very powerful environments may also produce significant personal change. Nevertheless, in no case studied or reviewed by Bloom did such powerful environments affect all individuals in it identically, though in some instances percentages ranged to 90 and 95 percent.

Bloom also notes (1964, p. 196) that "as individuals leave one environment and enter another, they seem to be especially susceptible to the effects of the new environment." Greater and more rapid changes tend to occur in initial exposure than in later and continued contact with the environment or setting. Bloom hypothesizes that this may be the result of a fuller acceptance of and openness to the environment and its demands while one is new to it. In addition, it is possible that during the initial period the individual is unable to locate more protective subenvironments or is as yet unable to develop and utilize an adequate set of defenses in and for it.

Less extreme and less powerful environments provide the individual with greater possibilities of resisting their effects, of interacting with them and modifying their effects, rather than being unilaterally molded and formed by them. These environments are less demanding and involve less social pressure. They may be less constant, less time-consuming, and less consistent. Or they may be more complex and differentiated, affording the individual greater opportunities to find agreeable and reasonably harmonious subenvironments from among the variety offered.

When differences among individuals or groups are observed, they may result either from *socialization* processes (the changing of personal traits, attitudes and other characteristics) or from *selection* processes (differential selection or concentration of certain kinds of people in a given setting or roles, without their actually undergoing personal change). In this chapter we are basically interested in socialization effects on participants in voluntary organizations or programs, *not* in selection effects.

Infancy is the only universal "total" experience and very likely the most "total" experience (due to lack of previous potentially modifying influences and lack of other reference standards to help interpret experiences). Here "socialization" influences are clearest, with few if any "selection" possibilities really available (i.e., children cannot pick and choose their preferred experience settings to any significant degree). Over time, the child clearly does have the potential to develop his own unique preferences for experience, as well as the opportunity to choose his peers to some extent. However, the general importance and impact of infancy and childhood experiences on the person and his future actions, reactions, growth, and development hold perhaps the firmest place of all social scientific findings and theories.

After the experience of infancy and childhood, the most total and encompassing experiences are probably those in political prisons and concentration camps, especially those involving brainwashing. These environments typically involve and/or seek fundamental and rapid breaks with the person's past and a concerted attempt to "resocialize" the person. Once more, a fairly clear socialization dimension is apparent, with relatively few individuals deliberately choosing this sort of experience with complete freedom. The adult individual is exposed in such settings to "infantilizing" experiences—totally dependent on others for all needs, permitted only the present status and denied all former ones, convicted of a faulty, deficient, and blameworthy self, threatened by and exposed to extreme sanctions and deprivations, and isolated from all countervailing influences of potentially competing groups, organizations, or institutions.

In "brainwashing" situations, where reform is sought in addition to punishment, various devices for isolating the individual are typically used. The props for "group feeling," group identity, and social support are systematically undermined by destruction of both formal and informal group structures among prisoners. Meanwhile, the individual is commonly urged to "change," to "confess," to "reform," and to become acceptable to "approved groups and their ideas," while nevertheless fully deserving humiliating and degrading treatment. The individual is encouraged to play an active role in his "redemption" through self-criticism and by confession of his past and present failings.

Although these settings generally succeed in inducing behavioral conformity and do have both short- and long-term impacts, there is some evidence that their long-term (postincarceration) impact tends to be smaller than might be expected. For example, brainwashing "successes" among American POWs in the Korean conflict were relatively few (and some of these nonenduring) in view of the total number exposed to brainwashing. In some measure this general lack of success may be attributable to program deficiencies such as lack of sufficient trained personnel capable of speaking English, a wide sociocultural gap which hindered the effective development and implementation of the program, the large numbers of individuals who were undergoing "treatment" at the same time, and so forth. Yet brainwashing often didn't also work because the experience could be successfully resisted in many ways. Prisoners were exposed to brainwashing techniques unwillingly and under severe sanctions. They were so radically unprepared for the experience that it could not readily be comprehended and accepted (brainwashing was not ordinarily perceived as legitimate by prisoners). Despite attempts to undermine formal and informal group support, subtle and covert resistance was not uncommon. In sum, these programs tended to be more successful in exploiting weaknesses, failings, and inconsistencies than in overcoming or rechanneling personal strengths (cf. Schein, 1957).

Other "total" but usually far more benevolent settings would also seem to have the best prospects of significant impacts on individuals. Goffman notes (1961, p. 6), "the central feature of total institutions can be described as a breakdown of the barriers ordinarily separating the spheres of life. Sequenced, coordinated, and regimented group activities largely isolated from involvement with noninstitutional personnel are typical. In addition to POW camps, Goffman includes in his listing of total institutions homes for the blind, aged, and orphaned, TB sanitaria, mental hospitals, jails, military boarding schools, ships, monasteries, and convents. However, other relatively "closed" communities might also be included such as small "voluntary communities" established by fundamentalist religious sects, communes, and *kibbutzim* (see Zablocki 1971).

It is clear that "total institution" as a concept covers a broad range of possible settings. For some, an impact by means of socialization would seem to be the likely emphasis, while for others, processes of *self-selection* would limit the extent of direct socialization impacts possible. Also, where lower-level participants see themselves as discriminated against or overly constrained in the activity and where they are less self-selected, subcultures and an "underlife" are likely to form in opposition to and mitigating the influence of the dominant participants of an organization (and their intended socializing efforts). Where participants are in some measure self-selected and are also selected (more or less exclusively) by the organization, cooperation and "intended" effects seem to be far more likely. These latter kinds of organizations are likely to have both high admission criteria and extensive socialization programs.

While much theory suggests that all "total institutions" are likely to have a powerful impact on the individual, some theory argues against this. Wheeler (1969) has argued, for example, against the view that prison is a setting within which fundamental changes in attitudes and values are likely to take place. He concedes the extensive findings on surface conformity, compliance, and external adjustment but holds that men do not enter prison seeking a "basically new and different vision of themselves." When change does occur, Wheeler states that it is produced as much by general reaction to confinement and separation as by the prison program and life. Society's definition of the prison is seen as being most relevant for the future life and career of prison inmates, since it has, does, and will serve as a major determinant of the prisoner's self-concept, self-image, and of his sense of personal worth.

There is some justification for terming psychotherapy as involving a "total experience"—a concerted, psychiatric attempt to break down the barriers ordinarily separating the spheres of life. The patient over a period of time establishes a unique relationship of trust and confidence with the therapist, discussing intimate aspects of experiences, thoughts, dispositions, emotions, fantasy, etc., in the joint attempt to resolve the patient's deep-seated problems. Along these same lines, we may note that "encounter groups" might well also be termed brief "total experiences," that is, a brief attempt to break down conventional intrapersonal and interpersonal barriers to free expression and behavior. Group psychotherapy is a longer term effort of a related sort.

A substantial amount of research has been done on the effects of psychotherapy, although there is much controversy over the conclusions to be drawn from this work. Eysenck (1952,1965) has been a prominent figure in arguing from the literature that psychotherapy has not demonstrated it has any consistent significant effects on patients. However, when careful studies with control groups are examined (and there are relatively few such studies), psychotherapy and personal counseling do seem to have some significant positive effects, but this is not always the case (see Cross 1964; Dittman 1966). Bergin (1966), in fact, concludes from a review of the literature that psychotherapy generally tends either to increase or decrease the adjustment of people receiving therapy. In short, it does change people, relative to similar people who do not receive therapy; but the change may be for the better or for the worse. Most important with regard to the aims of the present chapter, Bergin concludes that therapeutic results can occur from informal therapeutic contacts as well as from more formal therapeutic activity. The demonstrated presence of such effects suggests the possibility that participation in certain kinds of voluntary groups might have similar effects.

Another kind of relatively "total experience" that has received substantial investigation by behavioral scientists is very monotonous stimulation or the extreme restriction of stimulation (sensory deprivation). In their excellent book on these and related matters, Fiske and Maddi (1961) showed that the varied experience seems to be a requirement for the normal growth and development of organisms, especially in their early environment. And even in later life, monotonous stimulation or marked restrictions of experience over relative short periods tend to produce both reduced task performance and negative emotional states in human beings (Fiske and Maddi 1961; Schultz 1965). The longer term importance of varied stimulation and the impact of environmental variations on intelligence and capacities have received special attention. This body of research makes it clear that long-term variations in cultural and social class experience have an especially important impact on capacities (see Hunt 1961; Guilford 1967, chap. 16; Vernon 1969).

But there is more to the impact of environments on the individual than this. The fact that "total institutions" and various forms of extreme experience or stimulation of a special kind have significant impacts on the person does not deny the possibility that less extreme environments and experiences can also have important effects. The less extreme the environment and the less different it is from other environments the individual is accustomed to, the less likely and the less marked such change will probably be. But this is a relative and individual matter. What is an important contrasting experience for one person may not be for another.

Normal Experiences and Social Settings

Much of the prior research on the impact of the social environment upon individuals has focused on special or extreme aspects of that environment or else on the influence of that environment in the early years. But in recent years there has also been some research on how more ordinary kinds of experience and social environments can have important impacts on persons after childhood. For instance, Breer and Locke (1965) have shown that various kinds of task experience can be an important source of attitudes, quite apart from any aspects of direct socialization (verbal learning or teaching) that takes place in a social setting. They present evidence for a general theory of how and why this occurs, both through generalization from one situation to other similar situations as well as through generalization from a specific situation to more abstract principles.

In their forthcoming work entitled BECOMING MODERN, Inkeles and Smith (1973) present significant evidence from their study of individual modernization that work environments (e.g., the factory vs. the traditional farm), formal schooling, mass media exposure, and certain other experiences have a consistently significant modernizing impact on men in developing countries. Studying about six thousand men in six developing nations from three continents by means of four-hour interviews, they found that exposure to modernizing social environments affects attitudes, values, beliefs and behavior in similar ways in very different countries. They explain these findings in terms of the task experiences of the individuals involved, by and large, rather than in terms of direct tuition and verbal learning, since people are not generally taught consciously to be modern.

There are several other areas of research in the past decade that have lent supporting evidence to the general impact of social environments on the individual, and especially the impact of naturally occurring environments whose presence we take for granted but whose influence has been little investigated. One clear example of this is the research on political socialization (see Dawson and Prewitt 1969, Hess and Torney 1967, Sears 1969), although a number of other realms have also received careful attention (see Goslin 1969; Bicker 1964; Becker and Geer 1958; Becker et al. 1961; Blizzard 1956; Brim 1966; Campbell 1969; Dornbusch 1955; Elder 1968; and Moore 1969). To illustrate the kind of research that has been done on the impact of various kinds of "normal" social settings after childhood, we shall review briefly here some of the conclusions that have been drawn from research on the impact of school environments (especially college) upon adolescents and young adults.

A number of studies have been done detailing the impact of aspects of college experience on students (LeVine 1966, Sanford 1962, Wallace 1964, Webster et al. 1962, and Wilson 1960). Most often these have focused on values and value changes (those aspects which are less likely to be subject to significant change), though some have focused on attitudes and behavior. Perhaps understandably, the most apparent intended impact is the least documented—that is, as a result of college experience students are likely to acquire a good deal of information on a variety of topics and may also develop special skills at certain tasks.

One of the classic studies of attitude change in a college setting is Newcomb's (1943) study of Bennington College (a women's liberal arts college in Vermont). At that time (a four-year period during the middle thirties), but especially in the earlier part of the period studied, Bennington was a highly integrated community, unusually self-sufficient and self-contained. Incoming freshmen had largely conservative family backgrounds and tended to share their families' conservative attitudes. However, exposure to the faculty's liberal attitudes within this powerful environment tended to produce significant shifts toward more liberal positions over a four-year period. Freshmen scores were significantly more conservative than junior and senior scores for each year studied. During the first two years of the study even freshman-sophomore scores showed significant differentials. Exceptions to this general process occurred mainly among some subgroups which were largely isolated from the normal interaction patterns in the college setting, thus being better able to retain their initial conservative attitudes. Other colleges studied have not generally produced comparable changes or exerted comparable influence on political attitudes.

In a follow-up study twenty-five years later, Newcomb et al. (1967) found that graduates had in large measure retained their college-influenced (changed) political attitude orientations. They selected as mates and were in turn selected as mates by men sharing their attitude orientations. Indeed, in two-thirds of the cases, it was possible to predict accurately a future husband's political attitudes in 1960-61 on the basis of his wife's college attitude scores. Generally, when the graduate's social environment (spouse, friends, etc.) supported their Bennington attitudes, those attitudes were retained. Most frequently, the spouse's influence tended to be indirect, providing support for existing attitudes rather than directly instigating change. While having a number of friends with differing attitudes sometimes produced change, friends normally had similar political orientations.

Philip Jacob (1957) attempted to assess the impact of college experience on student values from a general review of the literature. Over the four years of college, he found a general trend toward greater homogeneity and consistency of values. No sharp breaks were found in the continuity of the main value patterns, changes rarely being drastic or sudden. Those changes which do occur are ordinarily on the periphery of the student's character, affecting not so much the values themselves as the student's personal application of them. McClintock and Turner (1962), similarly, found no significant impact of college upon political knowledge, values, or actions.

Overall, Jacob found no significant changes in student values attributable to the curriculum in general or any aspect of it, to the quality of teaching, or to the methods of instruction. Values may change in college, and that change may in some instances be substantial. However, the prime impetus does not seem to come directly from the formal educational process but rather from "the distinctive climate of a few institutions, the individual and personal magnetism of a sensitive teacher with strong value-commitments of his own, or value-laden personal experiences of students imaginatively integrated with their intellectual development" (Jacob 1957, p. 11). This has important implications for the potential impact of voluntary organizations on their participants.

A number of investigators have studied the role of peer groups in educational processes. Coleman (1961, 1966), for example, has documented the important role that peer groups can play in affecting the educational climate of a school. Peer groups may facilitate and stimulate learning or may create and sustain values and emphases that detract from some of the aims of the educational process. Newcomb (1966) has advanced a theory of peer group influence, noting that groups will be most effective in their impact when: (1) the groups are neither too large for stimulating interpersonal interaction nor too small for sustaining group support; (2) they are relatively homogeneous in the attitudes important for the group; (3) they are in "communicative isolation"—that is, not distracted or diverted by opposing views; and (4) the group supported attitudes are also very important to the individual. These same conclusions might well apply to the conditions of attitude change and personal impact of voluntary groups. Indeed, the peer groups Newcomb studied were simply informal voluntary peer groups.

In a recent study of a distinctive college environment, King (1967) reports that Harvard undergraduates do not ordinarily experience changes in the basic structure of their personalities but do change some values. Some opinions, attitudes, and ways of dealing with people and the world are subject to considerable change, however. A growth in concern for freedom of self-assertion and self-expression was noted along with a weakening of religious value positions. Attitudes toward political and social issues were subject to the greatest change. However, controls were not reported to provide assurances on the extent to which these changes are the result of broader sociocultural processes or maturational effects rather than the direct effects of college.

Feldman and Newcomb's THE IMPACT OF COLLEGE ON STUDENTS (1969), provides a very extensive and cogent more recent review of the literature on their topic. In their epilogue, they summarize their review and draw those generalizations and conclusions they believe are in order. Essentially, they note the general tendency for students' personalities to become more flexible, more open, more self-confident, and less dogmatic as a result of college experience. Students tended also to become more independent and less committed to organized religion.

Feldman and Newcomb point out that colleges differ in their student inputs—that student bodies may differ in their characteristics and tendencies as well as varying along the homogeneity-heterogeneity continuum. They feel that when some characteristics or tendencies are prominent and especially when the college setting is relatively homogeneous, reinforcement and intensification of those characteristics and tendencies is likely to take place, even though "deviant careers" in college are possible and do occur. In addition to the choice of a given college, the choice of a given major is also likely to result in the enhancement of certain tendencies and processes. While change may take place in college, it is also likely that some values and/or attitudes that in other contexts might have changed in some fashion will be maintained due to the college experience.

College environments may differ substantially in their potential for "impacts." Large, heterogeneous, commuter multiversities or junior colleges are unlikely to be sources of significant, consistent, campuswide impacts. The type of college that is most likely to produce a significant and reasonably consistent impact on students as persons is found to be small, homogeneous in faculty and in student characteristics, and residential. Overall, personal impacts seem most likely where there is relative homogeneity and substantial interaction, both formal and informal, of students with each other and with faculty.

Is one kind of student more likely to change than another? Feldman and Newcomb focus on two personal traits they feel facilitate change. One is an openness to change—an ability to cope with change, a tendency to find change potentially interesting and reasonably nonthreatening. The other change-facilitating trait is an openness to others—a willingness or a tendency to be influenced by others.

Finally, Feldman and Newcomb note that the impacts of the college experience are likely to persist after college when the graduate is in environments that support those impacts. Where selective processes have led the graduate to such settings, college impacts are likely to be continued, strengthened, and expanded.

Greeley and Rossi (1966), in their study of the impact of religious educational experience, THE EDUCATION OF CATHOLIC AMERICANS, provide a broader and more rigorous test of impacts than has commonly been the case, focusing on religious beliefs, attitudes, and behavior. Religiously oriented beliefs, values, and attitudes were found to be largely the same for Catholics who attended Catholic schools and those who did not, with the exception that attendees were likely to be more aware of the finer points of doctrine and showed a greater tendency toward orthodoxy on currently disputed questions.

Three variables were notably related to current adult (self-reported) religious behavior: (1) extended exposure to full-time religious education (elementary and high school and college), (2) the experience of a very religious family (especially parents) and family life (at least one parent receiving communion every Sunday), and (3) marriage to a religious Catholic spouse. For the young, the major predictor of religious behavior was current full-time attendance in a Catholic school. For those youth not in full-time attendance in a Catholic school, little relationship was found between attendance at Confraternity of Christian Doctrine classes (the equivalent of Sunday school, usually lasting about one hour per week) and religious behavior.

Attendance at Catholic high schools and colleges was found to affect religious behavior only when preceded by exclusively Catholic schooling. Whatever differences were apparent between those currently in attendance at Catholic high schools and colleges and those of the same age who were not attending such institutions eroded rapidly once schooling ended, unless the three most salient variables noted above were in effect. Thus, instead of finding that impacts were greatest where there was potential for change (where the parents were not notably religious and the child was sent to a Catholic school), instead impacts were greatest where children were most favorably disposed toward positive impacts of religious education through the beliefs and practices of their parents, despite a reduced potential for positive change.

In a study of several Latin American universities, Smith (1972a) found fairly consistent evidence for the impact of extracurricular aspects of college experience upon religious attitudes and behavior. The universities in question were generally public, secular ones, so that the direction of change was generally toward lower religiosity, measured in various ways. Smith's results agreed with those of Greeley and Rossi in finding that coming from a very religious family background had a powerful influence, with attendance at religious primary and elementary school having a secondary influence.

Summary

What type of group setting or social situation is most likely to have a significant "person-changing" impact on the individual?

Groups and social interaction settings are most likely to have strong impacts where their influence is intensive, extensive, well-integrated, and enduring, where the group is relatively homogeneous and consistent in its positions, where the group setting contrasts markedly with other, prior settings of the individual, and where the group norms, values, and role models are clear and successfully transmitted, being supported by a system of sanctions and rewards. The group with a personal impact tends to be highly attractive to members and of sufficient size to provide viable support for the individual but not so large that interpersonal relations are discouraged or hard to initiate and maintain. Groups also have a more powerful impact when the individual is dependent on them for significant satisfaction and the meeting of important needs, and when the group exposure comes at an earlier stage of the individual's development in a given area. Finally, groups have the strongest overt impacts on members where the group is seen as salient on an issue and its position is viewed as legitimate.

An individual is most likely to be influenced by a group or an interaction setting when he is in some way dependent on, committed to, strongly identified with and highly values the group—when he places trust and confidence in it and believes in the importance of group-supported attitudes. The person is also more open to group impacts when highly motivated and seeking to practice responses highly valued by that group.

The individual is often as much or even more likely to be affected by the informal aspects of a social setting as contrasted with direct, formal, consciously change-oriented aspects. A distinctive group climate, a charismatic or otherwise striking leader/teacher "model," or a moving personal experience in the group setting can produce more basic changes in personal values, attitudes, beliefs and behavior than any official training, orientation, or other direct didactic experiences.

All of the foregoing conclusions suggest that many kinds of voluntary action might well have significant personal impacts. But what empirical data do we have on the matter?

Impacts in Voluntary Action Settings

Having reviewed some general instances of personal impacts of social settings and having discussed some of the settings in which such impacts are likely, we now turn to the question of personal impacts in voluntary action settings specifically.

W. Keith Warner (1972) presents a listing of common characteristics of voluntary associations that, by extension and with adequate qualification, may apply to other voluntary action settings and roles. The list serves to highlight some aspects of voluntary action which in many instances may limit or circumscribe possible impacts on the participant. Warner notes that voluntary associations are generally avocational and of secondary importance to the individual in that they tend to be less pervasive, salient, and influential than familial and occupational facets of daily life.

Voluntary associations tend to rely on normative inducements for gaining membership, promoting participation, and maintaining social control. Although such inducements may be powerful and effective at times, being unable to call upon other sorts of inducements when necessary does reduce and lessen the ability of the voluntary organization to encourage and stimulate attitudes, dispositions and behaviors where the individual is apathetic, disinterested, recalcitrant, or reluctant.

Associations typically deal with specialized interests rather than the broader range of interests that the individual is likely to possess and pursue. Thus voluntary action personal impacts will usually be limited to a narrower range of interests. Since an individual is unlikely to be able to fulfill many of his varied interests by participation in a given voluntary action setting, he is likely to have segmental membership participation, being only partially involved in any given association or setting and thus being subject to competing influences and demands.

Voluntary associations tend to rely on intermittent activity on the part of most members rather than requiring continuous effort and activity. Meetings and other activities may be weeks apart. Activities may cease or diminish for some months. Thus, for long periods of time the association or program and its activities may not be at the forefront of the individuals' interests and attention.

Although subject to considerable variation, voluntary associations also tend to be subject to oligarchical control—a core of members being involved much more actively in leadership and participation than most members, owing to the special skills, knowledge, greater interest, power, influence, time, and so forth of the core members. Thus levels of involvement and levels of rewards may differ within any given setting, which in turn should have marked effects on how much personal impact the group has on a member. Finally, many voluntary associations have relatively low levels of formal organization, demanding relatively little of members in order to increase or maintain membership, but at the same time losing some of the organization's ability to mobilize members effectively.

In view of these characteristics, it would not be surprising if many voluntary associations had relatively low levels of personal impact on their members. On the other hand, the general findings of social science suggest that some kinds of voluntary associations might have powerful impacts on their members. We may expect the personal impact to be related to the distinctiveness, homogeneity, interpersonal closeness, size, degree of activity and other characteristics of the voluntary group, as suggested by the summary of the prior section of this chapter.

Expected Types of Personal Impact
of Voluntary Action

The personal impacts of voluntary action may be analytically grouped into five broad classes: those involving beliefs (knowledge, perceptions, images, information), dispositions (values, personality, and attitudes), emotions, capacities (skills, abilities), and behavior. Each of these classes is related to the others. Decrements, maintenance, or increments in one kind of impact are likely to influence appropriate aspects of the others.

Joining a voluntary association or a voluntary action setting commonly results in changing certain beliefs and providing certain information. New members and new participants will commonly come to know more about the group or setting after joining than they did prior to joining and participating. In some measure this may be the direct result of the organization's explicit and conscious attempts to teach the neophyte about the formal aspects of the organization (its rules, regulations, roles, programs, policies, procedures, rituals, officers, enemies, external barriers, sources of recruitment, etc.) and its informal aspects (customs, tendencies, what "really goes on," the actual "meaning" of activity for members, etc.).

Voluntary associations differ widely on the amount of formal and informal knowledge and beliefs the average newcomer is expected to attain or commonly gains. Where relatively little participation is expected and that participation is viewed by the organization as routine, not requiring special knowledge or beliefs, new members may not be encouraged or required to know much about the organization. Nevertheless, when people join or participate in a voluntary organization in some manner, they are likely to gain and retain at least some knowledge that they did not have previously about the organization, its operations, its ideology, and its environment. There is, unfortunately, only a little empirical data bearing on this point that we have found.

General and particular dispositions including values, personality dimensions or traits, and specific attitudes may also be influenced by membership in and participation in a voluntary association. Continued membership and participation would seem at least in part to depend on the maintenance of favorable attitudes toward the organization and the individual's past, current, and prospective involvement and place in it (see Mulford and Klonglan, 1972). Indeed, some voluntary associations may be especially sensitive to shifts in member's expectations and attitudes.

We expect participation in voluntary associations to affect individual dispositions because of social learning of several kinds. Most obviously, many kinds of voluntary groups and programs consciously attempt to influence the values and attitudes of their members. Political and issue-oriented voluntary groups have a vested interest in affecting their members' political attitudes and dispositions relevant to group goals. In fact, all kinds of instrumental voluntary groups, service-oriented as well as issue-oriented, have need of influencing their members' attitudes, values and other dispositions to act in order to make them consistent with accomplishing group goals.

But not all, in fact only a small proportion, of voluntary group influence on dispositions tends to be the result of conscious orientation/training activity by the group. Most of the impact is likely to come about as a result of "incidental learning"—the unintended consequence of experiences in the social environment created formally and informally by the voluntary group or program. In some cases, the learning occurs because of rewards (e.g., praise, recognition) and punishments (e.g., criticism, being ignored or left out) controlled by other members and leaders of the group. In other cases, the individual generalizes attitudes and dispositions from one specific situation to other similar situations inside or outside the group context. Still other attitudinal and value learning occurs through the modeling of one's own dispositions after those of respected and accepted members of the group, or through the acceptance of broad principles of action and the exemplification of those principles in specific attitudes and dispositions. As we shall see a bit later, there *is* some empirical evidence bearing on the impact of voluntary groups upon individuals' dispositions, though not on which of these kinds of social learning is most important in affecting dispositions in such groups.

Insofar as voluntary groups are able to engage the feelings as well as the minds of their members, we may expect them to have a significant influence on members' feelings and emotions. In particular, we may expect voluntary action to influence such emotional states as anxiety (especially where members are put in risky or difficult situations, in dealing with convicts for instance), anger and frustration (brought on by the inability to achieve desired goals because of external opposition, for instance), social belongingness and acceptance (the result of developing new friendships as part of a voluntary group or program, for instance), excitement (from active commitment to and participation in the achievement of an important community project, for instance), and of course general psychological well-being or happiness (growing out of the provision of various kinds of positive affect, with only minimal amounts of negative affect). There are some beginnings of research in this field, but only beginnings.

The potential impact of voluntary action upon individual capacities and skills is a much neglected area of research, even relative to the overall neglect of the general study of voluntary action impact upon individual volunteers/participants. It is obvious that participation in many kinds of social/expressive voluntary groups might have an important impact on social skills; that participation in instrumental and issue-oriented groups might enhance political, leadership, negotiation, public speaking, public relations and related skills; that participation in recreational, hobby, and artistic voluntary groups might increase skills in the corresponding games, sports, hobby areas, and artistic productions or performances; etc. Yet we have found no empirical research evidence bearing on these matters.

Finally, all of the foregoing kinds of potential impact of voluntary action on the individual can be manifested in his or her overt behavior. Voluntary action can not only change beliefs, dispositions, emotions and capacities; it can also result in different observable behavior patterns flowing from more "internal" changes in a person. And even without any significant or deep-seated internal changes (i.e., internalized changes, accepted as part of the self), there can be many changes in overt behavior as a result of voluntary action. Many such changes are simply the result of conformity to or compliance with group norms and pressures. Insofar as behavioral changes are simple matters of conformity or compliance, they are likely to be manifested mainly in situations where other group members are present or can indirectly monitor the individual's behavior. On the other hand, behavioral changes that result from changes in internalized values, beliefs, etc. are likely to be manifested not only in "public" social situations where group members are aware of what the individual is doing, but also in "private" situations where the group cannot easily monitor (formally or informally) the individual's behavior.

Impacts in Instrumental, Externally Focused Volunteer Groups and Settings

As we turn to an examination of the empirical studies relevant to our theme, we shall begin with those pieces of research which focus on volunteer groups or settings that are instrumental and that have an external focus. Such groups or programs are instrumental in seeking to accomplish some objective goal, rather than simply engaging in activity as an end in itself (expressive self-gratification). These kinds of voluntary groups or programs are to be viewed primarily as means to some end, not as ends in themselves.

However, an instrumental group can have either an internal or an external focus to its activities. If its focus is internal, then it is somehow trying to change or affect its members themselves and their situations (e.g., self-help groups). If its focus is external, its goal has to do with people or situations outside the membership of the organization itself. It is trying to affect or deal with clients, the public in contact, the community at large, or even the nation or other countries.

In seeking evidence of the impact of volunteer experience on the volunteer, we might expect to find the least impact on volunteers involved in instrumental activity with an external focus. In such volunteer experiences, the primary thrust of the activity is outward and away from the individual himself, so that any observed effects are likely to be accidental, unintended, or at least incidental to the main aims of the volunteer group or program. Therefore, if we find clear evidence of personal impact here, we might expect to find even stronger impacts in internally focused volunteer groups, especially self-help (vs. expressive) groups.

Some anecdotal evidence bearing on the impact of student volunteering in mental hospitals is given by Umbarger et al. (1962), reporting on the Harvard-Radcliffe student volunteer program operating at a nearby state mental hospital. According to the students involved, there were significant changes in their attitudes toward mental illness, generally in the direction of greater tolerance, understanding and acceptance. Holzberg and his colleagues have done several studies of a more experimental sort, using control groups, that shed more light on the personal impact of this kind of volunteer role.

Holzberg and Knapp (1965) summarize findings on the effects of a volunteer companionship program involving college students with chronically ill mental patients. The program consisted of volunteers spending one hour a week with a mental patient companion followed by small group discussions with a member of the institution's professional staff. These discussions enabled the students to share their program experiences, to have them interpreted and put into context by the staff, and to receive helpful information on problems of mental illness and of hospitalization.

After one year in the program, participants showed increased knowledge about mental illness and hospitalization. Their attitudes also changed as they became more "enlightened" about mental illness (Holzberg and Gewirtz 1963). Over a five-year period, volunteers tended to be slightly more religiously oriented, more morally concerned, more compassionate, and more introverted than the general student population (Knapp and Holzberg 1964). Knapp and Holzberg (1964) hold that the program served as an outlet for the volunteers' generosity and altruism. Comparing volunteers in the companionship program with a control group of fellow students who were matched on a number of background characteristics, Holzberg and Knapp (1965) noted that the volunteers tended, in part as a result of their participation in the program, to become more self-accepting and more tolerant, while also increasing in self-examination and self-awareness.

When a similar study was done with student volunteers in a companionship program and a control group of students in no volunteer program, Holzberg, Gewirtz and Ebner (1964) found a significant positive change in the volunteers' moral tolerance of sexual and aggressive behavior. They also found a significant increase in the volunteers' self-acceptance during the year, while that of the control group subjects actually declined by about the same amount. The companion volunteer students increased in introspectiveness and self-examination over this same period (Holzberg and Knapp 1965).

In still another study, this time with students from seven colleges working as volunteers in the companionship program, Holzberg, Knapp and Turner (1966) found that the volunteer experience helps the student develop his sense of personal competence and efficacy, as a result of successful accomplishment. The ability to make friends successfully with a mental patient opens the student "to a wider range of possible ways of classifying other persons and of possible ways in which he might relate to them" (ibid., p. 403). This helps clarify the student's perception of himself, his roles, and how they might be changed.

Related studies by Holzberg (1964), Holzberg and Gewirtz (1963), and Holzberg, Whiting, and Lowy (1964) provide additional confirmation that this kind of social service volunteering on a one-to-one basis with mental patients has various kinds of important impacts on the beliefs and dispositions of the college student volunteer exposed to the experience for an hour or so per week over a school year (nine months). These same kinds of programs, it should be noted in passing, also seem to have a positive impact on the patients involved (Beck et al., 1965).

A before-and-after study by King et al. (1970) used a careful testing procedure and control group to demonstrate that undergraduate psychology students who did volunteer work in a psychiatric hospital during their course were different in some ways from other students in the same class who did not. There was *no* observed signficant effect on moral tolerance but a significant increase in self acceptance scores did result from the volunteer work, corroborating further the results reviewed above.

Other studies of volunteering in hospital settings show that volunteer participation leads to increased knowledge and understanding of hospital routines and procedures (MacBain and Schumacher 1963), to increased understanding of abnormal psychology (Klein and Zax 1965), and to various general kinds of satisfaction (Klugman and Klugman 1964; Burke and Dye 1961).

Some of these and other studies indicate volunteer experience in hospitals may affect vocational choice decisions (MacBain and Schumacher 1963; Goldsmith 1963; Greenblatt and Kantor 1962). However, the effects on career choice are generally rather small in the sense that only a minority of students involved are affected. For example, on the basis of a small study Arffa (1966) suggested that most student volunteers, be they in high school or in college, make vocational decisions before volunteering—their volunteer experience serving to maintain or verify their choice rather than changing it. Of the forty volunteers at the hospital studied, only seven had "changed" their vocational choice. All seven were high school students. All had been initially unsure of their choices when they began their volunteer experience. Only three of the seven who changed stated they were directly influenced by their volunteer experience in that choice. Thus, although the evidence is scanty, it would seem that this type of volunteer experience is likely to influence the vocational decisions of only a few of those yet undecided while rarely altering (though perhaps confirming) already firm vocational choices. In general, this type of voluntary action does not uniformly affect the career plans of those who participate in it.

Although some of the studies noted earlier indicated that student volunteers working with mental patients undergo changed attitudes toward patients and mental illness, at least one study on adult volunteers challenges that conclusion. Vernallis and St. Pierre (1964) used an Opinions About Mental Illness scale on 163 hospital volunteers, comparing new and experienced volunteers. They found no significant evidence of change in attitudes as a result of volunteer experience, since the two groups did not differ significantly in scale scores.

A related kind of social service "companionship" volunteering is the "volunteer in the court," where adult volunteers work with delinquents. Ernest Shelley (1971), in a major review of recent studies dealing with volunteers in courts, cites only four studies (out of the thirty-five reviewed) that clearly included data dealing with the impact of such programs (or aspects of such programs) on the volunteer. One study, this by the Boulder County Juvenile Delinquency Project (1967), probed the current activities of volunteers who had left the program upon moving from the community, but who had been living for at least six months in a new location. Of the twenty replies, seven former volunteers indicated that they were currently involved in volunteer programs, three had applied for a program but were not yet active, and three intended to apply for a program. Of the seven who were already active in programs, only two were then involved with "problem youth." While it might be possible to argue that a possible impact of involvement in the Boulder Project was continued interest in and involvement in volunteer work and possibly in similar programs concerned for "problem youth," the study does not really establish that sequence and does not shed light on the actual effect that participation in the project had on an interest in volunteer work or in work in court-related programs. (There was no control group.)

The Joint Commission on Correctional Manpower and Training's "Volunteers Look at Corrections" (1967) reported that about two-thirds of the 541 volunteers questioned felt that their attitudes toward corrections had become more positive since they had become involved in corrections work, 70 percent also noting that they had interested some of their friends in corrections since themselves becoming volunteers. It would thus seem that continued involvement as a volunteer in a corrections program is likely to be associated with a more positive perspective on corrections and with advocacy of the program and of corrections among friends in the community.

Finally, Zaphiris, in conjunction with others (1968, 1970), provides insight into the impact of some training experiences on new volunteers. He found (1968) that volunteers who were not able to accept their probationers well before training, were able to accept their probationers well after receiving training. The 1970 study found that about half of the volunteers felt that their training made them more tolerant in attitude. The other half reported they were unchanged in that regard. Zaphiris also notes that while some volunteers had favored jail or fines as a deterrent prior to their training and experience in corrections, half of these changed their views after their training and as they gained experience in the field.

Shelley's overview (1971, p. 45) of the volunteer movement in courts and in corrections observes that "we have apparently passed through the period where the primary concern and interest is who is doing what, and how they are doing it, to the question of what kinds of impact is our practice having on the participants, volunteers, staff, clients, and community?" However, Shelley notes that these general impact questions, and the question of impact on the individual volunteer in particular remain quite open. As he phrases it (ibid.), still to be answered are the questions: "how does the experience change the attitudes and the general personality of the volunteer? Is there a difference in this impact depending upon the kind of activity the volunteer is engaged in with the offender or in terms of any of the demographic characteristics of volunteers?"

In an unpublished report to ACTION, Booz, Allen Public Administration Services (1972) has evaluated various aspects of the impact of the Foster Grandparent program. This program is intended to provide meaningful opportunities for the elderly to contribute to the community and to the welfare of institutionalized children, as well as to help the elderly enjoy feelings of greater self-respect and usefulness. The foster grandparents are 60 or older and receive a small stipend for giving four hours a day, five days a week to children seventeen or younger.

On the basis of 900 self-report questionnaires and interviews with numerous other people in 25 cities and counties around the U.S., several kinds of impact on the older volunteer (or "quasi-volunteer") were observed. Among the benefits received by these foster grandparents were increased feelings of independence, reduced loneliness, reduced concern for financial problems, increased feelings of being loved, and more general happiness, as well as some improvement in health (probably a result of increased physical activity).

Townsend (1972) has recently studied the impact of a still different kind of service volunteer program upon its participants. He drew samples of interested nonvolunteers (those expressing initial interest but not actually joining the program) and uninterested nonvolunteers from among the freshmen students at a large Eastern state university, using these two groups as control samples to compare with an "experimental" group consisting of all freshmen students who were actually participating in an off-campus community service volunteer program. Various questionnaire measures were administered just prior to the beginning of the volunteer program for the school year and again after a period of about six months. The focus of the tests was on organizational, political, and interpersonal attitudes and activities.

He found that all three sample groups reduced their organizational, political, and interpersonal activities, but increased their satisfaction and level of participation in selected activities. Interestingly, but quite unexpectedly, the volunteers (who were working a few hours per week in various community service agencies) showed a decline in their interest in organizational activity and in their sense of civic responsibility, while the nonvolunteers planned to expand their organizational and civic activities. All three sample groups showed a decreasing sense of political competence and increased alienation from the political process, as well as a growing concern with their own personal competence and ability to control their lives. In general, however, statistical tests indicated that "the changes reported for volunteers were not attributable to their volunteer service activities, but a process of change shared by the freshmen college students participating in this study" (Townsend 1972, p. 176).

The only area where there was clearly an impact of the volunteer program per se was in terms of the sense of citizen responsibility: the level of increased frustration and disillusionment expressed by the volunteers after their community service experience significantly differed from the increase in expressed civic concern by the nonvolunteers. Volunteers, for instance, significantly decreased their level of participation in health, welfare, or civic voluntary organizations, their interest in partieipating in organizations like the Peace Corps, and in their likelihood of selecting social service or social change as primary reasons for joining voluntary organizations. By contrast, the nonvolunteers (representing the bulk of the student body) showed significant increases on these items. The frustrations of meeting head-on a harsh and unyielding reality through community volunteer service are a possible explanation for these findings.

However, volunteers were also more likely to take action on specific issues that concerned them than were either of the nonvolunteer groups. This is interpreted by Townsend as a kind of increased selectivity on the part of the volunteers. They came into the program with high hopes, had them generally dashed, and retreated psychically to a more defensible position—not a general interest in civic activities and social service, but a willingness to engage in such activities if the outcome really concerned them personally.

It would be interesting to know whether the changes observed here persist in subsequent years. In any event, this study is an enlightening one in a negative way. The optimistic hypotheses regarding the impact of the program on the volunteers were not only not confirmed, but the only significant differential impacts on the volunteers were actually in the opposite direction. This study points up the complexity of the topic of this chapter, while once again making it clear how important it is to have appropriate control groups in impact studies. Were it not for the two control groups here, one might have concluded that the volunteer program per se (rather than the freshman year at college) had negative effects on nearly all of the attitude areas investigated.

Coles and Brenner (1965) examined the impact of a related but different kind of volunteer activity upon the participants. They studied a group of about 400 college students engaged in full-time summer volunteer civil rights work in Mississippi. The volunteers lived with rural poor families, and were involved in local community problems. Their primary aim was to aid with voter registration among blacks. On the basis of open-ended interview data and unstructured observation, Coles and Brenner described the impact of the volunteer experience in terms of several developmental stages that usually occurred.

The first stage was a kind of "culture shock," where the volunteers were overwhelmed by the problems presented and by the inadequacy of their own capacities to help. Then the volunteer attempted to transfer his sense of helplessness to the society in general for allowing such conditions to exist. At the same time the volunteer was trying to disengage himself emotionally both from the immediate situation and from society. In the third stage he engaged in intensive self-examination of his bitterness and disappointment, leading to the fourth stage where he generally recognized his own limitations as well as his strengths, and begins to work again for change. The impact overall, thus, is often one of increasing the emotional maturity of the volunteer as well as renewing his commitment to work for change.

A subsequent study by the same authors (Coles and Brenner, 1968) deals with two groups of college students working during two different summers as full-time community service volunteers in rural Appalachia. Again living with poor families, these volunteers worked on community projects like repairing school buildings, building roads, and teaching and gathering information about medical, legal, and educational needs of Appalachia. This study also confirmed the presence of the kind of developmental stages suggested in the earlier article.

Riechen (1952) studied a similar kind of volunteer experience over a decade earlier, focusing on college age youth who participated in the American Friends Service Committee "volunteer work camps" during the summer months in both the United States and Mexico. The volunteers constructed and repaired schools, homes, playgrounds, and other facilities in areas of "social or economic tension or conflict" (ibid., p. 26). About 200 volunteers were tested prior to the work camp experience, at the conclusion of the summer experience, and again nine months later.

Comparing before and after results with regard to the summer period, Riechen (1952, p. 98) found the volunteers became "significantly (0.05) less authoritarian, less prejudiced, and more democratic at the end of the summer than they were at the beginning." Other data on a subsample indicated the volunteers showed a significant increase in the need for autonomy and a significant decrease in the need for aggression. This means that the volunteers became less dependent and "more desirous of freedom from restraint, yet at the same time less aggressive and hostile in meeting opposition and frustration" (ibid., p. 120). At the time of follow-up nine months later, these changes generally had persisted. The lack of a control group makes the interpretation of these results ambiguous, but they are generally consistent with other results we have reviewed.

Hyman et al. (1962) evaluated the impact of volunteer summer work camps called "The Encampment for Citizenship." They used very careful techniques, including a series of testing points both before, immediately after, and several years after the six week summer volunteer experience for youth. The work camp experience included not only work on service projects but also educational and discussion activities, recreation, fellowship, etc.

They found (p. 166) as an immediate effect of the program little change in basic vocational values or social/political action orientation (all were initially very action-oriented and remained so). But they did find frequent and significant changes in cognitive and attitudinal areas, with few unanticipated negative changes. The greatest positive changes were observed in terms of scales measuring attitudes regarding civil liberties, civil rights, tolerance and authoritarianism. These findings take on special weight in view of the fact they appeared consistently in the evaluation results of four separate summer work camps. In the cognitive area, the volunteers showed significantly increased optimism with regard to the possible solution of social and racial problems in society. With regard to relations to society, the main impact was to increase diversity among the volunteers—some became more alienated from society while others increased their identification.

Although there were no external control groups, the extent of "natural improvement" was investigated by sending attitude questionnaires to one-third of the volunteers six weeks *before* the work camp, comparing their attitudes at this point with their attitudes just prior to the work camp. Large "natural improvement" was found only for the civil liberties scale, with some change also in tolerance. Little or none was found in authoritarianism, civil rights, or other attitude scales.

Longer term followups after four years showed that the attitude changes were generally maintained, with or without personal and reference group support from others. Changes in behavior, however, were generally maintained only if supported by the subsequent social milieux. Retrospective data on work camp "alumni" from earlier years generally supported the conclusions drawn from the before-and-after study. Both the didactic and communal aspects of the volunteer work camp experience were important causal elements in the changes observed.

The last few studies we have reviewed have concerned full-time, intensive, though relatively short-term volunteer experiences, in contrast with less intensive, part-time, but longer experiences (in terms of the total time period in which the part-time experience is embedded). From the general research on socialization and task experience that we reviewed earlier in the chapter, we would expect this latter, more intensive volunteer experience to have a greater impact than the less intensive, part-time kind of volunteer work in companionship type programs. This seems to be generally the case, although it is difficult to draw valid conclusions since no single study has ever compared the impacts of the two kinds of volunteer roles using a common set of measurement instruments and adequate methodology.

There has also been some research on the impact of longer term, full-time, "quasi-volunteer" roles, where the participant is paid a subsistence allowance and travel expenses. The Peace Corps and VISTA in the United States are examples of this kind of role, characterized by intensive full-time participation over a period of at least a year (VISTA) or even two years (Peace Corps).

Stein (1966) performed a panel study on Peace Corps volunteers over a period of three years, collecting data several times from the time of their first training through the first year of their return home to the United States after two years of service abroad. Since he did not use a control group, it is difficult to know whether the effects he finds are a result of the Peace Corps experience or more general maturational processes. Nevertheless, the results are interesting.

Although there was little change in the psychological well-being of the volunteers over the whole three-year period, the volunteer generally showed a significant decline in well-being while serving abroad. A similar trend occurred for anxiety: while serving abroad, the level of anxiety of the volunteer increased significantly, although this level generally decreased upon his return to the United States. As problems of adjustment were also faced at home, the level of anxiety again rose, so that at the end of the three-year period anxiety levels were generally higher than at the beginning. In the area of authoritarianism, very different results were found. The volunteers showed a sharply significant and persisting decrease in authoritarian values from the time of their training to all later testing points.

Volunteers rank ordered a set of twenty personality needs in terms of importance to themselves. One year of experience abroad tended to make them less deferent and less counteractive, but more aggressive and more orderly than they were in training. After the full three years had passed, the volunteer continued to be less deferent but now was also less nurturant (likely to help others) and less affiliative (likely to join with others). He was still more aggressive and orderly than while in training. In general, Stein (1966, p. 227-28) portrays the volunteer as becoming less concerned with how others view him, and more capable of accepting others for what they are; he becomes less submissive and more self-reliant and independent.

Finally, the Peace Corps experience tended to make volunteers more active and interested in participating in nonpolitical community affairs as well as in political activities. Stein (1966, p. 229-30) indicates that for *non*-political affairs, 21 percent (N=52) participated prior to their Peace Corps experience; after a tour of duty in Colombia, 62 percent said they expected to participate, and six months later 27 percent were actually participating—an admittedly small effect on actual behavior. However, reported *political* activities (vs. attitudes) went from 10 percent "before" to 34 percent "after."

Lou Harris and Associates, Inc. (1969) performed another longitudinal study of the impact of the Peace Corps upon volunteers, comparing returned volunteers who had entered in 1962, 1964, and 1966 with control groups of persons who manifested interest in joining but who declined the invitation ("declines") or who joined but failed to serve a full two-year term overseas ("early returnees"). The study concludes that the three main sample groups do not differ in their organizational memberships (in political and other voluntary groups). Hence, the Peace Corps volunteer experience seems to have had little or no impact on such related voluntary activities and community concerns. However, joining and participating in the Peace Corps seems to have had the effect of maintaining liberal or radical political attitudes, while the group of "declines" showed a marked tendency to become more conservative or "middle of the road." Hence, Peace Corps experience did not "radicalize" people or make them more liberal, but it did tend to prevent career and other pressures from making people more conservative over the two-year period between training and subsequent testing.

In the same way, both volunteers and early returnees were significantly likely to maintain their willingness to participate in political actions relevant to a cause or issue they felt strongly about, while "declines" became over the two-year period significantly less likely to state they would participate in such activities. Once again, the volunteer experience had the effect of maintaining an earlier orientation that otherwise probably would have changed. With regard to domestic problems of various kinds, the declines tended to become more conservative, while the volunteers and early returnees were more likely to maintain their original liberal positions.

In summary (ibid., p. 119), Harris and Associates point out that the primary impact of the Peace Corps volunteer experience was in the area of attitudes (especially political attitudes), since all three sample groups started out with essentially the same attitudes and the "declines" were significantly different on several attitude dimensions after two years. There was much less apparent impact on career choice and employment plans, or on community behavior expectations. The marked similarity between the attitudes of volunteers and early returnees further suggests that the length of service is not so critical in the impact as is the personal decision and commitment to accept the Peace Corps service assignment when offered.

Gottlieb and Gold (1971) performed a similar study on VISTA volunteers, who serve for only one year as a kind of domestic Peace Corps helping with the problems of urban and rural poor. They surveyed all former VISTA volunteers and all persons accepted into the program who did not accept the offer during the period 1965-69. Data from the questionnaire administered could be compared with corresponding data collected at the time of application to VISTA. Some reasonable conclusions can be drawn about the probable impact of the volunteer experience since the demographic background characteristics of the volunteers and declines show the two groups to be quite similar.

There was little difference between the two sample groups on attitudes regarding domestic and international problems. However, significantly more volunteers considered themselves "revolutionaries" in terms of a self-descriptive checklist. Over the period since application was made to VISTA, both groups became generally more liberal or radical in political attitudes. The VISTA experience was given specifically by over half of the volunteer group as an important reason for their change in political attitudes (ibid. p. 68). Gottlieb and Gold (1971, p. 4) also conclude that volunteers are better prepared and more willing to make a commitment for social change and to do so through existing channels than are the declines.

The last two kinds of volunteer roles (Peace Corps and VISTA) that we have examined lead us to a consideration of a whole other class of voluntary action than we have generally considered so far in this section. We have now looked at both short and longer term kinds of social service-oriented externally focused instrumental volunteer programs. But we have not dealt with the class of social and political issued-oriented voluntary groups that generally are instrumental and also externally focused. Many of the most powerful social movements in human history fall into this latter category.

Many social scientists have been concerned with the nature of social movements in general and with their impact both on the individual and society (see Cantril 1941, Smelser 1963, Toch 1965, Wilkinson 1971). However, these reviews of the nature of social movements generally have found only impression-istic evidence of the impact on individual participants, insofar as they have considered this specific matter. By far the greatest amount of scholarly attention has gone into the origins, membership composition, functioning, and larger societal impact of these movements, not the impact on the participant. In fact, the ideological impact on the member-participant is usually taken for granted, rather than being seen as something that needs any systematic empirical demonstration or that might be subject to variations among participants. Given the very effective indoctrination and social control techniques of many social movements, this may at times not be far from the truth, but we believe it is still an open question until demonstrated by adequate research.

The various issue-oriented and political movements are generally distinguished by having some fairly clear set of ideological beliefs, values, attitudes, and so forth, which are communicated to new members. For the Nazi movement the pro-Aryan and anti-Semitic beliefs and values were important (Bullock 1952, Kedward 1969). The Communist party has had to convey its own set of beliefs and values regarding a "classless society," the historical role of the proletariat, the defects of capitalism, the optimal structuring of production, and so forth, with variations according to the "brand" of communism involved and the time period and country looked at (see Schapiro 1970, Liu Shao-Ch'i 1952, Monnerot 1960). For both the Fascists and the Communists, who have wielded extensive power in many nations at various times over the past several decades, indoctrina-tion of the members of the society at large as well as party members has been a central concern of the "Organizational Weapon," as Selznick (1952) has termed the totalitarian, party-controlled state. Even the Anarchists have had a set of beliefs and values to convey to new members of their groups, although their very nature has been rather anti-ideological (see Apter and Joll 1972, Woodcock 1968).

But social movements with a powerful ideology have not been confined to the category of political parties and groups. Churches, sects, and religious movements have often had an externally focused and instrumental component, seeking social justice and protesting social wrongs. The roots of these activities have generally been in various powerful theological doctrines about the nature of man and human society (see Troeltsch 1931, McCoy 1964). Religious sects growing from among the oppressed themselves likewise often tend to have an outward, society-changing thrust (see Lanternari 1965).

The various labor movements and trade unionism comprise another example of a powerful social movement which, although often quite politicized, is still analytically separable from political movements per se. For labor and even peasant movements, one key ideological point is often the matter of changing the social status and access to resources of a whole category of people in society (a class, in Marxian terms), as Landsberger suggests in Chapter 13 of this volume. There are, of course, many other special matters of belief and value that distinguish labor movements from various other kinds of social movements, though this ideological quality is sometimes lost in highly advanced industrial or postindustrial states like the United States.

Several studies describe in general terms the educational and socializing impacts of unions on their members, often with an emphasis on political orientations (Matthews and Ford 1966; Zon 1960). When students get involved in trade unionism, this may be viewed as a kind of anticipatory socialization relevant to later career roles (Pinner 1964).

In addition there are some studies that have focused in detail upon the impact of union membership and activity upon political attitudes and alienation. Sheppard and Masters (1959), in a study of Detroit auto workers, found the union to play a significant part in the political thinking of most of them. In a similar study, Wilensky (1956) found activity in a Chicago union local to have a significant impact on members' political orientations and positions on specific issues relevant to the union.

Neal and Seeman (1964) add some additional evidence of the impact of unions and other work-related voluntary associations in a sample of the adult male population of Columbus, Ohio. In general they found a sense of individual powerlessness (anomia) to be associated with *lack* of work-related associational affiliation. However, the observed results might as well be the outcome of differential selection to these associations, rather than the socializing impact of the groups themselves, since no longitudinal design was employed.

Political scientists have shown an increasing interest in the whole question of political socialization in recent years, yet relatively little is known about the amount and type of political socialization arising from voluntary association experiences. Langton (1969) suggests that peer groups (presumably both formal and informal) are as important an influence on one's sense of political efficacy as are formal school experiences (p. 154), but both are much less important influences on youth than their families in this regard (p. 155).

Sears (1969) reviews some of the relevant literature on the impact of political parties and other political organizations upon their members. He concludes that the overall impact of the parties in the United States tends to be weak and rather non-specific (p. 337). He notes that there is relatively little data on the impact of experiences after adolescence, but that impressionistic evidence suggests the importance of peer groups, climates of opinion, mass media, and so forth (p. 373, 387, 397).

Maccoby (1958), Freeman and Lambert (1965), and Freeman and Showel

(1962) all provide more specific evidence on the impact of voluntary organizational affiliation and activity upon volunteers. The observed impacts vary widely, however, from organization to organization, and there is some evidence that identification, rather than activity or membership *per se*, is crucial.

In the past decade or so there has been a resurgence of social movements concerned with various kinds of disadvantaged persons—women, blacks, American Indians, Mexican-Americans and others of Latin American background, and so forth in the United States. Each of these movements has its own powerful ideology and tries to indoctrinate newcomers to its own distinctive beliefs and values. This socialization process has itself been raised to the status of a primary goal, among others, by many such movements. In current parlance, "consciousness raising" is one of the most critical tasks of women's liberation (see Friedan 1963; Morgan 1970; and, for a decades earlier view of this movement, Flexner 1959), black power and black liberation (see Barbour 1968; Carmichael and Hamilton 1968), and similar movements. And within any broad movement, such as the black liberation movement, there are always many shades of ideology, many variations in beliefs, values, plans, and projections of the future (see Hughes 1962 on the NAACP, Bell 1968 on CORE, Zinn 1964 on SNCC, and Foner 1971 on the Black Panthers).

For present purposes the problem is, quite simply, that although large variations in ideology can obviously be seen among the various social movements of today and yesterday, there have been practically no quantitative empirical studies on the extent to which such social movements have had demonstrable personal impacts on samples of specific people over time. This is not to deny such personal impacts of social movements—doubtless they exist. But it is to say that our evidence on the matter is almost nonexistent, beyond general impressions and the documentation of intensive efforts to bring about such ideological and behavioral impacts.

Among other important points yet to be settled by research is the degree to which differential selection vs. actual experience with the social movement accounts for major personal differences between members and nonmembers. Similarly, we do not know whether the personal impacts that do take place are the result of direct socialization by the group, or more the result of incidental learning from "task experience," as discussed in the previous part of this chapter. Hopefully, future research will begin to settle some of these important issues, rather than ignoring the problem of personal impact in social movements as if it were automatic—thus committing a kind of fallacy ably described by Wrong (1961) as the "over-socialized conception of man."

Conclusions

The foregoing studies are not terribly compelling as a set, especially considering the wide range of activities that voluntary groups engage in and the anecdotal, impressionistic evidence of its impact that is often adduced. Most importantly, there have been no really comparative studies of the impact of volunteer experience in different kinds of instrumental, externally focused groups. And even the studies that have been done often leave much to be desired in the way of methodological techniques. Control groups of an appropriate sort are often not included, or a study may depend for its conclusions on the administration of test instruments at a single point in time. And where both control groups and a longitudinal approach are used appropriately, the time period of the study is often a relatively short one.

It may be argued, of course, that many volunteer experiences are by their very nature rather short term (e.g., a summer work camp). But we know from socialization research in general that the impact of a social environment is likely to be greater, other things equal, if it is able to operate on an individual over a longer period of time. Therefore, it is quite possible that many kinds of volunteer programs that seem to show little personal impact when short-term longitudinal evaluation studies are performed would show significant longer term impacts if the appropriate follow-up studies were made.

In any event, we can draw some very tentative conclusions from the foregoing studies. First, instrumental, externally focused voluntary groups and programs do often have some significant kinds of personal impact on their participants. Hence, we may expect even stronger and more consistent personal impacts in instrumental, internally focused groups where personal impact is the explicit aim (see the next section). Nevertheless, the data are very patchy, the nature of the impacts vary from group to group, and there are volunteer groups and programs that do not show much personal impact, if any.

Second, at least some quantitative empirical evidence has been found to indicate that instrumental, externally focused volunteer groups and programs have an impact on most of the types of characteristics suggested at the beginning of this part of the present chapter—beliefs, dispositions, emotions, capacities and behavior.

Beliefs. The service-oriented kind of volunteer roles seem most likely to affect specific kinds of information and knowledge directly related to the voluntary group/program they are associated with and the environment in which it functions. If volunteers are working in a mental hospital, they will learn more about what goes on there and how mental patients behave, often breaking down formerly held stereotypes. If they are working in a poor rural community or a prison or elsewhere, they will develop correspondingly more realistic pictures of what prisons or rural poverty or a particular country are like, often destroying or at least altering major aspects of more stereotyped beliefs about these settings.

We have not found anything in the way of solid, quantitative empirical studies of the personal impact of more ideological social movements that are an important form of externally focused, instrumental, voluntary organization. Yet impressionistic and anecdotal evidence, often from sensitive observers and social scientists, suggest that social movements have marked personal impacts on the beliefs, knowledge, and information of their participants.

Dispositions. There is more evidence on the impact of voluntary groups upon the dispositions of members than there is for the other kinds of personal impact we are considering. Service-oriented volunteer groups and programs are especially likely to affect participants' attitudes toward specific aspects of the volunteer role or its setting and role partners. For instance, volunteer mental patient "companions" are likely to develop more favorable attitudes toward mental illness and toward mental patients as a class of people. In general, but not always, service volunteers seem to become more tolerant in their attitudes toward the negative aspects of the problems, settings, groups, or people to be helped (e.g., toward prisons, convicts, delinquents, unwed mothers, the handicapped, poverty, sexual behavior, aggressive behavior, etc.). We may state that social service volunteers working with the disadvantaged—whatever the particular problems of the latter (health, social deviance, poverty, etc.)—tend to become less "up tight" or conventionally moralistic about various kinds of deviations from the norms of middle-class respectability in their own society (norms that will vary with time and place, of course).

Community social service volunteers (as contrasted with personal problem service volunteers) seem also to be affected in the realm of political attitudes. If volunteers work intensively with community social problems of the disadvantaged in the United States or abroad, they tend either (a) to maintain more liberal or radical political attitudes (both regarding domestic and international matters) while the attitudes of control group persons decline, or else (b) to increase in such attitudes after several months or more of experience. Sometimes the volunteer's attitudes toward community organizations and civic responsibilities in general may decline, while his more specific commitment to social change and willingness to engage in political or social action, where the issue really concerns him, is enhanced.

This general "liberalizing" or, some might say, "radicalizing" impact of community social service volunteer roles does not seem to operate in a simple manner, but rather occurs as part of a cycle. The usual first reaction of the community social service volunteer is to be overwhelmed by the magnitude of the problems; he goes into a state of "culture shock." If a longitudinal evaluation study performs a follow-up at this point, as Townsend (1972) did, the results are likely to show that the volunteer experience has a depressive effect on civic responsibility and social involvement. However, if the volunteer experience continues, the participant is likely to be able to come to grips with the problems facing the disadvantaged people and community he is trying to help. At the same time he will tend to develop or at least maintain liberal or radical social and political attitudes that are seen to be facilitative of more basic reform and social change in society as a way of *preventing* community problems of the sort he is asked to deal with as a volunteer.

In sum, the scanty evidence reviewed here suggests fairly consistently that service-oriented volunteers working with various kinds of disadvantaged people are likely to become more accepting of others' foibles and deviations from middle-class norms; while those volunteers involved with community social problems (rather than more personal problems) tend also to become more social change oriented in their attitudes and more liberal politically.

With regard to more political or issue-oriented voluntary groups and social movements, the available evidence indicates that participation tends to enhance the political interests and focus more sharply the political attitudes of those involved, although the participants are likely to be self-selected and recruited as already fairly high on these dimensions. This effect may be most marked for the disadvantaged as volunteers (not clients). For most political and issue-oriented social movements, however, we lack adequate quantitative data to demonstrate the many kinds of other attitudes and values that anecdotal reports suggest are probably affected as well.

Several studies have focused on how volunteer experiences have affected personality traits and needs. Intensive social service volunteer experience, whether short or long term, seems to lead rather consistently to greater self-insight, self-acceptance, self-assuredness and what may be termed "ego strength." Facing and dealing, however imperfectly, with the problems of disadvantaged people tends to act as a kind of "tempering" experience, forcing people to recognize and accept both their own strengths and weaknesses if they are to cope with the volunteer role requirements, as well as changing their attitudes toward and acceptance of others as we have suggested above. This increased self-insight does not come easily, however, and usually results from a period of much soul searching, anguish, and even despair. Again, if one tested people while they were in the midst of this self-examination process, rather than after its successful conclusion, one would draw very different conclusions regarding the impact of the volunteer experience. It is doubtless also true that many volunteers (though an unknown percentage) are not able to achieve this heightened self-insight, perhaps dropping out when the going gets rough.

Research into other personality traits and characteristics has produced less consistent results. Sometimes volunteer experience increases aggressiveness, while in other cases it decreases this need. With some slight consistency, however, social service volunteer experience has tended to increase the needs for independence, achievement and expression of personal competence, while decreasing deference, authoritarianism, alienation, and anomie. Yet again volunteer experience has sometimes increased compassion while in other studies it has decreased the similar need to be "nurturant" (helpfulness to people). Hence, the most balanced conclusion here is that social service volunteer roles often do seem to have an impact on personality traits and needs, but this impact varies in direction and content from role to role. Much more research will be necessary before we know much about why and how these impacts vary systematically.

But at least we can be sure that there are some personality impacts, in addition to any impacts on attitudes discussed earlier.

Again anecdotal evidence suggests that issue-oriented voluntary groups and social movements will often have powerful impacts on the personality, as well as their impacts on beliefs and attitudes already alluded to. Milgram and Toch (1969, p. 594) suggest that for many social movements, perhaps most, "the member's needs and purposes become tied to the community of members, and to the movement's aims. A member may come to feel, in the long run, that his personal identity depends completely on his membership." The process whereby the member becomes so closely bound up with his social movement or group is frequently a kind of "conversion experience," affecting the deepest roots of selfhood and personality. Unfortunately, these kinds of processes are difficult to study, especially longitudinally. Partly as a result of this, as well as for other reasons, we can at present do little more than to make a plea for more adequate, quantitative research on the matter.

There are other areas of personal dispositions that might also be affected by voluntary action experience—plans, hopes, values, occupational interests, and so forth. These kinds of dispositions have been even less studied than attitudes, personality traits, and needs, however. We can therefore conclude little more than that they are likely to be affected by certain kinds of volunteer experiences, although we know of only anecdotal evidence indicating this, except for vocational choice, where there is conflicting evidence suggesting some impact at times.

Emotions. Only a small beginning has been made on seeing how volunteer experiences affect feelings and emotional states. The present evidence suggests most clearly, though still only tentatively, that service volunteer experience with disadvantaged people of various kinds tends to lead to anxiety, despair, bitterness, outrage, anger, and other related negative emotions. Unlike other personal characteristics, however, emotions show a great deal of variation within the individual over time. Hence, the above conclusion does not necessarily mean that service volunteer experiences with the disadvantaged lead to a permanent kind of continuous depression and/or anger. Yet some studies, like one of returned Peace Corps volunteers, even show that such emotional effects can persist over fairly long periods of time (in this case, the impact was to heighten anxiety levels).

Given the plight and problems of disadvantaged people, the generally negative emotional impact on volunteers working intensively or extensively with them is neither surprising nor unrealistic. Anyone who expects such volunteer work to be "a picnic" has a lot to learn (see the earlier section on beliefs). At least the volunteer can go home at night or can eventually (voluntarily) leave his confrontation with the problems of the disadvantaged. The disadvantaged usually cannot "leave."

Anecdotal evidence suggests that most kinds of social service volunteers also experience a very deep and personal sense of satisfaction with their activity (which is not inconsistent with the negative emotions noted above). So far, such feelings have not been captured by any of the quantitative research we have reviewed, yet we are still inclined to view this as a probable hypothesis on the basis of our reading of the literature. We suspect, however, that the general feeling of "pure" satisfaction with volunteer work may be more common among volunteers who are only superficially involved in social service programs, than among those volunteers who become more deeply committed to dealing with the real problems of real people whom they come to know and understand well. A "bittersweet" emotional mix of combined joys and sadnesses, satisfactions and outrages, seems more likely as a realistic outcome.

In the realm of social movements, the foregoing statement is likely also to hold true, although there is one kind of exception (which we shall take up more extensively in the next section). The exception is that in highly ideological social movements, especially where there is a religious or quasi-religious fervor and a kind of intensive community of fellowship among the members, a heightened state of psychological well-being and "excitement with life" may often be achieved and may persist over time. This is a frequent accompaniment to genuine conversion experiences, particularly when the "convert" then devotes himself to the cause wholeheartedly and works to bring others to "enlightenment." The evidence here is again only impressionistic and anecdotal, but the point is well worth pursuing in some quantitative research in the future.

Capacities. In spite of the theoretical suggestions by Rose (1954, Chap. 3) and others that voluntary action can be a training ground for democracy and an opportunity to learn social, verbal, physical and other skills, we have not found any quantitative research bearing on this matter. Therefore, we cannot draw any conclusions based on satisfactory empirical evidence here, but we can and do urge researchers give some concentrated attention to this kind of personal impact in the future.

Behavior. Since all volunteer roles, virtually without exception, require certain distinctive kinds of behavior of their participants, it is almost a tautology to ask whether voluntary action affects the behavior of the volunteer. Nevertheless, there is room for nonconformity to varying degrees in all voluntary groups and programs. There are also usually marked variations among different people in how much they will conform behaviorally to any given set of group norms. Further, there may be many unintended behavioral consequences of participation in a particular volunteer role, in addition to the kinds of behavioral conformity or compliance consciously sought from volunteers in a given group or program. There has been practically no quantitative research on the matter, however, as far as the present authors could ascertain. Researchers investigating the impact of voluntary action on the volunteer have seldom gathered records, structured observational material, or unobtrusive measures of various possible kinds regarding volunteer behavior. Where such data has been collected, it has usually been with regard to the behaviors required by the volunteer role.

Primarily anecdotal evidence suggests that most volunteers *do* have their behavior affected by the explicit social expectations of their role in a voluntary group or program. We have little or precise knowledge about the variations in such compliance across participants, roles, or types of groups, however, nor any information regarding why such variations might systematically occur. We also lack knowledge regarding the unintended and incidental behavioral consequences of volunteer roles. Finally, we lack knowledge of how the behavior of volunteers, either in or out of voluntary group contexts, is influenced by situational conformity factors as contrasted with more internalized dispositions, attitudes, traits, etc.

Third, as would be expected from social science research in other areas, the evidence we have examined suggests that voluntary action tends to have a greater personal impact where the volunteer is participating in more intensive, full-time, longer term, and more psychically involving roles than where the volunteer participates in a more superficial, part-time, short-term, or not psychically involving role. This means that within any volunteer program or voluntary group, the most active and involved members are likely to show the greatest personal impact of the experience. It also means that a summer work camp or other intensive volunteer experience is likely to have more impact than a volunteer experience for a few hours a week or month, even over a longer period. It means that quasi-volunteer experiences of an intensive sort over a period of a year or more, like Peace Corps and VISTA, are likely to have more impact than either of the former types of voluntary action, but this kind of limited commitment voluntary action will still not have the impact of a lifelong, intensive, if part-time commitment to some highly ideological and active social movement. This hierarchical series of relative degrees of impact has never been tested directly, however, so it must be more of a hypothesis than an empirical generalization. Our reading of the literature merely suggests such a hierarchy, based on the broad conclusion stated above. Of course, behavior is likely to be affected more while the volunteer is in a volunteer setting than after he or she has left it.

Fourth, in spite of the apparent association between intensity/extensity of volunteer experience and the amount of resulting personal impact, there is also some scanty but suggestive evidence that joining and participating in certain kinds of voluntary groups has almost immediate commitment/conversion personal impacts. In addition to the results along this line from Stein's (1966) Peace Corps study, there has also been some relevant experimental research by psychologists on the effects of severity of initiation on liking for a group (Gerard and Mathewson 1966; see also Smith 1972b). By far the largest amount of evidence, however, is from anecdotal sources regarding "conversion experiences" and the absorption into social movements that provide a powerful ideological/psychological/interpersonal atmosphere. More extensive quantitative research in this area would obviously be helpful, especially with regard to showing how, why, and under what circumstances such conversion/commitment effects occur.

Impacts in Expressive and Internally Focused
Instrumental (Self-Help) Groups

Where the previous part of this chapter dealt with externally focused instrumental groups, the present part reviews some of the literature on internally focused instrumental groups, as well as research on expressive groups. We treat these two different kinds of voluntary groups together here because in practice they are often difficult to distinguish, even though the polar cases may be clearly different. Both expressive groups and internally focused instrumental groups primarily aim at affecting their members, volunteers, or participants (i.e., both are internally focused). The primary difference between them is that the expressive group sees its activities primarily as ends in themselves, to be performed for their sheer enjoyment, edification, or satisfaction. By contrast, the primary aim of an internally focused instrumental group is to change or affect the members in some way—to make them better, more sober, more skilled, more healthy, thinner, more normal, more informed, and so forth. The two kinds of groups are hard to distinguish in a middle ground area where the group activity is both consciously enjoyable for its own sake as well as change-producing in some personal way (e.g., discussion groups, youth groups involving the learning of various skills, religious groups that aim at personal rehabilitation, etc.). In reviewing what literature we have been able to find regarding personal impact, we shall begin with more purely expressive groups, as we see them, and proceed toward more clearly instrumental internally focused groups, without attempting to make any clear line of demarcation in the middle.

William A. Scott's study (1965) of college fraternities and sororities provides some evidence on the impact of an expressive voluntary organization with notably higher levels of member interaction than most groups tend to have. Scott makes a strong case for selection processes when he notes relatively small value change among his respondents. Several groups ("houses") made no distinctive impacts on their pledge groups and there were probably no distinctive impacts on those considered most susceptible (the pledges most attracted to their organization).

Indeed, Scott found some evidence that, within any single fraternity or sorority house, a trend toward value heterogeneity was more likely than a trend toward value homogeneity. On each of the twelve measured values, there were no significant differences in changes over a one-year period between all pledges and all nonpledges. However, when the pattern of all twelve values was used, there was some evidence that pledges and nonpledges tended to shift in different directions, pledges moving toward the value patterns of active fraternity and sorority members.

Scott had hypothesized that fraternities and sororities would have relatively high potential for impact, since membership in them would likely be highly valued, clear ingroup-outgroup distinctions existed, and enduring and relatively high rates of member interaction prevailed. However, Scott found that these organizations tended to recruit new members holding values already similar in content and strength to those of the current membership. Hence, new members had little latitude for change in the direction of greater similarity to other group members. Extrapolating from his data, Scott (1965, p. 225) ventures that "perhaps it is in the nature of voluntary groups to attract new members who already believe strongly in the essential values by which the groups function." On this basis, Scott (ibid.) hypothesized that "value influence in natural settings is more apt to occur when a person unintentionally get himself into a compelling (i.e., enjoyable or necessary) circumstance in which new values are being promulgated, and he has little choice but to attend, and insufficient social support to oppose them." In short, he suggests value change is more likely as an unintended consequence of voluntary participation.

Some research on happiness or psychological well-being has looked at community and voluntary participation, including informal social activity, as one of several possible causal factors. For instance, Scott (1971) found that happy individuals tended to be more concerned with helping others, helping the community and mankind. Yet there was no explicit mention of voluntary participation here, nor any clear indication that such participation caused the greater happiness—merely some suggestive conclusions on the part of the investigator after studying hundreds of protocols written by various kinds of respondents in answer to questions tapping various aspects of happiness in their lives.

More explicit attention to social participation is found in Bradburn and Caplovitz's (1965) study of the determinants of happiness in normal populations in several towns. In this work they were able to make some major breakthroughs in understanding the nature and determinants of happiness. They established, for instance, that happiness has two essentially independent components—positive affect (feelings) and negative affect, with the two being relatively unrelated over short periods of time. That is, a person may have a lot or a little of either kind of feeling without necessitating a corresponding level on the other kind. In addition, they found that different kinds of background factors and experiences were associated with the two aspects or components of overall happiness. Thus sickness is associated with negative affect, but health does not significantly make for positive affect. On the other hand, going to a movie tends to be associated with positive affect, but failure to go to one in a given period does not usually cause negative affect.

Most relevant to present concerns, they found voluntary participation and social interaction to be associated with greater happiness and especially with positive affect, while marked absence of these experiences (i.e., social isolation) was associated with negative affect in general. This suggests that voluntary action, both formally and informally organized, may affect the happiness of members/participants significantly. Since there were no repeated measurements in this cross-sectional study, however, we cannot be sure whether the participation leads to greater positive affect, or whether some other confounding variable is affecting both participation and positive affect.

In a more recent study, Bradburn (1969) has extended and elaborated the findings of a earlier study using new area probability samples from the inner city, working-class suburbs, a middle-class suburban county, and from the ten largest metropolitan areas in the country. The people in each sample were interviewed at least twice, and in one suburban sample four times, with nearly three thousand people participating as respondents in the study as a whole. Bradburn was again able to show that overall happiness was the result of the relative balance of positive and negative affect in a person's life, with the latter two factors being essentially unrelated (ibid., chap. 4). Test-retest reliability of the happiness and affect items was quite high when a three-day interval intervened, and even after several months the stability was reasonably high, indicating that the measures might be used to draw reasonable conclusions about the determinants or at least the correlates of avowed happiness (ibid., chap. 5).

For present purposes, the key substantive results are presented by Bradburn in Chapter 8, where he describes the relationships he found between positive affect and social participation. It is unfortunate that Bradburn uses a composite measure of social participation, combining items dealing with activity in voluntary organizations, getting together with friends, chatting with friends on the phone, meeting new people, making new friends, being in touch with relatives, and longest noncommuting trip made recently. Nevertheless, all of these kinds of social participation can take place in voluntary groups, especially expressive or internally focused ones; and by a broad definition they all represent informal and formal kinds of voluntary participation. The various items are intercorrelated positively.

Once again the analysis showed social participation to be significantly associated with positive affect, though not with negative affect in general. Among the various social participation items, those dealing with the novelty aspect (new people, new places, new friends) tended to be somewhat more closely associated with positive affect than those items dealing simply with sociability per se (chatting with friends, activity in organizations, being in touch with relatives). When separate sociability and novelty indices were created, the novelty index (new and varied experiences) was more closely associated with positive affect than the sociability index (even when controlling for socioeconomic status), although they were both correlated significantly with each other and with socioeconomic status.

Most importantly, Bradburn examines how changes in social participation over a ten month interval between interviews relate to changes in positive affect (ibid., p. 136 ff). The results were not strong enough to be statistically significant, but they clearly and consistently went in the expected directions: Those who markedly increased their social participation (i.e., from low to high) showed marked increases in positive affect, while those who decreased their social participation tended to report decreased positive affect, and those who did not change their social participation levels or who showed only moderate increases did not change much in their levels of positive affect. The failure of these results to reach statistical significance was puzzling, however, and Bradburn refrains from drawing any direct causal inferences. He does suggest the likelihood of a feedback loop of causality here, with greater social participation leading to greater positive affect, which in turn may lead to enhanced social participation.

Smith (1970) and Phillips (1967a, b; 1969) have performed studies that generally corroborate the findings of Bradburn (1969) and Bradburn and Caplovitz (1965). In both instances, social participation—including voluntary organization activity and social participation measures similar to those used by Bradburn—has been found associated with greater happiness, even when variables such as socioeconomic status are controlled. Because these studies have been cross-sectional, however, causal inferences are even more difficult to make than in the case of the Bradburn study. All that we can be sure of is that overall happiness (and positive affect in particular) tends to be significantly associated with voluntary group participation as well as with various forms of informal social participation. The emphasis has been on the sociability and new experience aspects of such participation, rather than on instrumental accomplishment, however.

In a long-term longitudinal study dealing with the effects of 4-H Club activity, Wu (1968) examined data from 339 persons who had lived in their respective communities from first grade through high school and who were tested at grades one, six, twelve, and five years after high school. Controlling for extraneous variables, 4-H club membership was found to be associated with later participation in, and attitudes toward, adult education. Membership also was significantly related to rural youth interests, which in turn affected personal social behavior and adult occupational choices. Lack of a control group somewhat vitiates the results of this study, but the very long time span and focus on adult behavior make it interesting nonetheless.

A related study by Atkins (1969) investigated changes among 4-H Club members after their volunteer leaders had taken a short human relations course. The 200 youth members and their 30 adult volunteer leaders were divided into experimental and control groups, with the control group leaders receiving a short course in local government instead of the human relations course. Other aspects of the course and group interaction were controlled. The leaders and the club members filled out a personal checklist and self-portrait both before and after the training the leaders received. The members of the clubs exposed to the trained leaders gained significantly in "desirable positive behavior" and in "favorable self-evaluation," compared to the control group, while the trained leaders themselves gained significantly in level of achievement and acceptance of others.

Davis (1960, 1961) reports on the impact of participation in the Great Books Program. In Great Books, members meet in small voluntary groups about twice a month to discuss selected sections of the classics of Western literature. He found no change in basic values as a result of participation in the program. But, as the result of exposure to differing positions in an "intellectual" discussion context, a tendency toward a greater acceptance (but not necessarily espousal) of liberal and skeptical approaches to religion was discovered. Members commonly indicated some change in atttitudes toward some author or school of thought.

Members were typically "cosmopolitan" in orientation but not without relatively high levels of participation in the local community. A slight tendency toward increased participation (behavior) was noted along with a marked increase in understanding of local issues and problems (knowledge). Although members were already heavy readers, continued participation in the Great Books Program tends to increase the total amount of outside serious reading.

Not surprisingly, the strongest and clearest reported effect of participation in the program was increased knowledge of the liberal arts and humanities. Advanced year participants were found more knowledgeable in the liberal arts and humanities than first year participants. Indeed, with his measuring criteria, Davis found those having three years in the program and no college education scored as well as beginning members with bachelor's degrees. Nevertheless, there was no marked improvement in esthetic tastes in terms of current cultural standards. Although exposed to a considerable amount of verse in the program, advanced-year members were not better judges of "excellence" in verse than were new members. Members were also tested on another esthetic dimension, one not directly a part of the Great Books Program—their familiarity with classical music. Once more no "spillover" effect could be found.

Individuals typically join Great Books seeking intellectual stimulation from the works themselves as well as from the opportunity for discussing these works with others of similar orientations and aspirations. Levels of satisfaction run high in the program, with those initially dissatisfied commonly dropping out quickly. A high proportion of members report "genuine" impacts resulting from participation. However, it would seem that the program is sufficiently diffuse so that the "major determinant of an effect is the participant's motivation" (Davis, 1960, p. 113). Members indicating they sought a specific effect are markedly more likely to report having achieved it, especially when these goals could be attained through the normal processes of discussion in the group and were not focused on events or activities outside the group's ambit.

Davis notes that the impact of Great Books is itself mediated by prior and present patterns and habits of interaction learned in roles and situations outside the program. Of these, Davis especially pointed to the large influence of sex roles and marital status roles on the activity levels and quality of group role performance (1961, p. 84 and ff.), contrasting these with "the relative failure of intrinsic aspects of the group process, such as role function or leadership, to affect the outcome" (1961, p. 219).

Finally, Davis notes that the net effect of the Great Books Program on the total society provides but another confirmation of the general principle: "them as has, gets." That is, in general, "Great Books tend to keep, not those who have needed the most intellectual growth, but those whose preparation and interest are already strong" (1961, p. 217). However, Davis notes that the true relationship between preparation and participation is more likely curvilinear— with highest drop-out rates among those who are least prepared and most in need, as well as those who are most prepared and least in need.

In sum, personal impacts do take place as the result of the Great Books Program. The greatest measured changes result from exposure to and increased knowledge of the literature itself. The impact is, however, quite specific to the literature dealt with and is not generally transferable to the evaluation of other literature or of classical music. Although members tend to become more intellectually tolerant of differing positions, no general value changes were noted. Overall, the Great Books Program is sufficiently diffuse that members may report a variety of primary impacts—usually the ones they say they sought when entering the program.

It is important to note that the significant impact of this kind of voluntary group fits well with earlier theory and research on personal impact that we have reviewed. Great Books discussion groups are small, intensive, interpersonal action settings with rather clear general goals and implied norms. They are a kind of mild self-help group, rather than trying to change outsiders or the larger society. Hence, it is to be expected that they would have more impact than large, superficial, non face-to-face, externally oriented groups might have (e.g., many volunteer service programs or mass membership voluntary groups). However, the impacts found are likely to be less in a *self-improvement* group like Great Books as contrasted with *self-remedy* groups like Alcoholics Anonymous, which we consider later.

Three areas of partly expressive and partly self-help voluntary action have received very little systematic, quantitative research attention relevant to present concerns in spite of the probability of their having important impacts on participants. One area is religious groups, congregations, sects, and movements. In modern society, nearly all religions are essentially voluntary organizations, with a relatively small paid staff (clergy) and a large majority of volunteer participants (laymen). Although, as we saw in an earlier part of this chapter, the family and religious schooling have important impacts on individual religious behavior, the church and its many kinds of affiliated and auxiliary groups are also likely to have some effects themselves (e.g., through volunteer "Sunday Schools"). This is particularly likely to be the case for small, very close knit sects, especially if they are in some sense socially "deviant" or oppressed.

The works by Lincoln (1961) and Essien-Udom (1964) suggest at least impressionistically the kinds of far-reaching effects that conversion to the "Black Muslims" (the Black Nation of Islam) can have on blacks in the United States who have joined this movement. This sect stresses the suffering of the blacks at the hands of whites and Christians, and presents a world view and way of life that makes a complete break with prior habits and beliefs, in many cases. Black separatism and independence are emphasized rather than integration, a new Muslim name is adopted (as the boxer Cassius Clay became Muhammed Ali), and new habits of abstemiousness, "morality," achievement, hard work, and saving are substituted for previous life patterns. There seem to be no before and after quantitative research studies on this kind of transformation. But enough anecdotal material exists, even in the case of famous sports figures, to make it clear that the personal impact of joining and participating in this sect can be very real and far-reaching indeed.

An even smaller and less well established kind of sect, the "Doomsday Cult," has received some careful attention from Festinger et al. (1956). Their primary purpose in studying this group was to see how attitudes of the members were affected by the group and by the discrepancy between the group's beliefs and objective reality. Since the group's beliefs were so idiosyncratic, there could be no doubt that members of the sect came to hold these beliefs as a result of experiences within the group. A major belief of the group was that the world would end on a specified date and at a specified time, not too far off. Festinger was able to observe the group members on that very day at the appointed time. When nothing happened, some of the group members resolved the "cognitive dissonance" by realizing that their previously held beliefs were simply false. But other members seized upon a rationalization of the leader that predicted another date and explained why "doomsday" had not come at the appointed hour. The latter members tended subsequently to become even *more* fervent in their beliefs and more active in trying to recruit others to the group, an outcome that Festinger interpreted as an alternative way of reducing cognitive dissonance for these members (the unconscious logic being, roughly, that "if other people can be convinced to believe what I believe, then there must be something to it").

The second area of self-help voluntary action that could bear a great deal of attention is the whole question of scientific society/association participation. Insofar as such groups are dedicated to a greater scientific understanding of some kind of natural phenomena (rather than primarily toward enhancement of the economic position of their members), they fall into the category of internally focused instrumental groups. Many, perhaps most scientists are probably "pseudo-members" (see Smith 1972c) of scientific associations, their participation consisting of little more than paying dues and reading a particular journal at times. Yet for those who are more active participants, scientific societies may have a major impact on their general job and life satisfaction, their intellectual progress, their friendships, their attitudes toward particular scholars and particular areas of research, their perceptions of the proper role of science in contemporary society, even their general political attitudes. We know of no research that explores these matters, however.

The third area of instrumentally oriented but internally focused voluntary action that needs significant amounts of personal impact research is the realm of businessmen's groups, professional associations (with an economic rather than primarily scientific thrust), trade unions, and other economic self-interest (hence, self-help) voluntary groups. The large literature on trade unions (e.g., Clegg, Fox, and Thompson, 1964; Lorwin, 1953) and the much smaller amount of study devoted to other kinds of economic self-interest voluntary groups (e.g., Holtzman, 1963) make it clear that such groups do generally have important economic impacts on or for their members (or for the members of relevant occupations/professions/businesses in general). But practically no attention has been given, that we know of, to the more personal impacts of such voluntary groups upon the attitudes, beliefs, skills, emotions, and behavior of their members.

One kind of longer term, economic self-interest volunteer experience that has received some research attention is reported by Inkeles and Smith (1973). They focus on the probable personal impacts of participation by poor, uneducated subsistence farmers in a rural cooperative in East Pakistan (now Bangladesh). Their principle measure of impact was the "OM Scale," an overall measure of psychosocial individual modernity of attitudes, information, beliefs, and self-reported behavior. Comparing men who were members of the Comilla Cooperative with a control group of men from the same villages who were not members, they found the members to be significantly higher in modernity after an average exposure of about three years to the cooperative. This impact was attributable to experiences in the cooperative because other major influences had been controlled in a complex matching procedure. Statistical controls applied via multiple regression analysis led to a similar conclusion.

The Comilla Cooperative was a very special kind of cooperative, however, and it is not clear that similar results would be found in other instances. It was founded and run by a charismatic leader, with support from the national government, and functioned almost as a school for modernity. Among other things members were taught better farming and money management techniques and their wives were instructed in family planning and improved homemaking and child-rearing techniques. Still, this same kind of experience could be provided by other cooperatives, as well as other kinds of rural voluntary organizations. Of course, it may be questioned whether a particular cooperative *is* a voluntary organization, since it may be nothing more than a profit-making business. But in this case it was a highly ideological, public-interest oriented, essentially not-for-profit organization whose aim was to raise the living standards and quality of life of rural Pakistanis. Hence, we may term it a quasi-voluntary organization, at least.

The observed greater modernity of the cooperative members in this study may be interpreted as evidence that their voluntary participation in the cooperative caused them to become generally more efficacious, higher in aspirations, more open to change and new experiences, more aware of the world beyond their village, more politically involved, and so forth. This effect on OM scores was all the more striking since it rivalled in strength the impact of several years of formal education or factory experience that was found for other men in the study samples.

Zurcher (1970) performed a longitudinal study of the impact of voluntary participation on lower income individuals. He administered questionnaires to a very heterogeneous group—the board members of a local poverty program. The board consisted of "target neighborhood committee officers" representing the poor as well as government and agency officials, businessmen, professionals, religious and civic leaders, and so forth. The poor were significantly different from the rest of the board members in their level of annual family income, level of formal education, and their number of memberships in voluntary associations. On a battery of social-psychological questions, the poor were significantly different and low on activism, achievement orientation, and future orientation, while significantly different and high on anomie, isolation, normlessness, powerlessness, alienation, and particularism.

Seven months later the questionnaire was again administered to those who still remained on the board. The nonpoor were not significantly changed by their experiences during that period of time. But the poor showed significant increases in activism and achievement orientation, while particularism decreased significantly. Changes which did not reach statistical significance were found in decreased anomie, isolation, normlessness, and alienation, with increased integration with relatives. An insignificant increase in felt powerlessness was interpreted as being situation specific—that is, there was an ongoing dispute between the poor on the board and the director of the local community action agency over power-allocation and decision-making. Those among the poor board members who were more active in the board's efforts showed significantly greater increases in activism and achievement orientation, and decreases in normlessness and alienation.

Perhaps the most clearly instrumental and internally focused kind of self-help voluntary group is the "self-remedy" group of various kinds. As a class, this kind of group has been emerging into prominence in the United States, especially in the past decade or so, though its roots go back much further. In parallel to this development in the United States and other highly industrialized countries, there has been a corresponding growth (on a smaller scale) of indigenous self-help groups in lesser developed countries (Alvarez 1970). These have grown up partly as a reaction from the belief that "export volunteer" programs like the Peace Corps and its equivalent from the other developed countries of the world are a form of "neocolonialism," unless and until they focus on helping the people of developing countries to help themselves (see Roberts 1968).

The distinguishing characteristic of a self-help group of the self-remedy type is that its members recognize that they have a common personal problem that can be at least partially remedied by their own efforts in cooperation with others. The focus of the activity is on changing the members of the group in some way, although this may include changing the roles these members play outside the group in the larger community. Self-help groups of the self-improvement type focus on enhancing the characteristics of people (members) who do·not really have a basic problem, but would like to increase their skill, knowledge, etc. in some area. All self-help groups are definitely more than "social clubs"—they are dedicated to some kind of change in the personal characteristics or situation of their members, not simply to the enjoyment of common fellowship or recreation/amusement.

Because the primary purpose of self-help groups is an instrumental one, and because the focus of their activity is inward, toward changing the members/ participants/volunteers, we may expect the greatest amount of personal impact to be found generally within this category of groups rather than among simply expressive groups or among externally focused instrumental groups. There are numerous examples of this kind of group in the United States that have grown up in recent years, and still more seem to be arising each year.

One of the earliest, and perhaps the largest and best known self-remedy voluntary association in the United States is Alcoholics Anonymous, an organization where alcoholics and former alcoholics try to help each other "dry out" and stay sober, while resuming a more normal family, occupational and community life. Narcotics Anonymous, also one of the earliest self-help groups, does the same kind of thing for drug addicts and former drug addicts (see also Addicts Anonymous and Synanon). Similar organizations have arisen among people with mental health/illness problems (Neurotics Anonymous, Schizophrenics Anonymous), the overweight (Fatties Anonymous, Overeaters Anonymous), ex-convicts (Adults Anonymous, Recidivists Anonymous), forgers (Checks Anonymous), juvenile delinquents (Youth Anonymous and Delinquents Anonymous), unsuccessful suicides (Suicides Anonymous), gamblers (Gamblers Anonymous), smokers (Smokers Anonymous), child abusers (Parents Anonymous), and so forth. The best single work on this category of self-remedy organizations is Sagarin's (1969) *Odd Man In*.

There are many other kinds of self-remedy, self-help groups that have not adopted the "____ Anonymous" format. For instance, there are many clubs of ex-mental patients, handicapped, divorced or widowed persons, persons with rare blood, persons with special/rare diseases, unemployed executives and professionals over forty, and persons in poor physical condition desiring to improve themselves through exercise. In addition, there is a whole host of formal and informal self-improvement self-help groups aimed at one or another kind of adult education and psychological, mental, moral, or spiritual improvement of their members. Still other self-improvement groups attempt to improve the musical, artistic, dramatic, sports, speaking, writing, interpersonal relations, or practical/manual arts skills of their members. Many youth groups like the Boy and Girl Scouts, 4-H, Campfire Girls, and so on have a significant amount of this self-help and personal improvement quality, although the sociability component is also strong.

There have been a few studies of some kinds of self-help groups, but most kinds of self-remedy, self-help groups have not even been described adequately in the social science literature, let alone having their impact on members adequately evaluated. We shall mention briefly the research done on three of the most common and oldest types of self-remedy, self-help groups—Alcoholics Anonymous, Narcotics Anonymous, and ex-mental patient groups.

Alcoholics Anonymous (or "AA") occupies a very special and peculiar place among self-help groups. On the one hand, researchers in the field of alcohol studies generally recognize that it works—that it has a significant success with rehabilitating and "drying out" its members (see Trice 1966, p. 98 ff.; Root 1967, p. 142). Indeed, Maxwell (1962) states that "it is probable that more contemporary alcoholics have found sobriety through the fellowship of Alcoholics Anonymous than through all other agencies combined." Yet, he goes on to say, many people see the program of AA as an enigma. We would add that it is strange so little adequate evaluative research has been done on this group, given its apparent success. One key reason for its relative neglect by researchers may be simple egotism and pride. Most alcohol researchers are much more interested in (and rewarded for) studying the effects of programs they and their colleagues have devised and operated than in examining AA which has had no "professional guidance"—even though it apparently works much better than their "professional programs" in most cases. The lay language and "spiritual" concepts embodied in the AA program and ideology have also been a stumbling block preventing many social scientists from trying to understand what is going on (see Ritchie 1955).

The study done by Maxwell (1949) over twenty years ago remains perhaps the best piece of research we have evaluating the impact of AA, even though it is based on retrospective self-reports rather than on longitudinal data, control groups, and quantitative measures. As later summarized by Maxwell (1962), case studies of AA members made it clear that not only did group participation generally bring about sobriety, but "the majority exhibit additional and sometimes very substantial changes in personality." He goes on to summarize these changes as follows: "The list of reported changes was led on the one hand by the reduction of interpersonal anxieties, ego-inflation, hostility, and intolerance, and in a listing of values gained, by an increase in the ability to interact more satisfyingly with other persons. Reportedly gained was the greater enjoyment and appreciation not only of other persons but also of other facets of life; a greater ability to face and accept reality; greater objectivity with regard to self—honesty, humility, and sense of humor and of proportion; an increase in the sense of security, adequacy, confidence, worth, and accomplishment; physical and emotional relaxation; and finally—and frequently listed—peace of mind." In general, these changes indicate fundamental modification of "self-other attitudes."

Gellman's (1964) later study, entitled THE SOBER ALCOHOLIC, provides additional suggestive evidence of the powerful impact of AA on alcoholics. But this is not to say that AA would be successful in drying out and rehabilitating all or even most alcoholics, since only certain kinds of alcoholics are able to join and participate in AA (see Trice 1957, 1959; Maxwell 1951, 1954). Nevertheless, the overwhelming body of admittedly anecdotal, impressionistic, and case study evidence points to the powerful impact of AA on its members, both in terms of drinking behavior as well as in terms of personality and various kinds of social role behavior (jobs, family, etc.).

More research actually seems to have been devoted to explaining *why* AA has its consistent and powerful impact than has been devoted to demonstrating that impact. One approach to explanation uses the language of psychotherapy (see Stewart 1955; Ripley and Jackson 1959), while another approach is more sociological, stressing the interpersonal, subcultural, reference group, and differential association aspects of AA (Maxwell 1962; Gellman 1964; Root 1967).

Some key aspects of the impact of AA seem to be the following: The person who joins has to face finally the fact that he *is* an alcoholic (an uncontrolled drinker) and needs help. Hope is held out for rehabilitation through AA by seeing and hearing recovered alcoholics describe their experiences. The AA group has a very powerful and distinctive subculture facilitating recovery and personal change. There is a single, explicit purpose—to become and stay sober. Members are urged to avoid involvement in other voluntary groups and movements unless they relate to helping alcoholics.

AA provides a great deal of specific knowledge and information about the impact of alcohol on the body and the effects of alcoholism and alcoholics on society. Alcohol and drinking attitudes are attacked directly, with all kinds of negative associations and anxiety about drinking (even in small amounts) developed. There are frequent and extensive self-confessionals and problem-sharing sessions regarding drinking problems, both in formal and informal settings and before larger groups as well as in dyadic relationships. Members are encouraged to depend on other members for support and encouragement, and new members are quickly and warmly accepted into the group as "converts." There is a great deal of informal fellowship and many social activities to reinforce the meaning that members have for one another and their ability to influence each other's drinking behavior. The "significant others" of members are drawn into the culture of AA through auxiliaries like Al-Anon (for spouses) and Ala Teen (for their children).

Finally, recovered alcoholics and other members are urged to recruit other alcoholics into AA and continue to work with them in order that they might be helped too. Only ex-alcoholics can really understand and help alcoholics, it is argued. This activity maintains a sense of purpose and usefulness among those who have accomplished their own "self-help" and encourage continuing group participation, although the recruitment and other aspects of social influence in AA are generally "low pressure." The latter element is especially important, since it generally results more in internalization of new attitudes and values as a result of personal commitment, rather than mere overt compliance with external social pressures.

In many ways, then, AA provides an excellent learning and social influence environment. It embodies in its program many of the features that social science in general has found to be critical aspects of changing people's beliefs, attitudes, personality, and behavior. Still, there is much variation among AA groups, as for example in the degree to which they reach out actively for new members and provide a warmly accepting atmosphere for newcomers (see Maxwell 1962). Overall, however, AA is generally very successful in providing its members with a new "way of life"—a way of dealing with their problems and relationships that involves very different beliefs, attitudes, values, and behavior from what they were accustomed to before joining.

Before going on to the second kind of self-help group we shall consider here, we should mention that "halfway houses" and agency run "group therapy" of a voluntary sort also have some success with changing alcoholics. Halfway houses (or "recovery houses") are probably most similar to AA in their intensity of interpersonal relations and group support, being residential houses where an alcoholic can stay while trying to reintegrate himself into normal society. Many such houses act as a sort of extension of AA, according to Trice (1966, p. 100), and follow similar strategies.

Narcotics Anonymous and Synanon groups represent a second kind of self-help group that has received some social scientific attention. Both types of groups were set up by former drug addicts to help other addicts, and depend on the development of very close-knit, intensive, interpersonal primary group relationships for their success. Narcotics Anonymous is explicitly patterned after AA, using group norms, attitudes, and information to help an addict break out of former life patterns and take on new ones. Joining the group begins, like AA, with an admission that the member is powerless to control his drug use and needs the help of others. And as with AA, present members who have "kicked the habit" are instrumental in recruiting new members, describing their own past problems and steps to recovery in both informal and formal sessions (see Nyswander 1956, p. 144).

Synanon has a distinctive program of its own, with a "tightly controlled program of admission, indoctrination, and status promotion" (Trice 1966, pp. 115-16). The methods of the group, with continual mutual reinforcement for "staying clean" (off drugs) and severe group verbal chastisement for deviation from the norms, has many (though not all) of the elements of successful political "brainwashing." The use of an intensive small group culture to bring about personal change is similar to AA, but the kind of formal status hierarchy and "promotion" for good behavior (following group norms) are distinctive (see Yablonsky 1965), as is the residential, full-time nature of the program.

Although there has been little or no quantitative evaluation research on how these groups affect the personalities and attitudes of their members, there is some evidence of their impact on the specific behavior of returning to drug use. Trice (1966, p. 116-17) reports that three studies of drug users who were exposed to other kinds of treatments generally showed recidivism (relapse into drug use) rates of about 85 percent. By contrast, a study by Volkman and Cressey (1963) shows the residents of Synanon to have recidivism rates (one year or more after leaving) considerably lower, ranging from 52 percent of those who had stayed in a Synanon house for at least one month, to only 14 percent of those who had stayed at least seven months. Clearly, even a relatively brief full-time exposure to Synanon was markedly more successful than other change therapies, and the impact of the group increased with increasing amounts of exposure (at least over the range from one to three to seven months residence that was studied).

Member oriented self-help groups in the mental health field fall into two general categories—social and recreational clubs (predominantly expressive with therapy as a secondary goal) and therapeutic groups (predominantly instrumental with sociability as a secondary goal). Although not mutually exclusive in activities and goals, social clubs tend to concentrate on providing opportunities for the members to socialize, to regain and to grow in social skills, self-confidence, and social confidence through mutual interaction; while overtly therapeutic organizations commonly engage directly in group discussions of their common problems in adjustment. In some groups these are under direct professional guidance (e.g., Bierer, 1944), but in others an "inspirational" approach is taken with the aim of instilling and maintaining a group credo or ideology by which mental health is attained and preserved. (See Goertzel, Beard and Pilnick 1960; Jones 1953; Lerner 1960; Palmer 1958; Olshansky 1962).

Joshua Bierer in Britain was one of the prime instigators of social and recreational clubs for ex-mental patients, editing a book (1948) on social therapeutic clubs and helping to found a number of them. Bierer used clubs in his practice as a therapeutic device for his patients, enabling them to develop better self, other, and social attitudes and skills. In general, however, social clubs are today viewed as analogous "halfway houses" for mental patients, providing a source of both social support and recreation, protecting the ex-patient from the isolation and loneliness which may be his upon his return from institutionalization. Permissiveness, informality, a sense of social support, and friendliness are their goals. At times the social clubs are run primarily by hospitals and other social service agencies, especially at the local or county level. Often, however, social clubs are run entirely by ex-patients themselves. In some instances a single organization, such as the Fountain House Foundation, will sponsor a number of ex-patients clubs and other services.

Abraham Low (1950) was also instrumental in forming ex-patient clubs, initially for his own former patients but then open to the general populations, including eventually even those who had been neither hospitalized nor under therapy but who felt that they were suffering from nervous disorders of some sort. Each club follows a strict program for every meeting. Meetings combine a reiteration of Low's therapeutic principles ("Will-Training") with practical discussions of how to apply those principles to everyday situations and common problems. Hundreds of Low's clubs, under the name of Recovery, Inc., are now widely spread across the country.

However, despite the wide variety of such programs and despite the involvement and interest of professionals in some of the programs (notably in those dealing with mental health), to the authors' knowledge there has been no systematic study (either cross-sectional or longitudinal) of the impact any of these organizations has on its members, matching these with a control group of those who are eligible to be members of the group but who are not members. The literature that does exist on these groups tends to fall into two major categories, and neither category marshalls much data to support their contentions. The first category comprises testimonials to the efficacy of the organization by the organization, by satisfied members of the organization, or by professional personnel somehow involved with the organization. Limitations in the program and its failures are seldom mentioned and virtually never stressed in this category, and no quantitative information is given.

The second category contains the reflections of professionals on the various programs and groups. It is assumed that these groups do have impacts of sorts, but the primary theme is how these impacts might be considerably more positive if professionals were to play a more important role in the organizations, this especially being the case for groups of former mental patients. Professionals also voice doubts about the overall efficacy and appropriateness of some programs. There is at times a strong feeling that some groups' ideologies and antiprofessional biases may be harmful to those members who need professional help in addition to, or instead of, the experiences the group offers. Finally, some professionals have been sensitive enough to the membership attributes of some organizations to note that, especially in the field of mental health, supposedly "transitional" groups in some instances have tended to become more permanent groups, attracting many who tend to need and appreciate long-term dependency on the group.

In sum, the ex-patients organizations are a growing phenomenon. They are somewhat less successful than might otherwise be the case, since there is a low general popular acceptance of mental illness; hence many former patients want above all to forget their illness and their hospital experience. Also, unlike the alcoholic, who at least can claim common symptoms in addition to common social stigma, mental patients though stigmatized have been the victims of a wide range of symptoms. Where patients play major roles, adequate leadership is often hard to find and sustain in these self-help groups. In addition, where it is hoped that participation will be only temporary (commonly the social clubs see themselves as such), memberships for some may be sustained over a long period of time. However, despite the number of these organizations and their earnest and concentrated efforts, the present authors must agree with Wechsler (1960a, b) that the impact of these groups is yet to be adequately tested by any quantitative empirical research. Hence, for the present we can only conclude that impressionistic and anecdotal evidence suggest they often have a favorable impact, though with less consistency than AA or Synanon.

Conclusions

The studies we have reviewed bearing on the personal impact of expressive and self-help groups are not much more compelling than those we earlier looked at for instrumental externally focused groups. There are really very few adequate quantitative studies meeting high standards of scientific method. Nevertheless, let us again draw some tentative conclusions from our review.

First, even more than for instrumental externally oriented groups, instrumental internally oriented voluntary groups (self-help groups) seem impressionistically to have substantial personal impacts along a variety of dimensions. In a few instances, this evidence is overwhelming (e.g., Alcoholics Anonymous) and in a few more both overwhelming and adequately demonstrated by at least one quantitative study (e.g., Synanon). Hence, there can scarcely be any doubt that self-help groups can and often do have very important personal impacts upon their members/participants/volunteers.

Second, this impact doubtless varies according to the kind of self-help group considered (e.g., AA vs. Gamblers Anonymous vs. Great Books Club vs. 4-H), as well as varying according to the specific instance or chapter of a given kind of group (i.e., an AA chapter in a large central city vs. one in a smaller suburban town). Since research on the amount and kinds of impact these groups have is just beginning, nothing systematic is known about how group variations in goals, structure, and activities are associated with variations in personal impacts.

Third, as with externally oriented groups, self-help groups have been found to influence most kinds of personal characteristics—beliefs, dispositions, emotions, capacities, and behavior, although much of the evidence is anecdotal or case study material.

Beliefs and Knowledge. Self-help groups usually include an informational or ideological component to their program. As a result, their members usually show an increase in the particular kinds of knowledge or belief that are being presented by the group as part of its socialization of new members or its ongoing activity. For a self-improvement group, the additional knowledge may deal with literature and the arts (as in a Great Books Club) or with how to raise animals or crops (as in the 4-H Club). The active participant in a scientific association is likely to learn more about his own and others' specialties, and the union member may learn more about the wage scales in other companies or states. In a religious group or sect, the member is likely to be indoctrinated with religious beliefs, theology, moral principles, as well as with racial, economic, and political beliefs. In the self-remedy kind of self-help group, the focus is more likely to be on specific beliefs and information about the problem and its effect on oneself, one's family, and one's community—the effects of alcohol, drugs, mental illness, and so forth. In the most extreme case, a self-help group can lead the individual to see the whole world in a different light than before, as a result of a conversion experience.

Dispositions. It might be a fair summary to say that self-improvement kinds of self-help groups tend to have more impact on beliefs, knowledge, and skills; while self-remedy, self-help groups tend to have relatively more impact on dispositions, (although this statement, like most others in our conclusions, is more suggested hypothesis than empirical generalization). It also seems that, within the category of dispositions, self-improvement groups are more likely to influence the more superficially held attitudes, rather than more deeply rooted aspects of self-conception and personality traits. Conversely, self-remedy groups are more able to influence the latter kind of disposition as well as the former. For instance, 4-H Club experience seems to affect rural youth interests, and Great Books Clubs seem to affect attitudes toward various authors, literary schools, and so forth. And while such groups also may have some impact on self-conceptions, self-remedy groups are more likely to grapple successfully and directly with the deeper levels of attitudes toward self and relations to others. Self-remedy groups have been reported to increase tolerance, positive self-evaluation, pride in oneself, awareness of one's failings, tolerance of the weaknesses of others, humility, and so on. They have also been reported to decrease hostility and rejection of others and their ideas, values, and activities. Yet self-remedy groups always work at changing specific attitudes in one area—attitudes toward the particular problem the group is focused on (alcohol, drugs, etc.). Where the problem is a kind of behavior that the members wish to cease doing (drinking, smoking, etc.), the group tends to increase its members' negative attitudes toward that behavior. Where the problem is not something that is very likely to be eliminated (handicaps, schizophrenia, etc.), the group tends to increase its members' acceptance of the problem as preparatory to coping with it in a more nearly normal life.

Emotions. Not much has been done to study the impact of self-help groups on emotions. At most we may say that anecdotal evidence suggests significant impacts on lowering anxiety and on increasing general satisfaction and "peace of mind." Along with these feelings go correlative emotions like an increased sense of personal security, felt belongingness, and so on.

Skills. Quantitative empirical research has also largely ignored this area. Anecdotal evidence suggests that many kinds of self-improvement groups have marked effects on the skills of their members in areas of activity that are the focus of group goals and activity (e.g., public speaking, art, making clothes, etc.). In a sense, much of the grading system of adult education classes and groups, and the rating/awards system of youth groups like the Scouts and 4-H are associated with empirical evidence of increases in various skill areas, as well as in knowledge. What is less clear is how long these skills persist and to what extent there is incidental learning of social skills, and so on, not specifically taught by the group.

Behavior. As with externally oriented instrumental groups, self-help groups can show clear impacts on behavior, especially on behavior that is the focus of group norms and sanctions. What is special in the present instance is that some of this behavior represents a total change in the way of life of the group members. For an alcoholic to stop drinking or an addict to stop taking drugs means immeasurably more as a behavioral impact than for a service volunteer to spend his expected hour or two each week or month as a mental patient's "companion." Participation in self-help groups has thus been shown to have an impact on the specific problem behavior that is treated by self-remedy groups (alcohol, drugs, gambling, smoking, eating, etc.), although most of the evidence is anecdotal again. But self-help groups also seem to have a demonstrable impact on other kinds of behavior as well, especially on heightened participation in the recruitment and socialization of newcomers (self-remedy groups) and on forms of participation related to, but different from, the group's activities (self-improvement groups). An instance of the latter is the increased general serious reading done by Great Books Club members, over and above that reading specified as part of their club activity.

Fourth, expressive voluntary groups, whose goals involve primarily enjoyment, fellowship, sociability, and so on, do not seem to have much impact on beliefs/knowledge, dispositions (attitudes, values, personality traits), or skills, although there has been virtually no quantitative empirical research on this kind of group impact (but see Scott 1965). We would expect some impact on interpersonal and social skills, if nothing else, but there is no evidence even of an impressionistic sort that we know of here. As for behavior, it is unlikely that expressive groups have much impact beyond being able to enforce conformity on their members to "obey the rules" and generally to follow the written and unwritten norms of the group. Scott (ibid.) suggests generally that differential selection is much more important than socialization in the kind of expressive groups he studied.

However, fifth, expressive voluntary groups and social participation in general seem to have an important impact on increasing positive feelings (affect) and hence on general happiness. The causality here is likely to be a complex feedback loop, so that greater happiness is probably both a cause (at one time) and a consequence (at another time) of social participation. The key element of social participation that increases positive affect seems to be new and varied experiences ("novelty"), rather than simple sociability, although the latter is important too. The general finding here is supported by several pieces of quantitative research, unlike most other conclusions we have drawn.

Sixth, the more intensive, closely interpersonal, small-group oriented, time-consuming, and high commitment forms of self-help groups (notably self-remedy groups like Alcoholics Anonymous or Synanon, but also groups like a highly ideological cooperative, the Black Muslims, or the "Doomsday Cult") tend to have more powerful personal impacts than less intensive, less closely knit, large-group oriented, less time-consuming, lower commitment kinds of groups. The more of one's self one puts into a self-help group, the more likely one is to be changed as a person. This means that residential self-help groups tend to have more impact than nonresidential, and that longer exposure to self-help groups, other things equal, is likely to produce greater impacts. However, there must also be "plateau effects," or "ceiling effects." If seven months in a Synanon group is enough to keep 86 percent of former addicts "clean" for a year or more (Volkman & Cressey 1963), then additional months or years may not be able to increase this success rate and impact very much, if at all. There will probably always be some irreducible minimum number of "failures" for any kind of self-help group—members who for one reason or another simply cannot be reached by the methods and programs of the group, even though they have joined purportedly seeking the same help as others.

Seventh, there is some anecdotal evidence that powerful "conversion effects" occur both in self-help groups as well as in expressive religious groups, probably even more frequently than in externally oriented instrumental groups. The whole root meaning of "conversion" comes from the sphere of expressive religious groups, of course, but the presence of such effects in self-help groups like AA and Synanon is special and worth noting. It is also a matter worthy of some solid empirical research which, alas, we do not now have.

Some Reflections on Needed Future Research

This chapter does not purport to be an exhaustive review of the literature on the impact of voluntary groups upon the volunteer/participant. The literature is much too scattered and hard to identify, let alone track down, for this to have been possible. Moreover, as we have stated earlier, the "conclusions" to the last two parts of this chapter are really meant to be more suggestive than conclusive. We have tried to stretch beyond the few pieces of quantitative empirical research and fragmentary anecdotal evidence to see some of the broader trends or tendencies that emerge if one blends "educated guesses" with established facts. In this sense, we hope our conclusions will be taken with the appropriate skepticism until demonstrated more clearly by future research. But we also hope that future research can focus on broad conclusions like these as hypotheses for future testing, in order that this subarea of voluntary action research can begin to progress more rapidly and its results synthesized rather than allowed to lie scattered in the literature.

We would also like to touch on a few methodological and substantive questions here about which we did not even feel certain enough to hazard a guess as to the probable outcome. These, too, we hope will be taken as possible guides to some future research.

What is the relative effect of differential selection processes (certain kinds of people joining or staying in a group, other kinds not joining or dropping out) as contrasted with social learning processes in bringing about the apparent personal impacts of voluntary groups? Very few of the studies that have used sophisticated quantitative methodologies (themselves a class small in size) have considered differential selection as an alternative explanation for apparent personal impacts of group experience. Yet, as both Scott (1965) and Davis (1961) have remarked, such selection effects pretty clearly take place. Moreover, entry selection effects need to be carefully distinguished from apparent "conversion effects" as well as from differential retention effects.

Where true social learning effects on voluntary group members do exist, to what extent are these effects the result of various forms of socialization (in the sense of intended, conscious teaching, whether formal or informal) as contrasted with incidental learning from task experience (in the sense of learning from activities performed by the member and unintended stimuli that he is exposed to)? We have the impression that task experience in many cases can be quite as important, if not more important, than the direct socialization processes.

What are the structure and process characteristics that are most conducive to social learning in voluntary groups? Put another way, what do you do if you want to maximize (or to minimize) the personal impact of a particular voluntary group? By studying groups with especially powerful impacts (AA, Black Muslims, and so on) a number of common elements begin to emerge, most of which have some basis in the generalizations social scientists have drawn from social learning, attitude change, and socialization research in other contexts. At the very least, the role of normative pressure, public interpersonal sharing of problems, intensive social interaction and mutual support, manipulation of rewards and punishments, modeling after "successful" and respected others, group participation, and a variety of related factors seem to stand out as potentially important. But we really have no comparative research to tell us which of these might be more important than another, which crucial and which incidental, and so forth.

This leads us to a related question: How does the personal impact of voluntary groups vary with the type of the group? On the basis of very flimsy evidence, we have tried to review the literature here and draw conclusions differently for instrumental vs. expressive groups, for internally vs. externally focused groups, and for self-improvement vs. self-remedy groups. But perhaps these are not the most appropriate analytical categories. There are many ways of classifying voluntary groups, and any one of these classifications may be analytically useful—may help us to understand how and why the personal impacts of voluntary groups differ (cf. Smith et al. 1972). But we will never be able to draw valid conclusions here until we have some really comparative research on voluntary group impact, utilizing a common sampling strategy, measurement techniques, and analytical dimensions to investigate the impact of different kinds of voluntary groups on their members. Not a single study of this kind exists, to our knowledge, yet we will need many before we can hope to understand the differential impact of voluntary groups upon their participants.

Another key question is how and why does a voluntary group bring about a "conversion experience" in a person? Since the conversion experience seems to be the most drastic kind of personal impact that a voluntary group can have, it must be especially important to understand fully. Note, by the way, that conversion experiences are almost exclusively an impact of voluntary groups—very rarely, if ever, are such drastic changes the result of experience in work organizations or coercive organizations. (Would anyone speak of "conversion" to General Motors, the State Department, or a prison?) In a somewhat less vivid form, this question may be rephrased to ask about how voluntary groups are able to generate and allocate personal commitment. In an age of increasing alienation and a generation of "the uncommitted," what can be more important for our survival as a society in the long term than to understand commitment? Indeed, we would suggest that the loss or lack of commitment is the root social problem of our times, so that if it can be ameliorated, many other problems will likewise move toward resolution.

And for the last we have saved a *methodological exhortation*. Without true longitudinal studies, adequate control groups, careful sampling, and reliable and valid measures of personal impact, this area of voluntary action research is doomed to barely informed conjecture (as we would have to deem much of the present chapter). These are not mere "methodological niceties," in our view, but the very cornerstones on which any kind of social science must be built, voluntary action research included. But they depend on that kind of voluntary commitment we have spoken about in the preceding paragraph. Before more longitudinal studies with adequate control groups, and so on will be done in this area, there needs to be much more commitment to such a goal on the part of both researchers and funding agencies. We hope this chapter at least serves to make that need clearer.

References

Alvarez, Vladimir
1970   "National Voluntary Service Programmes in Developing Countries." 17th Conference Paper. Paris: Co-ordinating Committee for International Voluntary Service.

Apter, David E., and James Joll, eds.
1972   ANARCHISM TODAY. Garden City, N.Y.: Anchor Books, Doubleday and Co.

Arffa, Marvin S.
1966   "The Influence of Volunteer Experience on Career Choice." VOCATIONAL GUIDANCE QUARTERLY 14: 287-89.

Atkins, Wayne Lewis
1969   "Growth and Development of Adults Through Understanding Self and Others." Ph.D. dissertation, Univ. of Nebraska, Lincoln.

Barbour, Floyd
1968   THE BLACK POWER REVOLT. Boston: Porter Sargent Co.

Beck, James, David Kantor, and Victor Gelineau
1965   "Inpact of Undergraduate Volunteers on the Social Behavior of Chronic Psychotic Patients," INTERNATIONAL JOURNAL OF SOCIAL PSYCHOLOGY 11: 96-104.

Becker, Howard S.
1964   "Personal Change in Adult Life." SOCIOMETRY, 27: 40-53.

Becker, Howard S., and Blanche Geer
1958   "The Fate of Idealism in Medical School." AMERICAN SOCIOLOGICAL REVIEW 23: 49-56.

Becker, Howard S., Blanche Geer, Everett Hughes, and Anselm Strauss
1961   BOYS IN WHITE. Chicago: University of Chicago Press.

Bell, Inge
1968   CORE AND THE STRATEGY OF NON VIOLENCE. New York: Random House.

Bergin, A.
1966   "Some Implications of Psychotherapy Research for Therapeutic Practice." JOURNAL OF ABNORMAL PSYCHOLOGY 71: 235-46.

Bierer, Joshua
1944   "A New Form of Group Psychotherapy." MENTAL HEALTH 5: 23-26.
1948   SOCIAL THERAPEUTIC CLUBS. London: H.K. Lewis and Co.

Blizzard, Samuel
1956   "The Minister's Dilemma." THE CHRISTIAN CENTURY April 25: 508-510.

Bloom, Benjamin S.
1964   STABILITY AND CHANGE IN HUMAN CHARACTERISTICS. New York: John Wiley.

Booz, Allen Public Administration Services Inc.
1972   COST BENEFIT STUDY OF THE FOSTER GRANDPARENT PRO-
        GRAM Report prepared for ACTION, U.S. Government, Washington,
        D.C.
Boulder County Juvenile Delinquency Project
1967   "Boulder Ex-Volunteers in Other Communities." Boulder, Colorado:
        Boulder County Juvenile Delinquency Project.
Bradburn, Norman M.
1969   THE STRUCTURE OF PSYCHOLOGICAL WELL-BEING. Chicago,
        Ill.: Aldine Publishing Co.
Bradburn, N., and D. Caplovitz
1965   REPORTS ON HAPPINESS. Chicago, Ill.: Aldine Publishing Co.
Brim, Orville G., and Stanton Wheeler
1966   SOCIALIZATION AFTER CHILDHOOD: TWO ESSAYS. New York:
        John Wiley.
Breer, Paul E., and Edwin A. Locke
1965   TASK EXPERIENCE AS A SOURCE OF ATTITUDES. Homewood, Ill.:
        The Dorsey Press.
Bullock, Allen
1952   HITLER: A STUDY IN TYRANNY London: Odhams.
Burke, Libbie S., and Marty Dye
1961   " 'Adoptive Friend' Program in an Institution for the Mentally Re-
        tarded," AMERICAN JOURNAL OF MENTAL DEFICIENCY 66, No.
        3: 387-392.
Campbell, Ernest Q.
1969   "Adolescent Socialization." In HANDBOOK OF SOCIALIZATION
        THEORY AND RESEARCH. Edited by David A. Goslin. Chicago: Rand
        McNally.
Cantril, Hadley
1941   THE PSYCHOLOGY OF SOCIAL MOVEMENTS. New York: Wiley.
Carmichael, Stokely, and Charles Hamilton
1968   BLACK POWER. London: Jonathan Cape.
Clegg, Hugh A., Alan Fox, and A.F. Thompson
1964   A HISTORY OF BRITISH TRADE UNIONS SINCE 1889. Oxford,
        England: Clarendon Press.
Coleman, James S.
1961   THE ADOLESCENT SOCIETY. New York: Free Press.
Coleman, James S., et al.
1966   EQUALITY OF EDUCATIONAL OPPORTUNITY Washington, D.C.:
        U.S. Government Printing Office.
Coles, Robert, and Joseph Brenner
1965   "American Youth in a Social Struggle: The Mississippi Summer Project."
        AMERICAN JOURNAL OF ORTHOPSYCHIATRY 35, no. 5: 909-26.

1968 "American Youth in a Social Struggle (II): The Appalachian Volunteers." AMERICAN JOURNAL OF ORTHOPSYCHIATRY 38, no. 1:
31-46.

Cross, H.J.
1964 "The Outcome of Psychotherapy: A Selected Analysis of Research
Findings." JOURNAL OF CONSULTING PSYCHOLOGY 28: 413-17.

Darley, J.G.
1938 "Changes in Measured Attitudes and Adjustment." JOURNAL OF
SOCIAL PSYCHOLOGY 9: 189-199.

Davis, James A.
1960 A STUDY OF PARTICIPANTS IN THE GREAT BOOKS PROGRAM.
No city: The Fund for Adult Education.
1961 GREAT BOOKS AND SMALL GROUPS. New York: Free Press.

Dawson, Richard E., and Kenneth Prewitt
1969 POLITICAL SOCIALIZATION. Boston: Little, Brown.

Dittman, Allen T.
1966 "Psychotherapeutic Processes." In ANNUAL REVIEW OF PSYCHOL-
OGY. Edited by P.R. Farnsworth et al. Vol. 17. Palo Alto, Calif.: Annual
Reviews, Inc.

Dornbusch, Sanford M.
1955 "The Military Academy as an Assimilating Institution." SOCIAL
FORCES 33: 316-21.

Elder, Glen H. Jr.
1968 "Adolescent Socialization and Development." In HANDBOOK OF PER-
SONALITY THEORY AND RESEARCH. Edited by Edgar F. Borgatta
and William W. Lambert. Chicago: Rand McNally.

Essien-Udom, E.U.
1964 BLACK NATIONALISM: A SEARCH FOR IDENTITY IN AMERICA.
New York: Dell.

Eysenck, Hans J.
1952 "The Effects of Psychotherapy: An Evaluation." JOURNAL OF CON-
SULTING PSYCHOLOGY 16: 319-24.
1965 "The Effects of Psychotherapy." INTERNATIONAL JOURNAL OF
PSYCHIATRY 1: 97-144.

Feldman, Kenneth A., and Theodore M. Newcomb
1969 THE IMPACT OF COLLEGE ON STUDENTS. San Francisco: Jossey
Bass, Inc.

Festinger, Leon, H.W. Riecken, and S. Schachter
1956 WHEN PROPHECY FAILS. Minneapolis: University of Minnesota.

Fiske, Donald W. and Salvatore R. Maddi (eds.)
1961 FUNCTIONS OF VARIED EXPERIENCE. Homewood, Ill.: The Dorsey
Press.

Flexner, Eleanor
1959 CENTURY OF STRUGGLE. Cambridge, Mass.: Harvard University Press.

Foner, Philip
1971 THE BLACK PANTHER SPEAKS. Philadelphia: Lippincott.

Freeman, Howard E., and Camille Lambert
1965 "The Influence of Community Groups on Health Matters," HUMAN ORGANIZATIONS 24: 353-7.

Freeman, Howard E., and Morris Showel
1962 "The Political Influence of Voluntary Associations," In PUBLIC OPINION AND CONGRESSIONAL ELECTIONS. Edited by W.N. McPhee and W.A. Glaser. New York: Free Press of Glencoe.

Friedan, Betty
1963 THE FEMININE MYSTIQUE. New York: Dell.

Gellman, Irving
1964 THE SOBER ALCOHOLIC: AN ORGANIZATIONAL ANALYSIS OF ALCOHOLICS ANONYMOUS. New Haven, Conn.: College and University Press.

Gerard, H.B., and G.C. Mathewson
1966 "The Effects of Severity of Initiation on Liking for a Group: A Replication." JOURNAL OF EXPERIMENTAL SOCIAL PSYCHOLOGY 2: 278-87.

Goertzel, Victor, John H. Beard, and Saul Pilnick
1960 "Fountain House Foundation: A Case Study of an Ex-Patient's Club." JOURNAL OF SOCIAL ISSUES 16, no. 2 : 54-61.

Goffman, Erving
1961 ASYLUMS. Garden City, N.Y.: Anchor-Doubleday.

Goldsmith, Nancy
1963 "Volunteer Program Helps Teen-Agers Find Careers in the Health Field," MODERN HOSPITAL 100, no. 4: 6-8.

Goslin, David, ed.
1969 HANDBOOK OF SOCIALIZATION THEORY AND RESEARCH. Chicago: Rand McNally.

Gottlieb, David, and Carol Hancock Gold
1971 VISTA AND ITS VOLUNTEERS; 1965-69, A SUMMARY REPORT. Washington, D.C.: Office of Economic Opportunity.

Greeley, Andrew M., and Peter H. Rossi
1966 THE EDUCATION OF CATHOLIC AMERICANS. Garden City, N.Y.: Doubleday Anchor.

Greenblatt, Milton, and David Kantor
1962 "Student Volunteer Movement and the Manpower Shortage," AMERICAN JOURNAL OF PSYCHOLOGY 118: 809-814.

Guilford, J.P.
1967   THE NATURE OF HUMAN INTELLIGENCE. New York: McGraw-Hill
        Book Co.
Harris, Louis and Associates, Inc.
1969   A SURVEY OF RETURNED PEACE CORPS VOLUNTEERS. A survey
        conducted for the Peace Corps.
Hess, Robert D. and Judith V. Torney
1967   THE DEVELOPMENT OF POLITICAL ATTITUDES IN CHILDREN.
        Chicago: Aldine-Atherton.
Holzberg, Jules D.
1964   THE SIGNIFICANCE OF THE COMPANIONSHIP EXPERIENCE FOR
        THE COLLEGE STUDENT. Washington, D.C.: United States Govern-
        ment Printing Office.
Holzberg, Jules D., and Herbert Gewirtz.
1963   "A Method of Altering Attitudes toward Mental Illness." PSYCHIATRIC
        QUARTERLY SUPPLEMENT 37: 56-61.
Holzberg, Jules D., Herbert Gewirtz, and Eugene Ebner
1964   "Changes in Moral Judgment and Self-Acceptance in College Students as
        a Function of Companionship with Hospitalized Mental Patients."
        JOURNAL OF CONSULTING PSYCHOLOGY 28: 299-303.
Holzberg, Jules D., H. Whiting, and D.C. Lowy
1964   "Chronic Patients and a College Companion Program." MENTAL HOS-
        PITALS 15: 152-158.
Holzberg, Jules D., and Robert H. Knapp
1965   "The Social Interaction of College Students and Clinically Ill Patients."
        AMERICAN JOURNAL OF ORTHOPSYCHIATRY 35: 487-92.
Holzberg, Jules D., Robert H. Knapp, and John L. Turner
1966   "Companionship with the Mentally Ill: Effects on the Personalities of
        College Student Volunteers." PSYCHIATRY 29: 397-8.
Holtzman, Abraham
1963   THE TOWNSEND MOVEMENT: A STUDY IN OLD AGE POLITICS.
        New York: Bookman Associates.
Hughes, Langston
1962   FIGHT FOR FREEDOM: THE STORY OF THE NAACP. New York:
        Norton.
Hunt, J. McVickers
1961   INTELLIGENCE AND EXPERIENCE. New York: The Ronald Press.
Hyman, Herbert, Charles R. Wright, and Terence K. Hopkins
1962   APPLICATIONS OF METHODS OF EVALUATION: FOUR STUDIES
        OF THE ENCAMPMENT FOR CITIZENSHIP. Berkeley: University of
        California Press.
Inkeles, Alex, and David Horton Smith
1973   BECOMING MODERN. Boston: Little Brown, forthcoming.

Jacob, Philip E.
1957 CHANGING VALUES IN COLLEGE: AN EXPLORATORY STUDY OF THE IMPACT OF COLLEGE TEACHING. New York: Harper and Brothers.

Joint Commission on Correctional Manpower and Training
1967 "Volunteers Look at Corrections." Washington, D.C.: Joint Commission on Correctional Manpower and Training.

Jones, Maxwell
1953 THE THERAPEUTIC COMMUNITY. New York: Basic Books.

Kedward, H.R.
1969 FASCISM IN WESTERN EUROPE, 1900-1945. London: Blackie.

Kelly, E.L.
1955 "Consistency of the Adult Personality." AMERICAN PSYCHOLOGIST 10: 659-82.

King, Mark et al.
1970 "Personality Change as a Function of Volunteer Experience," JOURNAL OF CONSULTING AND CLINICAL PSYCHOLOGY 35: 423-4.

King, Stanley H.
1967 "The Harvard Influence." HARVARD TODAY (Autumn 1967): 27-33.

Klein, William L., and Melvin Zax
1965 "The Use of a Hospital Volunteer Program in the Teaching of Abnormal Psychology," JOURNAL OF SOCIAL PSYCHOLOGY 65: 155-65.

Klugman, S.F., and C.H. Klugman
1964 "High School Volunteers Find Summer Work Rewarding," MENTAL HOSPITALS 15: 274-5.

Knapp, Robert H., and Jules D. Holzberg
1964 "Characteristics of College Students Volunteering for Service to Mental Patients." JOURNAL OF CONSULTING PSYCHOLOGY 28: 82-85.

Langton, Kenneth P.
1969 POLITICAL SOCIALIZATION. New York: Oxford Univ. Press.

Lanternari, V.
1965 THE RELIGIONS OF THE OPPRESSED. New York: Mentor Books.

Lerner, R.C.
1960 "The Therapeutic Social Club: Social Rehabilitation for Mental Patients." INTERNATIONAL JOURNAL OF SOCIAL PSYCHIATRY 6: 101-114.

LeVine, Robert A.
1966 "American College Experience as a Socialization Process." In COLLEGE PEER GROUPS: PROBLEMS AND PROSPECTS OF RESEARCH. Edited by Theodore Newcomb and Everett K. Wilson. Chicago: Aldine.

Lincoln, C. Eric
1961 THE BLACK MUSLIMS IN AMERICA. Boston: Beacon Press.

Liu Shao-Ch'i
1952   "Training of the Communist Party Member." In MAO'S CHINA: PARTY
       REFORM DOCUMENTS, 1942-44. Edited by B. Compton. Seattle,
       Wash.: University of Washington Press.
Lorwin, Lewis L.
1953   THE INTERNATIONAL LABOUR MOVEMENTS: HISTORY, POLI-
       TICS, OUTLOOK. New York: Harper.
Low, Abraham A.
1950   MENTAL HEALTH THROUGH WILL-TRAINING: A SYSTEM OF
       SELF-HELP IN PSYCHOTHERAPY AS PRACTICED BY RECOVERY,
       INC. Boston: Christopher Publishing House.
MacBain, N. and L.R. Schumacher
1963   "Pre-Med Students Learn Hospital Routine as Volunteers." HOSPITALS
       37 (July 16): 73-75.
Maccoby, Herbert
1958   "The Differential Political Activity of Participants in a Voluntary
       Association," AMERICAN SOCIOLOGICAL REVIEW 23: 524-32.
Maslow, A.
1962   TOWARD A PSYCHOLOGY OF BEING. Princeton, N.J.: Van Nostrand
       Co.
Matthews, P.W.D., and G.W. Ford
1966   "Trade Union Education and Training in Australia," JOURNAL OF
       INDUSTRIAL RELATIONS 8: 158-74.
Maxwell, Milton
1949   "Social Factors in the Alcoholics Anonymous Program." Unpublished
       Ph.D. dissertation, Univ. of Texas, Austin, Texas.
1951   "Interpersonal Factors in the Genesis and Treatment of Alcohol Ad-
       diction." SOCIAL FORCES 29:443-48.
1954   "Factors Affecting an Alcoholic's Willingness to Seek Help." NORTH-
       WEST SCIENCE 28: 116-23.
1962   "Alcoholics Anonymous: An Interpretation," In SOCIETY, CULTURE
       AND DRINKING PATTERNS. Edited by David J. Pittman and Charles
       R. Snyder. New York: John Wiley & Sons.
McClintock, Charles G., and Henry A. Turner
1962   "The Impact of College Upon Political Knowledge, Participation and
       Values," HUMAN RELATIONS 15: 163-176.
McCoy, Charles S.
1964   "The Churches and Protest Movements for Racial Justice." In
       RELIGION AND SOCIAL CONFLICT. Edited by Robert Lee and
       Martin E. Marty. New York: Oxford Univ. Press.
McGuire, William J.
1969   "The Nature of Attitudes and Attitude Change. In THE HANDBOOK

OF SOCIAL PSYCHOLOGY. 2nd ed. Edited by Gardner Lindzey and Elliot Aronson. Reading, Mass.: Addison-Wesley.

Milgram, Stanley, and Hans Toch
1969   "Collective Behavior: Crowds and Social Movements." In THE HAND-BOOK OF SOCIAL PSYCHOLOGY, 2nd ed. Chapter 35 in Vol. 4. Edited by Gardner Lindzey and Elliot Aronson. Reading, Mass.: Addison-Wesley.

Monnerot, Jules (transl. by Jane Degras and Richard Rees)
1960   SOCIOLOGY AND PSYCHOLOGY OF COMMUNISM. Boston: Beacon Press.

Moore, Wilbert E.
1969   "Occupational Socialization." In HANDBOOK OF SOCIALIZATION THEORY AND RESEARCH. Edited by David A. Goslin. Chicago: Rand McNally.

Morgan, Robin, ed.
1970   SISTERHOOD IS POWERFUL. New York: Vintage Books, Random House.

Mulford, Charles, and Gerald Klonglan
1972   "Attitude Determinants of Individual Participation in Organized Voluntary Action." In VOLUNTARY ACTION RESEARCH: 1972. Edited by David Horton Smith et al., Lexington, Mass.: Lexington Books, D.C. Heath and Co.

Neal, Arthur G., and Melvin Seeman
1964   "Organizations and Powerlessness: A Test of the Mediation Hypothesis," AMERICAN SOCIOLOGICAL REVIEW 29: 216-26.

Nelson, Erland N.P.
1954   "Persistence of Attitudes of College Students Fourteen Years Later." PSYCHOLOGICAL MONOGRAPHS: GENERAL AND APPLIED. Vol. 68. Whole number 373.

Newcomb, Theodore M.
1943   PERSONALITY AND SOCIAL CHANGE. New York: Dryden.
1966   "The General Nature of Peer Group Influence. In PEER GROUPS: PROBLEMS AND PROSPECTS FOR RESEARCH. Edited by Theodore M. Newcomb and Everett K. Wilson. Chicago: Aldine.

Newcomb, Theodore M., Kathryn E. Koenig, Richard Flacks, and Donald P. Warwick
1967   PERSISTENCE AND CHANGE: BENNINGTON COLLEGE AND ITS STUDENTS AFTER TWENTY-FIVE YEARS. New York: John Wiley.

Nyswander, Marie
1956   THE DRUG ADDICT AS PATIENT. New York: Grune & Stratton.

Olshansky, Simon
1962   "Social Life." MENTAL HYGIENE 46: 361-369.

Palmer, Mary B.
1958   "Social Rehabilitation for Mental Patients." MENTAL HYGIENE 42: 24-28.
Phillips, Derek L.
1967a   "Mental Health Status, Social Participation and Happiness." JOURNAL OF HEALTH AND SOCIAL BEHAVIOR 8: 285-91.
1967b   "Social Participation and Happiness." AMERICAN JOURNAL OF SOCIOLOGY 72: 479-88.
1969   "Social Class, Social Participation, and Happiness: A Consideration of Interaction Opportunities and Investment." SOCIOLOGICAL QUARTERLY 19 (Winter): 3-21.
Pinner, Frank
1964   "Student Trade-Unionism in France, Belgium, and Holland: Anticipatory Socialization and Role-Seeking," SOCIOLOGY OF EDUCATION 37: 177-99.
Riechen, Henry W.
1952   THE VOLUNTEER WORK CAMP: A PSYCHOLOGICAL EVALUATION. Reading, Mass.: Addison-Wesley.
Ripley, Herbert S., and Joan K. Jackson
1959   "Therapeutic Factors in Alcoholics Anonymous." AMERICAN JOURNAL OF PSYCHIATRY 116: 44-50.
Ritchie, Oscar W.
1955   "A Sociohistorical Survey of Alcoholics Anonymous." QUARTERLY JOURNAL OF STUDIES ON ALCOHOL 9: 119-56.
Roberts, Glyn
1968   VOLUNTEERS AND NEO-COLONIALISM: AN INQUIRY INTO THE ROLE OF FOREIGN VOLUNTEERS IN THE THIRD WORLD. Paris: Coordinating Committee for International Voluntary Service.
Root, Laura Esther
1967   "Social Therapies in the Treatment of Alcoholics." In ALCOHOLISM. Edited by David J. Pittman. New York: Harper & Row.
Rose, Arnold M.
1954   THEORY AND METHOD IN THE SOCIAL SCIENCES. Minneapolis, Minn.: University of Minnesota Press.
Sagarin, Edward
1969   ODD MAN IN: SOCIETIES OF DEVIANTS IN AMERICA. Chicago: Aldine.
Sanford, Nevitt
1962   "Developmental Status of the Entering Freshman." In THE AMERICAN COLLEGE. Edited by Nevitt Sanford. New York: John Wiley.
Schapiro, Leonard
1970   THE COMMUNIST PARTY OF THE SOVIET UNION. 2nd ed. London: Methuen.

Schein, Edgar H.
1957 "Symposium Number 4: Methods of Forceful Indoctrination: Observations and Interviews." New York: Group for the Advancement of Psychiatry.

Schultz, Duane P.
1965 SENSORY RESTRICTION: EFFECTS ON BEHAVIOR. New York: Academic Press.

Scott, Edward M.
1971 AN ARENA FOR HAPPINESS. Springfield, Ill.: C.C. Thomas.

Scott, William A.
1965 VALUES AND ORGANIZATIONS: A STUDY OF FRATERNITIES AND SORORITIES. Chicago: Rand McNally.

Sears, David O.
1969 "Political Behavior." In HANDBOOK OF SOCIAL PSYCHOLOGY, 2nd ed. Edited by Gardner Lindzey and Elliot Aronson. Reading, Mass.: Addison-Wesley.

Selznick, Philip
1952 THE ORGANIZATIONAL WEAPON: A STUDY OF BOLSHEVIK STRATEGY AND TACTICS. New York: The Rand Corporation.

Shelley, Ernest L.V.
1971 "An Overview of Evaluation, Research, and Surveys." Boulder, Colorado: National Information Center on Volunteers in Courts.

Sheppard, H.L., and N.A. Masters
1959 "The Political Attitudes and Preferences of Union Members: The Case of the Detroit Auto Workers," AMERICAN POLITICAL SCIENCE REVIEW 53: 437-46.

Smelser, Neil J.
1963 THEORY OF COLLECTIVE BEHAVIOR. New York: Free Press.

Smith, David Horton
1970 "Personality and the General Activity Syndrome." Unpublished paper, Institute of Human Sciences, Boston College.
1972a "The Religious Behavior of Latin American University Students." Unpublished report, Boston, Institute of Human Sciences, Boston College.
1972b "Ritual in Voluntary Associations." JOURNAL OF VOLUNTARY ACTION RESEARCH 1, no. 4: 39-53.
1972c "Organizational Boundaries and Organizational Affiliates." SOCIOLOGY AND SOCIAL RESEARCH 56, no. 4: 494-512.

Smith, David Horton, Richard D. Reddy and Burt R. Baldwin
1972 "Types of Voluntary Action: A Definitional Essay." In VOLUNTARY ACTION RESEARCH: 1972. Edited by David Horton Smith et al. Lexington, Mass.: Lexington Books, D.C. Heath and Co.

Stein, Morris I.
1966   VOLUNTEERS FOR PEACE. New York: John Wiley & Sons.
Stewart, David A.
1955   "The Dynamics of Fellowship as Illustrated in Alcoholics Anonymous."
       QUARTERLY JOURNAL OF STUDIES ON ALCOHOL 16: 251-62.
Toch, Hans
1965   THE SOCIAL PSYCHOLOGY OF SOCIAL MOVEMENTS. New York:
       Bobbs-Merrill.
Townsend, Edgar J.
1972   "An Examination of the Effects of College Student Participation in
       Volunteer Service Activities on Selected Attitudes and Activities."
       Unpublished Ph.D. dissertation, American University, Washington, D.C.
Trice, Harrison M.
1957   "The Process of Affiliation with AA." QUARTERLY JOURNAL OF
       STUDIES ON ALCOHOL 18: 38-54.
1959   "The Affiliation Motive and Readiness to Join AA." QUARTERLY
       JOURNAL OF STUDIES ON ALCOHOL 20: 313-20.
1966   ALCOHOLISM IN AMERICA. New York: McGraw-Hill.
Troeltsch, Ernst
1931   THE SOCIAL TEACHING OF THE CHRISTIAN CHURCHES. 2 vols.
       New York: Macmillan.
Umbarger, Carter C., D. Kantor, and M. Greenblatt
1962   COLLEGE STUDENT IN A MENTAL HOSPITAL New York: Grune
       and Stratton, 1962.
Vernallis, Francis F., and Roderick G. St. Pierre
1964   "Volunteer Workers' Opinions About Mental Illness," JOURNAL OF
       CLINICAL PSYCHOLOGY 20: 140-43.
Vernon, Philip E.
1969   INTELLIGENCE AND CULTURAL ENVIRONMENT. London:
       Methuen & Co.
Volkman, Rita, and Donald R. Cressey
1963   "Differential Association and the Rehabilitation of Drug Addicts."
       AMERICAN JOURNAL OF SOCIOLOGY 69: 129-42.
Wallace, Walter L.
1964   "Institutional and Life-Cycle Socialization of College Freshmen."
       AMERICAN JOURNAL OF SOCIOLOGY 70: 303-318.
Warner, W. Keith
1972   "Major Conceptual Elements of Voluntary Associations." In VOLUN-
       TARY ACTION RESEARCH: 1972. Edited by David Horton Smith et
       al. Lexington, Mass.: Lexington Books, D.C. Heath and Co.
Webster, Harold, Mervin Freedman, and Paul Heist
1962   "Personality Changes in College Students." In THE AMERICAN COL-
       LEGE. Edited by Nevitt Sanford. New York: John Wiley.

Wechsler, Henry

1960a "The Ex-Patient Organization Summary." JOURNAL OF SOCIAL IS-
SUES 16, no. 2: 47-53.

1960b "The Self-Help Organization in the Mental Health Field: Recovery
Incorporated, A Case Study." JOURNAL OF NERVOUS AND MEN-
TAL DISEASE 130: 297-314.

Wheeler, Stanton

1969 "Socialization in Correctional Institutions." In HANDBOOK OF
SOCIALIZATION THEORY AND RESEARCH. Edited by David A.
Goslin. Chicago: Rand McNally.

Wilensky, Harold L.

1956 "The Labor Vote: A Local Union's Impact on the Political Conduct of
Its Members," SOCIAL FORCES 35: 111-20.

Wilkinson, Paul

1971 SOCIAL MOVEMENT. London: The Macmillan Press.

Wilson, Everett K.

1966 "The Entering Student: Attributes and Agents of Change." In COL-
LEGE PEER GROUPS: PROBLEMS AND PROSPECTS FOR RE-
SEARCH. Edited by Theodore Newcomb and Everett K. Wilson. Chi-
cago: Aldine.

Woodcock, George

1968 ANARCHISM. Harmondsworth, England: Penguin Books.

Wrong, Dennis H.

1961 "The Oversocialized Conception of Man in Modern Sociology." AMER-
ICAN SOCIOLOGICAL REVIEW 26, no. 2: 183-93.

Wu, Tsong-Shien

1968 "A Seventeen-Year Study of the Relationship of 4-H Club Work to the
Interests of Rural Youth and Their Selected Performances as Adults."
Ph.D. dissertation, Univ. of Wisconsin, Madison.

Yablonsky, Lewis

1965 THE TUNNEL BACK: SYNANON. New York: Macmillan.

Zablocki, Benjamin

1971 THE JOYFUL COMMUNITY. New York: Penguin Books.

Zaphiris, Alexander et al.

1968 "Volunteer Probation Counseling Program of the Jefferson County
Court." Denver, Colorado: Graduate School of Social Work, Denver
University.

1970 "Volunteer Probation Counselors in the Denver County Court." Denver,
Colorado: Graduate School of Social Work: Denver University.

Zinn, Howard

1964 THE NEW ABOLITIONISTS. Boston: Beacon Press.

Zon, Henry

1960 "Political Education in Labor Unions," JOURNAL OF SOCIAL ISSUES
16: 21-3.

Zurcher, Louis A., Jr.
1970　"The Poverty Board: Some Consequences of 'Maximum Feasible Participation.' " JOURNAL OF SOCIAL ISSUES, 26: 85-107.
Zurcher, Louis A., and Alvin E. Green
1969　FROM DEPENDENCE TO DIGNITY: INDIVIDUAL AND SOCIAL
CONSEQUENCES OF A NEIGHBORHOOD HOUSE. New York: Behavioral Publications.

Voluntary Associations and
Individual Involvement in
Public Policy-making and
Administration

W. Keith Warner

Introduction

Voluntary associations have been credited historically in the United States with helping to promote and represent the interests of individuals in society. This credit seems to be based on at least five factors: (1) the large number of such associations in existence, (2) the wide scope of interests they represent, (3) the large numbers of people and proportion of the total population involved in them, (4) the ease with which new associations can be formed to address new problems, or utilize different methods on old ones, and (5) the evidence that voluntary associations have been able to make substantial accomplishments both in direct action to solve problems, and in influencing public policy and administration.

Interest in voluntary associations as social instruments has taken various forms. One is a concern for volunteer action, and a belief that people can and should do more for themselves through private associations. A second form of concern is revealed in proposals for governmental decentralization, and the belief that big, centralized government should be de-emphasized in favor of greater local government, and more "grass roots democracy."

Two general modes of action by voluntary associations are: (1) direct action, whereby the group seeks primarily by its own efforts to bring about some expressive or instrumental end, and (2) what might be called mediative action, whereby the group seeks to further its aims by influencing the decisions and activities of other organizations such as public agencies and business enterprises.

A great many voluntary associations engage in both approaches to action, but the approaches are analytically separable, and make somewhat different requirements on the association.

It is the mediative action of voluntary associations to which this chapter is primarily addressed, although several of the implications are also important for considering the viability of those organizations that emphasize instrumental direct action. The importance of what can be accomplished by direct action of

This is a revision of a paper titled "Voluntary Associations and Public Involvement in Resource Policy Making and Administration," prepared for the seminar on Volunteer Action Theory and Research: Steps Toward Synthesis, at the annual meeting of the American Sociological Association, Washington, D.C., 1970.

239

voluntary associations should not be underemphasized. But neither should underemphasis be given to the fact that for most of the dominant problems in society, there are public agencies assigned responsibility and allocated funds. The mediation between these agencies and individual citizens is a major area of contribution to be made by voluntary associations.

The purpose of this chapter is to review some of the attributes of voluntary associations and of the interorganizational structure reflected by their relations with each other and with public agencies and (by implication) business enterprises. In view of these attributes, some implications and conclusions can be considered regarding facilitation of individual involvement in policy-making and administration.

Natural resources problems are taken as an illustrative area, although many other problem areas would reflect similar patterns of analysis. The aim is not to describe in detail the nature of such problems, or to document the role of voluntary associations in dealing with them. Rather it is to show in a general way that the mediative action of voluntary associations, if it is to be successful, requires particular relations both to the problems and to the public agencies and business enterprises concerned.

Resource Problems. A number of features of mediative voluntary association action are illustrated by natural resources problems.

One is that resource problems tend to be defined as technical issues of engineering, biology, economics, and so forth. Social aspects of the problem, when the "human factor" is recognized, tend to be relegated to brief and general terms. Relatively little specification is made of how organizations are involved, and particularly how voluntary associations are involved in the definition and solution of resources problems. When recognition is given, it often is restricted to a focus on two common functions: mobilizing public opinion and action of some kind, and "educating the public."

Second, natural resource problems are extremely complex and technical, as a whole. Substantial expertise in a great many fields—such as various kinds of engineering, biology, economics, and so on—is involved. Management problems must be handled for humans, wildlife, forests, parks, water and air quality, flood control, scenic beauty, etc.

In this general field of interest, with its technological basis as well as its economic and political interests, voluntary associations seeking to facilitate individual involvement in policy-making and administration must bring considerable expertise and skill.

Third, resource problems frequently extend beyond the domain of any single public agency. For example, problems of water pollution are not the sole province of any single level of government—local, state, or national—or any single agency of government. Consequently, if voluntary associations are to mediate between their members (or the general public) and the agencies responsible for policy and administration regarding water quality management, there is no one place to go, no one organization that is accountable, no one agency that could "effect a cure" if it tried.

Finally, natural resource problems are very much public problems, but ones in which there has not been dominant public concern. More often the concern has been fragmented into those special constituencies of business enterprises seeking the development and use of the resources, and the public agencies of resource administration which have their own agency interests to promote, along with some number of voluntary associations. Many public problems of this sort apparently have been handled in relatively private arenas among particular groups with the most immediate interests at stake (McConnell 1966, pp. 243-45). Despite earlier efforts by such people as President Theodore Roosevelt and others, and by voluntary associations in the conservation movement, the result has been the accumulation of a "quiet crisis" (Udall 1967) that has only recently been made noisy by the current ecology-environment movement.

Thus resource problems, although subject to substantial accomplishment via direct action, are very much the kinds of issues for which voluntary associations must undertake mediative action, or in other words must facilitate individual involvement in public policy-making and administration. Moreover, the mediation efforts occur in the context of powerful business and public agency interests.

The Mediation Problem. The mediative function of voluntary associations is the facilitation of individual involvement in both policy-making and administration. Mediation of the interests of various groups requires not only that policies be made in a form acceptable to those groups, but also that the administrative programs and actions be acceptable. This is crucial because many of the important decisions and actions do not enter the arena of general public policy debate. Instead, they are handled as either internal policy and program matters pertaining to particular agencies, and/or as interagency rivalries and disputes. Therefore, many important issues will have been decided outside the realm of public involvement, in a general sense, and those that are left to the public arena will be constrained within the boundaries and filtered through the decisions already made in these other contexts (McConnell 1966, pp. 244-45; Wengert 1955, pp. 55-56).

Policy-making and administration are both essentially political processes. Consequently, any intermediary organizations that seek to represent successfully their member interests must be able to engage adequately in political struggle. This requires power and other resources, especially economic and informational.

The representation process takes a variety of forms including such diverse ones as lobbying, court action, "negotiation" or "bargaining" with administrators, and mobilizing public opinion.

The mediation problem must account for particular application and expertise regarding a problem area, such as natural resources. It must also account for three general categories of factors relating to the instrumentality of voluntary associations: (1) involvement of individuals in the groups, (2) attributes of voluntary associations as viable, effective instruments, and (3) the involvement of the associations in policy-making and administration, and thereby in relations with public agencies and business enterprises.

Involvement of the Public in Voluntary Associations

Estimates of public involvement based on local and national samplings indicate that a substantial proportion of the American people belong to at least one voluntary association. At the same time, although the findings are not entirely consistent, they also show that an important number and proportion of people do not report affiliation with any voluntary association, and many more report no more than one affiliation.

Further interpretation is essential, however. The evidence also indicates that there is substantially less active participation than affiliation; hence, the affiliation figures alone would overestimate active involvement.

Additionally, only some voluntary associations are relevant for particular member interests. For example, affiliation with expressive or consummatory organizations has little or no relevance for facilitation of individual involvement in public policy and administration. Moreover, affiliation with many instrumental associations may be generally irrelevant for involvement in natural resources policy and administration (or any other specific policy or problem area).

In short, many persons are not affiliated with voluntary associations, more are not actively involved, and more yet are not involved in associations that are instrumental for mediation regarding resource policy and administration. The issue, then, is not simply being organized, but also whether one is represented by one or more relevant instrumental associations regarding a given problem area of personal concern.

Even though natural resources issues are vital to the entire population, it is doubtful that more than a small proportion of the total population is actively involved in voluntary associations with primary concerns for these issues. (The same could probably be said about most other areas of public concern.) Firm conclusions about this are difficult, however, because many organizations with primary interests elsewhere have been and are becoming actively concerned with problems of this type.

The available evidence shows that involvement in voluntary associations tends to be related in a positive direction to socioeconomic status (Payne et al. 1972). Therefore, those persons affiliated and involved tend to be relatively advantaged. On two counts, then, the instrumentality of voluntary associations may maintain or widen the gap of advantage deriving from involvement in policy-making and administration: the existence of significant segments of the public not organizationally represented, and the relative socioeconomic advantage enjoyed by those who are involved.

Problems of the Unorganized

A fairly popular view seems to be that people have the opportunity to join existing voluntary associations, or to form new ones, and therefore if they are not represented, it is is because they do not care enough to be. There is much evidence to support this view. Many people are not active in such groups who could be. And many have not formed new associations who could do so.

The problems of organizing the unorganized have not been understood sufficiently. Olson's "theory of collective action" is an important contribution to such understanding (Olson 1965). He points out some of the underlying conditions affecting the traditional presumption that people with common interests can and will voluntarily organize to pursue those interests. He also indicates some of the structural conditions of organizing, especially regarding size of group and benefit-contribution relations. Natural resource problems, often common to large groups or the entire population, repeatedly illustrate the problems of failing to organize in the common interest.

For whatever the reasons of the nonrepresentation in relevant voluntary associations, unorganized people do not have equal representation in policy making and administration. And the fact of nonrepresentation impairs the "balancing out" of the several interests among the public that is supposed to occur in democratic pluralism (Perrow 1964, 414-416).

Attributes of Voluntary Associations as Instruments

The mediative function of voluntary associations depends on more than getting enough of the population affiliated and actively involved in the organizations; in addition the associations must be viable instruments. Thus, in the political struggle of policy-making and administration, what is the nature of voluntary associations as instruments for representing number interests?

The instrumentality of voluntary associations can be considered by reference to ten attributes described briefly elsewhere (Warner 1972). They help to show in a general way what is the nature of this type of organization as a mediating mechanism in society.

The ten characteristics were:

1. Voluntary involvement—entry, performance, and exit being matters of choice, not determined by direct financial remuneration or legal coercion.

2. Secondary importance—low priority on time and resources, compared with occupational and family obligations, and consequent relegation to leisure-time activity and "surplus" resources.
3. Normative inducements—participation induced primarily by normative rather than utilitarian or coercive factors.
4. Specialization of interests—limited scope of objectives that generally include only some of the individual's interests and only parts of societal problems.
5. Segmental membership participation—usually partial, limited involvement of persons in any given organization, and limits on the number of organizations in which much involvement is feasible.
6. Avocational operation—leadership and other planning, implementation, and work carried on typically by persons whose primary training and occupational expertise is in some line of work other than that represented by their responsibility in the voluntary association.
7. Intermittent activity—organizational meetings and other activity occurring relatively infrequently, such as weekly or monthly, rather than on a daily basis as in the case of most government agencies and business organizations.
8. Oligarchical control—centralization of power and decision-making in the hands of a small proportion of the membership, with a tendency for the same general group to retain leadership over relatively long periods of time.
9. Low degree of organization—relatively informal structure and procedures, with typically less coordination and control of work and more frequent *ad hoc* arrangements.
10. Private organization—lack of substantial external, especially public, accountability for the activity and accomplishment of either the organization or the members.

To the extent these characteristics are reasonably accurate (as far as they go) in typifying voluntary associations, a picture of such groups emerges that suggests considerable disadvantage in mediating between individuals in society and those government agencies responsible for the formation and implementation of various public policies. It is difficult to generate much power (relatively) in organizations that have secondary priority for time and other resources, do not emphasize utilitarian remuneration (or coercion), have a partial, limited involvement of members, operate intermittently by people in an avocational role, and so on.

Indeed, this relative disadvantage does appear to be a generally reasonable portrayal of voluntary associations as a type of organization, compared with business firms and governmental agencies, as general types. These latter types tend to operate continuously, have much more financial resources, have more expertise for the work to be done, have more complete control over activities constituting organizational work, and so on.

Yet voluntary associations do generate considerable power in society, and they do have notable successes in representing the interests of large numbers of people on many issues. How is that possible?

One way derives from just some of the supposed disadvantages. The same features (such as intermittent activity, normative inducements, and avocational operation) that provide little base for organizational power in one sense provide in another sense a basis for considerable power. That is, a voluntary association may have difficulty in obtaining from each individual member (or potential member) a substantial quantity of work or other resources, or great compliance with organizational efforts at coordinating activity. But by pooling a large number of these small increments of contributions, a substantial organizational resource can be created.

The "costs" of affiliation and participation in voluntary associations tend to be small, especially for the general membership (compared with the leaders). It is the characteristics like segmental participation and intermittent activity that help make those costs small, and make it possible for people to become involved in organizations on a limited basis. The choice might be no involvement at all in given issue areas.

Secondary importance still means some importance; relatively small quantities of work by volunteers in intermittent organizations is still some work. And not having the most power in society does not mean such organizations have no power. By pooling large quantities of these leisure-time, surplus-resource activities, voluntary associations are able to avoid competing head-on with business organizations and governmental agencies as primary claims regarding a person's livelihood, and still do something useful for the other interests of the members.

A second way voluntary organizations are able to succeed in representing the interests of their membership derives from the aforementioned pooling of resources, usually through the accumulation of a large membership. This is the development of a paid staff. The larger, more expert, and better financed is such a staff, the more it can off-set the disadvantages from some of the other characteristics of voluntary associations in the organization's mediating efforts.[1]

Of course what the addition of a paid staff amounts to, in a certain sense, is the creation of a kind of "hybrid" organization: part voluntary and part nonvoluntary (see Smith, Reddy, and Baldwin 1972). A nonvoluntary component has been infused into the voluntary association.[2] This hybrid probably has some important advantages over both nonvoluntary and purely voluntary organizations: it can still provide involvement opportunities and representation for people who have only limited amounts of time and other resources available, and it can run a continuous organizational operation with professional leadership and substantial resources.

There are other ways, too, of generating greater resources and other advantages for voluntary associations than might appear likely for groups with the ten characteristics reviewed above. One of these, for example, is in the generation of social movements that can instill a great sense of commitment and sacrifice in its participants, and can bring, via normative inducements, many advantages that business organizations and government agencies have to purchase through wages and salaries. In fact, social movements can sometimes generate stronger participant commitment than work organizations can buy with wages.

In short, voluntary associations have both advantages and disadvantages that are seldom taken into account adequately in the context of discussions about how such organizations actually are used in efforts to mediate between individuals in society and institutional agencies. Taking these attributes into account more fully would reveal, for example, some of the limits to the mobilization of individuals simultaneously in behalf of multiple "causes," the extent to which interest groups' positions regarding given problems may be accepted a priori as representative of "the public interest," the extent to which voluntary organizations may fall short of representing the views of individuals relevant to their issue area, and other such important problems (see Warner 1972).

The Interorganizational Structure of Voluntary Associations

The proliferation of voluntary associations leads to important questions about how these many and diverse groups are coordinated to seek their supposedly common interests. The preceding discussion dealt with the intraorganizational characteristics of given voluntary associations. The question of coordination is one of the many that require consideration of the interorganizational structure (or lack of it) of voluntary groups. To what extent is a particular form or degree of individual involvement in public policy-making and administration the unintended result of the numerous intentions of diverse voluntary associations? (Warner 1971.) Put another way, the question is how the proliferation of voluntary associations adds up to a social structure that has identifiable outcomes which are intended and desired?

Two ways in which the question is important regarding how the organizations add up are: (1) How do they add up to the interests of "whole persons." That is, to what extent do the available specialized voluntary associations constitute adequate structure for representing the interests of the public? (2) How do they add up to "whole problems"? That is, to what extent do the available specialized voluntary associations constitute adequate structure for involving the public in all of the relevant policies and administration pertaining to a given problem, such as water pollution? Less sociological literature has accumulated systematically regarding these problems than regarding those concerned with intraorganizational matters.

From time to time views are expressed and proposals made that say the myriad of voluntary associations "ought to" cooperate with one another. This is sometimes accompanied by either a rational or moral presumption of "ought." Since all conservation groups must have a common concern for conservation, such an argument would go, there must be no good reason why they do not get together and present a united front to further their aims.

This argument overlooks the fact that for at least some purposes both the normative and rational basis of noncooperation are as compelling as those for cooperation. As a matter of fact, there seems to be a tendency for similar organizations to act more as rivals than as cooperators (McConnell 1969, p. 158).

Often it is precisely ideological differences that distinguish one group from another; these differences help explain why there are several and not just one. There is no reason to believe that normative or ideological differences can be overlooked in the quest for cooperation among voluntary associations any more than that utilitarian differences can be overlooked in urging business competitors to cooperate. Additionally, some voluntary associations are tied in with administrative agencies as advantaged clientele or constituencies, and some are seeking to change the policies and programs of those agencies. Calls for cooperation and coordination cannot overlook such differences.

It is tempting to assume that some "invisible hand" works among voluntary associations mediating interests of various segments of the public, as it has been presumed to work in other sectors of society. Such an assumption would hold that the cooperation, accommodation, and competition among the thousands of associations somehow balance out the diverse interests and effect the compromises necessary for public involvement and grass-roots democracy. If such a thing happens, or the extent to which it does and the mechanisms by which it occurs—these are issues needing more systematic knowledge.

In short, the interorganizational structure of voluntary associations in relation to given problem sectors in society (such as natural resources) is a subject about which we have relatively little codified knowledge, and a great need for more. Understanding both the intra- and interorganizational structure of relevant voluntary associations is an integral part of the policy and administrative issues in areas of concern like natural resources.

Relations of Voluntary Associations to Public Agencies

In addition to the involvement of individuals and the attributes of the groups, the mediation function of voluntary associations concerns the relations to public agencies. Even for a comparatively restricted societal problem area like natural resources, a very large number of public agencies are relevant.

Local, area, state, regional, national, and international levels of government are involved. This includes several departments and numerous bureaus of the federal and state governments, along with river basin commissions and other regional agencies. It also includes thousands of local municipalities and thousands of special districts dealing with such functions as flood control, irrigation, water supply, sewage, and soil and water conservation. (For water resources, as an example, see Water Resources Council 1968, Chap. 9.) Mediation efforts of voluntary associations must be based on knowledge and understanding of the relevant agencies in this maze of governmental units.

The problems of coordination and cooperation mentioned regarding voluntary associations apply to resource agencies as well. Thus another important problem is how the agencies add up to adequate interorganizational structure for handling important natural resource problems (see Gilliam 1967). The relations and processes are not simply additive and cooperative, however. They are characterized by substantial rivalry and competition among agencies. As indicated earlier, many important decisions and actions are colored by this rivalry.

In this context, voluntary associations ally with some agencies and struggle with some in the political processes of making policy and administering programs. Some of the intra- and interorganizational attributes that affect the instrumentality of voluntary associations in this struggle have been discussed.

As with the relations among voluntary associations, the relations between them and public agencies (as well as business enterprises) have received relatively little systematic sociological study. Much of the available work consists of case studies, and these need codification.

The general image of voluntary associations "expressing public opinion" and engaging in campaigns to "educate" members or the public does not take into account that some of the most effective mediation of members' interests occurs via working relationships with public agencies and representatives. It is the involvement of the associations in decisions and actions of the agencies that provides a mechanism for individual public policy-making and administration.

Some voluntary associations have special working relations as "clientele" or constituencies, whereas others are relatively isolated in society.

Selznick (1966), in his study of TVA, described two forms of special working relations: formal and informal co-optation. Formal co-optation was the use of voluntary associations to share the responsibility and burdens of power, but not power itself (p. 219). One of the uses of this process is to legitimize administrative policies and programs (p. 260). An agency can determine what it thinks should be done and then seek some grass roots legitimation of the decision (but not necessarily grass roots involvement in arriving at the content of that decision).

Informal co-optation, as Selznick described it, was exemplified by the construction of an administrative constituency and giving leadership of that constituency a place in the policy-making structure—in this case of TVA (p. 217). This is not necessarily a process of using voluntary associations, but such groups are often involved in the constituencies, as the Farm Bureau was in the TVA case (pp. 141-45; 262-63).

This discussion of co-optation looks at relations with voluntary associations, constituencies, and the public from the perspective of the administrative agency and its attempts to accommodate to its social environment. Another perspective has been described by the concept of "capture."

Administrative agencies tend to be "captured" by their constituencies, regulatees come to "capture" their regulators, and so forth (McConnell, 1966:7). Some, though by no means all, of such captors are voluntary associations. Kaufman (1960), for example, gives a brief discussion of some of the problem of "capture" and some organizational responses to it (pp. 75-80, 217-19). Another aspect of the problem, though not called by that name, is discussed by Huntington (1965).

A third mode of relation between voluntary associations and public agencies consists of the organization of agencies into voluntary associations. The Association of Bay Area Governments discussed by Scott and Bollens (1968, pp. 11-12) is apparently such an organizational form.

This points up not only the problem of determining where the boundaries of voluntary associations leave off and other forms of organization emerge, but also the problems and implications of the public-private dimension of voluntary associations, described earlier, and of public versus private association (see Pennock and Chapman 1969). Many voluntary associations thus take on a public or quasi-public character. Yet few of them have adequate machinery for public accountability when they take on public functions or character.

Finally, voluntary associations relate to public agencies as competing interest groups because the agencies themselves constitute interest groups (Freeman 1965, pp. 24-25; Henning 1970, p. 135). They and their constituencies are seeking to promote and protect interests in the political struggle just as voluntary associations are. It is especially in this context as interest groups that public agencies may organize into voluntary associations, seek to co-opt constituencies, and so on.

Thus voluntary associations enjoy differential access to the means of policy-making and administration. They also have attributes (e.g., as described by the ten variables discussed earlier) that put them at a disadvantage in competing with the public agencies and business enterprises, especially when they do not enjoy a preferential access to public policy-making and administration.

In addition, the aims of voluntary associations are often normative, and objectives of that type have a difficult time in this society competing with material technology and economic considerations (McConnell 1969, p. 159). Finally, the rules of taxation constrain the ways in which voluntary associations can facilitate public involvement in policy-making and administration and still obtain resources from the members (Patterson 1967, pp. 1028-29).

Discussion

A general view has been sketched of some elements involved in understanding the instrumentality of voluntary associations for individual involvement in public policy formation and administration. The discussion has been both abstract and tentative. If the general "model" or framework of analysis seems useful, the details implied by it can then be explored with some confidence as to prospective utility.

The object of this brief overview has been to describe some of the main issues of mediative instrumentality that might fairly characterize both a diversity of specific voluntary associations and a diversity of problem areas. The natural resources area was used only for general illustrative purposes.

Whether the focus is on natural resources problems or some other kind, the foregoing discussion points out that the nature of those problems to be solved is an important element in understanding the instrumentality of voluntary associations. The problems help specify the work to be done, the organizational interrelationships involved, the resources needed, and some of the requirements for success.

Applicability to Direct Action Associations

What of the prospective applicability of this framework to direct action voluntary associations, as well as to those oriented toward mediative action? If the foregoing points do have reasonable validity and utility for portraying voluntary associations as instruments for individual involvement in public policy matters, do they have similar validity and utility for "direct action" groups?

Response to this requires first a recognition of the distinction between consummatory or expressive organizations (those for which the programs of activity are predominantly ends in themselves) and instrumental organizations— those in which the activity is aimed at accomplishing some objective beyond the enjoyment of that activity (Gordon and Babchuk 1959; Warner and Miller 1964). Voluntary associations that for purposes of this discussion have been called direct action include both consummatory and instrumental groups.

The foregoing analysis is presumed to have considerable relevance for understanding instrumental associations oriented toward direct action, but is not intended to portray consummatory voluntary associations. Competition with other groups in society, for example, is part of much direct action effort, as well as of mediative efforts. And the discussions of involvement of the public in voluntary groups, problems of the unorganized, attributes of voluntary associations as instruments, and the interorganizational structure of voluntary associations seems important for both kinds of associations, although their implications likely will differ for the two kinds of groups. Nevertheless, considerably more knowledge is needed about the differences in those instrumental organizations predominantly oriented toward direct action and those primarily seeking mediative action.

It is especially important to see more clearly the kinds of problems addressed by each kind of group, and to determine how accurate the organizations generally are in adopting one approach or the other (direct action or mediative) in view of the requirements of the problems they are trying to solve. Voluntary associations must make some diagnosis of where the fundamental problems lie: in individual behavior, or in structural arrangements and programs in society? Presumably, direct action associations will be more viable instruments for problems having their solutions in mobilizing and using, or changing individual actions. Similarly, mediative associations will be more viable instruments, presumably, for problems having "structural blockage" in their roots and changes in organizational arrangements and/or programs in their solutions.[3]

This is not to say, however, that all important problems neatly divide into those having individual or those with structural solutions. Most such problems undoubtedly require both individual and structural changes. Nor is it to say that voluntary associations divide neatly into either direct action or mediative categories. Many groups use both approaches at least to some degree.

The empirical basis and implications of these presumptions about instrumentality for individual and structural solutions to problems need more study. More than that, such study appears to be worthy of investment in research.

Needed Study

The foregoing discussion has been offered as a tentative overview and interpretation of some important aspects of voluntary associations as mediating mechanisms in society. Hence, the entire discussion can be considered appropriately as a suggestion for further study that is worth substantial investment. Many of the points need further elaboration, refinement, and empirical testing. Throughout the discussion, several more specific suggestions for further research have been made. Following are a few examples of the issues involved.

1. The extent to which the organizational and interorganizational structures and programs "add up" to viable instrumentality for dealing with: (a) the needs and interests of "whole persons," and (b) the requirements of "whole problems."

    This additivity problem could be approached only for voluntary associations, but eventually it should deal with voluntary associations, public agencies, business firms, and other organizations in society, altogether.

2. The extent to which voluntary associations may help maintain or widen gaps between the advantaged and disadvantaged categories of people in society. Because of socioeconomic differences in who gets organized and who is most active, as well as because of other factors, the disadvantaged may get relatively little benefit from mediative voluntary associations,

whereas the advantaged (who are more likely to have other access to representation of their interests) may get more advantage from the work of such voluntary groups. To what extent is this empirically the case?

3. Related to the foregoing are the problems of the unorganized people, differential power for mediation success among various voluntary associations, and the representativeness of such groups.

   That is, what are the empirical consequences, put together into a whole picture, of (1) voluntary associations not representing a certain segment of the public (the unorganized), (2) some voluntary associations have vastly greater resources and power for representing their memberships than is true for other groups, and (3) the possibility that some organizational leaderships do not represent a majority of their membership in any event. How does the "balancing out" of interests in democratic pluralism occur under varying conditions of the above?

4. The extent to which limits on the mobilization of persons into diverse associations constrains the opportunity for individuals to have their various interests represented. Simultaneously, how do the limits on mobilization and the nature of voluntary associations influence the weights and interpretations that are made by policy-makers and administrators regarding voluntary associations as representative of "the public?"

5. How do organizations come to emphasize direct action or mediative action as their primary strategies, and what are the differential requirements on organizational and interorganizational structures and programs that are made by these two approaches? Moreover, to what extent is it the case that direct action approaches are more successful or "efficient" for problems grounded in individual behavior, whereas mediative approaches better fit problems dealing with structural blockage and requiring structural solutions?

In addition to empirical studies along lines illustrated above, there remains a continuous need for interpretation, synthesis, and codification of knowledge about voluntary associations. Repeated studies on a given problem are needed to establish much confidence in empirical generalizations, and repeated refinements are needed to advance methodological procedures. Similarly, repeated efforts in the realm of theory are needed to find more useful interpretations or frameworks, more powerful and accurate propositions from diverse studies, and so forth in the study of voluntary associations.

Summary and Conclusion

Summary

There is a great proliferation of voluntary associations in the United States, and millions of people have affiliation and active involvement in these groups with substantial accomplishments resulting. These general facts are not sufficient, however, for understanding the instrumentality of voluntary associations for either direct or mediative action.

This chapter has focused on the general mediative function of voluntary associations and has suggested that understanding this function requires knowledge of: (1) the interest area in which mediation is sought, (2) the involvement of people in the voluntary associations, (3) the attributes of voluntary associations as instruments for representing individuals' interests, as well as the interorganizational structure of the associations, and (4) the involvement of voluntary associations in the policy-making and administrative processes, as manifest in part by relations with public agencies and to some extent with business enterprises.

Natural resources problems were taken as an illustrative interest area. The point of the illustration was that, whatever the problem area, the nature of the problem is an important consideration in understanding the instrumentality of voluntary associations.

Effective mediation of individual interests requires involvement or representation in both policy-making and administration. One reason is that many important issues are not dealt with in the general public arena, but are handled as agency and interagency matters. Both policy and administration are essentially political processes, and therefore mediation by voluntary associations requires their successful competition in political struggle.

An important number and proportion of people are not affiliated with voluntary associations, more yet are not actively involved in them, and still more are not involved in associations that are instrumental for mediation regarding particular interests such as natural resources. Since involvement in voluntary associations is related in a positive direction with socioeconomic status, the accomplishments of such groups may maintain or widen the gap of advantage derived from involvement in policy and administration. Therefore, problems of the unorganized are important policy matters because lack of organization not only deprives some segments of the population of some advantage, but also impairs the "balancing out" of diverse interests that is supposed to occur in democratic pluralism.

Ten variables were suggested as characteristic of voluntary associations: (1) voluntary involvement, (2) secondary importance, (3) normative inducements, (4) specialization of interests, (5) segmental membership participation, (6) avocational operation, (7) intermittent activity, (8) oligarchical control, (9) low degree of organization, and (10) private organization. These interrelated attributes help describe the nature of voluntary associations as instruments for facilitating individual involvement in public affairs.

The issue is also interorganizational in at least two senses: to what extent do the voluntary associations available to individuals add up to the total range of interests of "whole persons," and to what extent do they add up to adequate structure for all the components in "whole problems?"

The problems of cooperation and coordination among the many voluntary associations cannot be handled by mere admonition. There are organizational and ideological bases for noncooperation and even rivalry. In any event, there is no adequate basis for believing that the many voluntary associations in society do somehow add up to the kind of interorganizational structure that yields the intended outcomes regarding particular interest areas. The nature and consequences of this interorganizational strucuture (or lack of it) are important problems needing much further study.

The public agencies through which public involvement in policy and administration may be sought are numerous and complex. Thousands of organizational units in all levels of government are involved. An understanding of this organizational maze in relation to the particular interest areas is another requirement of successful mediative action.

Four forms of relations of voluntary associations to public agencies were briefly reviewed: (1) cooptation, formal and informal, (2) "capture," (3) voluntary associations of public agencies, and (4) competition with public agencies as interest groups. The first three of these reflect special working relationships that differ markedly from the general image of voluntary associations as "free standing" units in society that appeal to public agencies for consideration of particular points of view, as well as attempt to mobilize public opinion and "educate the public." The fourth mode of relation points up the importance of understanding the nature of voluntary associations in comparison to their competitors.

Although the discussion was focused on instrumental mediative associations, the suggestions were made that (1) the general framework was also applicable to direct voluntary associations (but not consummatory groups), and (2) it would be valuable to learn how voluntary associations come to emphasize either direct action or mediative action and the organizational consequences that flow from this decision.

Finally, some general suggestions were made regarding further study that would appear to be productive and worthwhile.

Conclusion

Large expectations are often assigned to voluntary associations. They are supposed to accomplish important things directly, represent the interests of their members, help integrate society, make grass roots democracy work, and so forth. The more seriously such expectations are taken, the more important it becomes to extend, codify, and refine the available knowledge about such associations.

Some aspects of the physical environment are regularly or periodically tested or monitored. Some aspects are counted, tabulated, and publicly reported. Measurements and reports are made of water, weather, wildlife, land—and dollars. We also need to measure and monitor in some fashion those social instruments by means of which we expect to develop, control, or preserve natural resources for human welfare, justice, democracy, and other important values.

Voluntary associations are instrumental for individual involvement in public policy-making and administration. But how instrumental, for whose gain and whose loss, and with what effects on the quality of the outcome for the public and for the resources? What improvements need to be made? Questions like these are important for public policy—just as important as many of those to which the funds and expertise of physical technology are now being addressed.

Notes

1. The empirical question remains as to how representative is any program of mediating voluntary associations with large memberships. Particularly, how representative do paid staffs and the programs they promote tend to be of the general membership? (note Barber 1950.)

Additionally, of course, the characteristic of oligarchy raises the representation question even regarding volunteer leadership, especially in large associations. The point of this is that the interests of the general membership, or given segments of it, cannot automatically be considered to be those represented in the programs advanced by either volunteer leaders or paid staff. Representativeness is, of course, an empirical problem requiring evidence.

2. This point simply recognizes one of the sources of variation (in this case a structural variation) in the "voluntariness" of organizations traditionally called voluntary associations and notes that many organizations are neither purely voluntary nor completely nonvoluntary.

3. For a discussion of structural blockage and structural solutions, see Morrison 1971. For a general discussion of social organization as facilitating or blocking change or development, see Warner 1971.

References

Barber, Bernard
1950 "Participation and Mass Apathy in Associations." In STUDIES IN LEADERSHIP: LEADERSHIP AND DEMOCRATIC ACTION. Edited by Alvin W. Gouldner. New York: Harper.
Freeman, J. Leiper
1965 "The Bureaucracy in Pressure Politics." In BUREAUCRATIC POWER IN NATIONAL POLITICS. Edited by Francis E. Rourke. Boston: Little, Brown and Co.

Gilliam, Harold
1967 "The Fallacy of Single-Purpose Planning." DAEDALUS 96 (Fall):
1142-57.

Gordon, C. Wayne, and Nicholas Babchuk
1959 "A Typology of Voluntary Associations." AMERICAN SOCIOLOGICAL
REVIEW 24 (February): 22-29.

Henning, Daniel H.
1970 "Natural Resources Administration and the Public Interest." PUBLIC
ADMINISTRATION REVIEW 30 (March/April): 134-40.

Huntington, Samuel P.
1965 "The Marasmus of the ICC." In BUREAUCRATIC POWER IN NA-
TIONAL POLITICS. Edited by Francis E. Rourke. Boston: Little, Brown
and Co.

Kaufman, Herbert
1960 THE FOREST RANGER: A STUDY IN ADMINISTRATIVE BE-
HAVIOR. Baltimore: Johns Hopkins.

McConnell, Grant
1966 PRIVATE POWER AND AMERICAN DEMOCRACY. New York: Knopf.
1969 "The Public Values of the Private Association." In VOLUNTARY ASSO-
CIATIONS. Edited by J. Roland Pennock and John W. Chapman. New
York: Atherton.

Morrison, Denton E.
1971 "Some Notes toward Theory on Relative Deprivation, Social Movements,
and Social Change." AMERICAN BEHAVIORAL SCIENTIST 14 (May/
June): 675-690.

Olson, Mancur, Jr.
1965 THE LOGIC OF COLLECTIVE ACTION: PUBLIC GOODS AND THE
THEORY OF GROUPS. Cambridge, Mass.: Harvard Univ. Press.

Patterson, Robert W.
1967 "The Art of the Impossible." DAEDALUS 96 (Fall): 1020-33.

Payne, Raymond, Barbara Pittard Payne, and Richard D. Reddy
1972 "Social Background and Role Determinants of Individual Participation in
Organized Voluntary Action" in VOLUNTARY ACTION RESEARCH:
1972 edited by David Horton Smith et al., Lexington, Mass: Lexington
Books, D.C. Heath and Co.

Pennock, J. Roland, and John W. Chapman (eds.)
1969 VOLUNTARY ASSOCIATIONS. New York: Atherton.

Perrow, Charles
1964 "The Sociological Perspective and Political Pluralism." SOCIAL RE-
SEARCH 31 (Winter): 411-22.

Scott, Stanley, and John C. Bollens
1968 GOVERNING A METROPOLITAN REGION: THE SAN FRANCISCO
BAY AREA. Berkeley: Univerisyt of California, Institute of Governmental Studies.

Selznick, Philip
1966 TVA AND THE GRASS ROOTS: A STUDY IN THE SOCIOLOGY OF FORMAL ORGANIZATION. New York: Harper & Row, Harper Torchbooks.
Smith, David Horton, Richard D. Reddy and Burt R. Baldwin
1972 "Types of Voluntary Action: A Definitional Essay." In VOLUNTARY ACTION RESEARCH: 1972. Edited by David Horton Smith et al. Lexington, Mass.: Lexington Books, D.C. Heath and Co.
Udall, Stewart L.
1967 THE QUIET CRISIS. New York: Avon Books, Discus Books.
Warner, W. Keith
1971 "Structural Matrix of Development." In SOCIOLOGICAL PERSPECTIVES OF DOMESTIC DEVELOPMENT. Edited by George M. Beal, Ronald C. Powers, and E. Walter Coward, Jr. Ames: Iowa State University Press.
1972 "Major Conceptual Elements of Voluntary Associations." In VOLUNTARY ACTION RESEARCH: 1972. Edited by David Horton Smith, Richard D. Reddy, and Burt R. Baldwin. Lexington, Mass.: Lexington Books, D.C. Heath and Co.
Warner, W. Keith, and Sidney J. Miller
1964 "Organizational Problems in Two Types of Voluntary Associations." AMERICAN JOURNAL OF SOCIOLOGY 69 (May): 654-57.
Water Resources Council
1968 THE NATION'S WATER RESOURCES. Washington, D.C.: U.S. Government Printing Office.
Wengert, Norman
1955 NATURAL RESOURCES AND THE POLITICAL STRUGGLE. Garden City, N.Y.: Doubleday & Co.

10

Citizen Participation in Federal Programs: A Review

Hans B.C. Spiegel

Introduction

Citizen participation in governmental programs, though not exactly invented during the past five years, has recently received dramatic attention and visibility. A number of federally sponsored programs have begun to require resident or consumer participation and the resultant effects have caused widely divergent expressions. "Maximum feasible misunderstanding" is the opinion of a well-known urban specialist, who goes on to raise the spector of "private nullification" of the legislative will (Moynihan 1969, p. 182). "Let's stop all this nonsense," pronounces an exasperated local housing official who has had his fill of rhetoric and requirements about citizen participation (Louis Danzig, quoted in Campbell 1969, p. 24). A husband and wife team of lawyers, well versed in the war on poverty, offer a choice between genuine citizen participation and rebellion, declaring that the former is "probably the only guarantee, frail though it may be, that people will be willing to abide by the terms of today's social contract. . . ." (Edgar S. and Jean Camper Cahn 1968, p. 222.) Another observer likens citizen participation to eating spinach, "no one is against it in principle, because it's good for you," but the principle explodes when the "citizens" are defined as the "have-nots" (Arnstein 1969, p. 216). All these observers would probably agree that "citizen participation virtually defies generalization and delights in reducing abstractions to dust" (Spiegel 1968a, p. 3).

Indeed, the various sets of activities and roles that are subsumed under the rubric of citizen participation create serious definitional problems in the context of volunteerism. "Citizen participation" can be the label applied to relatively powerless advisory committees that gather at the beck and call of a mayor; it can also be applied to a paid group of area residents exercising veto power over policy decisions about the area's physical development. It can mean the opportunity for groups of citizens to join governmental bodies in a coalition

The assistance of Sherry Arnstein in gathering crucial data under fierce time pressure is gratefully acknowledged. Mrs. Arnstein is a Washington-based Urban Affairs Consultant who was working under a grant from the Center for a Voluntary Society in investigating current policies and practices of various federal agencies in the realm of citizen participation as background for this chapter. This chapter was previously published as JOURNAL OF VOLUNTARY ACTION RESEARCH MONOGRAPH NO. 1 (Dec. 1971), by The Association of Voluntary Action Scholars.

(Mogulof 1969, pp. 225-26) where "convergent action" (Soysel 1966, p. 46) is encouraged and where citizens are expected to give opinions while respecting the proactive role of the professional (Pomeroy 1953, pp. 31-34). But it can also result in confrontation, divergent action, and political challenge.

Smith and his colleagues (Smith, et al. 1972) define voluntary action at the level of individuals as "behavior that is primarily motivated by the expectation of psychic benefits, rather than being primarily motivated by: (1) expectations of the application of physical force or punishment for noncompliance, (2) expectations of strong social-legal-economic sanctions for failure to act in a certain manner. . . ." While this definition is broad enough to cover most aspects of citizen participation in federal programs, I continue to have a nagging sense that even this thoughtful conceptual net is not quite subtle and tightly knotted enough to catch all its squirming and divergent activites. For one thing, citizen participation is a mandated, not a permissive, facet of a number of programs. A given jurisdiction of persons, then cannot opt not to engage in "voluntary" action—unless, of course, the federal program itself is rejected by the intended consumers. Furthermore, I wonder whether psychic benefits are the prime motivational force behind individuals engaging in, say, the Tenant Committee of a public housing project (see "Tenant-Management Issues" 1970) rather than the desperate attempt at avoidance of physical disbenefits. Many persons who are the object of federal programs appear to be motivated into actual participation, at least initially, for essentially negative psychic reasons, such as avoidance of "maximum feasible manipulation" (Arnstein 1970). The scope of citizen participation is so vast that examples can be placed in all of the cells describing various forms of voluntary action in figure 1 of Smith, et al. (1972). That is, citizen participation in federally sponsored activities can be remunerated or not, can take place in formal or informal settings, and can take on autonomous and nonautonomous organizational forms.

Perhaps the basic reason why the elusive concept of "citizen participation in federal programs" tends to sprawl all over—and sometimes beyond—"volunteer action" (even of federally sponsored volunteer action such as VISTA and the Peace Corps) revolves around the term "citizen." A citizen, presumably, not only has responsibilities toward the state, but his will helps to master the state. As will be pointed out later, many federal programs now permit or even require affected citizens to help formulate local policies concerning the program, in addition to discharging program-implementing or assisting functions. In other words, "citizen participation" can go considerably beyond citizens assuming service-supplementary or program-advisory roles; it can also mean that local citizens carry policy and decision-making responsibilities. The current debate about the question of citizen participation revolves exactly around this question of citizen power: how much decision-making power should be maintained by the elected officials and "the essential machinery of conventional democracy" (Soysel 1966, pp. 23-25) and how much power should be delegated to those directly affected by a given program, be they known as "consumers of services," "citizens," "the poor," or "residents"?

How then can we define citizen participation in federal programs? As we shall use the term here, "citizen participation" represents the acts of those who are not formally part of the legislative or public administrative hierarchy but who nonetheless intend to influence the efficacy of the program and the behavior of those public officials responsible for ultimate policy and operational decisions. This definition should accommodate a wide spectrum of activities, including individual and collective citizen acts, that may be convergent with or divergent from the goals of a given governmental unit. Citizen participation thus includes altruistic and Machiavellian acts; acts of high and low social change potential; acts that can be focused on all residents of a given area and those focused on a specific target population such as the poor; and remunerated or nonremunerated acts.

It should be noted that all these acts are performed in the context of a given governmental program and thus vis-à-vis certain political structures. Citizen participation in this context involves decisions—and often struggles—over the allocation of scarce resources. It follows that the present essay stresses the political aspect inherent in this form of voluntary action. I have chosen to highlight the fascinating interplay between deliberate citizen acts and a given administrative governmental program. Excluded from the present essay, there-fore, are citizen acts that are independent of and have no immediate need for federal program assistance, such as a local church's Clean Block Campaign.

It is high time that more be said about these federal programs and their evolving policies and practices toward citizen participation.

Stances of Selected Federal Programs

Participation by Legislative and Administrative Fiat: An Historical Sketch

Participation—An Historical Value? "Why in a democracy that has embraced to the point of excess the tradition of public control of the executive, should it be necessary for the Congress to emphasize the role of the citizen in a governmental undertaking? . . ."

"Why in a federal system where at every level of government elected representatives claim exquisite sensitivity to the needs of their constituents should residents be called on to participate in the administration of a program?" (Wood 1969, pp. 5-6.)

Why, indeed, should the federal government bother to set up mechanisms outside the regularly established representative and administrative channels to deal with the individual citizen and his grass roots organizations? One suspects that there are several answers to the above questions, including tactical ones. Fundamentally, however, it may be said that Americans have a particular penchant for accepting participation in community affairs as an historical value.

DeToqueville wrote about citizen involvement in innumerable civic projects just as today a sociologist observes:

"Citizen participation is a social invention which is characteristic of American community life. The idea of ordinary citizens taking part in improving the commonweal is very congenial to our conception of democracy in which superior wisdom is imputed to an enlightened citizenry" (Rossi 1960, p. 17).

Other writers, such as deHuszar (1945, pp. 12-17), have pointed to the historical advantages and persistent need to supplement "consent-democracy" with "do-democracy." President Nixon joins those paying tribute to this historical value by pointing out that "The principle of voluntary action is not something lately grafted onto America's ways; it goes back as far as the Nation's founding" (Nixon quoted in HUD, 1970a, Foreword).

Building on this value, interest groups for many years have attempted to hold government responsive to the deficiencies of representativeness (Kaufman 1969, p. 3). All manner of private organizations have urged that governmental programs flowing from Washington should not only have the crucial and decisive legislative approval, but a consequential program-oriented nongovernment input, particularly as the program reaches its intended consumer. And government has increasingly acquiesced to these urgings.

Beginning in the 1930s. Mathews (1968, pp. 38-39) points to the U.S. Department of Agriculture as one of the first manifestations of deliberate programmatic attempts to involve a consumer population. The national network of extension services provides one instrumentality (together with various other USDA-related voluntary action groups like the boards of soil conservation districts) to involve individual farmers. But, claims Mathews, when it comes to policy oriented decisions, these efforts tend to be dominated by federal government administrators, resulting in legitimizing centrally determined plans.

There have been other governmental programs such as TVA and Selective Service that have counted on citizen groups to implement their programs. Most of these efforts appear to entail a measure of administrative decentralization, permitting certain well-prescribed discretionary powers and/or advice functions to be locally exercised. Mathews expresses great skepticism about TVA efforts since it, like the Extension Service, depends on staff intermediaries who are accountable to the central program administration. Concluded Mathews (1968, p. 41): "citizen participation from the top, given overriding program goals, ended in mere administrative involvement and a dismal record of participation. That all this happened to TVA, the greatest shining example of incorruptibility, liberalism, and progress, adds to its significance. . . ."

It should be mentioned here that these early attempts at citizen involvement cannot be adequately written about, much less written off, by one whose experience focuses on contemporary urban policies. I merely wish to indicate that citizen participation in governmental programs has an antecedence beyond the start of the poverty program and that such efforts, though surely much more complex than indicated above, illustrate some of the same problems as the later experiences in the 1960s. The remainder of this chapter will concentrate on more recent programs specifically oriented to urban development.

The Kennedy-Johnson Years. The Kennedy administration marks the beginning of a bend in the road of legislative and administrative mandates for citizen participation. Of course, participatory requirements predate 1961, as in housing programs when in 1954 the Workable Program for Community Improvement was written into the law. It stipulated that citizen participation should henceforth be one of the prerequisites to a locality's receiving federal housing funds. However, the local participatory structures thus created were often decidedly middle class and blue-ribbon in character, meeting infrequently, and were more renowned for producing publicized, but innocuous advisory involvement of city-wide citizen leaders than for creating a forum where decision-making confrontations found an airing (see Wilson 1963, pp. 242-43; Van Til and Van Til 1970, p. 314). Mathews suggests (1968, p. 49) that these city-wide citizen advisory committees "were established to meet formal requirements," but in reality represented co-optation by the city in an attempt to legitimize its renewal agency. The Administrator of the Housing and Home Finance Agency could still say in 1961 that "We mean [by citizen participation] not just a passive acceptance of what is being done but the active utilization of local leadership and organization which can profitably assist in the community's efforts" (Weaver 1961). "Profitable assistance" is still miles away from the often shrill and powerful model cities neighborhood board which, with the federal housing department's sanction and money, challenges city hall over the allocation of Washington's money. The transition of "socially legitimate, integrative and non-controversial citizen participation" to the abrasive and power-oriented struggles we experience today was, in retrospect, abrupt and sudden (Mittenthal and Spiegel 1970, p. 32).

Starting in 1964 the War on Poverty, whether by design or not, helped to lend legitimacy to a new level of citizen participation. Its well publicized requirements of "maximum feasible participation" helped usher into American communities a series of innovative participatory structures and practices (see Moynihan 1969; Donovan 1967; Sundquist 1969; Kramer 1969; Mogulof 1969; Zurcher 1970). Thousands of community action agencies were created on whose boards, by administrative regulation, target area residents had to be represented and who, at times, controlled the policy-making machinery. Unprecedented opportunities for citizen participation in program development, federal grantsmanship, paraprofessional work, and—not insignificantly—in negotiating and manipulating the political system were made available by the War on Poverty. A new breed of neighborhood leader emerged—the head of the citizen participation component of the local community action program.

Though himself a target to be co-opted by the city, he had the potential to lead his constituency in opposition to the desires of the mayor and established community pillars. It is hardly surprising that the community action program of the War on Poverty, which permitted and supported such opposition, drew the ire of several city halls.

Housing and other urban development programs could hardly stand pat in the light of these developments that were having an impact on the very same urban poverty pockets in which they also were operating. Indeed, the War on Poverty swept a considerable portion of the federal establishment toward endorsement of citizen participation even if only grudgingly and incrementally. Starting in Fiscal Year 1965, a number of regulations were administratively introduced to encourage citizen participation, mostly by permitting participatory activities to become "an eligible project cost," as in the case of the urban renewal program. In effect this meant that the local renewal agency could, if it wanted to, expend its funds (mostly derived from Washington) for community organizers, for establishing on-site offices, or for hiring indigenous program aides. In the mid-sixties there were not yet mandatory rules to set up a resident project committee. But the trend was unmistakable and may well have been triggered by the Economic Opportunity Act of 1964 and its innovations for consumer participation.

Present Regulations in Selected Programs

Where does the federal government presently stand (as of early 1971) in regard to citizen participation? To really understand the existing federal posture, or more correctly its plurality of postures, one must not only look at the administrative regulations of the various agencies (in itself a Herculean task of compilation—to my knowledge there is no single source listing them comprehensively), but one must also examine the manner in which these regulations are enforced. I will touch on both of these aspects though obviously the second task of judging the administration of programs is much more subjective than the first.

Department of Housing and Urban Development. The federal department bearing primary responsibility for the American city is HUD and thus might be expected to have established the most far-reaching citizen participation policies of any Washington agency. As will be indicated below, one HUD program—Model Cities—has such a set of policies, while many other HUD activities appear far more cautious about the subject. The closest to a Department-wide policy statement on citizen participation appears to have been made, significantly enough, by HUD's general counsel. In it, the purposes of citizen participation are defined as making "the experience, ideas, and needs of those who are to be affected by the program available to city government" (Unger 1970, p. 37). It is repeatedly pointed out that HUD is in the business of "strengthening, not weakening, of local government. We have no desire to carve out new quasi-governmental entities mothered in Washington to administer Federal programs" (ibid, p. 36). In another part it is claimed that "the Department does not prescribe specific requirements for the form that citizen participation must take" (ibid, p. 34). While thus assuring the mayors and city managers that their managerial prerogatives will not be abrogated, the statement nevertheless emphasizes that in the case of the Model Cities Program HUD prescribes "performance standards which must be met . . . that city residents should be fully involved in policy-making, planning, and the execution of all program elements" (ibid, p. 35). One is left with the impression that the HUD front office desires to soft-pedal citizen participation as a potential threat to municipal officials while at the same time meeting the Congressionally legislated mandate for "widespread citizen participation" in its Model Cities program.

The Workable Program for Community Improvement. As has been previously mentioned, the "Workable Program" that was initiated in 1954 is a threshold that localities must cross to qualify for most HUD financial assistance. It contains several elements including codes, planning, relocation, and citizen participation. A number of observers, as cited above, believe that the resulting citizen committees often have performed a rubber-stamp function for the city authorities.

Samuel Jackson, the HUD assistant secretary responsible for the Workable Program—and one of the highest ranking blacks in the Nixon administration—has reportedly been trying to "put teeth" into the citizen participation element. The 1970 edition of regulations show two significant additions to policies. Firstly, the new regulations no longer insist on a Citizen Advisory Committee (a city-wide organizing structure that tended to be fairly static), but require continual participation of citizens with particular emphasis on the poor and minority group members. The language employed, though still general, is more pointed than before:

The Workable Program requires continuing effort on the part of the community to improve and expand the opportunities for creative forms of participation and collaboration that ensure representation by poor and minority groups. . . . (HUD 1970b, MPD 7100.1a, Chapter 7, p. 1.)

Secondly, the new statement specifically requires the poor and minority groups to be involved in the "community's plan to expand the supply of low and moderate income housing" (HUD, ibid, p. 1). These innovations may be seen as discouragingly minor increments to a policy that has only a few fixed requirements. Nevertheless, these new regulations slightly enlarge the toehold of those citizen organizations that wish to influence a housing program. It increases the possibility for successful administration and legal challenges by aggrieved citizen groups.

It is difficult to judge the effectiveness of the administration of the Workable Program at this time. However, there does not appear to be any one Washington staff member who has the responsibility for riding herd on the citizen participation requirement and for training regional staff in rendering technical assistance about it to localities or, for that matter, for imposing appropriate enforcement sanctions. Any federal program, regardless of Washington department, that has broad-gauged requirements and that permits considerable local option, must rely on a perceptive and skilled staff to work effectively vis-à-vis local officials. Whether or not such staff is, in fact, available to HUD and how willing it is to impose negative sanctions on communities that are "soft on citizen participation" remains to be seen. One indication of HUD willingness to act in this arena would be the number of localities denied funding because of failure to comply fully with the citizen participation requirements. As yet we have no such data.

Public Housing. This program contains no requirement for citizen participation or perhaps more properly "tenant participation." HUD encourages participation, but with one exception noted below, appears not willing at this time to insist that local housing authorities implement it. HUD's assistant secretary for the public housing and renewal programs admitted as much when he declared: "It may seem strange in this era of participatory democracy, but the fact is that we really have not addressed ourselves at HUD in any comprehensive way to the issue of tenant participation in public housing management, except for the modernization program" (Watson 1970, p. 2). Encouragement of tenant participation has meant, for example, suggesting that tenants should serve as Housing Authority Commissioners. In the words of a recent circular, HUD "wishes to encourage local communities to consider the appointment of tenants as commissioners of local housing authorities to increase tenant participation in the management of low-income housing projects" (HUD 1970c, RHM 7401.1, p. 1). No doubt, if implemented by LHAs, this form of representation could become consequential. It will be interesting to see how many housing authorities are stirred into action on this recommendation and, if they are, to what extent the protestations of tenant rights groups may have been responsible.

It should be emphasized parenthetically that the local public housing front has been anything but quiet in recent months. A National Tenants Organization has made representations to HUD and its local affiliates have pressed housing authorities around the country for greater participation (see "Tenant-Management Issues" 1970, pp. 534-43).

The one exception to the no-requirement stance of the public housing program is the modernization program which operated on the basis of a set of draft guidelines that are three years old and that appear to be recognized, like Communist China, as a *de facto* though not a *de jure* reality. This draft statement talks of "an officially recognized resident council structure with advisory responsibility in well-defined and mutually agreed upon areas . . . broadly representative of the tenant population and democratically chosen . . . not management appointees" (HUD 1967b, p. 2).

Just as was cited in the case of the Workable Program this requirement may seem minimal, but it does provide an element of leverage. Both LHAs and the organized tenants know that Washington has said something on the subject thus lending a measure of legitimacy to their negotiations.

Urban Renewal. It was 1969 when the urban renewal program made the step from encouraging citizen participation to requiring it—at least in renewal efforts involving residential rehabilitation. The pertinent guideline states that "a Project Area Committee (PAC), made up of residents of the project area, shall be established in cooperation with local residents and groups. It shall be representative of a fair cross-section of the residents of the urban renewal area and shall adopt no financial deterrents to membership or participation by residents of the urban renewal area" (HUD 1969b, RHA 7217.1, p. 1). It should be noted that, unlike HUD's Model Cities Program, the urban renewal requirements make technical assistance and utilization of residents as employees permissive, not mandatory. Significantly, if the local renewal agency agrees, it can pay for the PAC's staff, office space, and technical assistance. A PAC may even help prepare the urban renewal plan for its area.

Again, the evidence on how many local renewal authorities have actually taken advantage of this permissive provision is, unfortunately, not available. One knowledgeable person estimated that between one and two dozen local renewal agencies have actually obtained funds for their PACs; if this figure is anywhere near correct, it would represent a tiny portion of several hundred LRAs around the nation.

Metropolitan Development Planning Program. Citizen participation has even invaded the territory of the regional planner, formerly considered a relatively safe preserve for highly trained professionals. The new regulations, promulgated in 1969, provide for, in general: (1) the designation of "some form of organizational structure, mechanism, or otherwise formalized process, which will directly involve residents of the planning area, . . ." (2) assurance that "the views of low-income and minority groups must be explicitly solicited and recognized, . . ." and (3) the obligation that applications for planning assistance grants contain "a description of arrangements for citizen participation meeting the requirements and performance standards. . . ." (HUD 1969c, MD 6041.1 CHG1, Chapter 1, pp. 7-8).

As is the case with the Workable Program, there appears to be no staff member on national or regional office staffs specifically and exclusively assigned to monitoring citizen participation requirements.

Another planning program, the Community Renewal Program, has provided funds to almost 200 communities. There are no citizen participation requirements in this program and apparently no application for Washington funds has ever been rejected for lack of resident in-puts.

Model Cities. It was the Model Cities Program, enacted in 1966, that enunciated the most far-reaching policy statement concerning citizen participation in HUD's history. Tucked into the enabling legislation were the words "widespread citizen participation," thus creating a congressional mandate of sorts. (For the history of this phrase, see Mittenthal and Spiegel 1970, pp. 38-41.) Part of the official 1967 program guide stated that:

"there must be some form of organizational structure . . . which embodies neighborhood residents in the process of policy and program planning and program implementation and operation. The leadership of that structure must consist of persons whom neighborhood residents accept as representing their interests. . . . The structure must have the technical capacity for making decisions. This will mean that some form of technical professional assistance, in a manner agreed to by neighborhood residents, shall be provided. . . . Where financial problems are a barrier to effective participation, financial assistance should be extended to neighborhood residents" (HUD 1967a, MCGR 3100.3, pp. 1-2.)

It should be noted that this policy not only mandated locally chosen participatory structures but also put at the neighborhood's disposal technically competent advocates of its own choosing, and offers to foot the bill. A number of citizen participation bodies in Model Cities attempted to utilize this HUD pronouncement to gain neighborhood control over the program. HUD lowered the boom. "There can be no exclusive control by citizens," said Washington headquarters, "or by any single citizen group" (Taylor 1968).

There followed an uneasy toleration by Washington of several citizen participation schemes, but the minimal and maximal thresholds of permissible participation were never rendered explicitly firm. The present Nixon administration appears to be more determined to put control and responsibility into the hands of city hall (Baida 1969, and Unger 1970) though considerable variations continue in various locations.

The latest available regulation on citizen participation comes over the signature of HUD Secretary Romney and Office of Economic Opportunities Director Rumsfeld. Entitled "Joint HUD-OEO Citizen Participation Policy for Model Cities Program," it appears to be more concerned about explicating the limitations of citizen participation (what it can't and shouldn't do) than to enlarge its functions. There is no equivocation about the phrase, "The ultimate responsibility and authority for final decisions lie with the officials of local government" (HUD 1970d, MC 3135.1, p. 1). Translated this means that no model neighborhood resident group shall have *de facto* or *de jure* veto power over the program.

The joint statement also reintroduces the requirements of city-wide, as contrasted to neighborhood participation in the Model Cities Program, an idea rather reminiscent of the broad-based boards in the old Workable Program. The architects of the Model Cities Program had talked about city-wide involvement and representation of professional, commercial, religious, and civic groups. While this notion was never explicitly disputed, it was soon forgotten and "citizen participation" became, in fact, "target area resident participation" (Mittenthal and Spiegel 1970, p. 41). Now, however, the local participatory organizations may likely be expanded to include city-wide interests as indicated below. How target area residents will respond to this relative diminution of their role is yet to be seen.

[The citizen participation component] shall be so structured as to afford fair representation to representatives of major elements of the city as a whole, (e.g., religious, charitable, private, and public organizations), having an interest in the Model Neighborhood. (HUD 1970d, p. 2.)

Interestingly enough, this new policy statement does not appear to supersede the 1967 issuance mentioned above and for the moment at least, the two declarations represent somewhat incongruent bed-fellows.

Department of Health, Education and Welfare. In turning to the Department of Health, Education and Welfare we find, once more, policies concerning citizen participation that differ in degree, character, staff enforcement, and even semantics from those of other federal departments and from one another in HEW itself. While HUD had "citizen" and "resident" participation (each susceptible, as we have discovered, to interpretative nuances), the HEW programs speak of "parent participation" (see HEW 1968), "consumer involvement," or "community involvement." The term "citizen participation" is conspicuous by its absence, though its function appears vibrantly strong in some of the department's programs examined below.

Two caveats should be remembered before turning to a few of HEW's programs. One is that the department houses dozens of programs that appear to have regulations concerning citizen participation (including Adult Basic Education, Compensatory Education Program, Equal Educational Opportunities, Dropout Prevention Program, to mention only a few in education). HEW is a programmatic mammoth and is thus particularly resistant to generalizations about department-wide policies. The second caveat is that most HEW programs operate through the state before reaching the locality. The state filter may well complicate the administrative machinery in exercising direct sanctions on the local level.

Elementary and Secondary Education Act (Title I). New regulations require that each school system (though not necessarily each individual school) receiving Title I funds create a Parent Council "composed of parents of children to be served in public and non-public schools." A recent memorandum states that "members of such a council must be chosen in such a manner as to insure that they are broadly representative of the group to be served" (HEW 1970a, OE, p. 2). Also required is "open access to information" about the program for such parents (ibid, p. 2).

So much for the bare-bones outline of the new regulations. To put this new policy into context, however, it must be remembered that local school systems are likely to exercise considerable influence over these Parent Councils. For one thing, the members of the councils can be appointed by the school system, which can also control such vital functions for the councils as training, technical assistance, and allowable expenses for participation. For another, the monitoring of parent participation appears to be primarily the task of state education officials.

A footnote about the enactment of this regulation may be of interest to those concerned with the process that leads to the issuance of such policy statements. It appears that an HEW draft policy was circulated to interested parties after basic staff work had been finished—a common practice in federal agencies. Civil rights groups, poverty organizations, and some educational groups are said to have been supportive of this and stronger participatory policies; reportedly lining up against any proposed participation were the Washington representatives of school administrators, teachers, school board members, and state education commissioners. One suspects considerable *Sturm und Drang* within the Office of Education to move even the present statement into policy over such formidable opposition.

Head Start. This program had its genesis in the Office of Economic Opportunity but was shifted to HEW. It might have been reasoned that this change in Head Start's umbrella agency would result in a down-playing of parent participation as a key program requirement. Quite the opposite seems to have occurred.

Not only do official regulations seem to stress participation more now than previously, but there is a Washington staff specifically carrying the parent involvement portfolio, a central monitoring process seems to be functioning, literature on the subject is abundantly available, and funds are being expended on relevant training and technical assistance.

It is instructive to compare the 1967 regulations with the 1970 edition. For example, the 1967 issuance talks of Policy Advisory Groups of which 50 percent must be parents of participating children (HEW 1967, p. 10), whereas the 1970 statement speaks of Head Start Policy Groups (HEW 1970b, p. 2). The implication is clearly that the groups formerly were advisory to policy-makers while now the groups themselves are responsible for policy.

Equally significant is the corresponding strengthening of functions to be carried out by the policy groups. The 1967 regulations, for instance, stated that the policy advisory groups, as a minimum, should participate in the selection of the program director and "have a voice in establishing criteria for the selection of staff personnel" (HEW 1967, p. 10). In 1970 the policy groups "must approve or disapprove" the hiring and firing of both director and staff.

How much of this Washington stance filters through the federal regional offices and eventually to the local Head Start programs is a matter open to conjecture. Whatever the local performance may be, the Washington regulations appear strong and are there to be acted upon.

Comprehensive Health Planning. This wide-ranging program, covering the planning for "people's total health needs ... of all the population, and all means—services, manpower, facilities, ..." (HEW 1970c, p. 1) uses the term "consumer participation."

The total program has several component parts: state planning (314 a), areawide planning (314 b), training (314 c), state services (314 d), and service development (314 e). The description below centers on area-wide planning where citizen participation takes the form of advisory councils or membership on the policy-making group itself. The regulations of the (314 b) program are instructive in this respect:

An organization receiving a grant to conduct planning ... must have made formal provision for participation in planning decisions by representatives of providers of preventive, environmental, and personal health services as well as by consumers broadly representing the geographic and socioeconomic distribution of the area's population. An organization whose sole purpose is areawide comprehensive health planning must provide for such participation in its governing body, i.e., board of directors, and a majority of that body must be consumer representatives. (HEW 1970c, p. 9.)

Unlike the other HEW programs described above that have as their target a disadvantaged population, area-wide health planning is concerned with the total population of a given geographical entity. Thus "consumers" can be a varied group that, by regulations, only excludes health providers such as physicians, insurance company representatives, and the like. The guidelines urge the inclusion of the poor and minority members on such bodies, but there are no minimal percentages prescribed for such representation.

Again, the nature of the staff running the program is an important variable in terms of the potential consequentiality of citizen participation as a program element. One might speculate that if the staff responsible for a program such as this looks upon health planning in a fairly narrow, prevention-of-disease fashion, the enforcement of the limited participatory provisions would be routine. If, however, the staff views the promotion of health as an endeavor that requires constant consumer input and support, then citizen participation can be expected to receive higher priority in program administration. It appears, for example, that judging by the funding pattern of the pre-Nixon National Institute of Mental Health, a number of its staffers viewed health in the latter fashion and must have been persuasive within the Public Health Service. Unfortunately, I lack evidence concerning the comprehensive health planning program's staff and can do no more than point to the staff role as a variable worthy of further examination.

Department of Transportation. Observers of both the urban renewal and public roads programs have wondered why, in the past, citizen protests about land-takings in urban renewal were much louder than those for highways, which also resulted in massive displacements of residents. Times have changed. Today, highway officials are increasingly aware of public opposition to expressways in populated areas. "Strident citizen protest," says a DOT staff sociologist, "will increasingly interfere with our most accomplished and sophisticated planning efforts, unless and until we learn the techniques of working together at the grassroots" (Larrabee 1970, p. 2). See also Feldman, "Brief History of the Inner Belt Issue in Cambridge" in Spiegel 1969a, pp. 195-211. New regulations for citizen participation in the highway-planning process seem to reflect this administrative unease. The guidelines are still general, but citizen participation has at least impacted an agency that had virtually no regulations on the subject in the past. The following permissive language should be compared with the HUD mandates for participation cited earlier. Both agencies, of course, deal with similar population groups and are equally involved in land-use operations.

Citizen participation is needed at all stages of the planning process. . . . Lines of communication should be established and maintained which will not only seek the views of those affected by proposed programs but demonstrate to them in ways they understand that their views receive full and sincere consideration. This may well require the aggressive use of newspapers, radio, and television in addition to public meetings and organized citizen committees. (DOT 1969, p. 9.)

There are, of course, requirements for public hearings, which do represent opportunities for residents to be heard, but hardly to participate. As yet, there does not appear to be more than an emerging concern and suggestive rumblings at DOT.

Office of Economic Opportunity. So much has been written about citizen participation in the War on Poverty that, in the minds of some people, OEO and participation go naturally together like a horse and carriage. Who has not heard of "maximum feasible participation" that was mandated in the 1964 legislation? It may be useful to take a brief retrospective view of how the participatory provisions of OEO fared soon after the agency's establishment. Elsewhere I wrote:

The fledgling Office of Economic Opportunity had the difficult task of issuing regulations affecting citizen participation in the community action program. On the one hand, the new poverty agency was obligated to advocate consequential, meaningful resident involvement while on the other, it was equally responsible to avoid overstepping a tenuous Congressional mandate. Initially, OEO pursued a course of calculated ambiguity. It advised local antipoverty programs on a number of ways to help the poor to participate through the establishment of new, indigenous-based organizations, actual employment in component projects, and assurances of representation in the governing bodies of the community action agencies. At this point OEO policy took two simultaneous courses. It virtually mandated the inclusion of representatives of the poor to the amount of 1/3 of the CAP Board membership. At the same time, the agency insisted on an open-ended flexible stance . . . Eventually, the duality of policy positions was resolved when OEO issued firm administrative regulations establishing the one-third quota (Spiegel 1968a, pp. 75-76.)

Today OEO still struggles with the administration of participation. A number of its programs have been taken over by other federal agencies, such as the Head Start program. While there still is a Community Action Program, a number of its features have been considerably sandpapered. Perhaps the roughest sandpaper has been applied to the power of the target area residents in running their own programs with minimal outside influence. It should be pointed out that legislative amendments in 1967 and administrative guidelines since then kept intact many aspects of the local Community Action Agency's (CAA's) composition and function. For example, the one-third or more representatives of the poor rule has been retained. And so has the role of CAA as "advocate for the poor on matters of public policy." But now CAAs must operate under considerably intensified restrictions. The net effect of the 1967 amendments was to put the CAA under the mayor's umbrella by making it necessary for the "state or political subdivision" to designate the agency (OEO 1968a, p. 1). Furthermore, one-third of the membership of the CAA Board must be public officials (OEO 1968b, p. 10), there are rather stringent restrictions on political activities (OEO 1968c) and, lately, there has been an emphasis of the CAA's role as catalyst working closely not only with the target area poor, but also the public sector and private sector (OEO 1970). These actions can be seen as a diminution of function and power of poverty area citizen participation in the program.

The above encapsulated interpretation hardly can do justice to the legislative and administrative road OEO and particularly CAP citizen participation regulations have travelled. It must not be forgotten that OEO was the agency that served, in Shriver's terminology, as "the point of the lance" in requiring consequential citizen participation in governmental programs. Perhaps OEO's ultimate legacy is not the recent development of its own participatory policies, but the pervasive attention to grassroots participation it helped to unleash in uncounted programs of the federal establishment.

Office of Voluntary Action. One new Washington agency that may give important clues as to the Nixon administration's attitude toward volunteerism and citizen participation is the Office of Voluntary Action. The Office is the outgrowth of President Nixon's Executive Order 11470 in which he authorized the establishment of a national voluntary action program and a cabinet committee on voluntary action. The program is to "encourage and stimulate more widespread and effective voluntary action for solving public domestic problems." The term "voluntary action" as used in the Executive Order is defined as "contribution or application of non-governmental resources of all kinds (time, money, goods, services, and skills) by private and other organizations of all types (profit and non-profit, national and local, occupational, and altruistic) and by individual citizens. Such contributions or applications of resources are deemed 'voluntary' to the extent they are made without legal compulsion or compensation." (White House News Release 1969.)

This Order seems to be an extension of President Nixon's admonition in his Inaugural Address to "reach beyond government, to enlist the legions of the concerned and committed. What has to be done, has to be done by government and people together or it will not be done at all." This call for voluntary action was to be implemented by a cabinet committee composed of Secretary Romney as chairman and five other Department Secretaries plus former-Director Rumsfeld of OEO. Romney, in turn, started the Office of Voluntary Action to staff and energize the new mission.

OVA, according to its descriptive pamphlet has set itself the task to:

Provide information and referral services for voluntary groups on request concerning the availability of federal domestic program assistance, both financial and technical, . . . provide a point of contact through which voluntary groups can effectively make their needs and concerns known to government, . . . develop, on a selective basis projects designed to relate effectively federal resources and voluntary groups in addressing specific problems, . . . propose, where appropriate, changes in federal legislation, policy, or practice to enhance the government's capability to assist voluntary groups in becoming more creative. (OVA 1970.)

To start on this ambitious task, OVA is cooperating with its opposite organization in the private sector, the National Center for Voluntary Action. The two groups are expected to work in tandem. It appears that the Office (which has as yet no funds with which to make grants and is dependent upon a limited budget for administrative salaries and expenses) is expected to be the intragovernmental agent while the National Center (whose Board Chairman is Henry Ford, II) is to be the monied partner, free from governmental restrictions to conduct an aggressive national program. Besides a Ford Foundation grant of $600,000 (VOLUNTARY ACTION NEWS 1970, p. 6) and "the availability of one million dollars in Federal monies granted through the Office of Management and Budget which will be used in the organization of a network of local voluntary action centers" (ibid, p. 1), there are no indications what other funds are presently available to the National Center for Voluntary Action.

From reading the National Center's newsletter it seems that both it and OVA are concerned about bringing together a broadly-based and apolitical coalition of groups and individual citizens motivated to volunteer their services. Neither the Office nor the National Center appear to wish to focus special attention on any one segment of the population such as the poor or any one problem area such as pollution. A casual perusal of printed material did not disclose the term "citizen participation" once and the term "power" was only discovered in a story entitled "Volunteer Bureaus Tap People Power" (ibid, p. 7).

It is still unclear precisely what additional forces and policies will emerge from the recent merging of OVA and various Federal volunteer programs (VISTA, Foster Grandparents, the Peace Corps, etc.) into an umbrella agency called ACTION. Formed officially on July 1, 1971, ACTION is still in the process of formulating an overall "game plan," although most of its formerly separate component volunteer programs are continuing to operate pretty much as before.

Where We're At

In terms of federal policy on citizen participation, where does this leave us? The above discussion may justify the following observations:

Proposition 1: Administrative regulations concerning citizen participation have permeated Federal domestic programs in several Washington agencies.

Proposition 2: Existing regulations are more cognizant of, more numerous, more developed, and more consequential toward participation than they were a decade ago.

Proposition 3: A single, explicated uniform and consistent Federal policy concerning citizen participation has neither been established legislatively nor administratively.

Proposition 3.1: The federal administration at its highest levels favors citizen participation that is congruent with and not disruptive of municipal and federal program management.

Proposition 3.2: The federal administration at its highest levels opposes citizen participation that results in citizen control over, as contrasted with citizen involvement in, any key aspects of programs.

Proposition 4: Administrative regulations concerning the nature, purpose, support, and enforcement of citizen participation activities vary from Federal agency to agency and even from program to program within any given agency.

Proposition 4.1: Administrative regulations concerning citizen participation range from being vague and permissive to being specific and mandatory (e.g., they vary from general encouragement for informing affected citizens to requiring specific involvement of citizens in organizational structures in which they must be able to exercise certain irreducible powers).

Proposition 4.2: There is no correlation between the amount of financial expenditures of a given federal program and the citizen participation regulations. (E.g., an "expensive" program such as public roads has rather limited regulations, whereas the relatively low budget Head Start program has extensive regulations.)

Proposition 5: The crucial variables determining the stance of a federal program toward citizen participation appear to be: (a) the statutory language of the legislative enactment; (b) the availability of and willingness to utilize administrative sanctions to enforce administrative regulations; (c) the power that can be generated by the program's citizen clientele (often dependent on the degree to which such citizens are organized); (d) the power generated by those opposing strong citizen participatory regulations (often the program's local managers as detailed below); and (e) the availability and performance of staff in the federal program (especially at middle and upper management levels) in monitoring and supporting citizen participation activities.

The Local Scene

How do the federal regulations unfold themselves locally? Who are some of the key actors? What characterizes some of the emerging institutions in the neighborhoods? How can the evolving participatory processes best be described and categorized?

Hard, empirical findings concerning these questions are still relatively sparse. I shall try to concentrate on those aspects of participation that are directly connected with the federal policy stance previously described. Generalizations about the participatory or volunteer process per se I gladly leave to others.

A Phenomenology of Citizen Participation

Two crucial local actors step into the foreground as a federal program finally arrives at the local level: (1) the governmental program manager who is responsible for the program's local administration and (2) the spokesman representing the citizens who are affected by the program (which, in urban-related programs, often means a neighborhood target population). It may be useful to examine quickly the manner in which these two important actors view citizen participation. In short, we want to sketch an abbreviated phenomenology which, hopefully, will illustrate how "citizen participation" generally, and the federal laws and regulations cited earlier, are perceived differentially. It can be expected, of course, that each actor pursuing an active role in the citizen participation drama will define the term to fit his own function, convenience, and perspective.

The Program Manager. This person may be the head of a municipal urban renewal program, or a city's anti-poverty or Model Cities program. He is likely to have been appointed by the mayor or the local governing body and therefore is directly reponsible to the mayor or city manager. He is often the city's entree to the coffers of a specific program.

It may be superfluous to say that the urban program manager is oriented toward program results and efficiency. He wants program applications to be locally approved and sent to Washington for formal approval there. He wants to deliver a program's goods and services as efficiently and quickly as possible. (His definition of both "efficiency" and "goods and services" may, of course, be at variance with that of the intended recipient.) The federally-endorsed Planning–Programming–Budgeting System (PPBS) puts a premium on the program manager being able to maximize limited resources and to control some of the essential variables in municipal programming. The powers and responsibilities of an executive character must be clearly lodged in the mayor and not in two or three bodies, insists New York City's former budget director, who warns that "a return to the divided executive responsibility and accountability and the sheer red tape of the prior system would have severe adverse effects upon the quality of government." (Hayes 1970, p. 31.)

It is not surprising that a number of program managers declare, "from a bureaucrat's viewpoint, there is always trouble in citizens organizations. . . ." (Herman 1969, p. 602.) Program managers appear to think in terms of "production versus participation" (Ascher 1970, pp. 9-10), and this polarization may lead to a perceived inverse correlation between the degree and strength of citizen participation and the production of program results.

To be sure, program managers usually endorse a style of citizen participation that is essentially collaborative-integrative in nature. In this context, citizen participation can be seen as a device whereby public officials induce nonpublic individuals in a way the officials desire (Moynihan 1970, p. 13). It is the oppositional-conflicting style that is perceived as disruptive to the governmental program pipeline that has its fountainhead in Washington and flows through a carefully patched-together and complex system to the eventual consumer. "I share enthusiasm for maximum feasible participation in the process of local governments," states an experienced public administrator, "but I also favor orderly administrative processes and governmental action not unduly impeded by neighborhood power struggles and competing squabbles. . . ." (Hamilton 1969, p. 7.)

The fear of citizen participation resulting in programmatic stalemates and paralysis is repeated often. Roger Starr devotes the better part of his book (Starr 1967) to the need for public officials to make decisions, even in the face of objections or of conflicting preferences of residents and "that action which is taken imperfectly . . . is ultimately more popular than no action at all" (p. 275). Otherwise, many program managers would argue, urban programs will never get off the ground and get fouled up in "the mutual stymie," a phrase attributed to Paul Ylvisaker (Campbell 1969, p. 24). The anguished words of the director of a local housing authority concerned with the production of badly needed shelter well illustrates this fear:

When I think of all the pieces that have to fall together before a public housing unit is constructed, you can see why mankind's first effort at a high-rise as the Tower of Babel never came through. . . .

We've got people like me and the people who work for me. We've got to listen to board members. One of them says, "I want big projects." One of them says, "I want little projects." One of them doesn't want anybody to build unless he's a member of the home builders association.

We've got the city planning commission; we've got the city council; we've got half a dozen other public agencies.

We've got civic associations, pros and cons; we've got neighborhood groups.

We've got the Federal Housing Assistance Office . . . and they don't always agree with us.

We've got the developer and the matter of whether he's making a bundle or not making a bundle.

We might have a non-profit sponsor.

We've got the prospective tenants.

All of these people have got to agree in some way, shape, or form before anything's done. But don't get exercised. This is democracy in action.

For the process to work someone's got to say, "Okay, Mr. Neighborhood Group, you can plan with us; but remember, there's a limit as to what you can do. And there sure is a limit on what you can stop us from doing." (Brignac 1969, p. 604.)

The Neighborhood Spokesman. This person may be the head of a neighborhood council, community corporation, or Model Cities citizen organization. He is usually appointed by his organization and sometimes by a special, publicly supervised election. He may be the executive and paid director of an organization or the elected president. He probably is indigenous to the area and, even if he is not, he is accountable to an indigenously-based policy-making group. In short, he is the spokesman for the neighborhood or for that element in the neighborhood that has a dominant voice in the respective neighborhood organization.

There is growing evidence (see, for example, the case studies of Oakland, New Haven and the South Bronx in Mittenthal and Spiegel 1970) that a number of neighborhood spokesmen are viewing federal citizen participation requirement as political levers which can be utilized to gain advantages for the neighborhood far beyond the boundaries of a specific program. While the program manager looks toward program efficiency and utilizes citizen participation to enhance the flow of program services, so the neighborhood spokesman may be said to regard redistribution of power as his main objective and, likewise, looks to citizen participation to accomplish *his* ends. He may advocate, for example, the delegation of considerable governmental responsibilities to the neighborhood organization and away from city hall. And, in a number of significant instances, he has accomplished just that (Warren 1969, p. 248). Though such a shift in power may not have been anticipated or desired by the Congress when it passed recent social legislation (Moynihan 1969, pp. 88-100), the neighborhood spokesman can utilize the new-found legitimacy of citizen participation for whatever political leverage it may yield.

The theme of redistribution of power appears particularly evident in black neighborhoods. The following statement made by the head of a Model Cities citizen group to a white representative of HUD, who had urged him to consult with city hall, is revealing. Note how the contempt of white-controlled institutions is utilized to draw political battle-lines over issues that presumably go beyond the limitations of a specific federally sponsored program.

The time has passed for me that I will be defined by you or others like you and be told what is reasonable by folk like you. . . . Whether you wish to agree or not, Congress and City Halls around the country are the enemy of the poor because they control the public institutions which oppress many of the poor. And if the poor happen to be black the oppression seems more acceptable and rational. That kind of polarity existed before my time and will in all probability continue after my time. . . . The problem is to recognize a polarity and move toward a bargaining situation in which the interests of parties in conflict can be negotiated. I intend that the representatives of the black community of the poor in West Oakland approach that situation with a strong bargaining position with hat on head and not in hand. . . . (Percy Moore, quoted in Spiegel and Mittenthal 1968, p. 82).

The above is probably not the most typical example of neighborhood spokesmen. There are surely numerous citizen group leaders who presently don't have the political skills or motivations to maximize the potential foothold on neighborhood power facilitated by citizen participation regulations. But to others, the foothold has been eagerly grasped and enlarged into a beach-head. As HUD's former chief advisor for citizen participation in the Model Cities program states, "citizen participation is a categorical term for citizen power. It is the redistribution of power that enables the have-not citizens, presently excluded from the political and economic processes, to be deliberately included in the future" (Arnstein 1969, p. 216).

As a corollary to the presumed goal of power distribution, the neighborhood spokesman will also enter a federally sponsored program with a high degree of skepticism. He often perceives government-citizen partnership as, in reality, an arena for power struggles which he enters at a distinct disadvantage. In the words of frustrated Model Cities neighborhood leaders in North Philadelphia: "If only we had known two years ago what we now know about city and Federal politics, it might have been a different story. But we were political novices, and they were experts in political chicanery. We were trying to change things, and they were trying to keep us boxed in. . . . They had the upper hand, particularly the money and the sophisticated methods for maximum feasible manipulation" (Arnstein 1970, p. 31).

This same group, the North Philadelphia Area Wide Council, concludes with eight lessons that were reportedly learned in the process of dealing with the city and the federal government, the first two of which are, "No matter what HUD says, Model Cities is first and foremost a politician's game," and "You can't trust City Hall or HUD" (ibid, p. 37).

Participation as Political Process

From the foregoing it can be surmised that one way of viewing citizen participation in Federal programs as a local phenomenon is in a political and power context. Indeed, my colleague Mittenthal and I (Mittenthal and Spiegel 1970, pp. 6-9) ventured to make the following statements which I am slightly altering for presentation as propositions.

Proposition 6: Participation of organized local citizen groups in federal programs cannot be considered apart from a context of power. Issues of organizational development and survival, power and control become transcendent themes in consideration of specific issues, especially those issues that deal with the planning and execution of delivery of services to low income areas. (The lexicon of citizen participation has lately been interspersed with repeated references to power not only by neighborhood spokesmen such as the ones cited, nor by social actionists such as Saul Alinsky (see, for example, Spiegel 1968a, pp. 149-205), but also by students of the subject who find the concept of power a convenient context to help understand the dynamics of participation. Indeed, it might be argued that an exclusion of power in the consideration of participation in governmental program is something akin to describing free enterprise capitalism without talking about the profit motive.)

Proposition 7: Organized local citizen groups that have gained a measure of power and/or control over aspects of the local allocation of federal program resources tend to trigger a set of sociopolitical processes that often engender community-wide conflict. (Once the neighborhood organization has resisted or challenged city hall, the issue no longer remains localized to the target area but becomes a city-wide political conflict, as the controversies over Model Cities in West Oakland, South Bronx, and New Haven illustrate (Mittenthal and Spiegel 1970). While conflict is not predestined, there frequently is struggle over the allocation of scarce resources that plays itself out in confrontation between rival actors—and each actor attempts to involve sympathizers to his cause.)

Proposition 8: Dominance in the frequently protracted struggle between neighborhood groups and city hall over control of program resources is often a function of the ability to sustain a permanent, bureaucratic, and financially viable organization over an extended period of time. (As Austin 1970 points out, the city can often "wait out" the neighborhood by the simple expediant of inaction over a period of time. The neighborhood organization often is unable to survive a period of time when no funding is forthcoming. Austin stresses the inherent advantage of established and financially viable community agencies over more vulnerable neighborhood organizations as they compete for the federal dollar.)

Proposition 9: Responding to local political contingencies involving city hall and local citizen organization, federal policies appear to permit considerable local option that varies in time and place and to allow the local citizen participation pendulum to swing once toward the city, then toward the neighborhoods, as the body politic requires. (As has been demonstrated, the federal government has no single citizen participation policy that is uniformly enunciated from Washington. But even if it were, the federal program would have to take local political contingencies into consideration and make adaptations, even if only in nuances. Mittenthal (1970), Rosenbaum (1970), and Warren (1969) write about citizen participation practices that are, to a considerable degree, adjusted and sand-papered to meet local political realities.)

Proposition 9.1: When both city and neighborhood are determined and strong, a major stalemate tends to occur with both parties rallying federal policies and regulations to bolster their respective arguments. (In Newark, N.J., for example, the battle between city hall and a neighborhood group over the location of a medical and dental complex forced the high level intervention of a joint memo by both HUD and HEW undersecretaries explicating specific ground rules. This attempt at *ad hoc* policy interpretation, incidentally, appears to have left both local parties considerably less than satisfied. See Altshuler (1970, pp. 178-80), Williams (1970), and Duhl (1969, pp. 537-72, plus rejoinders pp. 573-88).)

A Typology of Participation

There have been a number of writers trying to categorize the styles of action of citizen groups vis-a-vis a governmental program. A continuum is frequently drawn from little or no participation to much or full participation. As Marcuse (1970, p. 5) has pointed out, this linear approach to participation frequently begs the question of the goals of participation. It also uses concepts such as power, control, involvement, and participation in a unitary sense and places them on a continuum as though they were synonymous when, in reality, important differentiations should be drawn. Despite these shortcomings, the literature is beginning to dissect the conceptual umbrella of "citizen participation."

Arnstein (1969, p. 217) speaks of "a ladder of citizen participation," the lower rungs of which are characterized by manipulation, therapy, information-giving, consultation, and placation. The higher rungs represent partnership, delegated power, and resident control. Arnstein acknowledges that her ladder is a homogenizing abstraction, but insists that human perceptions often appear to be shaped more by image than by substance. "In most cases," she says, "the have-nots really do perceive the powerful as a monolithic 'system', and the powerholders actually do view the have-nots as a sea of 'those people'."

Spiegel and Mittenthal talk of "levels of participation . . . as steps in an evolutionary scale" in the context of Model Cities planning (1968b, pp. 31-33) which are derived from Arnstein's formulations in an earlier memo: information, consultation, negotiation, shared policy and decision-making, joint planning, delegation of planning responsibility, and neighborhood control.

Burke (1968, pp. 287-94) establishes five types of participation: education-therapy, behavioral change, staff supplement, cooperation, and community power. Again, power in the hands of residents is the ultimate type of participation but not necessarily, as Burke takes pain to underline, the most functional for all planning activities.

Other writers do not describe a linear continuum, but emphasize basic modalities of participation which can be differentiated from one another. Ascher (1970, p. 2) makes the useful distinction of citizen participation as service "to supplement the services of paid civil servants . . . " and as decision-making. Mogulof (1969, pp. 225-32) historically traces citizen participation through an elitist model (as characterized by the juvenile delinquency program of the early 1960s), to a coalition or broker model (as in the War on Poverty), to what he describes as an adversary of confrontation model. Other scholars such as Marris and Rein (1967), Hyman (1969), and Warren (1969) have mentioned different sets of typologies.

As has already been noted in a previous proposition, governmental agencies seem to oppose citizen participation that result in their control over a program. There is less empirical evidence that most citizen groups desire maximal power, though it is a hypothesis worth testing. Regardless of whether we speak of "rungs" or "steps" or "models" of citizen participation, it is difficult to predict exactly where the governmental unit and/or the citizen organization will finally draw a line of *modus operandi* demarcation. What appears to be emerging from the previously cited literature, however, is that at the local level this line is often negotiated.

Who Participates, How Much, in What Structures and with What Results?

At this time, these vital questions cannot really be answered with any degree of certainty. To the extent that the literature sheds some light on these issues I have so indicated below in abbreviated fashion. The evidence at hand, however, is too skimpy in my estimation even to formulate reasonable propositions.

What local institutional structures for citizen participation have evolved? They range from advisory councils with relatively few powers to neighborhood boards with *de facto* veto powers. We know of no national survey critically examining the varied structures of community action and model cities agencies. Among the studies touching on this matter are Kramer (1969), Spiegel and Mittenthal (1968), Mittenthal and Spiegel (1970), Mogulof (1969, 1970a, 1970b), MARC (1968), HUD (1969), Austin (1970).

What leadership has evolved from this participatory process with what impact on the program, constituency, and political structures? One of the most perceptive analyses is contained in Zurcher (1970), which is limited, however, to one city. See also Mann (1970), Hunter College (1969).

How Many Participants Are Really Involved—and to What Degree—Under the Banner of "Maximum Feasible" and "Widespread" Participation? We know of no national empirically-based studies on how many "rank and file" residents participate in what program planning and execution tasks. Brandeis University's study of Community Representation in Community Action Agencies, under contract with OEO, studied twenty city programs and reports that "target area residents across all CAAs had very little impact on the major program strategies" (Austin 1970, p. 24). The full Brandeis study may shed welcome light on this area. The number of citizens responding to opportunities to vote for their representatives on citizen boards may be another clue as to "widespread" participation. Mathews (1968, p. 56) cites election results from five cities for local antipoverty boards with an average voter turnout of 4 percent of those eligible to cast a ballot. Hallman (1969, p. 174) writes about an election turnout of 25 percent in voting for representatives of a community corporation. Arnstein and Fox (1968) report an even higher level (up to 40 percent) in some Model Cities elections.

Cross-cutting the Above Is the Basic Efficacy Question: Does Participation Work? How Are the Outputs of a Program with High Degree of Participation Different Compared with Those Evidencing Little Citizen Participation? Observers have taken hold of this question from different vantage points without coming to definitive judgments. Crain and Rosenthal (1967) and Van Til and Van Til (1970) are among the writers who suggest that citizen participation can lead to stalemates where action in any direction may become paralyzed. Mogulof (1969, 1970b) and Spiegel and Mittenthal (1968) point to citizen participation as a political lever for power redistribution, but both authors deliberately leave unanswered the question of improved programmatic outputs. MARC (1968a, p. 248) concludes that the required involvement of the poor is "no assurance of effectiveness of these programs" and, "while theoretically and democratically sound, [it] is more illusory than real." Mathews (1968, p. 56) claims that citizen representatives on poverty boards "have shown more interest in personnel and program control than in program content." However, Kaplan, Gans, and Kahn (HUD 1969a) are rather supportive of the efficacy of citizen participation in their recent evaluation of the Model Cities Program.

Where to Now?

Crystal-ball gazing concerning the future of citizen participation is an enterprise fraught with more than the usual uncertainties. The variables involved, to the extent that they can be identified, spread across many classifications. At the risk of skating on very thin empirical ice, let me venture the following generalization.

Proposition 10: Among the factors that will influence the future utilization of citizen participation in federal programs are: (a) the developing nature and strength of minority and protest movements, particularly the black and consumer movements; (b) the establishment of new federal statutes and guidelines and the manner in which old and new regulations are interpreted and enforced; (c) the degree to which technical assistance and training can be given to both citizen groups and the bureaucracies that administer programs; (d) the availability of federal commitment and resources to urban programs so that there is something about which to participate; and (e) the extent to which local participatory structures can be institutionalized.

In attempting to justify the above predictions, let me cite some brief, personal observations about each factor: (a) It appears to me that one of the chief pressures upon Washington that resulted in stronger citizen participation regulations came from the civil and black power movements. I don't see any other groups in the wings to continue to exercise this pressure, save perhaps a new consumer coalition. Unless such black or consumer pressures are exercised, citizen participation regulations from Washington will likely diminish. The idea of citizen participation as an integral aspect of federal programs just doesn't have enough spokesmen with political muscle to coast on its own momentum.

I previously discussed item (b) concerning the importance of enactment and enforcement of new federal policies. As to (c), technical assistance and training, I have the strong feeling that governmental agencies continue to expect impressive results from citizens and bureaucrats to whom only the most modest assistance is given. Both parties must have training available to accomplish the often delicate task of negotiating and implementing the social contracts involved. (It would be useful to compare those local programs where training and technical assistance have been maximal with those where this assistance was absent or only present in token form.) Citizen groups, it seems to me, must be able to secure their own technical advice, and local program management staff must likewise receive technical support and training. The university may be one institution to play a significant role in this endeavor (Spiegel 1968b, pp. 316-18).

Factor (d), about federal commitment and resources, seems self-explanatory. Obviously, if there is no federally sponsored program or money, citizens can't participate in them. Thus, if Model Cities should be scuttled, participatory regulations and existing practices will cease. A legacy will continue, but many of the neighborhood participatory structures would be doomed.

The last factor, (e), concerning institutionalization of citizen participation, may be less obvious than the others cited above. Let me explain in a few paragraphs.

The vulnerability of the citizens' organizational base concerns me. As it is, such organizations and/or their leadership can be co-opted or derailed with relative ease. Arnstein (1970) tells such a story from the point of view of a model neighborhood resident group. Austin (1970, p. 48) informs us how antipoverty agencies with their neighborhood participation often fell prey to co-optation by established and traditional public and private agencies. How can such participatory neighborhood structures be strengthened to function with relative staying power and independence? This line of inquiry is particularly pertinent when considering that there will likely come times when federal and/or city support for this role diminishes, or when resident apathy reasserts itself, and when the need for an institutional base will prove to be critical. It must be one that displays the resiliency, staying power, and functional utility that enables it to be placed beyond the fickle moods of the culture. At the end of their own assessment of citizen participation the Van Tils point to the "critical importance of the development of new institutional forms that will represent the interests of the poor and will build those interests into the larger political and social structure. . . ." (Van Til and Van Til 1970, pp. 321-22.)

As for particular institutions that appear to be most effective in meeting this goal, there are suggestive models that have been developed but that require testing. For example Hallman (1969) describes the community corporation and neighborhood board that carry out a number of private and quasi-governmental functions in the neighborhood. These community corporations and boards present a suggestive organizational pattern, one that could be utilized as the final part of a triple tiered machinery of federal program administration (Washington, city hall, and the neighborhood). They are accountable to the neighborhood electorate, can enjoy considerable independence from arbitrary city hall actions, and can even generate independent income through commercial enterprises. Advocates of neighborhood control and neighborhood government such as Altschuler (1970) and Kotler (1969) have elaborated on this theme.

Another alternative, of course, would have existing governmental structures become dramatically more responsive to the needs of neighborhoods and accessible to their inhabitants (Mann 1970). Rather than creating new quasi-independent neighborhood units, according to this line of reasoning, a number of existing bureaucracies can be redirected toward serving the public and the neighborhood with greatly intensified effort and sensitivity, but without radical structural changes. Thus a housing program would hire indigenous housing aides, train its existing staff to better relate to citizens, establish many more field offices, consult with community groups, organize participatory planning charettes, and possibly introduce a housing ombudsman. Measures such as these, it will be argued, will tend to correct the temporary imperfections of what still can be a truly representative and response-able liberal democracy. Publicly funded citizen participation will thus take place around a single governmental network without necessitating pitting a separate neighborhood paragovernmental structure against the city. Many observers would insist that effective decentralization rather than "evading or avoiding the jurisdiction of established local authorities" (Moynihan 1970, p. 12) will meet the needs of the neighborhood.

Finally, a mixed model, somewhere between community control and enlightened neighborhood-oriented administration of centrally-controlled programs, suggests itself. New York City's recent efforts at the creation of neighborhood governments appear to be such a mixed model. Mayor Lindsay (1970) wants to meld the separate functions of community planning boards, urban action task forces, neighborhood city halls, neighborhood conservation bureaus, and Operation Better Block into sixty-two districts throughout the city. While the districts would be intimately involved with their respective communities and responsible for the neighborhood administration of various programs, their policy-setting boards would initially be appointed jointly by city governmental officials and resident constituency and only eventually selected totally by direct election. Precisely how this delicate matter of transfer of powers is to be accomplished is not yet clear.

The problem with the institutional forms mentioned above lies in the impetus

287

for their creation, the resources to sustain them, and, once established, their capacity to foster and broaden the popular participatory base. The ultimate irony of course would be to see such institutions become another oligarchical layer that stifles broad-based community dialogue and decision-making. Then citizen participation (the institution) would have helped to kill citizen participation (the process).

One final thought about the future of governmentally sponsored citizen participation deals not so much with participation-as-involvement but with the goals of participation. As Bertram Gross reminds us, participation can become a device for manipulation under the banner of enlarging human welfare. In his disturbing essay on "friendly facism," he perceives the possibility that, "under the combined blessings of HEW, HUD, OEO, and new coordinating agencies, ever new and changing community participation games and carnivals would be staged to allow low-income and low-status leaders—from both white and black ethnic groups—to work off their steam harmlessly without endangering the system" (Gross 1970, p. 48). Indeed, the twentieth century has an abundance of historical evidence that the totalitarian state often seeks to enlist "widespread citizen participation" in its programs. It is the more subtle and benign forms of such participation that worries Gross and the unnamed French student who penned the poster declaring "Je participe, tu participes, il participe, nous participons, vous participez, ils profitent" (Arnstein 1969, p. 216).

Perhaps the best insurance against the dangers of participation-as-manipulation is the assurance that citizen groups will have the power to do more than engage in genteel advice giving but to carry some fundamental decision-making responsibilities about the program's impact on a specific consumer population. The creation of such citizen organizations and the encouragement of truly democratic and productive decision-making processes is an endeavor, to put it mildly, fraught with difficulties. It seems clear that, whichever organizational pattern citizen participation in governmental programs will follow during the next few years, our nation's states', and cities' administrative capacities and willingness to innovate will be severely tested.

References

Aleshire, Robert A.
    "Power to the People? An Assessment of the Community Action and Model Cities Experiences." Date and source unknown.
Altshuler, Alan A.
1970 COMMUNITY CONTROL: THE BLACK DEMAND FOR PARTICIPATION IN LARGE AMERICAN CITIES. New York: Pegasus.

Anton, Thomas
1963 "Power, Pluralism and Local Politics." ADMINISTRATIVE SCIENCE QUARTERLY 7:448-57.

Arnstein, Sherry R.
1969 "Ladder of Citizen Participation." JOURNAL OF THE AMERICAN INSTITUTE OF PLANNERS 25:216-24.

_____ (as told to)
1970 "Maximum Feasible Manipulation in Philadelphia: What the Power Structure Did to Us." CITY 4, no. 3.

Arnstein, Sherry R., and Fox, Dan
1968 "Developments, Dynamics and Dilemmas." Internal Staff Memorandum on Citizen Participation in the Model Cities Program, HUD, August 1968.

Ascher, Charles S.
1970 "The Participation of Private Individuals in Administrative Tasks." Paper delivered at International Academy of Comparative Law, Pescara, Italy.

Ash, Joan
1965 PLANNING WITH PEOPLE, U.S.A. London: Ministry of Housing and Local Government.

Austin, David M.
1970 "The Black Civic Volunteer Leader: A New Era in Voluntarism." Harriet Lowenstein Goldstein Series, Issue no. 5; THE VOLUNTEER IN AMERICA. The Florence Heller Graduate School for Advanced Studies in Social Welfare, Waltham, Massachusetts: Brandeis University.

Babcock, R., and Bosselman, F.
1967 "Citizen Participation: A Suburban Suggestion for the Central City." LAW AND CONTEMPORARY PROBLEMS 33:220-31.

Baida, Robert
1970 "Local Control Essential in Model Cities Program." Speech reported in HUD NEWS, July 18, 1969.

Bell, Wendell, and Force, Maryanne
1965 "Urban Neighborhood Types and Participation in Formal Associations." AMERICAN SOCIOLOGICAL REVIEW 21:25-34.

Bike, E.
1966 "Citizen Participation in Renewal." JOURNAL OF HOUSING 23:18-21.

Boone, Richard
1970 "Reflections on Citizen Participation and the Economic Opportunity Act." Paper prepared for the National Academy of Public Administration.

Brignac, Ronald L.
1969 "Public Housing Official Reacts to Citizen Participation Menages with One-Man Drama." JOURNAL OF HOUSING 26:604-605.

Buchanan, Jeffrey D.
1970   "Urban Renewal in DeSoto-Carr: Citizen Participation Comes of Age."
       URBAN LAW ANNUAL. St. Louis: Washington University, 103-132.
Burke, Edmund M.
1966   "Citizen Participation in Renewal." JOURNAL OF HOUSING 33:18-25.
1968   "Citizen Participation Strategies." JOURNAL OF THE AMERICAN
       INSTITUTE OF PLANNERS 34:287-94.
Cahn, Edward S., and Cahn, Jean C.
1964   "The War on Poverty: A Civilian Perspective." YALE LAW JOURNAL.
       73, no. 8, 1317-52.
1968   "Citizen Participation." In CITIZEN PARTICIPATION IN URBAN
       DEVELOPMENT: CONCEPTS AND ISSUES. Edited by Hans B.C.
       Spiegel. Washington, D.C.: NTL Institute for Applied Behavioral Science.
Campbell, Louise
1969   "Paul Ylvisaker: The Art of the Impossible." CITY 3, no. 2.
"Citizen Participation in Urban Renewal"
1966   COLUMBIA LAW REVIEW, 486-607.
Crain, Robert, and Rosenthal, Donald
1967   "Community Status and a Dimension of Social Decision-Making. AMER-
       ICAN SOCIOLOGICAL REVIEW 32:132-35.
Cunningham, James
1965   THE RESURGENT NEIGHBORHOOD. Notre Dame: Fides Publishers,
       Inc.
Dahl, Robert A.
1960   "The Analysis of Influence in Local Communities." In SOCIAL SCI-
       ENCE AND COMMUNITY ACTION. Edited by Charles Adrian. East
       Lansing: Institute for Community Development and Services, Michigan
       State University.
Davies, J. Clarence, III
1966   NEIGHBORHOOD GROUPS AND URBAN RENEWAL. New York:
       Columbia University Press.
Davis, James W., and Dolbeare, Kenneth M.
1968   LITTLE GROUPS OF NEIGHBORS. Chicago: Markham Publishing Co.
Davis, Lloyd
1965   "With Citizen Participation: New Haven Has Neighborhood Rehab
       Success Story." JOURNAL OF HOUSING 22:132-35.
DeHuszar, George B.
1945   PRACTICAL APPLICATION OF DEMOCRACY. New York: Harper and
       Bros.
Denhardt, Robert
1968   "Organizational Citizenship and Personal Freedom." PUBLIC ADMINIS-
       TRATION REVIEW 28: 47-53.

Denise, Paul
1969 "Some Participation Innovations." In CITIZEN PARTICIPATION IN
URBAN DEVELOPMENT: CASES AND PROGRAMS. Edited by Hans
B.C. Spiegel. Washington, D.C.: NTL Institute for Applied Behavioral
Science.

Donovan, John C.
1967 THE POLITICS OF POVERTY. New York: Pegasus.

Duhl, Leonard J.
1969 "Community or Chaos—A Case Study of the Medical School Controversy." JOURNAL OF APPLIED BEHAVIORAL SCIENCE 5, no. 4.

Edelston, Harold, and Kolodner, Fern
1967 "Are the Poor Capable of Planning for Themselves?" Address before the
National Association of Social Welfare Conference, Dallas.

Gross, Bertram
1970 "Friendly Facism: A Model for America." SOCIAL POLICY 1, no. 4,
44-53.

Hallman, Howard
1969 COMMUNITY CONTROL: A STUDY OF COMMUNITY CORPORA-
TIONS AND NEIGHBORHOOD BOARDS, Washington, D.C.: Washington Center for Metropolitan Studies.
1970 "Federally Financed Citizen Participation." Paper prepared for the
National Academy of Public Administration.

Hamilton, Randy
1969 "Citizen Participation: A Mildly Restrained View." PUBLIC MANAGE-
MENT 51, no. 7, 6-8.

Hayes, Frederick
7/3/70 "Text of Hayes Memorandum on Consultant Contracts." THE NEW
YORK TIMES, p. 31.

Herman, M. Justin
1969 "Renewal Official Responds to Citizen Participation Statements of
Messrs. Burke and Rutledge." JOURNAL OF HOUSING 26, no. 11.

Hunter College, Department of Urban Affairs
1969 THE CITIZEN PLANNER SPEAKS: CITIZEN PARTICIPATION IN
THE NEW YORK CITY MODEL CITIES PLANNING PROCESS. Hunter College, Department of Urban Affairs, New York.

Hyman, Herbert H.
1969 "Planning With Citizens: Two Styles." JOURNAL OF THE AMERICAN
INSTITUTE OF PLANNERS, 35:2, 105-112.

Kaplan, Harold
1963 URBAN RENEWAL POLITICS: SLUM CLEARANCE IN NEWARK.
New York: Columbia University Press.

Kaplan, Marshall
5/68 "The Role of the Planner in Urban Areas: Modest, Intuitive Claims for

Advocacy." Paper presented at the National Association of Social Welfare Conference, New York City.

1970 "HUD Model Cities—Planning System." Paper prepared for the National Academy of Public Administration.

Kaufman, Herbert

1969 "Administrative Decentralization and Political Power." PUBLIC ADMINISTRATION REVIEW 29, 1: 3-15.

Keyes, Langley

1969 REHABILITATION PLANNING GAME: A STUDY IN THE DIVERSITY OF NEIGHBORHOOD. Cambridge: M.I.T. Press.

Kohn, Sherwood

1969 EXPERIMENT IN PLANNING AN URBAN HIGH SCHOOL: THE BALTIMORE CIGARETTE REPORT. New York: Educational Facilities Laboratories.

Kotler, Milton

1969 NEIGHBORHOOD GOVERNMENT: LOCAL FOUNDATIONS OF POLITICAL LIFE. Indianapolis, Indiana: The Bobbs-Merrill Company.

1967 "Two Essays on the Neighborhood Corporation." In URBAN AMERICA: GOALS AND PROBLEMS. Edited by Subcommittee on Urban Affairs, Joint Economic Committee, U.S. Congress, Washington, D.C.: Government Printing Office.

Kramer, Ralph M.

1969 PARTICIPATION OF THE POOR. Englewood Cliffs, N.J.: Prentice-Hall, Inc.

Larrabee, Kent R.

1970 "Highway Project Planning with Local Citizens." Remarks at Highway Management Institute, University of Mississippi, March 13, 1970.

Lewis, Gerda

1959 "Citizen Participation in Renewal Surveyed." JAIP 16:80-87.

Lindsay, John V.

1970 "A Plan for Neighborhood Government for New York City." City of New York.

Lipsky, Michael

9/69 "Toward a Theory of Street-Level Bureaucracy." Paper delivered at the American Political Science Association, New York City.

Mann, Seymour Z.

1969 "Participation in Model Cities Planning." Paper presented at the 75th National Conference on Government, National Municipal League, Philadelphia, Pa.

1970 "Participation of the Poor and Model Cities in New York." Paper prepared for the National Academy of Public Administration.

Mann, Seymour Z., ed.

1970 PROCEEDINGS OF NATIONAL CONFERENCE ON ADVOCACY

AND PLURALISTIC PLANNING, Urban Research Center, Department of Urban Affairs, Hunter College, New York.

Marcuse, Peter
1970   TENANT PARTICIPATION—FOR WHAT? Working Paper, The Urban Institute, Washington, D.C.

Marris, Peter, and Martin Rein
1967   DILEMMA OF SOCIAL REFORM. London: Atherton.

Mathews, Vincent
1968   CITIZEN PARTICIPATION: AN ANALYTICAL STUDY OF THE LITERATURE. Catholic University, Washington, D.C.

Metropolitan Applied Research Center (MARC)
1968a   A RELEVANT WAR AGAINST POVERTY. New York.
1968b   "The Future of Maximum Feasible Participation." Unpublished paper delivered at the Alumni Meeting, Columbia University School of Social Work, New York.

Mittenthal, Stephen D.
1970   "The Power Pendulum: An Examination of Power and Planning in the Low-Income Community." Ph.D Dissertation, Columbia University, New York.

Mittenthal, Stephen D., and Spiegel, Hans B.C.
1970   URBAN CONFRONTATION: CITY VERSUS NEIGHBORHOOD IN MODEL CITY PLANNING PROCESS. New York: Institute of Urban Environment, Columbia University.

Mogulof, Melvin
1969   "Coalition to Adversary: Citizen Participation in Three Federal Programs." JAIP 35: 225-32.
1970a   CITIZEN PARTICIPATION: A REVIEW AND COMMENTARY ON FEDERAL POLICIES AND PRACTICES, pt 1, working paper for the Urban Institute, Washington, D.C.
1970b   CITIZEN PARTICIPATION: THE LOCAL PERSPECTIVE. Pt 2. Working paper for the Urban Institute, Washington, D.C.

Moynihan, Daniel P.
1969   MAXIMUM FEASIBLE MISUNDERSTANDING: COMMUNITY ACTION IN THE WAR AGAINST POVERTY. New York: Free Press.

Moynihan, Daniel P., ed.
1970   TOWARD A NATIONAL URBAN POLICY. New York: Basic Books.

Office of Economic Opportunity
1965   COMMUNITY ACTION GUIDE. Washington, D.C.: OEO.
1968a   Community Action Memorandum 80—Designation and Recognition of Community Action Agencies Under the 1967 Amendments.
1968b   Community Action Memorandum 81—The Organization of Community Action Boards and Committees under the 1967 Amendments.
1968c   OEO Instruction #6907-1. "Restrictions on Political Activities, Community Action Program." September 6, 1968.

1970   OEO Instruction #6320-1. "The Mission of the Community Action Agency." November 16, 1970.

Office of Voluntary Action

1970   NATIONAL CENTER FOR VOLUNTARY ACTION—OFFICE OF VOLUNTARY ACTION, as of November 1970, Washington, D.C.

Peattie, Lisa R.

1968   "Reflections in Advocacy Planning." JAIP 34:80-88.

Perloff, Harvey, and Hansen, Royce

1967   "Inner City and a New Politics." In URBAN AMERICA: GOALS AND PROBLEMS. Edited by Subcommittee on Urban Affairs, Joint Economic Committee, U.S. Congress, Washington, D.C.: Government Printing Office.

Piven, Frances

1966   "Participation of Residents in Neighborhood Community Action Programs." SOCIAL WORK 1, no. 1.

Pomeroy, Hugh R.

1953   "The Planning Process and Public Participation." In AN APPROACH TO URBAN PLANNING. Edited by Gerald Breese and Dorothy E. Whiteman. Princeton: Princeton University Press.

Rein, Martin

1969   "Social Planning: The Search for Legitimacy." JAIP 35:233-44.

Robinson, David Z., ed.

1968   REPORT OF HUD/NYU SUMMER STUDY ON CITIZEN INVOLVEMENT IN URBAN AFFAIRS. Report to the U.S. Department of Housing and Urban Development, Washington, D.C.; New York: NYU.

Rosenbaum, Allen

1970   "Participation Programs & Politics—The Federal Impact on the Metropolis." Paper presented at the American Political Science Association, Los Angeles, California.

Rossi, Peter

1960   "Theory in Community Organization." In SOCIAL SCIENCE AND COMMUNITY ACTION. Edited by Charles Adrian. East Lansing, Michigan: Institute for Community Development & Service.

Rossi, Peter, and Dentler, Robert A.

1961   THE POLITICS OF URBAN RENEWAL: THE CHICAGO FINDINGS. New York: Free Press.

Seaver, Robert

1966   "The Dilemma of Citizen Participation." PRATT PLANNING PAPERS. No. 4:6-10.

Siegal, Roberta

1967   "Citizen Committees—Advice vs. Consent." TRANS-ACTION. May, 4, no. 6:47-52.

Smith, David Horton; Reddy, Richard D.; and Baldwin, Burt R.

1972   "Types of Voluntary Action: A Definitional Essay. In VOLUNTARY

ACTION RESEARCH: 1972. David Horton Smith, et al., eds. Lexington, Mass.: Lexington Books, D.C. Heath and Co.

Soysel, Mumtaz, ed.

1966 PUBLIC RELATIONS IN ADMINISTRATION: THE INFLUENCE OF THE PUBLIC ON THE OPERATION OF PUBLIC ADMINISTRATION. Brussels, International Institute of Administrative Science.

Spiegel, Hans B.C.

1968b "Human Considerations in Urban Renewal." UNIVERSITY OF TORONTO LAW JOURNAL 18:308-18.

Spiegel, Hans B.C., ed.

1968a CITIZEN PARTICIPATION IN URBAN DEVELOPMENT: CONCEPTS AND ISSUES. Washington, D.C.: NTL Institute for Applied Behavioral Science.

1969b CITIZEN PARTICIPATION IN URBAN DEVELOPMENT: CASES AND PROGRAMS. Washington, D.C.: NTL Institute for Applied Behavioral Science.

Spiegel, Hans B.C., and Alicea, Victor G.

1969 "The Trade-Off Strategy in Community Research." SOCIAL SCIENCE QUARTERLY 50:598-603.

Spiegel, Hans B.C., and Mittenthal, Stephen D.

1968 NEIGHBORHOOD POWER AND CONTROL: IMPLICATIONS FOR URBAN PLANNING. Report to the U.S. Department of Housing and Urban Development. Washington, D.C.; New York: Institute of Urban Environment, Columbia University.

Starr, Roger

1967 "An Attack on Poverty: Historical Perspective." In URBAN AMERICA: GOALS AND PROBLEMS. Edited by Subcommittee on Urban Affairs, Joint Economic Committee, U.S. Congress. Washington, D.C.: Government Printing Office.

Sundquist, James L., ed.

1969 ON FIGHTING POVERTY. New York: Basic Books.

"Symposium on Alienation, Decentralization and Participation." PUBLIC ADMINISTRATION REVIEW (January/February 1969), 29:2-64.

Taylor, Ralph C.

9/28/68 Speech to the National Association of Housing and Redevelopment Officials, Minneapolis.

1970 "Tenant-Management Issues." JOURNAL OF HOUSING 27, no. 10: 534-43.

Unger, Sherman

1970 "Citizen Participation—A Challenge to HUD and the Community." URBAN LAWYER 2:29-39.

U.S. Department of Health, Education and Welfare

1967 HEAD START CHILD DEVELOPMENT PROGRAM: A MANUAL OF POLICIES AND INSTRUCTIONS. Office of Child Development.

1968   PARENTS AS PARTNERS IN DEPARTMENT PROGRAMS FOR CHILDREN AND YOUTH. Report to the Secretary of HEW by the Task Force on Parent Participation.

1970a   "Memorandum to Chief State School Officers: Advisory Statement on Development of Policy on Parental Involvement in Title I, ESEA Projects." Washington, D.C.

1970b   "Transmittal Notice: Head Start Policy Manual 70.2." August 10, 1970.

1970c   PROJECT GUIDE FOR AREAWIDE COMPREHENSIVE HEALTH PLANNING. Public Health Service.

1970d   "Joint HUD-OEO Citizen Participation Policy for Model Cities Programs." CDA Letter #10B.

U.S. Department of Housing and Urban Development

1966   PROGRAM GUIDE: MODEL NEIGHBORHOODS IN DEMONSTRATION CITIES. Washington, D.C.

1967a   CITIZEN PARTICIPATION. CDA Letter #3.

1967b   "Draft Guidelines for the Social Service Program." Housing Assistance Administration. Washington, D.C.

1968a   CONTENT ANALYSIS OF FIRST ROUND MODEL CITIES APPLICATIONS. Washington, D.C.

1968b   CITIZEN PARTICIPATION TODAY. Proceedings at a Staff Conference, Region IV. Chicago, Ill.

1969a   THE MODEL CITIES PROGRAM: A HISTORY AND ANALYSIS OF PLANNING PROCESS IN THREE CITIES. Prepared by Marshall Kaplan, Gans, and Kahn, Washington, D.C.: GPO.

1969b   URBAN RENEWAL HANDBOOK. LPA Administration, chap. 5, Washington, D.C.

1969c   COMPREHENSIVE PLANNING ASSISTANCE HANDBOOK 1, MD 6041.1, chap. 61, Washington, D.C.

1970a   CITIZEN AND BUSINESS PARTICIPATION IN URBAN AFFAIRS: A BIBLIOGRAPHY. Washington, D.C.

1970b   WORKABLE PROGRAM FOR COMMUNITY IMPROVEMENT. Washington, D.C.

1970c   "Circular: Appointment of Tenants as Local Housing Authority Commissioners." Washington, D.C.

1970d   "Joint HUD-OEO Citizen Participation Policy for Model Cities Program." CDA Letter #10B.

U.S. Department of Transportation

1969   "Policy and Procedure Memorandum, Transmittal 162." Federal Highway Administration, November 24, 1969.

Van Til, Jon, and Van Til, Sally Bould

1970   "Citizen Participation in Social Policy: End of Cycle?" SOCIAL PROBLEMS 17:313-23.

Verba, Sidney

1967   "Democratic Participation." THE ANNALS 11:53-78.

VOLUNTARY ACTION NEWS
1970   1, no. 2, November 1970. National Center for Voluntary Action, 1735
       Eye Street, NW, Washington, D.C.
Warren, Roland
1969   "Model Cities First Round: Politics, Planning and Participation." JAIP
       35:242-52.
Watson, Norman V.
1970   "The Role of Tenants in Public Housing." Remarks at the Conference of
       the National Tenants Organization by HUD Acting Assistant Secretary.
       Winston Salem, N.C., November 21, 1970.
Weaver, Robert C.
1961   Speech to Family Service Association of America. New York City,
       November 13, 1961.
White House News Release
1969   "Executive Order Prescribing Arrangements for the Structure and Con-
       duct of a National Program for Voluntary Action, May 26, 1969."
Williams, Junius W.
1970   "The Impact of Citizen Participation." Paper prepared for the National
       Academy of Public Administration.
Wilson, James Q.
1963a "Planning and Politics: Citizen Participation in Urban Renewal." JAIP
       39:242-49.
1963b "The Citizen in the Renewal Process." JOURNAL OF HOUSING
       20:622-27.
Wood, Robert C.
10/68 "Science: The Urban Witch." Unpublished paper delivered at the Second
       Annual Symposium of the American Society of Cybernetics. Washing-
       ton, D.C.: October 1968.
3/28/68 "Citizen Participation in the Administrative Process." Address to the
       National Conference of the American Society of Public Administration.
       Boston, Massachusetts.
1969   "A Call for Return to Community." PUBLIC MANAGEMENT 51:7, 2-9.
Zurcher, Louis A.
1970   POVERTY WARRIORS: THE HUMAN EXPERIENCE OF PLANNED
       SOCIAL INTERVENTION, Austin, Texas: University of Texas Press.

11

The Voluntary Participation of College Students as a Catalyst for Change

Athena Theodore

Introduction

American college students, like other social beings, are also voluntary participants in the affairs of their society. On their own initiative and outside their academic roles as college students, they band together without benefit of remuneration in an attempt to effect change in their society. Our definition of voluntarism includes both the student who resembles his adult counterpart in the institutionalized role of "volunteer" and also the student who disrupts the campus and demands reform: the two types differ only in the means they use to achieve change. Why should we study the voluntary participation of college students?

To answer, we need only point to important events occurring in present-day America in which college students are directly involved. At the beginning of the decade of the seventies, colleges and universities are in unusually visible prominence as they attempt in various ways to respond to crisis situations of increasing proportions on their campuses, while the issue of student unrest is the foremost concern of the public. Thus, what students do as voluntary participants in their extracurricular roles may have immediate consequences for the academic community, the society, and perhaps for other societies as well.

The purpose of this chapter is to summarize the major research, theory, and other information which is available on the voluntary participation of American college students oriented towards social-political change; to point out some of the major gaps; and to suggest a few directions and implications for further research. In addition, the concept of voluntarism will be reexamined in the light of the information gained from the investigation of college students.

Early Research

The Extracurricular Activities and
Organizations of College Students

Negligible systematic empirical research has been conducted on the voluntary participation of American college students, even when voluntarism is defined

---

This chapter was originally presented as a paper at the American Sociological Association Seminar Session on "Volunteer Action Theory and Research: Steps Toward Synthesis," Washington, D.C., August-September 1970, and revised for inclusion here.

under the conventional definition of "joining" a recreational club or other type of college organization. As a matter of fact, until the late fifties and sixties the need to study any of the nonacademic or "exrracurricular" activities of students or the organizations with which these activities were affiliated either on or off campus was not considered to be urgent. This is surprising not only in view of the fact that it was generally conceded that what students did in their time away from studies was important and even necessary to their personal, social, and academic development, but also that those students not involved in such activities were suffering from personality and social adjustment problems (Hand 1938; Remmers 1940). Even the political organizations and activities of college students have not been carefully scrutinized by social scientists prior to 1960 despite some student political protest during the thirties and fifties and societal concern as to its proper place on the college campus (Stroup 1955).

Part of the explanation for this early research disinterest may be attributable to the fact that in the past a kind of laissez faire attitude has prevailed among social scientists, who are also often likely to be members of college faculties, that what students did in their spare time was none of their concern and that too close observation of their nonacademic interests and their organizations might be construed as interfering with their "rights." One of the first sociologists to study in detail the extracurricular activities of students, Angell (1928) observed that faculty meddling produced damaging results to the morale of the student organization. Yet even where information has been easily accessible, as in college athletic teams and student government organizations having administrative and faculty liaisons, student participation in these organizations and the organizations themselves have been largely ignored. And reference to any groups or organizations performing social service functions, those more clearly identifiable as "volunteer," is virtually nonexistent.

Political Apathy and Conservatism

A brief examination of the few available studies of student organizations, most of which are lacking in systematic rigor, together with studies on extracurricular activities, peer-group subcultures, and student values, provides us with a background for some understanding of present patterns of college student voluntarism in social-political action.[1] In these studies we can find no history of student involvement or interest in the problems of the world or, for that matter, even a concerted effort to change anything in the immediate college environment. The closest suggestion found in the early literature on the topic of social responsibility was indicated in the stated objectives of student government organizations—to help students gain skills in citizenship and to help train society's leaders.[2] A decade or so ago students were shown to be politically apathetic and extremely conservative, and they looked to their families and careers for their greatest satisfactions. The four-year period of college life had little impact on their political knowledge, involvement in social problems, or ideological beliefs. They showed little or no concern for the welfare of others, and they shunned civic responsibility although they were dutifully responsive toward government. They had little personal interest to crusade for discrimination.[3] Despite the fact that as students they were more liberal than the general population, a substantial proportion even admitted to being intolerant of others' beliefs and prejudiced against minority groups.[4] For most students, college constituted a period of life in which dating, sports, bull sessions, and fun all had priority over academic matters and social responsibility. Social service is nowhere mentioned as an extracurricular activity which might even help to shape student values. The Greek-letter fraternity system, which has received the lion's share of the research on student organizations, apparently contributed substantially to the uniformity and stability of the entire academic social system, providing *in loco parentis* and status to its members, distributing power among the various campus groups, and producing a high degree of conformity and conservativeness within the entire student body.[5]

Research During the Sixties

Research interest on college students in social and political action arose during the decade of the sixties. Two areas of college student voluntarism were rather substantially studied during this period, both independently of each other. The first concerned the general area of political "activism," and the second concerned the role of the volunteer in the mental health organization.

The College Student Political "Activist"

Participation in "New-Left" Extremist Groups. Beginning with the Berkeley "student revolt" of 1964, the power of a small minority of students to disrupt the quiet and relatively orderly processes of American institutions both off and on campus directed a considerable amount of both societal concern and research enthusiasm to the general question of student unrest, mass protest, and organized acts of violence on campuses across the country. The substantial number of investigators who kept pace with the political activities of American college students have included sociologists, psychologists, political scientists, educators, historians, and social critics of various backgrounds and dispositions, all of whom—both independently and collaboratively—have studied and reported on the "crisis" of the campus. Included in this literature of rather uneven quality are both systematic analyses and impressionistic accounts, surveys of local and national samples, in-depth interviews, and on-the-spot observations and "instant" analyses of the political behavior of college students. Even the student himself has been permitted to record his own personal history for both authenticity and posterity.[6]

The emphasis on the research on college student political behavior has been mainly on those students identified as belonging to the radical or New Left extremist groups to be found in large universities where size, location, and ethos facilitate such a pattern of political participation.[7] The fact that only a handful of universities have been included in these studies presents us with a very limited view of the political behavior of college students and points to a need for future study of other colleges and universities, especially those having distinctly different structures.

Reports vary somewhat as to membership in the New Left group, but it is generally agreed that such participation comprises between 1 and 2 percent of the total college population. It is also generally agreed that membership has been increasing.[8] We are, however, confronted with a problem in identifying the various groups of students. The term "activist" is loosely used to include various types of students, some who are centrally involved in the most dramatic events, and others who are only marginal, that is, participating in one or more activities. Thus, insofar as those students called the "activists" may consist of left-wing extremists, radicals, liberals, moderates, or even counteracting conservatives, we may even question the sociological utility of this concept. We might suggest, in fact, that the concept of social role still has some considerable potential for analyzing college students who are constantly making instrumental decisions to effect change and who occasionally deviate from existing normative patterns. Why has no one studied rock-throwing students as deviants?[9] At any rate, the subject of how many students are actually involved—regardless of identification—in the riots, demonstrations, and other forms of protest is an extremely important one, especially when communication media distort the public image of the college student through emphasis on the most dramatic activities in which only a small portion of the student population is involved. It is also important to identify and study the noncollege extremist who invades the campus social system without the legitimacy of student status, a task which may be far less easy than identifying tuition-paying students.

Political Organizations. The political organizations of student activists have received much less systematic attention than have the activities of the students themselves.[10] Political activism does not take place within the traditional political party organizations but rather in a highly decentralized, pluralistic, nonauthoritarian, and generally amorphic system of formal voluntary organizations with national headquarters on the one hand, and various other overlapping and loosely structured groupings of differing degrees of impermanency on the other. Most of the latter spring up to express grievances on specific issues as *ad hoc* pressure groups in the form of committees, projects, "movements," caucuses, councils, and coalitions having interorganizational connections and splintering-off relationships of considerable scope. Groups of this type also arise spontaneously among the opposition groups whose members feel compelled to counter both the Left group and other nonideological campus-issue protestors.[11] Lack of a rigid organizational structure allows for both spontaneity and flexibility in the choice of actions which occur, facilitating the instant mobilization of large segments of the concentrated university population. Considerable ideological diffusion occurs even among the most radical students and within any one group. At the same time, fluid membership and stress on a participatory style of decision-making minimizes the importance of the leader, thus diffusing power and control among the radical groups and making them virtually ineffective once the attack or confrontation has ended. Where leaders are present, they are usually self-appointed, and their roles are restricted to applying for permits, holding press conferences, and other such tasks.

There is need to study these groups and organizations systematically. Other than including them as important forms of collective behavior in the literature on social movements, we have little empirical knowledge of their internal structure, their interrelatedness both among themselves and with other kinds of structures, their leadership patterns, and the processes by which they change or dissipate.[12] In addition, our investigation on college student political organizations and groups suggests a fertile field for research at all levels of social relationships. How does political activism affect friendship patterns, authority, prejudice, and social commitment? Is there a new subculture which develops around protest in the various group forms and rituals such as those of demonstrations, sit-ins, and marches? There are indications that this type of collectivity which demands "instant" reform is becoming institutionalized in the society, not only in the academic community, but also in the wider society among other kinds of groups. What are the implications for social change?

Student Protest. The subject of why students protest on college campuses has received wide attention in the literature. Yet a good portion of this literature is speculative and ungrounded in systematic inquiry. Some consensus, with varying degrees of emphasis and interrelatedness, is that students are protesting because of discontent and disillusionment with the war in Indochina, civil rights, poverty, education, and civil liberties. Many other reasons are also given in the literature at different levels of generalization, usually based on the few studies available from those universities involved in crisis situations.[13]

We are really not too sure why students protest. For example, Peterson (1966, 1968) reports that in the summer of 1965 only one in five students was protesting the war and that civil rights had clear priority in the largest number of campuses. He also reports that during the academic year 1964-65 students were protesting more about dormitory and other living group regulations than they were about United States actions in Vietnam. On the basis of several surveys testing student opinion, Lipset (1967) also concluded that war was of far less concern to students than other aspects of American life.[14] Katz's (1968) study of students at Berkeley and Stanford during 1961-65, which included the period of the crisis during the Free Speech Movement of 1965, indicated that only a small proportion—less than 10 percent—singled out political activities as having any influence on them, and that social and other recreational activities had a far greater influence.

The Politicization of College Students. On the other hand, the time variable is important, and changes may be occurring which have yet to be closely studied through research. In this respect Lipset (1967) has identified two phases of the student movement, one before and one after 1965, marking a change from acceptance of basic values and norms of the American political community to a progressive deterioration in acceptance of national and university authority. However, although present patterns of protest have still to be revealed, we do have information which suggests that American college students are becoming more politicized and radicalized as the decade of the sixties has progressed.

In their sample of seniors and freshmen at Miami University where no major campus crisis had taken place, Christenson and Capretta (1968) found that a trend toward political liberalism manifested itself in every student group tested, at the same time producing a wider range of opinion regarding controversial public issues. In addition, students majoring in the social sciences were more liberal than their class average on entering college and also more liberal on departure. The activists in Paulus' (1966) study also revealed themselves as moving towards radical politics, and Lane (1968) also concluded that college produces politico-economic liberalism and increases political participation. A large-scale mail survey of students and faculty at Columbia conducted by Barton (1968) revealed that while only a minority of students favored the tactics of the sit-in demonstrators during the Columbia riots of 1968, most students and faculty favored many of the major stated goals. This was the conclusion reached by Somers (1965) earlier at Berkeley and it has also been suggested by others who have based their opinions on observation during the campus disturbances in other universities.[15]

Some important theoretical questions are raised by these findings. Who becomes more liberalized, politicized, and radicalized? What are the processes by which liberalization, politicization, and radicalization take place? What aspects of the social structure affect these processes? What is the contribution of voluntary participation in the radicalization process? How are students influenced towards becoming radicals?

One approach to finding answers to these questions would be to study students who have not yet reached the extremist position of the New-Left radical groups. However, if all college students become more liberalized as they proceed through college, we must of necessity be selective as to which group(s) of students in the general "activist" category to place under close scrutiny. A logical place in which to begin a study of these important processes might be the college student volunteer engaged in "constructive" social action in the neighboring community.

There are a few clues provided in both the data-based studies and those which are merely descriptive for seeking out the college student volunteer as an object of focus in the politicalization process. Paulus' (1966) findings that students were mainly protesting the university's position concerning traditional extracurricular activities—a position which they roundly rejected—leads us to assume that at least some students have turned elsewhere for meeting both their personal and social needs. As mentioned earlier, extracurricular activities have always provided the main source of satisfaction to college students, a fact which is demonstrated in the mid-sixties as well as for the preceding decades (Katz 1968). Barton's study (1968) indicates that students would even include neighborhood residents to share in university policy. In addition, the various categories of students identified in the literature as liberal, moderate, and constructive are frequently mentioned as mingling with the radicals or participating in some of their protest activities; and reference has also been made that many northern college students participated as volunteers in the civil rights struggle during the early sixties.[16]

Another point relevant to the politicalization process has been raised by Peterson (1968) who has suggested that not only have the campus-issue activists borrowed the tactics and strategies of the student left but that one campus imitates another campus. Although this is hardly a surprising finding in view of the closely knit campus community, the publicity given to campus unrest in the communication media, and the existence of several national student organizations, it does indicate an expanding network of student relationships across the country. But whether the goals are political or not, we need to study how the voluntary effort spreads from one locality to the next and how this process is facilitated under a democratic system of freedom of expression and a modern communication technology; and we need to make comparisons with other countries, both totalitarian and democratic, in relation to this process.[17]

Background Factors Related to College Student Activism. Several studies have been made of the personal and social characteristics of the political activist to determine if there is indeed a protest-prone personality.[18] For the most part, the activist is compared with the nonactivist. Since these studies vary both in the definition they give to activism and membership in the activist group, they are both difficult to compare and lack the degree of reliability needed to render them useful for the very purpose for which they were designed. They also do not explain why some nonactivists may also have many of these same characteristics.

However, considerable consistency is evident in the conclusions of these researchers. Activists appear to be more liberal, more intellectually oriented, more independent, more socially committed, more altruistic, and less conventional and career-oriented than are nonactivists. They also come from homes of higher socioeconomic status and greater liberalness than do the nonactivists.[19] As might be expected, it is difficult to distinguish a clear liberal-conservative dichotomy in the ideologies of the two types of students, as the majority of students consider themselves to be liberal anyway.[20] Thus we may ask the crucial question which is related to these studies: whether and to what extent volunteer participation in neighborhood service projects, political campaigning for "peace" candidates, or marches in behalf of poverty or civil rights are intervening variables in influencing the activist students towards greater social awareness, altruism, independence, or even less career orientation and conventionality. The fact that these students tend to come from higher socioeconomic backgrounds provides one important clue that they have the time to be both politically active and involved in social and political action. It may well be that further research which includes variables other than those studied might reveal some different clusters of protest determinants.

As already suggested, the participation of black students in protest activities has been the subject of far less study than has been the case for whites. Available studies suggest that black status in relation to white status and different goals between the two groups account for differences in protest patterns. Orbell (1967) found that proximity to the dominant white culture increased the likelihood of protest involvement on the part of Southern black college students. Donadio's (1968) conclusion on the role of black students at the Columbia demonstrations in 1968 was that they received more support from the administration than did white students because they demonstrated for concrete goals and behaved in an orderly manner. These studies raise questions which need to be explored, not only with respect to the participation patterns of black and white college students, but also with respect to their relationships on campus and in the urban neighborhoods concerning both protest activities and community projects. Are there different patterns of volunteerism between white and black students?

The Social Impact of Political Activism. The impact of political activism and campus unrest on the public was clearly evident during the first half of 1970. Student unrest was indicated as the greatest source of concern on the part of the American public during 1970,[21] and a conservative swing among adults during this same year was attributed in part to their reaction to protest movements among young people and the turmoil on college campuses.[22] The establishment of a President's Commission to Study Campus Unrest and various other study groups is further proof of the strong public reaction and government concern.

The impact of political activism and campus unrest on the university may not have yet been fully felt. Discontent with the educational content and impersonality of the large university has already been noted as a major source of student unrest. Mention has also been made of the rejection of the university's "collegiate" brand of extracurricular activities (Paulus 1966). Donadio's (1968) study suggests a decline of student loyalty and a fading confidence in authority based on self-sacrificing devotion to the university. Wider demands for power by students have been noted by Barton (1968), Somers (1965), and many others. The inclusion of neighborhood groups in university policy-making as a demand from students and faculty at Columbia (Barton 1968) all portend marked changes in the academic community. Finally, the demand for "relevance" by college students on all campuses raises questions concerning the role structure and authority patterns of the academic system and the very meaning of education itself.[23]

The College Student Volunteer in Mental Health Therapy

Research on College Students in Mental Health Organizations. The second area of major research effort during the sixties concerned the role of the college student volunteer in mental health settings, mainly the large-scale public hospital. Although a few studies were published in the late fifties, it was not until the first half of the following decade that they reached considerable proportions. The recruitment of student volunteers beginning in the fifties was precipitated by the acute manpower shortage in the mental health field (Kantor 1959; Greenblatt and Kantor 1962; Macbain and Schumacher 1963; Holzberg 1963), and the research by the medical hypothesis that college students contribute to the therapy of mentally ill people. Several scores of studies have been published on the college student volunteer in mental health settings, including not only the complex hospital organization but also half-way houses, prisons, and home and school environments.[24] The most rigorous studies have been conducted by psychologists and psychiatrists on hospital staffs.

Most of our knowledge about college student volunteering is limited to the volunteer in mental health. Although information is lacking on the number of college students who work in mental health, some data on trends is nevertheless available.[25] During the period from 1955-65, a concerted attempt to recruit college students witnessed a rapid growth in the number of state hospitals using students.[26] The location of these hospitals in relatively isolated settings related to their stigmatic qualities appears to be an important factor in the distribution pattern of volunteer assistance.

The Role of the Volunteer. The research on college students in mental hospitals has concentrated on the treatment process, with both students and patients receiving roughly comparable attention. There is considerable repetition in the objectives set for these studies and also considerable unanimity in the conclusions reached.

What is revealed is a rather unique role in which youthfulness, student status, and motivation are important variables. College students are represented as involved in a broad spectrum of projects, tasks, time allotment, age of "clients," type of mental illness, and treatment stage.[27] However, although the volunteer role is seemingly structured around specific tasks (or no tasks, if being one's self would be so considered), the central role function appears to be a symbolic one—that of providing the forgotten patient with a link back to the community to assure his social acceptance. In this respect the volunteer role takes on a different emphasis than that of service as it has been institutionalized in the adult volunteer role. The idea that college students may perform functions which their adult counterparts do not perform presents a considerable challenge for such comparative research.

The Motivation of College Students in Mental Health Volunteerism. An important question which has yet to be answered concerning the role of the volunteer in the mental hospital concerns the motivation of the student. Why should students want to be with mentally sick people if other choices are also presented for volunteer work? The research has yet to come to grips with this aspect of the volunteer role. Our appraisal of the completed research suggests that the emotional support needed to enter the stigmatized world of mental illness may, in fact, derive from some source other than the student's own willingness to perform a service or even to learn about abnormal psychology. A few studies have been conducted in which college students assume the volunteer role in relation to a specific psychology course and through assignment by an instructor. (Wanderer and Sternlicht 1964; Klein and Zax 1965; Rooney 1967). Further study of the two types of student groups on a comparative basis may shed some needed light on the question of motivation, and longitudinal studies of the postcollege volunteer may reveal some additional knowledge about the college student volunteer in mental health.

The Impact of the Volunteer Role on the Volunteer and "Client." The greatest concentration of the research effort has been on the impact of the volunteer role on both the patient and the volunteer. For the most part the student is considered as substantially contributing to the mental therapy of the patient. Studying volunteers over a period of several years Beck et al. (1963, 1965) concluded that students had a positive effect on patients, although it was not clear if other aspects of the social context were also relevant. An even more ambitious undertaking by Holzberg and his associates to study the college student in the companion role with chronically ill patients resulted in the same general conclusion—that students had a favorable impact on patients. Added to this was the conclusion that the volunteer experience also had a favorable impact on the volunteer, the hospital personnel, and the entire hospital milieu.[28]

Beery's (1963) experiment with college students in a maximum security prison also resulted in the conclusion that college students received acceptance from the inmates whom they befriended.

Considerable attention has also been given in the controlled studies to attitude change in students through their interaction with patients. From these experiments it was concluded that students showed more enlightened attitudes towards mental illness and manifested a series of personality changes, becoming more aware of self and more accepting, more self-reliant, and more tolerant of others.[29] Scheibe (1965) and Levine (1966) also noted that attitudes toward and interest in increased social action were favorably and positively enhanced by the experience. Sinnett and Niedenthal's (1968) concern with peer group interaction in a university setting revealed that the academic dropout rate in the client group was relatively low.

Bias in Research on College Student Volunteers in Mental Health. A possibility of bias in the research on college student volunteers should not be excluded. As participants in experiments in which they were accorded considerable attention and support from the professional personnel, students might be expected to experience a greater degree of satisfaction from the status which they derived from interaction with the psychiatric professionals who were observing them, particulary. if nonexperimental volunteer reference groups were also present in the hospital. In these situations students are likely to be given clear directions as to how to proceed and they are consulted frequently for their opinions.

The importance of supervision in the mental hospital was stressed by all hospitals replying to the questionnaire of state mental hospitals.[30] The need for supervision is also indicated by Reinherz (1967) who found that the volunteer's motivations, goals, and length of stay were seriously affected by the quality of the professional supervision given. Contact with patients was positively or negatively affected by contact with the professional supervisory staff. Brown (1968) notes that students who are inducted into traditional mental hospital services are expected to define a role for themselves which has little or no relevance to the larger hospital system. We need to study college student volunteers in mental hospitals who do not receive either preferential treatment or supervision, and we need to compare these volunteers with volunteers in other kinds of treatment settings. The research surveyed also indicates the need to study more systematically the volunteer's relationship with all the hospital roles in terms of usurpation of the central role function—"curing" the patient.

The College Student Volunteer in Social-Political
Action in Community Settings

Dearth of Research on College Student Volunteers in Community Settings. Our empirical knowledge about college student voluntarism in community settings is extremely limited, attributable at least in part to the fact that college volunteering of any sizable proportion is a rather recent phenomenon. As indicated earlier, even during the early period of the sixties, college students were demonstrating relatively little involvement in international, national, or civic affairs. Further evidence is provided by Katz (1968) who indicates that as late as 1965 students at Berkeley and Stanford ranked service to other people as astonishingly low, and he further found little change from the freshman to the senior year. Only 8 percent of all students reported participating in service projects.

We know more about college student volunteers in community settings from the communication media, campus newspapers, and volunteer community organizations. They have been clearly identified as "volunteers" and described by Randolph (1964) as part of the "Northern Student Movement" of the early sixties, by Coles and Brenner (1968) as the "Applachian volunteers," and by Kahn (1968) as the "McCarthy volunteers." They have also received passing reference in the literature on student movements, political behavior, and campus unrest, usually as the students who participated in the civil rights movement of the early sixties and the students who work at projects in the urban ghettos (Altbach 1966; Lipset and Altbach 1967). Several local and national organizations also collect and distribute data about them, some of which is published as reports of conferences, orientation and training manuals, and descriptions of projects.[31] Thus, what appears in the following brief summary can be offered only tentatively, based on conversations, correspondence with numerous local and national organizations, miscellaneous printed reports and other information, and personal experience with volunteers.

Increasing Participation in Volunteer Activities. There is one important conclusion which has a fair degree of statistical support. College student volunteers constitute an empirical reality of somewhat surprising proportions with participation in projects increasing dramatically between 1965 and 1970, varying considerably from campus to campus, and presently comprising as much as one-fourth of the student population at one of the nation's largest universities.[32]

How do we account for this development? First, we can account for at least part of the demand. The shortage of female volunteers occasioned by an increasing female labor force,[33] plus the student's availability in urban locations near established volunteer service organizations, plus the Office of Economic Opportunity Act of 1964 which actively recruits college students in some of its programs—all these have provided some impetus for volunteer work.[34] But we lack the facts to account for the supply. Although we may suspect that social concern constitutes an important determinant, we do not know how prevalent this attitude is among college students and to what extent it differs from one college to another. Further research might well reveal other reasons for volunteer participation in community projects such as peer group pressures, excitement, career information, or even a way to spend one's leisure time or achieve status.

College Student Volunteer Organizations. Beyond the fragmentary evidence on membership trends, we may present a few structural aspects in relation to organizations and organizational affiliation. There is usually a dual organizational base from which students operate, one in the college itself which acts as a clearinghouse or central coordinating group for community organizations recruiting volunteers, and the other in the community organization itself. The college-based organization, which has financial and other types of support from the college in varying degree, also initiates and carries out projects with or without other organizational affiliation. In addition, other special-purpose campus organizations such as clubs, fraternities, and student government organizations may also sponsor volunteer programs.

Goals of College Volunteer Organizations. An examination of the stated objectives of a sample of student organizations reveals three aspects of student volunteering. The first is the clear intent to effect change; the second to provide rewards for the student as well as for the "client"; and the third emphasizes the interpersonal relationship based on equalitarian values. For example, one of the earliest organizations to institute community programs for its college students, the Phillips Brooks House of Harvard University, has as its two-fold purpose "to facilitate social change in the community at large and to provide educational and meaningful fieldwork for students."[35] The United States National Student Organization, through its Tutorial Assistance Center, mentions among its tutorial objectives "to develop motivation for positive change in all important areas of living," "to give volunteers a chance to understand and confront the complex social problems of a large city," in addition to various other objectives emphasizing the "tutee's emotional, educational, and cultural benefits."[36] Available information from other college organizations and projects undertaken across the country reveal similar objectives. These projects range from tutoring on a one-to-one basis (apparently the most prevalent task) to organizing neighborhood groups for rent strikes and setting up storefront schools (Janowitz 1964). These tasks are performed with groups of all ages, for varying periods of time, and in varying distances from the college. The Appalachian volunteers described by Coles and Brenner (1968) are reported as building roads, repairing schools, teaching, farming, and handling legal and medical problems of the residents.

Impact on Students. One important bit of evidence which lends support to the conclusion that the college volunteer experience has a strong impact on at least some college students is to be found in the reports from VISTA and the Peace Corps. The antipoverty program called Volunteers in Service to America reports that most of the volunteers in the program have had some part-time volunteer experience in poverty programs or related activities before entering VISTA service and that college students going into VISTA rose from 33 percent in 1965-66 to 73 percent in 1969 (VISTA 1970). The Peace Corps, which trains college students for work in undeveloped countries, has also relied on college students as its chief source of volunteers (Colmen 1966). The fact that these volunteers are trained in the colleges themselves and are given college credit and degrees makes these programs highly visible to undergraduate students. The Peace Corps and VISTA volunteers also raise definitional questions concerning the minimally paid volunteer, a growing phenomenon of the sixties and applicable to the college student as well as to the indigenous urban volunteer.[37] A survey of student manpower in eight southern colleges in the Atlanta area revealed that money was a major determinant of volunteer participation along with academic recognition for the work performed.[38]

Gaps in Research on College Student Volunteers in Community Settings. Where does one begin to suggest research directions? Other than the few points already raised concerning college volunteers, a few additional questions may be added: To what extent does volunteer work replace the earlier patterns of participation in extracurricular activities in clubs, fraternity houses, and sports events? How does the volunteer role in the ghetto differ from the volunteer role in the more highly structured mental hospital organization? How does student volunteering differ from adult volunteering? To what extent and in what manner does socialization into a new community-based subculture reflecting more humane and democratic values stimulate the college student volunteer toward increasing political expression and radicalism? Is there a pattern of mobility through various stages or experiences before the role "within the system" is abandoned for that of the political activist seeking reform through irrational and illegal means?

Some Concluding Remarks

Major Gaps in Theory and Research

The preceding summary of the available research and other information on college student volunteer action points to a major gap in the literature, amounting to an inadequate understanding of the nature and scope of voluntarism. We have seen that the focus has been on two groups of students and their activities: one oriented toward purely political goals in crises situations, the other oriented toward health goals of a specialized nature. Yet, except for the volunteer who works in mental health, we know little about those students who work in other volunteer activities, particularly in the neighborhoods of the nation's large cities. The omission of a substantial segment of the college population is especially serious in view of the fact that these students are involved in constructive social-political action: they do not repudiate the existing channels through which such action may occur. In addition to contributing to this distortion, emphasis in the research on the radical student has serious implications for academic institutions and, ultimately, for the entire society. That such incomplete or distorted findings on a subject as volatile as campus uprisings may be used imprudently cannot be discounted. They may provide the basis for the enactment of new legislation to institute campus disciplinary reforms, for withholding of financial assistance to colleges and students, and for other public or private interference which may threaten academic freedom.[39]

Failure to study these student volunteers who work "within the system" may be attributed to a number of reasons. Among these would undoubtedly be the fact that they constitute too recent a phenomenon, they are relatively invisible in their off-campus locations, and they do not take over administration buildings or throw stones at police officers. But it is nevertheless surprising that sociologists, psychologists, and educators, all of whom have been accused of overresearching college students, have failed to give attention to an emerging social phenomenon of rapidly growing proportions.

What appears as neglect in the research effort of college student political action may also derive from the main theoretical framework which has been used—that of collective behavior. This approach views student voluntary participation mainly as part of a social movement and within the framework of mass society, not as individuals in social roles organizing themselves to bring about social and political change. A systems approach is needed which will present college student voluntarism in all its interrelated roles and group structures extending beyond the boundaries of the immediate campus into the community where education of a different kind is taking place. And while a theory of collective behavior provides a needed orientation for the study of college students engaged in protest activities on college campuses, we need to give attention first to all the elements of the social structure on which these movements arise.[40]

The Need for a Reexamination of the Concept of Voluntarism

Our brief examination of college students engaged in social-political action also suggests the need to reexamine the concept of voluntarism, a suggestion which has also been made by others (Palisi 1968; Bode 1970). This need is even more urgent during a period of rapid social change in which all the institutions of society are becoming more flexible and open. And because college students are at the forefront of social change today and will become society's "activist" leaders of the future, our present knowledge concerning them may provide an opportunity for a critical appraisal of the present multidefinitional approaches to voluntary participation. Thus the following three examples based on the review of college student voluntarism are presented merely as a starting point toward establishing a pivotally focused framework which will have some utility both in its theoretical and practical implications.

New Organizational Forms and Structures. College student voluntarism tends to move away from the formal organizational structure rather than towards it, creating new organizational forms and structures in the process and compelling established institutions to change also. The concept of formal volunteer organization thus becomes less relevant to voluntarism insofar as it reflects conservativeness, rigidity, boundary maintenance, and an orientation toward organizational goals other than those which will bring about change. We need to reexamine the concept of formal volunteer organization and the entire process of "joining" and membership in the formal volunteer organization, and we need to examine the new organizational forms and social patterns becoming institutionalized around more loosely structured groups and organizations which are more functional for effecting change.

New Volunteer Role Definitions. Secondly, college student voluntarism does not convey the stereotype of the "lady bountiful" or "do-gooder" image where the benefactor and the benefitted receive different kinds of rewards. There is need to examine a new kind of social relationship whereby nonpatronizing interaction, mutual benefits, and humane values take the place of one-way "service." The relatively recent appearance of both the college student volunteer and the indigenous volunteer of the inner-city ghetto appear to be instrumental in changing this stereotype, but the significance of such roles may lie more in the important latent functions they perform by breaking down the rigid class structure the service orientation has helped to perpetuate in the past. In addition, college student voluntarism suggests more creative and challenging experiences rather than dull and routine ones that have contributed to the persistent problem of high turnover plaguing the volunteer effort. But it also suggests the need to examine voluntarism in terms of its symbolic manifestations leading to social change.

Orientation Towards Social Change. The need to reexamine the concept of voluntarism becomes most imperative in relation to the crises occuring on today's college campuses. As never before in American history, college students are oriented towards change—"instant" change. While much of this impatience may be charged to youthful idealism and lack of knowledge, such impatience also has its counterparts in other segments of the society and it cannot be ignored. What is suggested is that if voluntarism is to have any utility whatsoever, it must be a dynamic concept, defined within a framework of change—urgent and change-oriented action—whether such action occurs as irrational and illegal disruption or as rational and "system"-oriented reform.

Practical Implications for Further Research

Channeling of Student Energy. In view of the transitory nature of both the college student role and voluntarism itself, why should we put any further energy into research concerning the voluntary participation of college students? For one thing, it is highly likely that we have not yet seen the end of campus turbulence and discontent. For another, we cannot be sure that those students not involved in disruptive tactics will not do so in the future. A recent poll taken of a cross-section of college students reveals that 32 percent believe that resorting to violent tactics, if necessary to bring about basic changes in the system, would be either very or somewhat effective, and 33 percent do not believe that the democratic process can work.[41] On this basis it seems clear that one important goal of colleges and universities is the termination of destructive and disruptive campus activities. However, since no magic formula apparently exists for reinstituting overnight previous conditions of calm, one answer may lie in the ability of the academic organization to channel student energy away from dysfunctional roles into more productive directions and build up some degree of countervailing power which is socially acceptable, socially "relevant," and academically sound. In this respect college student voluntarism of the kind which seeks the needed changes "within the system" appears to offer considerable promise.

What is needed—and perhaps urgently—is more information and systematic research that will assist college administrators to assess the potential of student voluntarism in all its dimensions, not merely as a measure of social control but in the degree of support necessary for its development as a stable institution within the academic community.

Integration of Volunteer Role into College Curriculum. In addition, our limited data suggests that student voluntarism is self-socializing, liberalizing, tension-releasing, emancipating, and integrating. It also suggests that voluntary participation and learning are not unrelated and that academic objectives and social goals should also be combined. The necessity occurs for both experimentation and evaluation of this relationship between voluntarism and the entire academic experience, including the curriculum.[42] Such a union may provide the needed link between knowledge and social action without jeopardizing the university's obligation to maintain a pluralistic position and a certain degree of detachment from the immediate environment. It might also constitute an important first step toward the more humanistic and equalitarian community most college students seem determined to achieve.

But additional research can only diagnose the nature of new forms of voluntarism and recommend socially functional alternatives. One of the greatest short-comings of our present system of government is the apparent lack of coordinated effort between the research findings of academia and the decision-making powers of government. For without systematic coordination of the two, no effective implementation of the research findings can be made.

Summary and Conclusions

The research on college students engaged in social-political voluntary action spans the decade of the sixties and relates to a small proportion of students in selected colleges across the country. Two types of voluntary participation have received attention: one group oriented towards political goals in crisis situations in campus settings, the other group oriented towards health goals in large-scale public mental hospitals in the community. However, negligible attention has been given to the off-campus social-political voluntary activities of college students. This neglect has contributed both to serious gaps in the literature and to an inadequate understanding of the nature and scope of college student voluntarism.

Both quantitative and nonquantitative approaches have been used by the social scientists and educators who have studied college student voluntarism. The combined effort is of uneven quality with many studies lacking in several respects: sound sampling techniques, adequate sample size, explicitly stated research design, properly constructed data collection instruments, sufficient controls for testing sample representativeness, and theoretical perspective. With few exceptions, virtually all the studies appear within a narrow specialized context consisting of one particular campus, one type of college, and one type of voluntary activity. Most of the research constitutes reliable "evidence" only insofar as it offers tentative generalizations for greatly needed further systematic research in this area.

The following are some of the major substantive propositions supported by the foregoing review of literature.

Propositions

Until the decade of the sixties American college students were extremely conservative, politically apathetic, and socially indifferent to voluntary participation for social-political change. (Strength and direction: strong; consistency: high.)

However, during the sixties college students became increasingly active as voluntary participants in "causes" such as renunciation of war, civil rights, and campus reform. Activities which were most disruptive to the educational process were political in nature and involved a small minority of the student population—the so-called radical New-Left activists. (Strength and direction: weak; consistency: low.)

In a relatively short period of a few years, college student voluntary participation oriented toward political goals has had a strong impact on colleges, the public, and the students themselves. Similarly, participation oriented toward mental health goals has had a strong impact on both students and patients. (Strength and direction: strong; consistency: high.)

College students engaged in social-political action display a diversity of social backgrounds, personality characteristics, and motivation. Distinctions are especially made between the radical activists and nonactivists and between black and white students. One recent challenge is noted concerning the adequacy of some of the social correlates explaining radical behavior. (Strength and direction: strong; consistency: high.)

The role, group, and organizational structure of college student voluntarism suggests more varied and flexible forms than those institutionalized in off-campus organizational settings among nonstudent populations. (Strength and direction: moderate; consistency: high.)

Finally, as demonstrated through their voluntary participation, American college students are becoming increasingly radicalized and politicalized. (Strength and direction: strong; consistency: high.)

Hypotheses for Further Testing

1. That the voluntary participation of college students is more oriented towards social change than is the voluntary participation of adults.
2. That, as college student voluntary participation oriented towards social-political change increases, college student voluntary participation in traditional social and recreational "extracurricular" activities decreases.
3. That college students who participate in voluntary activities oriented towards social-political change are more likely to become radicalized and politicalized than college students who do not engage in such activities.
4. That there is a progressive sequence from institutionalized forms of voluntary participation among college students to radical political activism.
5. That the causes of college student radicalism are rooted in the family rather than on the campus or in the wider society and are essentially psychological in nature.
6. That college students who volunteer to work in mental hospitals are themselves predisposed towards mental illness.
7. That the extent and intensity of college student voluntary participation may be considered as a social indicator of social-political change in a society.

The Role of Theory

Conventional definitions of voluntary action are inadequate to explain this phenomenon during periods of rapid social change. The theoretical position taken here is to view all voluntary behavior in terms of effecting (or controlling) social change. Such a framework appears on a higher level of generalization than other definitions and makes it possible to explain the broad variation which occurs with respect to roles, organizational forms, and other patterns of voluntary action, and also to separate voluntary behavior from nonvoluntary behavior.[43]

Notes

1. A few studies which deal wholly or in part with student organizations, including fraternities and sororities, are those of Angell (1928), Chapin (1926), Hand (1938), Goldsen (1960), Bach (1961), J. Scott (1965), W. Scott (1965), and Gerson (1969). Related studies which deal with college peer subcultures associated with the extracurricular activities of college students are Cowley and Waller (1935), Warren (1941), Hartshorne (1943), Sutherland (1950), Riesman (1959), and Gottlieb and Hodgkins (1963).

2. In actual practice, however, it is known that student government organizations succeed only in supervising the social activities of all the students (Klopf 1960).

3. The many studies conducted on college student values all reinforce each other. See, for example, Allport (1951), Kahl (1953), Jacob (1957), Goldsen et al. (1960), McClintock and Turner (1962), Warren (1966), Freedman (1967), Newcomb and Feldman (1968), Kapote and Zolbrod (1969).

4. Goldsen et al. (1960), p. 181, report that as many as 23 percent of the eleven-college student sample indicated that "some religious groups are inferior," 17 percent that "generally speaking, Negroes are lazy and ignorant," and 7 percent that "although some Jews are honest, in general Jews are dishonest in their business dealings."

5. W. Scott (1965), who studied the impact of fraternities and sororities in college students, was forced to conclude that a distinct "value culture" was transmitted primarily through processes of selection rather than influence. McClintock and Turner (1962), who studied ten southern California colleges, concluded that either no forces were operating on students or equivalent sets of antagonistic forces were operative.

6. Only a few of these studies will be mentioned here. They all deal in one way or another with the campus crisis and differ from one another mainly in the extent to which they emphasize student politics, protest, and general student unrest. A good number of these sources also include studies concerning the

political activities of students in countries outside the United States—Avorn et al. (1969), Barton (1968), Bell and Kristol (1968), Califano (1970), Cohen and Hale (1966), Draper (1965), Jacobs and Landau (1966), Lipset (1967), Lipset and Wolin (1965), Losch (1965), Miller and Gilmore (1965), Peterson (1966), and Skolnick (1969). Special issues of professional magazines have been devoted to these same topics: COMPARATIVE EDUCATION REVIEW 10 (June), 1966; THE JOURNAL OF SOCIAL ISSUES 23 (July), 1967; DAEDALUS 97 (Winter), 1968. The reader is also referred to a comprehensive bibliography compiled by Altbach (1968), together with a summary of the most fruitful studies dealing with historical, psychological, sociological, and related factors on the subject of student politics and campus unrest in the United States, and to the forthcoming bibliography by Keniston (1973).

7. Studying the extent to which colleges allow their students to express beliefs on controversial issues, Williamson and Cowan (1966) found considerable variation among colleges. In the larger private and public universities not only were students granted more freedom to discuss controversial topics, invite off-campus speakers, and demonstrate actively and engage in civil rights activities, but these universities were more likely to have many social and political action groups on campus.

8. Peterson (1968) places the *organized* student left, those students formally affiliated with various radical national organizations, to fewer than 15,000. Califano (1970) places the total membership of Students for a Democratic Society, the most significant group, at about 5,000-7,500 in 1969, with the ability to arouse about 70,000 sympathetic colleagues during a period of campus crisis. Blumenthal (1967) states that SDS grew from 1,200 members and 30 chapters in 1965 to more than 6,000 members and 227 chapters in 1967.

9. See Heise (1968) for a discussion of how moral norms, personal motivations, and situational pressures all contribute to student deviance.

10. The summary of political organizations and other groups is based mainly on the various accounts of campus protest movements described in the literature cited in n. 6.

11. Young Americans for Freedom (YAF), established in 1960, constitutes the most stable organization. It has as its stated objectives "to mobilize support among American youth for conservative political candidates and legislation and to act as spokesmen for conservative opinion on key issues affecting young people." In actual practice, however, the student right does not direct protest at the *status quo* but is actively involved in the student movement (Evans 1961).

12. See Smelser (1963), THEORY OF COLLECTIVE BEHAVIOR for an analysis of such groups.

13. For example, the decline of the college function *in loco parentis* and influence of graduate students (Katz and Sanford 1965), rejection of many prevailing American institutions (Peterson 1968), revolt against liberalism (Eisen and Steinberg 1969), and alienation (Keniston 1960, 1965, 1970). Alienation as

a cause of student discontent has been refuted by Kahn (1968) and by Oppenheimer (1968), the latter concluding that the New-Left themes are oriented toward social rather than personal alienation. The entire issue of THE JOURNAL OF SOCIAL ISSUES, Spring 1969, is devoted to the topic of alienation.

14. Lipset (1967), pp. 231-34.

15. See the collection of articles in Lipset and Wolin (1965) for many on-the-scene accounts and analyses.

16. Altbach (1967a), Lipset (1967). See also Zinn (1964) for an account of the participation of students in the civil rights movement.

17. Several studies have been made of student political activities in other countries. See Soares (1966) for a summary of these studies. See also Smith (1969) for an analysis of student activism in six Latin American countries.

18. Peterson (1968) identifies nine of these studies. Another review of this literature may be found in Keniston (1967).

19. Connors et al. (1968) also found a relationship between religious behavior and opposition to war in a sample of 1,062 students from four eastern campuses. Catholics were most accepting of modern war and more likely to demonstrate prowar; while students of no religion were most opposed. Quakers and those having no religion were most likely to demonstrate against war. Kerpelman's (1969) findings that the left-oriented student was less concerned with social acceptance than either the right or middle-oriented student led him to conclude that ideology should be separated from activism in any investigation of student political activists.

20. A nationwide Gallup poll taken in March 1970, asking college students to classify themselves as liberal or conservative found 61 percent to be liberal, 26 percent conservative, and 13 percent with no opinion. Report 60, June, 1970.

21. Ibid., p. 15.

22. Ibid.

23. The National Association of State Colleges and Universities, in a survey of its 114 members, reports that the nation's state universities are responding to student demands for more "relevant" courses and a greater voice in designing their educational programs. CHRISTIAN SCIENCE MONITOR, August 6, 1970.

24. Two comprehensive bibliographies are available on the volunteer in mental health. See Arffa (1966) on college and high school volunteers and Sobey (1969a) and (1969b) on all volunteers, college students included).

25. The National Institute of Mental Health includes college students in the young adult category (ages 18-21) and indicates that this group is roughly equal in number to that of adult volunteers over 21 (Sobey 1969b).

26. In a nationwide survey of state mental hospitals, 86 of the 109 hospitals reported programs as originating during that time period. (College Student Volunteers in State Mental Hospitals 1968).

27. Tasks reported by the National Institute of Mental Health, in addition to

companionship, include all kinds of recreational activities, individual tutoring, assisting professionals in occupational and speech therapy, taking case histories, teaching music and dance, and going shopping (NIMH 1968).

28. See Holzberg (1963, 1964); Holzberg and Gerwirtz (1963); Holzberg, Gerwitz and Ebner (1964); Holzberg and Knapp (1965); Holzberg, Whiting and Lowry (1964); Holzberg et al. (1966).

29. See n. 24.

30. COLLEGE STUDENT VOLUNTEERS IN MENTAL HOSPITALS (1968), pp. 7-8.

31. Conferences for which reports are available include "Beyond the Ivory Tower—Social Responsibility and the College Student, Report of a Conference," Cornell University, 1968; the "University and Voluntary Service," 1969; "Atlanta Service-Learning Conference Report, 1970," and "College Curricula for the Leadership of Human Service Volunteer Programs: A Report of a Conference" (1970). Examples of books and pamphlets which are primarily intended as manuals to assist students include Janowitz (1964) and (1965), Tanck (1969), and U.S. National Student Association Tutorial Center, which publishes approximately twenty-five pamphlets to assist students in tutoring alone. (Publications List, USNSA, undated).

32. As early as 1963 the Northern Student Movement was described as consisting of more than 65 campuses across the country in a highly structured organization which at the height of its popularity had seven city projects and affiliated groups involved in tutorial and other efforts for ghetto residents (Randolph 1964). In 100,000 HOURS A WEEK (1965), it is reported that more than 4,000 college students were involved in volunteer work across the country during that year. In 1969 the American Association of State Colleges and Universities conducted a study of state colleges and universities in which well over half of the 125 colleges and universities responding to the questionnaire indicated some form of organized student volunteer activity ("Report of a Study on College Student Volunteers in State Colleges and Universities" (1970). In "Campus Activists Reflect Social Concerns through Volunteer Programs" (1970), it is estimated that in 1969 about 50 percent of the nation's colleges and universities, both public and private, had some sort of organized student volunteer programs involving about 250,000 students with rapidly expanding programs in 25 or 30 colleges similar to that of Michigan State, where perhaps the most extensive volunteer operation on any one campus is taking place. Activities on this campus are reported to involve about 10,000 of the university's nearly 39,000 students in some 50 agencies in the Lansing area with three full-time employees staffing the Office of Volunteer Programs and with a pool of 15 university-owned vehicles assigned exclusively to the volunteer programs.

33. See Americans Volunteer (1969) for a summary of the present state of voluntarism in the United States, including some of its research needs. See also Curtin (1960) for a general view of the future role of youth in relation to volunteering.

34. In 1965 the National Student Association published a pamphlet containing more than 27,000 summer openings in 96 organizations for college students. (USNSA, SCOPE 1965). A DIRECTORY OF SERVICE ORGANIZATIONS (1968) lists hundreds of agencies and other resources for young people seeking social action involvement. The 25-year-old Commission on Voluntary Service and Action, a consultative council of more than 100 private North American organizations, publishes an annual catalogue of service opportunities of which thousands specifically require the services of college students for summer programs. (INVEST YOURSELF, 1970).

35. Harvard University, Phillips Brooks House Association (1969), p. 1.

36. Noce (1967), pp. 4-5. Noce refers to tutoring as the "tutorial movement," which included 200,000 tutors in more than 1,000 tutorial projects across the country during that year.

37. "Americans Volunteer" (1969), p. 2.

38. "Atlanta Service-Learning Report" (1970), pp. 9-10.

39. Jacobs (1966) attributes the significant increase in studies of radical student movements by sociologists to the reward structure within departments of sociology along with the availability of research funds which greatly influences the kinds of problems sociologists investigate.

40. Kobrin (1967) has not only stressed this point but suggests that movement into adult status should be viewed as mobility, not socialization.

41. Harris Poll, reported in the Boston Globe, July 22, 1970, p. 34. The poll interviewed a cross-section of 820 students from 50 colleges.

42. The idea of volunteer service experience as an integral part of the curriculum is not new and has been tried in various colleges. One such successful experiment is reported by Theordore (1970) in relation to a course in sociology. See also Eberly (1968a) for a summary of some of the college programs in which credit is granted for a "service curriculum," and also for some of the implications of such a curriculum. In addition, colleges are being suggested as training grounds for a National Voluntary Service program which has been recently proposed as a replacement for the military conscription of American youth (Eberly 1966, 1968b). An International Corps of Volunteers for Development is also being proposed by the United Nations which favorably views integration of such a volunteer corps into the college curriculum (United Nations, 1968a, 1968b).

43. For an elaboration of the author's position, see Theodore (1972).

References

Adams, Ethel M. and Suzanne D. Cope
1968 VOLUNTEERS—AN ANNOTATED BIBLIOGRAPHY. New York: United Community Funds and Councils of America.
Allport, Gordon, P.E. Vernon, and Gardner Lindsey.
1951 STUDY OF VALUES Rev. ed. Boston: Houghton-Mifflin.

Altbach, Philip A.
1966   "The Future of the American Student Movement." LIBERAL EDUCA-
        TION 52 (October): 313-24.
1967a   "Students and Politics." In STUDENT POLITICS. Edited by Seymour
        M. Lipset. New York: Basic Books.
1967b   "A Select Bibliography on Students, Politics, and Higher Education."
        Cross-cultural Studies on Student Activism. Cambridge, Mass.: Center for
        International Affairs, Harvard University.
1968   STUDENT POLITICS AND HIGHER EDUCATION IN THE UNITED
        STATES; A SELECT BIBLIOGRAPHY. Rev. ed. St. Louis, Mo.: United
        Ministries in Higher Education, and Cambridge, Mass.: Center for
        International Affairs, Harvard University.
Americans Volunteer.
1969   "Manpower-Administration Research Monograph No. 10." U.S. Dept. of
        Labor, April.
Angell, Robert C.
1928   THE CAMPUS: A STUDY OF CONTEMPORARY UNDERGRADUATE
        LIFE IN THE AMERICAN UNIVERSITY. New York: D. Appleton and
        Co.
Arffa, Marvin S.
1966   "High School and College Student Volunteers in Community and
        Psychiatric Settings: A Bibliography with Selected Annotations." Center
        for Continuing Education, Northeastern University, April.
"Atlantic Service-Learning Conference Report 1970." Atlanta, Georgia: South-
1970   ern Regional Education Board.
Avorn, Jerry L. et al.
1969   UP AGAINST THE IVY WALL: A HISTORY OF THE COLUMBIA
        CRISIS. New York: Atheneum.
Bach, Mary L.
1961   "Factors Related to Student Participation in Campus Social Organiza-
        tions." THE JOURNAL OF SOCIAL PSYCHOLOGY 54, no. 2: 337-48.
Barton, Allen H.
1968   "The Columbia Crisis: Campus, Vietnam, and the Ghetto." PUBLIC
        OPINION QUARTERLY 32 (Fall): 333-51.
Beck, James C., D. Kantor, and V.A. Gelineau.
1963   "Follow-up Study of Chronic Psychotic Patients 'Treated' by College
        Case-Aide Volunteers." AMERICAN JOURNAL OF PSYCHIATRY 120,
        no. 3: 269-71.
1965   "Impact of Undergraduate Volunteers on the Social Behavior of Chronic
        Psychotic Patients." INTERNATIONAL JOURNAL OF SOCIAL
        PSYCHIATRY 11 (Spring): 96-104.

Beery, Evelyn.
1963   "Volunteer Program Penetrates a Maximum Security Setting." MENTAL
        HOSPITALS 14, no. 9: 503.
Bell, Daniel and Irving Kristol (eds.)
1968   CONFRONTATION: THE STUDENT REBELLION AND THE UNI-
        VERSITIES. New York: Basic Books.
"Beyond the Ivory Tower—Social Responsibility and the College Student." Re-
1968   port of a Conference, Cornell University.
Block, Jeanne H., N. Haan, and M. Brewster Smith.
1967   "Activism and Apathy in Contemporary Adolescents." In CONTRIBU-
        TIONS TO THE UNDERSTANDING OF ADOLESCENCE. Edited by
        James F. Adams. New York: Allyn and Bacon.
Blumenthal, Richard.
1967   "SDS: Protest Is Not Enough." NATION, May 22.
Bode, Jerry G.
1970   "Toward a Definition of Formal Voluntary Associations." Paper pre-
        sented at the American Sociological Association Meetings, Washington,
        D.C., August.
Braungart, Richard G.
1966   "SDS and YAF: Backgrounds of Student Political Activists." Paper
        presented at the American Sociological Association meetings, Washing-
        ton, D.C., August.
Brown, Barry S.
1968   "Some Reflections on the Role of the Student in the Mental Hospital."
        COMMUNITY MENTAL HEALTH JOURNAL 4 (December): 509-518.
Califano, Joseph A.
1970   THE STUDENT REVOLUTION: A GLOBAL CONFRONTATION. New
        York: W.W. Norton.
"Campus Activists Reflect Social Concerns through Volunteer Programs."
1970   TEACHING TOPICS. 19, 1: entire issue.
Chapin, F. Stuart.
1926   "Extracurricular Activities of College Students: A Study in College
        Leadership." SCHOOL AND SOCIETY 23 (February): 212-16.
Christenson, Reo M. and Patrick J. Capretta.
1968   "The Impact of Colleges on Political Attitudes: A Research Note."
        SOCIAL SCIENCE QUARTERLY 49 (September): 315-20.
Clark, Burton R. and Martin Trow.
1966   "The Organizational Context" In COLLEGE PEER GROUPS. Edited by
        Theodore M. Newcomb and Everett K. Wilson Chicago: Aldine.
Cohen, Mitchell and Dennis Hale, eds.
1966   THE NEW STUDENT LEFT: AN ANTHOLOGY. Boston: Beacon Press.
Coles, Robert and Joseph Brenner.
1968   "American Youth in a Social Struggle (II): The Appalachian Volun-
        teers." AMERICAN JOURNAL OF ORTHOPSYCHIATRY 38, no. 1:
        31-46.

"College Curricula for the Leadership of Human Service Volunteer Programs: A
1970 Report of a Conference." Boulder, Colorado, November 9-10, The National Information Center on Volunteers in Courts.
"College Student Volunteers in State Mental Hospitals." Public Health Service
1968 Pamphlet No. 1752. Chevy Chase, Maryland: National Institute of Mental Health, Citizen Participation Branch.
Colmen, Joseph G.
1966 "A Discovery of Commitment." ANNALS OF THE AMERICAN ACADEMY OF POLITICAL AND SOCIAL SCIENCE 365 (May): 12-20.
Connors, John F., Richard C. Leonard, and Kenneth E. Burnham.
1968 "Religion and Opposition to War among College Students." SOCIOLOGICAL ANALYSIS 29 (Winter): 211-19.
Cowley, W.H. and W. Waller.
1935 "A Study of Student Life." JOURNAL OF HIGHER EDUCATION 6 (March): 132-42.
CRISIS AT COLUMBIA: REPORT OF THE FACT-FINDING COMMISSION
1968 APPOINTED TO INVESTIGATE THE DISTURBANCES AT COLUMBIA UNIVERSITY IN APRIL AND MAY 1968. New York: Vintage Books.
Curtin, Thomas J.
1960 "Youth in a Space Age." In PROCEEDINGS OF THE VOLUNTEER BUREAU WORKSHOP. Atlantic City, June 7-9, United Community Funds and Councils of America, pp. 1-9.
DIRECTORY OF SERVICE ORGANIZATIONS. Washington, D.C.: National
1968 Service Secretariat.
Donadio, Stephen.
1968 "Black Power at Columbia." COMMENTARY 45 (Sept.): 67-76.
Draper, Hal.
1965 BERKELEY: THE NEW STUDENT REVOLT. New York: Grove Press.
Eberly, Donald J. ed.
1966 A PROFILE OF NATIONAL SERVICE. New York: Overseas Educational Service.
1968a "Service Experience and Educational Growth." EDUCATIONAL RECORD. Washington, D.C: American Council on Education (Spring).
1968b "National Service: A Report of a Conference." New York: Russell Sage Foundation.
Eisen, Jonathan and David Steinberg.
1969 "The Student Revolt Against Liberals." ANNALS OF THE AMERICAN ACADEMY OF POLITICAL AND SOCIAL SCIENCE 382 (March): 83-94.
Evans, M. Stanton.
1961 REVOLT ON THE CAMPUS. Chicago: Henry Regnery.
Feldman, K. and T.M. Newcomb.
1969 THE IMPACT OF COLLEGE ON STUDENTS. San Francisco: Jossey-Bass.

Freedman, Mervin B.
1967   THE COLLEGE EXPERIENCE. San Francisco: Jossey-Bass.

Gerson, Walter M.
1969   "The College Sorority as a Social System." SOCIOLOGY AND SOCIAL
        RESEARCH 53 (April): 385-94.

Goldsen, Rose, M. Rosenberg, R.M. Williams, and E.A. Suchman.
1960   WHAT COLLEGE STUDENTS THINK. New Jersey: Van Nostrand.

Gottlieb, D. and B. Hodgkins.
1963   "College Student Subcultures: Their Structure and Characteristics in
        Relation to Student Attitude Change." SCHOOL REVIEW 71 266-89.

Greenblatt, Milton and David Kantor.
1962   "Student Volunteer Movement and the Manpower Shortage." AMER-
        ICAN JOURNAL OF PSYCHIATRY 118 (March): 809-814.

Hand, Harold C., ed.
1938   CAMPUS ACTIVITIES. New York: McGraw Hill.

Hartshorne, E.Y.
1943   "Undergraduate Society and the College Culture." AMERICAN SOCIO-
        LOGICAL REVIEW 8 (June): 321-332.

Harvard University Phillips Brooks House Association, Fall, 6 pp. Mimeo. 1969.

Heise, David R.
1968   "Norms and Individual Patterns in Student Deviancy." SOCIAL PROB-
        LEMS 16 (Summer): 78-91.

Heist, Paul.
1966   "The Dynamics of Student Discontent and Protest." Paper presented at
        the American Psychological Association Meeting, New York, September.

Holzberg, J.D.
1963   "The Companion Program: Implementing the Manpower Recommenda-
        tions of the Joint Commission of Mental Illness and Health." AMER-
        ICAN PSYCHOLOGIST 18 224-26.

1964   "The Significance of the Companionship Experience for the College
        Student." Washington, D.C.: U.S. Government Printing Office.

Holzberg, J.D. and H. Gerwirtz.
1963   "A Method of Altering Attitudes toward Mental Illness." PSYCHIATRIC
        QUARTERLY SUPPLEMENT 37: 56-61.

Holzberg, J.D., Herbert Gerwirtz, and Eugene Ebner.
1964   "Changes in Moral Judgment and Self-Acceptance in College Students as
        a Function of Companionship with Hospitalized Mental Patients."
        JOURNAL OF CONSULTING PSYCHOLOGY 28, no. 4: 299-303.

Holzberg, J.D. and R.H. Knapp.
1965   "The Social Interaction of College Students and Chronically Ill Pa-
        tients." AMERICAN JOURNAL OF ORTHOPSYCHIATRY 34 (April):
        487-92.

Holzberg, J.D., H. Whiting, and D.C. Lowry.
1964   "Chronic Patients and a College Companion Program." MENTAL HOS-
        PITALS 15 (March): 152-58.

Holzberg, J.D. et al.
1966   "Companionship with the Mentally Ill: Effects on the Personalities of College Student Volunteers." PSYCHIATRY 29, 4: 395-405.

"Invest Yourself: A Catalogue of Service Opportunities, 1970." New York: The
1970   Commission on Voluntary Service and Action.

Jacob, Philip E.
1957   CHANGING VALUES IN COLLEGE. New York: Harper.

Jacobs, Paul and Saul Landau.
1966   THE NEW RADICALS: A REPORT WITH DOCUMENTS. New York: Vintage Books.

Janowitz, Gayle.
1964   "After-School Study Centers—Volunteer Work in Reading." Chicago: Hyde Park Neighborhood Club.

1965   HELPING HANDS: VOLUNTEER WORK IN EDUCATION. Chicago: University of Chicago Press.

Kantor, David.
1959   "Inducing Preferences for Mental Health Careers." Monograph 75, NASW, October.

Kahl, J.A.
1953   "Educational and Occupational Aspirations of 'Common Man Boys.'" HARVARD EDUCATIONAL REVIEW 22: 186-203.

Kahn, Melvin.
1968   "Students for McCarthy—What Unites Them?" TRANS-ACTION 5 (July-August): 30.

Kapote, Christopher G. and Paul G. Zolbrod.
1969   BEYOND BERKELEY: A SOURCEBOOK IN STUDENT VALUES. New York: Harper and Row.

Katz, Joseph and Nevitt Sanford.
1965   "Causes of the Student Revolution." SATURDAY REVIEW 48 Dec. 18: 64-66, 76, 79-80.

Katz, Joseph and Associates.
1968   NO TIME FOR YOUTH: GROWTH AND CONSTRAINT IN COLLEGE STUDENTS. San Francisco: Jossey-Bass.

Keniston, Kenneth.
1960   "Alienation and the Decline of Utopia." AMERICAN SCHOLAR 29 1-40.

1965   THE UNCOMMITTED: ALIENATED YOUTH IN AMERICAN SOCI-ETY. New York: Harcourt, Brace.

1967   "The Sources of Student Dissent." THE JOURNAL OF SOCIAL ISSUES 23: 108-137.

1970   "What's Bugging the Students." EDUCATIONAL RECORD 51 (Spring): 116-129.

1973   RADICALS AND MILITANTS: AN ANNOTATED BIBLIOGRAPHY OF EMPIRICAL RESEARCH ON CAMPUS UNREST. Lexington, Mass.: Lexington Books, D.C. Heath and Co.

Kerpelman, Larry C.
1969   "Student Political Activism and Ideology: Comparative Characteristics of Activists and Non-Activists." JOURNAL OF COUNSELING PSYCHOLOGY 16, 1: 8-13.

Klein, William L. and Melvin Zax.
1965   "The Use of a Hospital Volunteer Program in the Teaching of Abnormal Psychology." JOURNAL OF SOCIAL PSYCHOLOGY 65: 155-65.

Klopf, Gordon J.
1960   COLLEGE STUDENT GOVERNMENT. New York: Harper and Bros.

Kobrin, Solomon.
1967   "Sociology and the Study of the Young Group." et al. 1 (Fall): 5, 10.

Lane, Robert E.
1968   "Political Education in the Midst of Life's Struggles." HARVARD EDUCATIONAL REVIEW 38 (Summer): 468-94.

Lasch, Christopher.
1965   THE NEW RADICALISM IN AMERICA. New York: Knopf.

Levine, Carl
1966   "Impact of Work with Mental Patients on Student Volunteers." JOURNAL OF HUMAN RELATIONS 14: 422-33.

Lipset, Seymour M., ed.
1967   STUDENT POLITICS. New York: Basic Books.

Lipset, Seymour M. and Philip G. Altbach.
1967   "Student Politics and Higher Education in the United States." In STUDENT POLITICS. Edited by Seymour Lipset. New York: Basic Books.

Lipset, Seymour M. and Sheldon S. Wolin, eds.
1965   THE BERKELEY STUDENT REVOLT: FACTS AND INTERPRETATIONS. New York: Doubleday.

Macbain, Nancie and Richard L. Schumacher.
1963   "Premedical Students Learn Hospital Routine as Volunteers." HOSPITALS 37 (July): 73-75.

McClintock, Charles G. and Henry A. Turner.
1962   "The Impact of College Upon Political Knowledge, Participation, and Values" HUMAN RELATIONS 15, no. 2: 163-76.

Miller, Michael and Susan Gilmore, eds.
1965   REVOLUTION AT BERKELEY. New York: Dell.

Newcomb, T.M. and K.A. Feldman.
1968   "The Impacts of Colleges upon their Students." New York: Carnegie Foundation for the Advancement of Teaching.

Newcomb, T.M. and E.K. Wilson, eds.
1966   COLLEGE PEER GROUPS: PROBLEMS AND PROSPECTS FOR RESEARCH. Chicago: Aldine.

Noce, James S.
1967   RESEARCH AND EVALUATION IN TUTORIAL PROGRAMS. Washington, D.C.: Tutorial Assistance Center, U.S. National Student Association.

100,000 HOURS A WEEK—VOLUNTEERS IN SERVICE TO YOUTH AND
1965 FAMILIES. New York: National Federation of Settlements and Neighborhood Centers.

Oppenheimer, Martin.
1968 "The Student Movement as a Response to Alienation." JOURNAL OF HUMAN RELATIONS 16, no. 1: 1-16.

Orbell, John.
1967 "Protest Participation among Southern Negro College Students." AMERICAN POLITICAL SCIENCE REVIEW 61 (June): 446-56.

Palisi, Bartolomeo J.
1968 "A Critical Analysis of the Voluntary Association Concept." SOCIOLOGY AND SOCIAL RESEARCH 52 (July): 392-405.

Paulus, George.
1966 "A Multivariate Analysis Study of Student Activist Leaders, Student Government Leaders, and Non-activists." Unpublished Ph.D. dissertation, Michigan State University.

Peterson, Richard E.
1966 THE SCOPE OF ORGANIZED STUDENT PROTEST IN 1964-65. Princeton, New Jersey: Educational Testing Service.
1968 "The Student Left in American Higher Education." DAEDALUS 97 (Winger): 293-317.

Randolph, Harland.
1964 "The Northern Student Movement." THE EDUCATIONAL RECORD 45: 389-394.

Reinherz, Helen.
1967 "Professional Supervision as a Means of Achieving Volunteer Program Goals" in VOLUNTEERS IN MENTAL HEALTH. Springfield, Illinois: Charles C. Thomas.

Remmers, H.H., ed.
1940 "Studies in Extra-Curricular Activities." In STUDIES IN HIGHER EDUCATION. Edited by H.H. Remmer, Lafayette, Indiana: Purdue University.

"Report of a Study on College Student Volunteers in State Colleges and Uni-
1970 versities," American Association of State Colleges and Universities, Office of Information and Research.

Riesman, David.
1959 "College Subcultures and College Outcomes." In SELECTION AND EDUCATIONAL DIFFERENTIATION. Berkeley, California: Field Service Center and Center for the Study of Higher Education.

Rooney, Herbert L., May Cummins, Margaret Sebastian, and Robert Wood.
1967 "The Field Work Student as a Volunteer: An Added Dimension in Social Work Education." SOCIAL WORK EDUCATION REPORTER 15 (December): 51, 55.

Scheibe, Karl E.
1965 "The Effects on College Students of Eight Weeks in Chronic Wards in

Mental Hospitals." Paper presented at Eastern Psychological Association Meetings, Atlantic City, April.

Schumer, Harry and Robert Stanfield.
1966   "Assessment of Student Role Orientations in College." Proceedings of the 74th Annual Convention of the American Psychological Association, Washington, D.C.

Scott, John F.
1965   "The American College Sorority: Its Role in Class and Ethnic Endogamy." AMERICAN SOCIOLOGICAL REVIEW 30, no. 4: 514-27.

Scott, William A.
1965   VALUES AND ORGANIZATIONS: A STUDY OF FRATERNITIES AND SORORITIES. Chicago: Rand McNally.

Sinnett, E. Robert and Linda K. Niedenthal.
1968   "The Use of Indigenous Volunteers in a Rehabilitation Living Unit for Disturbed College Students." COMMUNITY MENTAL HEALTH JOURNAL 4, no. 3: 232-243.

Skolnick, Jerome H.
1969   THE POLITICS OF PROTEST. New York: Ballantine Books.

Smelser, Neil J.
1963   THEORY OF COLLECTIVE BEHAVIOR. New York: Free Press of Glencoe.

Smith, David H.
1969   "Latin American Student Activism: Participation in Formal Volunteer Organizations." Manuscript submitted to Latin American Center Monograph Series at the University of Texas, October.

Soares, Glaucio A.D.
1966   "The Active Few, Student Ideology and Participation in Developing Countries." COMPARATIVE EDUCATION REVIEW 10 (June): 205-219.

Sobey, Francine S.
1969a VOLUNTEER SERVICES IN MENTAL HEALTH: AN ANNOTATED BIBLIOGRAPHY: 1955-1969. Chevy Chase, Maryland: National Institute of Mental Health.
1969b NON-PROFESSIONAL PERSONNEL IN HEALTH PROGRAMS: A SURVEY. Chevy Chase, Maryland: National Institute of Mental Health.

Somers, Robert H.
1965   "The Mainsprings of the Rebellion: A Survey of Berkeley Students in November, 1964." In THE BERKELEY STUDENT REVOLT: FACTS AND INTERPRETATIONS. Edited by S.M. Lipset and S.S. Wolin, New York: Doubleday.

"Special Section on Involved Youth" AMERICAN EDUCATION 5, no. 7: 11-27.
1969

Stroup, Herbert.
1955   "The Role of Student Activities in the University" ASSOCIATION OF AMERICAN COLLEGES BULLETIN 41: 436-47.

329

Sutherland, Robert L.
1950 "Some Aspects of the Culture of a Campus" In TRENDS IN STUDENT PERSONNEL WORK. Edited by E.G. Wonson University of Minnesota Press, 350-355.
Tanck, James.
1969 COLLEGE VOLUNTEERS—A GUIDE TO ACTION. Washington, D.C.: National Program for Voluntary Action.
Theodore, Athena
1970 "Integrating the Volunteer Role into the College Curriculum: an Experiment," VOLUNTEER ADMINISTRATION 4 (Winter): 14-18.
1972 "Social Change and Voluntary Action," in VOLUNTARY ACTION RESEARCH: 1972. Edited by David Horton Smith et al. Lexington, Mass.: Lexington Books, D.C. Heath and Co.
United Nations. "Participation of Young People in Community Development."
1968a Report prepared by the Secretary-General of the United Nations. December.
1968b "Report of the 19th Session of the Commission for Social Development." New York: United Nations.
U.S. National Student Association. "SCOPE: A Directory of Summer Oppor-
1965 tunities for College Students in Community Service." Washington, D.C.: USNSA.
U.S. National Student Association. "Publications List." Tutorial Assistance Center, (undated).
"The University and Voluntary Service." The 25th Annual Autumn Consulta-
1969 tion of the Commission on Youth Service Projects. Princeton, New Jersey, September.
VISTA (Volunteers in Service to America). "Who, What, Where, How." Office of
1970 Economic Development Pamphlet 4100-2 (rev.) March.
Wanderer, Zev. W. and Manny Sternlicht.
1964 "Psychologists Discover Value of Volunteers" and "Psychology Students Work with Retardates." MENTAL HOSPITALS 15 (May): 271-72.
Warren, Jonathan R.
1966 PATTERNS OF COLLEGE EXPERIENCE. Claremont, California.
Warren, R.L.
1941 "A Sociological Analysis of Student Activities." EDUCATIONAL FORUM 5: 442-57.
Westby, David L. and Richard G. Braungart.
1966 "Class and Politics in the Family Backgrounds of Student Political Activists." AMERICAN SOCIOLOGICAL REVIEW 31 (October): 690-692.
Williamson, Edmund and John Cowan.
1966 THE AMERICAN STUDENT'S FREEDOM OF EXPRESSION. University of Minnesota Press.
Zinn, Howard.
1964 SNCC: THE NEW ABOLITIONISTS. Boston: Beacon Press.

12

The Nature and Impact of Interorganizational Relations

Gerald E. Klonglan, Benjamin Yep,
Charles L. Mulford, and Donald Dillman

Introduction

The study of interorganizational relations (IOR) has been receiving increased attention by scientists and practitioners. This increased interest has been noted by several writers. Heydebrand (1971) indicates that organizational research has passed through two distinct phases and is beginning a third phase. Phase I, which occurred primarily during the 1950s, was concerned with the exploration of organizational prototypes. Phase II, during the 1960s, emphasized comparative and quantitative organizational analysis. The emerging Phase III is concerned with larger units of analysis (community) and by an increased emphasis on the nature of the relationships among organizations (organizational networks). Hall notes the increasing interest in interorganizational relations among organizations but stresses, "There are too few empirical studies for a firm basis of understanding" (1972a, p. 316). The recent interest in IOR as a special focus of study is further emphasized by a review of some of the most influential organization books of the 1960s. For example, the index to March's (1965) HANDBOOK OF ORGANIZATIONS, has no reference to interorganizational relations as such. And Blau and Scott (1962) devote only seven pages to "interorganizational processes." The current interest in IOR has not, however, been valued completely positive by everyone. At the 1972 meetings of the American Sociological Association, Scott (1972) stated a concern that those studying IOR may try to develop a unique subdiscipline of study rather than viewing the study of IOR as an integral part of the broad study of social organization. He hopes that the concepts, propositions, and theories developed to understand and explain IOR will be consistent with other frameworks used to explain other types of social organization.

Aldrich (1970), Marrett (1971) and Turk (1970) have all recently reviewed certain aspects of this emerging interest in IOR. White and Vlasak (1971) have prepared a selected bibliography of approximately 400 entries written during the 1960s focusing on interorganizational research in health. A secondary analysis of the entries in the White and Vlasak bibliography provide one framework to view current interests in IOR and to clarify some present needs re IOR research. The IOR articles which they found to be strong theoretically were not strong methodologically (see Table 12-1) and did not have a pragmatic (application) focus (Table 12-2). The strong methodological studies were also weak in theory (Table 12-1) and did not have a pragmatic focus (Table 12-3). Thus it appears that a gulf exists among the IOR theoreticians, methodologists, and practitioners. A need for integrating extant knowledge and its application exists.

The purpose of this chapter is to review, integrate and make applications of some of the work that has been done in recent years in the area of interorganizational relations (IOR). The specific objectives are (1) to present a general model that organizes much of the past research in IOR, (2) to present an applied model of IOR that has its basis in past theory and research and (3) to briefly discuss some of the applications of the applied IOR model. This chapter will focus primarily on cooperative forms of IOR rather than competitive or conflicting IOR situations. It will also focus primarily on IOR that occurs at the local community level rather than that which occurs at the nation-state level. Further, most studies of IOR seem to focus on what Blau and Scott (1962) refer to as "service organizations" where the client group is the prime beneficiary.

Table 12-1

Comparison of IOR Studies by Degree to which Theory and Methods are Emphasized

Theoretical Emphasis	Methodological Emphasis			
	Primary	Secondary	Minor	Total
Primary	0	7	73	80
Secondary	5	10	71	86
Minor	7	1	218	226
Total	12	18	362	392

Source: Based upon secondary analysis of data presented in Paul E. White and George J. Vlasak (1971).

Table 12-2

Comparison of IOR Studies by Degree to which Theory and Pragmatics are Emphasized

Theoretical Emphasis	Pragmatic Emphasis			
	Primary	Secondary	Minor	Total
Primary	0	4	76	80
Secondary	5	13	68	86
Minor	158	60	8	226
Total	163	77	152	392

Source: See source note for Table 12-1.

Table 12-3
Comparison of IOR Studies by Degree to which Methodology and Pragmatics are Emphasized

Methodological Emphasis	Pragmatic Emphasis			
	Primary	Secondary	Minor	Total
Primary	0	0	12	12
Secondary	0	2	16	18
Minor	163	75	124	362
Total	163	77	152	392

Source: See source note for Table 12-1.

Most of the publications re IOR such as Marrett (1971) and Aldrich (1970) that attempt to survey the literature make similar assumptions.

Objective 1: A General Research Model of IOR

Several writers have suggested preliminary frameworks for analyzing (theoretically and/or empirically) interorganizational relations. Hall and Clark (1969) suggest a list of variables to be considered in IOR research. Lehman (1971) develops an abstract paradigm for the analysis of IOR. Rogers (1971) has developed a taxonomy for studying IOR. White et al. (1971) use exchange theory as an organizing framework for IOR. Paulson (1971) goes beyond the listing of variables and develops a time-phased causal model to explain IOR. He also tests his causal model using seven different measurement models. Leadley (1969) also presents a general framework to study IOR.

The general research model utilized herein to organize some of the past research in IOR was developed as an organizing device by the authors while completing several recent studies of interorganizational relations (Klonglan et al. 1969a; Klonglan et al. 1969b; Klonglan et al. 1969c; Dillman 1966; Dillman 1969; Dillman 1970; Dillman et al. 1970; Yep 1970; George M. Beal et al. 1967; Klonglan and Beal 1970; Mulford et al. 1970; Klonglan and Paulson 1971; Klonglan et al. 1971; Klonglan and Yep 1972; and Mulford and Klonglan, 1972).

The research model (see Figure 12-1) will be used to answer a series of questions: (1) What are relevant units of analysis—see box A in Figure 12-1? (2) What is the focal field of IOR—box B? (3) What impact (social change) results from IOR—box C? That is, does IOR make any difference, i.e., improve impact—line 1? (4) What type of interaction activity can occur—box D? (5) What are the factors (box E, as prior social situation; and box F, organizational decision-making) that determine the level of interaction—box D? And, is the effect through lines II and III on interaction activity and thus through line I on

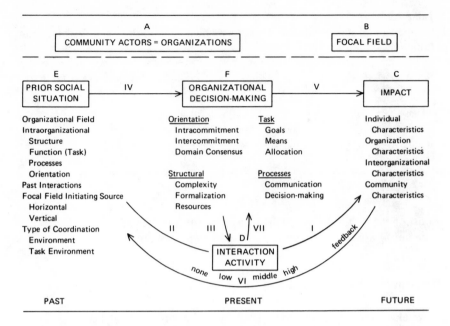

Figure 12-1. A General Reasearch Model of Interorganizational Relations

impact greater than the single organizational impact implied through lines IV and V? We also assume that feedback (line VI) is an important component of any IOR analysis over time. Each of these five questions will be discussed in the following sections.

A general distinction that may be useful at this point is the classification of the model into the general categories of past, present, and future (see bottom of Figure 12-1). Impact (box C) is seen as a future state. Organizational decision-making (box F) and interaction activity (box D) can be seen as some meaningful present action period, with the prior social situation (box E) being some past time period.

On Units of Analysis

The model assumes that the community is the most general unit of analysis and that the actors in the community are organizations, not individuals (see box A in Figure 12-1). Thus organizations may be seen as the smallest unit of analysis in the model. An intermediate unit of analysis is the relation between two organizations. The entire matrix of organizational interaction can be conceptualized as a third unit of analysis. A fourth unit of analysis is the larger environment of the community. (Brinkerhoff and Kunz 1972; Aldrich 1970; Turk 1970; Marrett 1971; Hemphill and Westie 1955; Kendall and Lazarsfeld 1955; Lazarsfeld and Menzel 1969; Tannenbaum and Bachman 1964; Dill 1958).

Some Assumptions about Interorganizational Relations

Most studies of IOR have made one or more implicit assumptions about interorganizational relations. Aldrich (1970, pp. 8-10) has stated three implicit assumptions that have helped encourage the study of interunit relations. One assumption is that cooperative relations are "good" in and of themselves because performance is thought to be higher and the resources used more efficiently when there is nonduplication of services (Warren 1967b; Reid 1964; Douds and Rubenstein 1966). A second unstated assumption is that resources are going to be maximized and innovations developed when organizations cooperate (Aiken and Hage 1968; Levine et al. 1963). The third assumption is that contracts, overlapping boards and other kinds of cooperation are the best ways to deal with a changing federal, state, and community environment. Aldrich discusses some of the problems associated with these assumptions.

Klonglan et al. (1972) have summarized six basic assumptions relevant to the theory and measurement of IOR. They are outlined briefly below with the references that were used to illustrate the assumptions:

1. Organizations are faced with a situation of limited resources (Levine and White 1961; White et al. 1971; Aiken and Hage 1968; Reid 1964; Litwak and Hylton 1962; Mott 1968).
2. Organizations must obtain resources from other units in their task environment (Goetzkow 1966; Evan 1966; Reid 1964; Levine and White 1961; Perrow 1961; Thompson 1967).
3. Drawing on outside resources reduces an organization's autonomy (Perrow 1961; Thompson 1967; Goetzkow 1966).
4. Organizations prefer autonomy and engage in interaction only when resource needs cannot be met within the unit (Gouldner 1959; Thompson and McEwen 1958; Aiken and Hage 1968; Warren 1969).
5. Organizations prefer low level IOR and will engage in higher level IOR only after lower levels have failed to fulfill resource needs (Thompson 1967; Parsons 1956; Yuchtman and Seashore 1967; Katz and Kahn 1966; Evan 1966).
6. Different levels of IOR can be ordered in terms of form and intensity of interaction (Thompson and McEwen 1958; Aiken and Hage 1968; Finley and Capener 1967; Leadley 1969; Hall and Clark 1969; Levine and White 1963; Parsons 1951; Litwak and Hylton 1962; Finley 1969; Klonglan et al. 1969b; Klonglan et al. 1972; Rogers and Vacin 1972).

The Focal Field of IOR

The model assumes that a focal field (Warren 1967b), or areas of concern (a problem) can be specified, i.e., alcoholism, community development, drugs, youth, smoking, etc. (see box B, Figure 12-1). The definition of focal field is critical in that it is one of the major criteria for delineating the organizations in a community which are most relevant to be coordinated in any given program. The specification of a focal field has been discussed by Braito et al. (1972) as one aspect of domain consensus.

Some of the focal fields or empirical arenas of concern that have been studied and selected references are outlined below.

Health (White and Vlasak, ed. 1970; Klonglan and Paulson 1971; Aiken and Hage 1968; and Levine and White 1963). Social Welfare (Caplan and Kohout 1966a and 1966b; Manley and Jensen 1966; Benson 1972). Poverty (Endo 1972; Dillman 1970). Model Cities (Richards and Goudy 1971). Delinquency Prevention and Control (Miller 1958; Hall 1972b). Voluntary Organizations (Beal et al. 1967; Dillman et al. 1970; Klonglan et al. 1969; Aldrich 1970). Disasters (Form and Nosow 1958; Dynes 1969; Dynes and Quarantelli 1969; Griffin et al. 1972; Griffin 1972). Rural Community Development (Finley and Capener 1967; Rogers and Vacin 1972; Rogers and Glick 1972; and Vacin 1972). Alcoholism (Klonglan et al. 1969b and Klonglan et al. 1969c). Education (Clark 1965; Hollister 1972). Industry (Cyert and March 1963). Municipal Governments (Friesema 1968). International (Bernstein and Welden 1968; Davis 1972). Rehabilitation and Mental Health (Black and Kase 1963). Services for the Elderly (Morris and Randall 1965).

What Impact (Social Change) Might Result from IOR?

We will focus on three parts of the impact question: (1) What are the social units that might be impacted? (2) What characteristics of the social units might be changed? and (3) Has there been any impact because of IOR?

At least four units of analysis have been specified as possible impact targets in the IOR literature: clients, organizations, interorganizational relations themselves, and the community. Some of the characteristics of each unit of analysis studied, or suggested to be studied are respectively: for clients, changes in attitudes, knowledge and behavior; for organizations, changes in characteristics such as structure (complexity, formalization, etc.), functions (services offered), process (innovativeness, internal communication, decision making, etc.); for interorganizational relations, changes in the quality (content) and quantity (frequency) of IOR; and for community, changes in community power decision-making and in the organizational set itself.

Both researchers and practitioners are interested in determining what kind of impact results from IOR (box C). The practitioner may be interested in clearly stating the positive outcomes (social progress) he desires. The researcher may be interested in ascertaining any type of outcome (positive or negative) resulting from IOR. The present day emphasis for delineating social indicators (Wilcox et al., 1972) and implementing evaluation research (Tripodi et al., 1971) reflect the current interest in assessing the impact of social programs.

Although there is an extensive amount of writing on IOR, there are very few studies that have attempted to empirically evaluate whether or not IOR does, in fact, have impact (line I). Hall (1972a, p. 321) states, "The effects of interorganizational interactions on the organizations has received some attention. (It is interesting to note that there has been almost no attention given to the effects on clients in the case of service organizations.)" In a more recent paper Hall (1972b) suggests the need to focus on the impact of IOR on the interorganizational relations themselves. He also suggests looking at the impact of IOR on the organizational set itself (one characteristic of a community).

In most studies of IOR it appears that IOR (box D) is treated as the dependent variable or result; i.e., that which needs to be explained; rather than being an independent variable or determinant used to help explain impact. It appears that most writers are assuming IOR will have a (positive) impact if it (IOR) occurs. What follows is a brief review of articles which have focused to some extent on the impact of IOR.

As noted above almost no one has done research to assess the impact of IOR on individual clients. Klonglan et al. (1969b and 1969c) compared the outcomes of 400 alcoholic clients to the quantity of IOR in four different communities. They found no clear relationship between quantity of IOR and improved client outcomes in these four communities. The community with the highest IOR score had the lowest client outcome score. However, in the other three communities the rank order of amount of IOR and client outcome was perfect; i.e., the greater the amount of IOR, the greater the client outcome score. Richards and Goudy (1971) found that a model cities IOR program did not change clients' perceptions of amount of coordination among agencies. In other words, clients perceived no differences in their contact with agencies after the initiation of a Model Cities IOR effort.

Aiken and Hage (1968) reviewed several of the studies which have examined the impact of the environment on internal organizational process and then proceeded to assess the impact of organizational interdependence (IOR) on intraorganizational structure. They found that IOR (interdependence according to joint programs) leads to increased complexity in organizational structure, increased organizational innovativeness, more internal communication channels and more decentralized decision-making structures. Price (1968) has developed hypotheses about impact when one organization co-opts members of other organizations to serve on its advisory board. He concluded that organizations which have co-optation (increased IOR) are more likely to have a higher degree of effectiveness than organizations which do not have such IOR. Sriram (1969) found a significant positive relationship between the use of IOR with elites and organizational effectiveness in her analysis of over 300 different organizations. Thompson and McEwen (1958) hypothesized that differential IOR would have differential impact on the organization's formal goals. Klonglan et al. (1969b) found that changes were made by a number of agencies in their procedure and policies re working with alcoholics. They found that agencies with high IOR made more changes than agencies with low IOR. Hall (1972a) summarizes some of the effects of external pressures (not necessarily interorganizational interactions) on organizations. Reviewing work by Thompson (1967), Udy (1965) and Goetzkow (1966), Hall suggests that external pressures resulted in increased communications and interactions among members of an organization, greater commitment to the organization, more authority exercised at various levels in the organization, and increased cohesiveness among members in the organization.

The authors are unaware of studies specifically designated to assess the impact of IOR on IOR.

Dynes and Quarantelli (1969) have found a greater amount of IOR in a community prior to a disaster results in more effective community recovery after a disaster. Griffin et al. (1972) found the same relationship in a study of 160 disaster communities. Perrucci and Pilisuk (1970) concluded that IOR has major impact for community power decision-making activity in that it serves as a source of mobilization.

What Type of Interaction Activity Can Occur
Between Organizations (See Box D)?

The concept of IOR is often discussed at a very general level where certain items which are output for one organization represent input for another (Parsons 1956; Blau 1964; Thompson 1962; Evan 1966; and Terreberry 1968). At the theoretical level one of the most frequently cited taxonomies of types of organizational interaction is that given by Thompson and McEwen (1958, pp. 23-31). These authors dichotomize organizational relations into cooperation and competition. Cooperation is further divided into: (1) bargaining, or "the negotiation of an agreement for the exchange of goods or services between two or more organizations"; (2) co-optation, or "the process of absorbing new elements into the leadership or policy-determining structure of an organization"; and (3) coalition, or "the combination of two or more organizations for a common purpose." Other schemes for delineating types of relationships exist in the literature but it appears as if most of these conform at a general level to Thompson and McEwen (Aiken and Hage 1968; Finley and Capener 1967; Leadley 1969; Hall and Clark 1969).

A second conceptual consideration of interorganizational relations is the area of environmental preconditions for the establishment and maintenance of interaction. Again, although several schemes exist, they are similar in that they specify certain needs which must exist in order for interaction to take place (Levine and White 1963; Parsons 1951). One system proposed by Litwak and Hylton (1962, p. 397) includes three preconditions for coordination or interaction: (1) partial interdependence, (2) awareness of this interdependence, and (3) expression in standard units of action.

At the operational research level Levine and White (1961) have utilized a series of more specific indicators of exchange, but they did not develop a composite measure of IOR. Aiken and Hage (1968) measured this complex phenomena with a single indicator in which they count the number of joint programs with other organizations. Finley (1969) delineated seventeen potential activities that might be part of IOR patterns. Using these items he was reasonably successful in developing Guttman scales of IOR. Klonglan et al. (1969b) developed seven potential activities in their analysis of organizations involved in alcoholism related IOR: (1) acquaintance, (2) frequency of interaction, (3) service on advisory board, (4) client referrals, (5) staffing sessions, (6) training interactions and (7) other interactions. Klonglan and Paulson (1971) developed eleven potential activities in their measurement of IOR among health related organizations. Klonglan et al. (1972) utilized eight of these eleven activities to develop a deterministic model of IOR (utilizing Guttman techniques) which met acceptable levels of analysis. The eight activities and their relation to the theoretical works of Finley (1969), Thompson and McEwen (1958) and Litwak and Hylton (1962) are outlined in Table 12-4. Rogers and Vacin (1972) are further developing deterministic models of IOR utilizing items similar to Klonglan and Paulson.

Table 12-4
The Forms of Interorganization Relations

1. Director Awareness of Existence of Other Organization	Litwak
2. Director Acquaintance	and
3. Director Interaction	Hylton
4. Information Exchange	Finley
5. Resource Exchange (Bargaining)	Thompson
6. Overlapping Board Membership (Cooptation)	and
7. Joint Programs (Coalitions)	McEwen
8. Written Agreements (Standardized Action)	Litwak and Hylton

Source: Klonglan et al. 1972.

The present authors believe that the recent analysis of specific activities sharpens focus on the intensity of cooperative organizational interaction as a key variable in IOR research. Following Finley (1969), we suggest that different types of IOR activities may be categorized as being indicative of low, middle, or high level cooperation between organizations as follows:

LOW LEVEL COOPERATION BETWEEN ORGANIZATIONS

1. Acquaintance with relevant personnel from other organizations.
2. Familiarity with relevant programs of other organizations.
3. Informal unscheduled communication.
4. Exchange of general information: program emphasis, etc.
5. Joint interagency council membership.

MIDDLE LEVEL COOPERATION BETWEEN ORGANIZATIONS

6. Formal exchange of information, in-house newsletter reports.
7. Exchange of personnel, resources, materials, and equipment.
8. Joint projects between organizations.

HIGH LEVEL COOPERATION BETWEEN ORGANIZATIONS

9. Joint budgetary considerations and money exchange or transfer.
10. Formal overlapping boards.
11. Joint ownership of facilities.
12. Formal written agreements regarding organizations policy and programs.

In addition to studying the intensity of interaction activity, some writers have focused on which levels of organizations interact. Figure 12-2 briefly outlines some of the possible levels of organizations which may interact. Thompson (1962) refers to boundary spanning roles which link an organization to its environment, including linking to other organizations. Kahn et al. (1964) conceptualized a boundary role to denote those organization roles which include in their role set persons outside the organization. Organ (1971) further develops the notion of boundary role, particularly as the incumbents of such roles perform a negotiating function with other organizations. Aldrich (1971) also analyzes organizational boundaries and IOR. Klonglan and Paulson (1971) found that some organizations delineate their director to perform the key linkage role; while other organizations have specified an assistant to take primary responsibility for linkage activity with other organizations. Hage and Aiken (1972) analyzed the relationship between boundary spanners and other organizational characteristics.

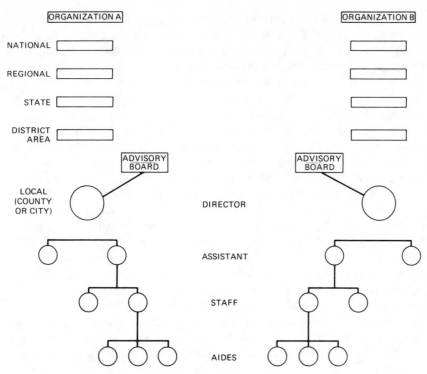

Figure 12-2. What Levels of Organizations Interact?

What Are the Factors that Determine the
Level of Interaction? (See Figure 12-1.)

If we assume that the level of interaction (box D) affects impact (box C), then we are interested in determining those factors (boxes E and F) which will affect (positively or negatively) the level of interaction (box D). Some research has focused on the affect (see line II) of the class of variables we label "Prior Social Situation" (box E) on interaction activity (box D). Other researchers have focused on the class of variables we label "Organizational Decision-making" (box F) and their effect (see line III) on interaction (box D). A detailed review of the research findings related to these questions is found in Klonglan and Paulson (1971). Briefly, the prior social situation and organizational decision variables are those variables common to intraorganizational or general social system studies. For example, prior social situation variables include (1) the organizational field or the organizations in the community relevant to the focal field of concern (Turk 1970); (2) intraorganizational variables such as structure, functions, processes and orientation of organizational actors (Paulson 1971); (3) past interactions among the members of the organizational field; (4) the focal field initiating source, i.e., was the program initiated by the local community (horizontal) or from outside the community (vertical) (Warren 1968); (5) the environment in general (Brinkerhoff and Kunz 1972); and (6) the task environment (knowledge and technology) directly relevant to the focal field of concern (Thompson 1967).

When we look at organizational decision-making (box F), we are focusing on each of the organizations in the organizational field as it tries to decide whether or not to become involved (line III) in interaction activity (box D). Four categories of factors are specified as possibly affecting the organization's decision to interact (line III): orientation, structural, task, and processes (Klonglan and Paulson 1971). Using these criteria, the organization may decide to interact with other organizations (line III), or to act in the focal field but independently of others (line V), or not to participate in this focal field at all. The prior social situation will affect an organization's decision (line IV).

In a social systems framework, we further assume that over time feedback occurs (line VI), i.e., evaluations are made as to whether or not the impact (social progress) from IOR (or lack of IOR) is "good" or "bad." This feedback becomes part of the prior social situation for the next "round" of organizational decision-making and interaction activity. A very important part of the next round will be each organization's evaluation (line VII) of the interaction activity to date.

Space will not permit a detailed specification of the many factors affecting IOR. Instead a more in-depth presentation of one factor, what we refer to as type of coordination, will be developed. Several writers (Finley and Capener 1967; Finley 1969; Warren 1969; Thompson and McEwen 1958; Thompson 1967; Lindblom 1966; Mott 1968; Litwak and Hylton 1962; Klonglan and Beal 1970; Mulford et al. 1970), have emphasized how different models of coordination may affect the intensity of interaction activity. Thompson's (1967) terminology will be used here. He delineates three basic types of coordination: vertical coordination or coordination by standardization, coordination by plan and coordination by mutual adjustment. The three types of coordination differ on a number of key characteristics (see Table 12-5); type of power relations (authority, influence and persuasion, respectively); extent of formalization (respectively, formal written expectations developed by central authority, written expectations developed by participating organizations, and informal, unwritten expectations); and potential use of sanctions (high, some, almost none). Coordination by plan may be either dyadic or systemic (see Figure 12-3). If it is dyadic only, the central coordinating unit relates to each of the other units; these units do not relate to each other. If the plan is systemic, each unit can relate to the coordinating unit and to each other. It would seem that coordination by plan based on systemic relations would be more efficient than

343

Table 12-5
Three Models of Coordination

Some Differentiating Characteristics	Models of Coordination		
	Standardization	Plan	Mutual Adjustment
Power Relations	Authority	Influence	Persuasion
Formalization	Formal written expectations developed by central authority	Written expectations developed by participating organization	Informal unwritten expectations
Potential for Sanctions	High	Some	Almost none

those based on the dyadic ones. Coordination by mutual adjustment may be asymetric-dyadic or symetric-dyadic (see Figure 12-4); or systemic (Figure 12-5).

The introduction of the three models of coordination provides a logical link to a major concern of several writers: who or what is the coordinating unit? Several alternative social mechanisms have been developed in attempts to facilitate IOR under all three models of coordination. Some IOR efforts have been coordinated by a council (Mott 1968). Some have been coordinated by a professional staff person hired to be a full-time coordinator (Klonglan et al. 1969b). Other IOR efforts have been coordinated by a "coordinating unit" composed of paid staff representatives from participating organizations. Still other IOR efforts are coordinated by "volunteers" (Klonglan and Beal 1970). Some agencies (Mulford et al. 1970) have created special change agent roles which they have titled coordinator (rather than director) since most of the role expectations involves linking the agency to other organizations. More research is needed to ascertain the differential impact, if any, from these alternative coordinating mechanisms.

The concern for who is doing the coordinating has generated much interest in organizations active in interorganizational relations. Some are very interested in developing training programs for their boundary personnel. This applied interest has motivated the authors to develop an applied model of IOR which can be used to improve an organization's abilities for IOR. The preliminary model is briefly outlined in the next section.

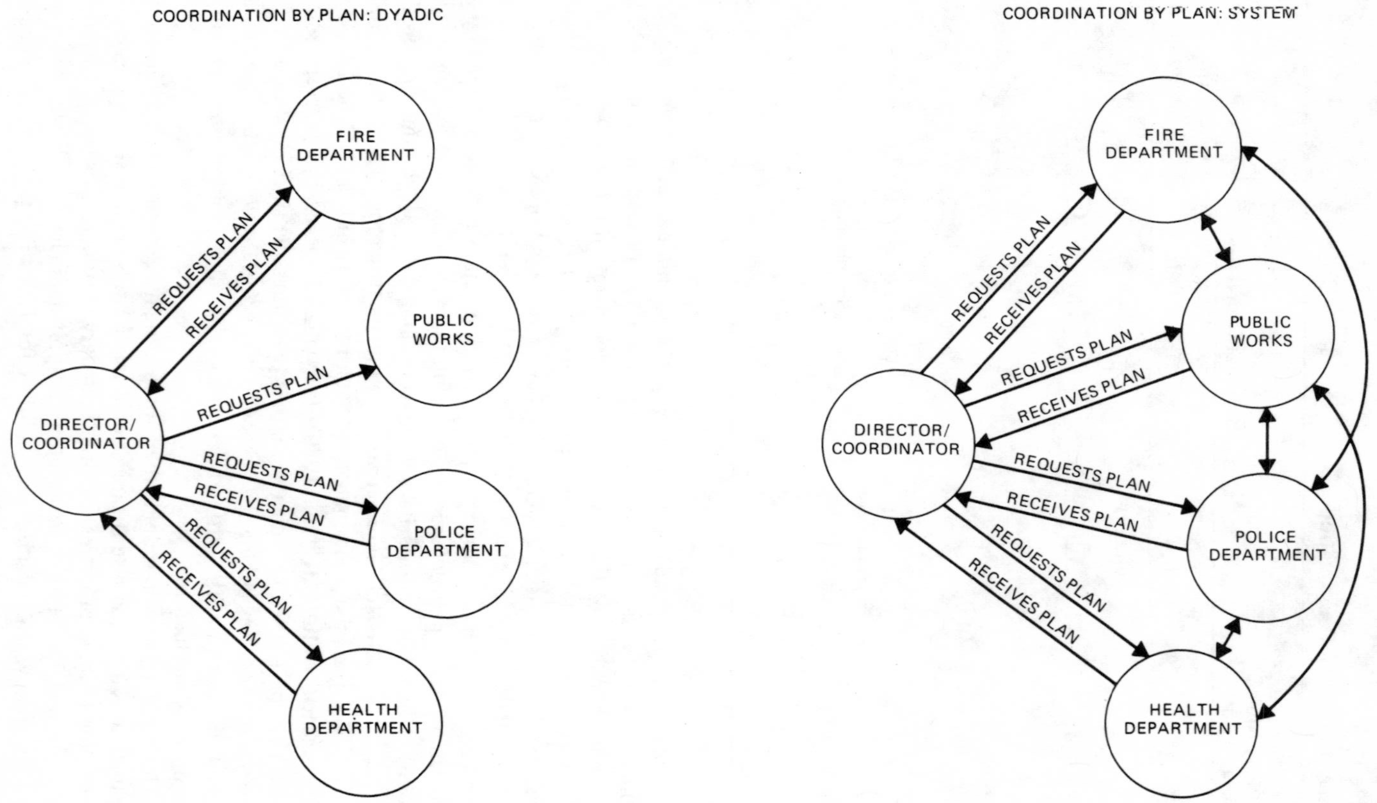

344

COORDINATION BY PLAN: SYSTEM

COORDINATION BY PLAN: DYADIC

Figure 12-3. Coordination by Plan

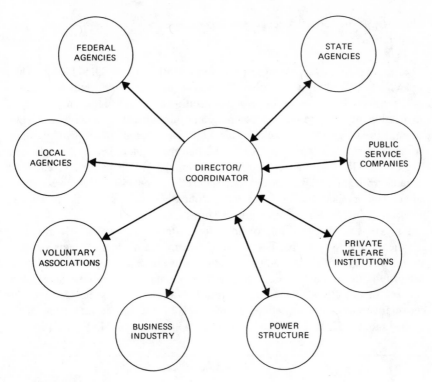

Figure 12-4. Coordination by Mutual Adjustment of Community Organizations

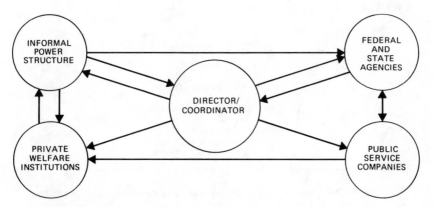

Figure 12-5. Symetric and Asymetric Mutual Adjustment Coordination in a Systems Model

Objective 2: An Applied Model of Interorganizational Cooperation

At a recent national conference on interorganizational research in health (White and Vlasak 1970), an initial attempt was made to integrate the existing theories and research in the area of interorganizational relationships and to make application of this research to planning and administrative practice. A further attempt to synthesize and make application of the cumulative research findings in the area of interorganizational relations has been undertaken by Klonglan and Yep (1972). They have developed an applied model of IOR which is essentially a research utilization package for practitioners concerned with interagency cooperation. The applied model presents a sequential analysis of the process of cooperative interaction between organizations.

An extensive review of interorganizational literature as well as a synthesis of the theory and research has been used to identify ten distinct planning stages or steps which appear sequentially in the cooperative interaction process, and when successfully negotiated, appear to result in increased cooperative interaction between organizations in the areas of health, education, and social services. This cooperative interaction is defined as five levels of interaction. An outline of the applied model of interorganizational cooperation is presented in Figure 12-6.

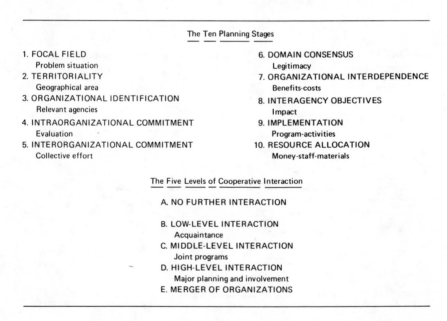

The Ten Planning Stages

1. FOCAL FIELD
   Problem situation
2. TERRITORIALITY
   Geographical area
3. ORGANIZATIONAL IDENTIFICATION
   Relevant agencies
4. INTRAORGANIZATIONAL COMMITMENT
   Evaluation
5. INTERORGANIZATIONAL COMMITMENT
   Collective effort

6. DOMAIN CONSENSUS
   Legitimacy
7. ORGANIZATIONAL INTERDEPENDENCE
   Benefits-costs
8. INTERAGENCY OBJECTIVES
   Impact
9. IMPLEMENTATION
   Program-activities
10. RESOURCE ALLOCATION
    Money-staff-materials

The Five Levels of Cooperative Interaction

A. NO FURTHER INTERACTION

B. LOW-LEVEL INTERACTION
   Acquaintance
C. MIDDLE-LEVEL INTERACTION
   Joint programs
D. HIGH-LEVEL INTERACTION
   Major planning and involvement
E. MERGER OF ORGANIZATIONS

Figure 12-6. An Applied Model of Interorganizational Cooperation

The ten sequential planning stages in the applied interorganizational cooperation model follow.

Planning Stage 1. Creation of the focal interagency field attempts to examine the basis for interagency cooperation. At any given time there are many potential and actual interagency fields or opportunities for cooperative interaction between organizations (Warren 1967b). However, a practitioner or change agent is usually concerned with a specific focal interagency field or situation. The focal interagency field is usually created as a proposed strategy for the resolution of problems requiring the involvement of two or more organizations. Examples of focal fields are health, poverty, juvenile delinquency, etc.

Planning Stage 2. Establishing the territoriality of the focal interagency field represents the attempt to define the geographical boundaries where this interagency cooperation is to take place (Loomis 1960). Beal (1965) defines territoriality as the geographical base or space dimensions of the social system that are formally, informally, or psychologically designated as meaningful areas of interaction. The territoriality of the focal interagency field could be state, county, community, or be as broad as national and international.

Planning Stage 3. Identification of relevant organizations for inclusion in the focal interagency field addresses itself to the question of what organizations and groups should be included in this focal field since very few interagency projects include all the organizations in a given area or community. Organizations usually identified or selected to participate in an interagency project usually have one or more of the following characteristics: (1) high organizational commitment to the purpose of the interagency project; (2) represents a potential resource base; (3) representative of the target population or client group; and (4) potential sources of legitimation and prestige (Litwak and Rothman 1970).

Planning Stage 4. Intraorganizational commitment is an evaluation of how committed in terms of resource allocation each of the relevant organizations are to the focal field. What percentage of an organization's resources have been or will be allocated to the problem under consideration in this interagency project (Klonglan and Paulson 1971; Aiken and Hage 1968; Finley 1970; and Rogers 1972).

Planning Stage 5. Interorganizational commitment within the focal interagency field examines how predisposed or willing each of the organizations is to working with other organizations rather than alone and independently (Babchuk 1959; Aiken and Hage 1968; Finley 1970; and Rogers and Glick 1972).

Planning Stage 6. Domain consensus between organizations in the focal inter-agency field analyzes the perceptions of each organization regarding the legitimacy and credibility of the other organizations in the interagency project. Domain consensus defines a set of expectations both for members of an organization and other organizations about what the organization will or will not do (Thompson 1967). Domain consensus appears to be a necessary prelude for interagency cooperation. Domain consensus refers to agreements between organizations regarding their respective goals, functions and services, and population served (Levine and White 1961; Braito et al. 1972; Rogers 1971).

Planning Stage 7. Perceived areas of organizational interdependence within focal interagency field examines how the organizations see the costs and benefits accruing in the interagency relationships within the focal interagency field (Thompson 1967). Organizational interdependence suggests the minimum condition for any form of linkage or relationship between agencies. By interdependence is meant that two or more organizations must take each other into account in order to best achieve their individual goals (Litwak and Rothman 1970; Rogers and Vacin 1972).

Planning Stage 8. Acceptance or agreement on interagency objectives within focal interagency field. Interagency cooperation is typically viewed by partici-pating organizations as a strategy for the resolution of a given problem (Klonglan et al. 1969b). Acceptance or agreement by organizations regarding a common definition of the problem area and methods for solving the problems appears to be an important condition for organization participation in an interagency project (Rogers and Vacin 1972).

Planning Stage 9. Acceptance or agreement on procedures for implementation of interagency objectives within focal interagency field. Following agreement on interagency objectives, the agencies must accept or agree upon a series of activities directed toward the resolution of the problem (Rogers and Vacin 1972). This stage is similar to Beal's plan of work in his Social Action Construct (1965). In this stage, the agencies accept or agree upon the type of structure needed to implement the interagency objectives (Warren 1969) and the neces-sary programs, activities, schedules, deadlines, budgeting, and evaluation pro-cedures.

Planning Stage 10. Organization allocation of resources for implementation of the interagency objectives is an important intermediary or linking stage between the planning and higher cooperative interaction stages in the applied model. Field studies suggest that the failure to obtain commitment and allocation leads to no further interaction or low level interaction between organizations. Organizational resources are defined as funds, staff, materials, facilities; and organizational support includes both legitimation and endorsement of the interagency activity.

The extent of acceptance or agreement in the preceding planning stages by organizations in the focal interagency field in conjunction with the constraints imposed by the models of coordination will usually result in one or a combination of the following five levels of interaction between organizations (Finley 1969; Leadley 1969; Starkweather 1970; Klonglan and Paulson 1971; and Klonglan et al. 1972).

Goetzkow (1966), Marrett (1971), and Mulford and Klonglan (1972) discuss the degree of reciprocity in the different levels of cooperative interaction ranging from unilateral—one-way cooperation to reciprocal—two-way cooperation to joint cooperation where the interaction is with a third party.

The five levels of cooperative interaction are:

1. No further interaction.
2. Low level interaction with informal and infrequent communication and minimal exchange of resources between organizations.
3. Middle level interaction with more formal and frequent communication and increased exchange of organizational resources.
4. High level interaction with highly formalized networks of communication and high exchange of organizational resources.
5. Merger of organizations represents a complete integration of organizational resources.

Relationship of Planning Stages to Levels
of Cooperative Interaction

If the first three planning stages of the applied model of interorganizational cooperation are successfully negotiated by participating organizations or a recognized third party, the organizations will usually have only reached the low level of interaction specified in the model.

Middle and high levels of cooperative interaction usually require agreement between participating organizations of planning stages 4 through 10. If serious disagreement occurs between organizations during the negotiation of the last seven planning stages, the level of interaction reverts to low level or no further interaction between organizations.

Interrelationship of Applied Model of Interorganizational
Cooperation and Applied Models of Coordination

The ten planning stages and five interaction stages of the Applied Model of Interorganizational Cooperation must be viewed in conjunction with the three models of coordination presented by Thompson (1967). Coordination is defined as strategies for regulating or affecting the type and level of interaction between two or more organizations (Klonglan and Yep 1972). Beal (1972) in analyzing Thompson's models of coordination emphasized the power dimension in each of the three models of coordination. Beal defined coordination by standardization as involving the use of authority where units in an organization or organizations are placed in clear cut hierarchical order with lines of authority explicit and sometimes designed to give power to the vertical lines of authority. This model has been described as a vertical model of coordination by Mulford and Klonglan (1972) and under this model of coordination there are maximum constraints on the organizations in both the planning and interaction stages. Coordination by plan involves the use of influence rather than authority and is similar to Dahl and Lindblom's (1953) notion of "manipulated field control." Thompson (1970) defined manipulated field control as deliberate action on another's field in order to get a definite response, by manipulating signals about rewards and deprivations, or manipulating rewards and deprivations themselves, or both. Organizations under coordination by plan establish plans or written agreements whereby the organizations agree to engage in a particular level of cooperative interaction. Coordination by mutual adjustment is the least powerful of the three models of coordination and involves rational persuasion or emotional appeal among organizations to motivate the organizations to engage in the planning and interaction stages in the Applied Model. This model of coordination has been described as "horizontal" (Mulford and Klonglan 1972) because it does not involve an hierarchical relationship. Coordination by mutual adjustment tends to be quite informal and *ad hoc* when compared to coordination by plan.

The three applied models of coordination exert varying degrees of constraints on organizational actions in the focal interagency field. Maximum constraints occur under coordination by standardization and plan, and minimum constraints occur under coordination by mutual adjustment. These models of coordination affect the organizations' responses in both the planning and cooperative interaction stages described in the preceding Applied Model of Interorganizational Cooperation. Low level cooperative interaction between organizations usually occurs under coordination by mutual adjustment. Higher levels are not required or consistent with the merits of mutual adjustment. Middle or high level cooperative interaction between organizations usually requires coordination by standardization or plan.

Current efforts are underway at Iowa State University to further integrate environmental factors into the applied models of cooperation and coordination which will enable the practitioner to more fully understand the nature of interorganizational relations.

Objective 3: The Empirical Use of the Applied Model of Interorganizational Relations

At the present stage of development, the applied model of interorganizational relations appears to be primarily useful as a diagnostic and evaluation guide for change agents in analyzing situations where two or more organizations are cooperating in planning and implementing a project. Three brief case examples will be presented in which the applied model was used in analyzing interorganizational relationships. The reader should note that each of the three types of coordination are illustrated.

The first case example involved the United States Department of Agriculture and the formation of rural development committees (focal field) at the state and county level (territoriality). The USDA issued a directive (coordination by standardization—authority) to five of their agencies (organizational identification) to cooperate (interagency objectives not specified) and form rural development committees at the state and local level. These federal agencies under USDA then notified their state agencies of this directive and requested compliance (vertical coordination). The stage agencies complied (intraorganizational and interorganizational commitment) and formed state rural development committees (low level interaction). Because the USDA was not more specific in defining interagency objectives and procedures for evaluation and in stating proposed sanctions, most state and local rural development committees appear to be operating at a low level of cooperative interaction with minimal impact.

Case example two was initiated when an administrator with a state department of education sent a letter to administrators of the state department of health, social services, state office of economic opportunity, and the state extension service (organizational identification) asking assistance from these organizations in locating low income children throughout the state (territoriality) for the purpose of participation in the free and reduced price school lunch program (focal field). All the contacted state organizations agreed to cooperate with the state department of education (intraorganizational and interorganizational commitment) and a plan was developed by the participating agencies (coordination by plan—influence) to form interagency committees at the area and county level. The direction of the low level cooperative interaction was primarily joint—directed to a third party, the schools rather than reciprocal—between participating organizations and minimizing the need for agreement on domain and organizational interdependence. Since resource allocation was small, agreement between participating organizations was quickly reached regarding interagency objectives and implementation.

The third case example focuses on the informal meetings of local (territoriality) executives and staff of health and social service organizations (organizational identification) who meet periodically to discuss topics of mutual concern (focal field). Coordination is horizontal and by mutual adjustment—persuasion or appeal and agreement is needed only for the first three planning stages. Low level interaction is the most common relationship between organizations and impact is minimal.

The applied model of interorganizational relations has been used in training programs by three organizations: United States Public Health Service, United

States Department of Agriculture-State Rural Development Committee (Iowa), and the University Extension Service (Iowa).

In using the applied models of interorganizational relations, we have found the most essential questions to the practitioner appear to be:

1. What is the desired level of cooperative interaction between participating organizations?
2. What is the most appropriate model of coordination for achieving this level of interaction?
3. What are the most important planning stages?
4. In what planning stages is disagreement most likely to occur?
5. What are the most effective strategies for resolving these disagreements?

Summary and Conclusions

The purpose of this chapter has been to review some of the work that has been done in recent years in the area of interorganizational relations, not limiting ourselves to relations among voluntary groups, since there is little research specifically on such groups alone. Specifically, we have presented a general model that organizes much of the past research in IOR and also provides a guide for future research. We have also presented an applied model of IOR that may be useful to practitioners. Three case studies using the applied model as a diagnostic device for practitioners were presented.

This analysis of the theory, methodology, and empirical studies in interorganizational relations suggests directions for future IOR study. Major research is needed to assess the real impact of IOR. Is a coordinated interorganizational effort superior to a noncoordinated organizational approach? Also, further research is needed to clarify the impact of overlapping IOR focal fields and the subsequent effect of this multiple IOR on one IOR focal field. Further analysis is needed on the effect of cumulative IOR in one focal field over a period of years in affecting a specific IOR situation. Additional study is needed to evaluate the significance of the frequency and content of interaction activities.

Although many variables have been delineated as actually or potentially affecting interaction activity, there is need to specify which are the most important variables in predicting the establishment of different levels of IOR. Of specific interest should be the variables which can be manipulated by individual organizations or coordinating bodies. This chapter has focused primarily on cooperative rather than competitive or conflict IOR situations. One special focus of study could be the affects of the three different models of coordination on competitive and conflict situations. More focus should be given to the effects on interorganizational relations of informal relations among IOR actors. Future research and action should clearly specify the unit of analysis being studied.

There is a need to further specify the relationship between the process of IOR and the role of change agents in communities. From the applied perspective, there is need to further develop IOR research utilization packages which can be used in training programs for organizational personnel.

Particular studies could focus on the importance of the size of resource investment made by any organization in IOR; particularly compared to its total agency resources. And theoretical perspectives other than exchange and field theory should be brought to bear on understanding IOR. In summary, there is considerably theoretical, empirical, and applied work to be done in order to better understand interorganizational relations.

This latter conclusion applies even more strongly to the study of IOR involving voluntary organizations. Yet what research there is on the impact of interorganizational relationships suggests that these relations may have an important impact on the level of mobilization of community resources to deal with a particular problem. Hence, voluntary action scholars should pay special attention to the interorganizational level of voluntary action as a new and exciting field of research on impacts.

References

Aiken, Michael and Jerald Hage
1968 "Organizational Interdependence and Intra-organizational Structure." AMERICAN SOCIOLOGICAL REVIEW 33, no. 6:912-30.

Aldrich, Brian C.
1970 "Relations between Organizations: A Critical Review of the Literature." Minneapolis: University of Minnesota. A paper presented at the annual meeting of the American Sociological Association, Washington, D.C. at the seminar session on "Voluntary Action Research: Steps Toward Synthesis."

Aldrich, Howard
1971 "Organizational Boundaries and Inter-Organizational Conflict." HUMAN RELATIONS 24, no. 4:279-293.

Babchuk, Nicolas and C. Wayne Gordon
1959 "A Typology of Voluntary Organizations." AMERICAN SOCIOLOGICAL REVIEW 24:22-30.

Beal, George M.
1965 "A Guide to Community Action." Des Moines, Iowa: Iowa Comprehensive Plan to Combat Mental Retardation.
1971 "Inter-Organizational Coordination: The Setting and Propositions." Ames, Iowa: Iowa State University.
1972 "Interorganizational Coordination." Ames, Iowa: Iowa State University. A paper presented at a conference on Agriculture in a Quality Environment, Cedar Rapids, Iowa.

Beal, George M., Gerald E. Klonglan, Paul Yarbrough, Joe M. Bohlen and Don A. Dillman
1967 "System Linkages among Women's Organizations." Ames, Iowa: Iowa State University. Sociology Report No. 42.

Benson, J. Kenneth
1972 "Two Levels of Analysis in the Study of an Interorganizational Network." Columbia, Missouri: University of Missouri. A paper presented at the annual meeting of the American Sociological Association. New Orleans, Louisiana.

Bernstein, Robert A. and Peter D. Weldon
1968 "A Structural Approach to the Analysis of International Relations." JOURNAL OF CONFLICT RESOLUTION 12, no. 2:159-81.

Black, Bertram J. and Harold M. Kase
1963 "Inter-Agency Cooperation in Rehabilitation and Mental Health." SOCIAL SERVICE REVIEW 37:26-32.

Blau, Peter M.
1964 EXCHANGE AND POWER IN SOCIAL LIFE. New York: Wiley.

Blau, Peter M. and W. Richard Scott
1962 FORMAL ORGANIZATIONS. San Francisco: Chandler Publishing Company.

Braito, Rita, Steven K. Paulson and Gerald E. Klonglan
1972 "Domain Consensus: A Key Variable in Interorganizational Analysis." In COMPLEX ORGANIZATIONS AND THEIR ENVIRONMENTS. Edited by Merlin B. Brinkerhoff and Phillip R. Kunz. Dubuque, Iowa: Wm. C. Brown Company.

Brinkerhoff, Merlin B. and Phillip R. Kunz
1972 COMPLEX ORGANIZATIONS AND THEIR ENVIRONMENTS. Dubuque, Iowa: Wm. C. Brown Company.

Caplan, Eleanor K. and Frank J. Kohout
1966a "Evaluation of Interorganizational Coordination in an Action Program: Preliminary Findings and Methodological Problems." Cleveland, Ohio: Department of Sociology, Western Reserve University. Unpublished mimeographed paper presented at the annual meeting of the Society for the Study of Social Problems, Miami, Florida.
1966b "The Welfare System: Hypotheses on Organization and Adaptation." Cleveland, Ohio: Department of Sociology, Western Reserve University. Unpublished mimeographed paper presented at the annual meeting of the Ohio Valley Sociological Society, Dayton, Ohio.

Clark, Burton R.
1965 "Interorganizational Patterns in Education." ADMINISTRATIVE SCIENCE QUARTERLY 10 (September):224-37.

Cyert, Richard M. and James G. March
1963 A BEHAVIORAL THEORY OF THE FIRM. Englewood Cliffs, New Jersey: Prentice-Hall, Inc.

Dahl, Robert and Charles Lindblom
1953   POLITICS, ECONOMICS AND WELFARE. New York: Harper and Row.

Davis, Stanley M.
1972   "Coordinating the Multinational Enterprise." Cambridge, Massachusetts: Harvard University. A paper presented at the annual meeting of the American Sociological Association. New Orleans, Louisiana.

Dill, William R.
1958   "Environment as an Influence on Managerial Autonomy." ADMINIS-TRATIVE SCIENCE QUARTERLY 2 (March):409-443.

Dillman, Don A.
1966   "Systemic Linkages between Voluntary Associations: A Theoretical Model." Ames, Iowa: Iowa State University. An unpublished M.S. thesis.
1969   "Analysis of Interorganizational Relations." Ames, Iowa: Iowa State University. An unpublished Ph.D. dissertation.
1970   "Relations between Social Agencies: A Preliminary Attempt at Measurement and Analysis. Ames, Iowa: Iowa State University. A paper presented at the annual meeting of the American Sociological Association, Washington, D.C.

Dillman, Don A., Gerald E. Klonglan, Paul Yarbrough and Paul F. Schmitz
1970   "Voluntary Associations and Community Structure." Ames, Iowa: Iowa State University.

Douds, Charles F. and Albert H. Rubenstein
1966   "Some Models of Organization Interfaces in the R+D." Evanston, Illinois: Department of Industrial Engineering and Managerial Sciences, The Technological Institute, Northwestern University.

Dynes, Russell R.
1969   "Community Conflict: An Explanation of its Absence in Natural Disasters." Columbus, Ohio: Ohio State University, Disaster Research Center, Working Paper No. 41.

Dynes, Russell R. and E.L. Quarantelli
1969   "Interorganizational Relations in Communities under Stress." Columbus, Ohio: Ohio State University, Disaster Research Center, Working Paper No. 19.

Endo, Russell
1972   "Participation of the Poor and Interorganizational Relationships." Seattle: University of Washington. A paper prepared for presentation at the annual meeting of the American Sociological Association. New Orleans, Louisiana.

Evan, William M.
1966   "The Organization-Set: Toward a Theory of Interorganizational Relations." In APPROACHES TO ORGANIZATIONAL DESIGN. Pittsburgh, Pennsylvania: University of Pittsburgh Press.

Finley, James Richard
1969 "Relations between Development Organizations: A Preliminary Report of Scaling Interorganizational Relations." Ithaca, New York: Cornell University.
1970 "A Study of Interorganizational Relationships." Ithaca, New York: Cornell University. Unpublished Ph.D. dissertation.

Finley, James R. and Harold R. Capener
1967 "Interorganizational Relations: Concepts and Methodological Considerations." Ithaca, New York: Cornell University. A paper presented at the annual meeting of the Rural Sociological Society, San Francisco, California.

Form, William H. and Sigmund Nosow
1958 COMMUNITY IN DISASTER. New York: Harper and Row.

Friesema, Harry Paul
1968 "Metropolitan Political Structure: Inter-governmental Relations and Political Integration in the Quad-cities." Iowa City, Iowa: University of Iowa. Unpublished Ph.D. dissertation.

Goetzkow, Harold
1966 "Relations among Organizations." In STUDIES ON BEHAVIOR IN ORGANIZATIONS. Edited by Raymond V. Bowers. Athens, Georgia: University of Georgia Press.

Gouldner, Alvin
1959 "Reciprocity and Autonomy in Functional Theory." In SYMPOSIUM ON SOCIOLOGICAL THEORY. Edited by Llewellyn Gross. New York: Harper and Row.

Griffin, Charles T.
1972 "A Causal Model Analysis of Role Performance of Coordinators in the Operating System Following a Disaster." Ames, Iowa: Iowa State University. Unpublished Ph.D. dissertation.

Griffin, Charles T., Charles L. Mulford and Gerald E. Klonglan
1972 "An Analysis of Operating System Effectiveness: Focus on the Behavior of Local Coordinators." Ames, Iowa: Iowa State University. Sociology Report No. 102.

Hage, Jerald and Michael Aiken
1972 "Organizational Permeability, Boundary Spanners and Organizational Structure." Madison, Wisconsin: University of Wisconsin. A paper presented at the annual meeting of the American Sociological Association. New Orleans, Louisiana.

Hall, Richard H.
1972a ORGANIZATIONS, STRUCTURE AND PROCESS. Englewood Cliffs, New Jersey: Prentice-Hall, Inc.
1972b "Perspectives from Outside Medical Sociology: Research on Large Scale Organizations." Minneapolis: University of Minnesota. A paper presented

at the annual meeting of the American Sociological Association. New Orleans, Louisiana.

Hall, Richard H. and John P. Clark
1969 "Toward the Measurement of Interorganizational Relations." Minneapolis: University of Minnesota. A paper presented at the annual meeting of the American Sociological Association. San Francisco, California.

Hemphill, John R. and Charles M. Westie
1955 "The Measurement of Group Dimensions." In THE LANGUAGE OF SOCIAL RESEARCH. Edited by Paul F. Lazarsfeld and Morris Rosenberg. New York: The Free Press.

Heydebrand, Wolf
1971 "New Directions in Research on Organizations." St. Louis, Missouri: Washington University. A paper presented at the annual meeting of the American Sociological Association, Denver, Colorado.

Hollister, C. David
1972 "School Bureaucracy as a Response to Parents' Demands." Duluth, Minnesota: University of Minnesota. A paper presented at the annual meeting of the American Sociological Association. New Orleans, Louisiana.

Kahn, Robert L., Donald M. Wolfe, Robert P. Quinn, J. Diedrich Snoek and Robert A. Rosenthal
1964 ORGANIZATIONAL STRESS. New York: Wiley.

Katz, Daniel and Robert L. Kahn
1966 THE SOCIAL PSYCHOLOGY OF ORGANIZATIONS. New York: Wiley.

Kendall, Patricia and Paul F. Lazarsfeld
1955 "The Relation between Individual and Group Characteristics in 'The American Soldier.'" in THE LANGUAGE OF SOCIAL RESEARCH. Edited by Paul F. Lazarsfeld and Morris Rosenberg. New York: The Free Press.

Klonglan, Gerald E. and George M. Beal
1970 "Structure of the Systems Inputs: Roles and Mission." In Proceedings of the Office of Civil Defense Research Symposium entitled, FRAMEWORK FOR EVALUATION OF SURVIVAL AND RECOVERY SYSTEMS. Arlington, Virginia: Institute for Defense Analysis.

Klonglan, Gerald E., George M. Beal, Steven K. Paulson, Richard D. Warren and William Fleischman
1971 "Organizational Coordination as an Intervention Process: Applied to the Problem of Cigarette Smoking and Health." Ames, Iowa: Iowa State University. Sociology Report No. 91.

Klonglan, Gerald E., Don A. Dillman, O. Andrew Collver and Paul Yarbrough
1969a "Determinants of Membership Linkages among Women's Voluntary

Organizations." Ames, Iowa: Iowa State University. A paper presented at the annual meeting of the Rural Sociological Society, San Francisco, California.

Klonglan, Gerald E., Don A. Dillman, Joel S. Wright and George M. Beal
1969b "Agency Interaction Patterns and Community Alcoholism Services." Ames, Iowa: Department of Sociology, Iowa State University. Sociology Report No. 73.

Klonglan, Gerald E., Joel S. Wright and Don A. Dillman
1969c "Alcoholism Services: Client Characteristics and Treatment Outcomes." A Description of personal characteristics and an analysis of factors related to treatment-rehabilitation outcomes of problem drinkers mutually served by the Iowa Comprehensive Alcoholism Demonstration Project Service Centers and other community agents. Ames, Iowa: Iowa State University. Sociology Report No. 74.

Klonglan, Gerald E. and Steven K. Paulson
1971 "Coordinating Health Organizations: The Problem of Cigarette Smoking." Ames, Iowa: Iowa State University. Sociology Report No. 90.

Klonglan, Gerald E., David L. Rogers and Steven K. Paulson
1972 "Measurement of Interorganizational Relations: A Deterministic Model." Ames, Iowa: Iowa State University. A paper presented at the annual meeting of the American Sociological Association. New Orleans, Louisiana.

Klonglan, Gerald E. and Benjamin Yep
1972 THEORY AND PRACTICE OF INTERORGANIZATIONAL RELATIONS. Ames, Iowa: Iowa State University.

Lazarsfeld, Paul F. and Herbert Menzel
1969 "On the Relation between Individual and Collective Properties." In A SOCIOLOGICAL READER ON COMPLEX ORGANIZATIONS. Edited by Amitai Etzioni. New York: Holt, Rinehart and Winston.

Leadley, Samuel M.
1969 "An Integrative Model: Cooperative Relations among Organizations." University Park, Pennsylvania: Pennsylvania State University. A paper presented at the annual meeting of the Rural Sociological Society, San Francisco.

Lehman, Edward W.
1971 "Toward a Paradigm for the Analysis of Inter-organizational Relations." New York: New York University. A paper presented at the annual meeting of the American Sociological Association. Denver, Colorado.

Levine, Sol and Paul E. White
1961 "Comments on: Exchange as a Conceptual Framework for the Study of Interorganizational Relationships." AMERICAN SOCIOLOGICAL QUARTERLY (March).
1963 "The Community of Health Organizations." In HANDBOOK OF MEDI-

CAL SOCIOLOGY. Howard Freeman, Sol Levine and Leo Reeder. Englewood Cliffs, New Jersey: Prentice-Hall.

Levine, Sol, Paul E. White and Benjamin D. Paul
1963 "Community Interorganizational Problems in Providing Medical Care and Social Services." AMERICAN JOURNAL OF PUBLIC HEALTH 53 (August):1183-95.

Lindblom, Charles E.
1966 THE INTELLIGENCE OF DEMOCRACY: DECISION MAKING THROUGH MUTUAL ADJUSTMENT. New York: The Free Press.

Litterer, Joseph A.
1965 THE ANALYSIS OF ORGANIZATIONS. New York: Wiley.

Litwak, Eugene and Lydia Hylton
1961- "Interorganizational Analysis: A Hypothesis on Coordinating Agencies."
1962 ADMINISTRATIVE SCIENCE QUARTERLY 6:395-420.

Litwak, Eugene and Jack Rothman
1970 "Towards the Theory and Practice of Coordination between Formal Organizations." In ORGANIZATIONS AND CLIENTS. Edited by William R. Rosengren and Mark Lefton. Columbus, Ohio: Charles E. Merrill Publishing Company.

Loomis, Charles P.
1960 SOCIAL SYSTEMS. Princeton, New Jersey: Van Nostrand Company, Inc.

Manley, Vaughn P. and Allen C. Jensen
1966 "Equalizing Access to Social Services through Area Inter-agency Approaches." IOWA BUSINESS DIGEST. Iowa City, Iowa: University of Iowa.

March, James G.
1965 HANDBOOK OF ORGANIZATIONS. Chicago: Rand McNally.

Marrett, Cora Bagley
1971 "On the Specification of Interorganizational Dimensions." SOCIOLOGY and SOCIAL RESEARCH 56, no. 1 (October): 83-99.

Miller, Walter B.
1958 "Inter-institutional Conflict as a Major Impediment to Delinquency Prevention." HUMAN ORGANIZATION 17 (Fall):20-23.

Morris, Robert and Ollie A. Randall
1965 "Planning and Organization of Community Services for the Elderly." SOCIAL WORK 10:96-102.

Mott, Basil J.F.
1968 ANATOMY OF A COORDINATING COUNCIL: IMPLICATIONS FOR PLANNING. Pittsburgh, Pennsylvania: University of Pittsburgh Press.

Mulford, Charles L. and Gerald E. Klonglan
1972 "Developing Coalitions for Social Action." Ames, Iowa: Iowa State University. A paper read at the National Conference on Voluntarism and America's Future: Prologue to the Third Century. Washington, D.C.

Mulford, Charles L., Gerald E. Klonglan and Ralph M. Brooks
1970 "Training Local Coordinators: Implications for Civil Defense." Ames, Iowa: Iowa State University. Sociology Report No. 84.

Organ, Dennis W.
1971 "Some Variables Affecting Boundary Role Behavior." SOCIOMETRY 34, no. 4:524-537.

Parsons, Talcott
1951 THE SOCIAL SYSTEM. New York: The Free Press.
1956 "Suggestions for a Sociological Approach to the Theory of Organizations—1." ADMINISTRATIVE SCIENCE QUARTERLY 1:63-85.

Paulson, Steven K.
1971 "Comparison of Causal Theories Constructed from Alternative Measurement Models of Complex Organizations." Ames, Iowa: Iowa State University. Unpublished Ph.D. dissertation.

Perrow, Charles
1961 "Organizational Prestige: Some Functions and Dysfunctions." AMERICAN JOURNAL OF SOCIOLOGY 66 (January):335-341.

Perrucci, Robert and Marc Pilisuk
1970 "Leaders and Ruling Elites: The Interorganizational Bases of Community Power." AMERICAN SOCIOLOGICAL REVIEW 35 (December): 1040-57.

Price, James L.
1968 ORGANIZATIONAL EFFECTIVENESS: AN INVENTORY OF PROPOSITIONS. Homewood, Illinois: Richard D. Irwin.

Reid, William
1964 "Interagency Coordination in Delinquency Prevention and Control." SOCIAL SERVICE REVIEW 38 (December):418-28.

Richards, Robert O. and Willis J. Goudy
1971 "Evaluations of Citizen Participation and Interagency Cooperation in the Des Moines Model City Program." Ames, Iowa: Iowa State University. Sociology Report No. 96.

Rogers, David L.
1971 "Organizational Coordination in Rural Development: A Research Proposal." Ames, Iowa: Department of Sociology, Iowa State University.

Rogers, David L. and Edward L. Glick
1972 "Public and Private Organizational Response to Rural Development." Ames, Iowa: Iowa State University, Center for Agricultural and Rural Development.

Rogers, David L. and Gary L. Vacin
1972 "A Deterministic Model of Interorganizational Relations: An Application to the Community Development Process." Ames, Iowa: Iowa State University.

Scott, W. Richard
1972 "Some Worries about the Developing Field of Interorganizational Research." Palo Alto, California: Stanford University. A paper presented at
the annual meeting of the American Sociological Association. New
Orleans, Louisiana.
Sriram, Carolyn Marzec
1969 "Towards a Theory of Organizational-Environmental Relationships."
Houston, Texas: University of Houston. M.S. Thesis.
Starkweather, David B.
1970 "Health Facility Merger and Integration: A Typology and Some Hypoth-
eses." Interorganizational Research in Health: Conference Proceedings.
Baltimore, Maryland: The Johns Hopkins University.
Tannenbaum, Arnold S. and Jerald G. Bachman
1964 "Structural versus Individual Effects." AMERICAN JOURNAL OF
SOCIOLOGY 69 (May):585-95.
Terreberry, Shirley
1968 "The Evolution of Organizational Environments." ADMINISTRATIVE
SCIENCE REVIEW 12:590-613.
Thompson, James D.
1962 "Organizations and Output Transactions." AMERICAN JOURNAL OF
SOCIOLOGY 68, no. 3:309-321.
1967 ORGANIZATIONS IN ACTION. New York: McGraw-Hill.
1970 "Thoughts on Interorganizational Relations: A Conclusion." Interorgani-
zational Research in Health: Conference Proceedings. Baltimore, Mary-
land: The Johns Hopkins University.
Thompson, James D. and William J. McEwen
1958 "Organizational Goals and Environment: Goal Setting as an Interaction
Process." AMERICAN SOCIOLOGICAL REVIEW 23 (February):23-31.
Tripodi, Tony, Phillip Fellin and Irwin Epstein
1971 SOCIAL PROGRAM EVALUATION. Itasca, Illinois: F.E. Peacock
Publishers, Inc.
Turk, Herman
1970 "Interorganizational Networks in Urban Society: Initial Perspectives and
Comparative Research." AMERICAN SOCIOLOGICAL REVIEW 35, no.
1 (February):1-19.
Tweed, Dan L.
1972 "A Developmental Methodology for the Study of Interorganizational
Relationships." Ames, Iowa: Iowa State University. Unpublished M.S.
Thesis.
Udy, Stanley H., Jr.
1965 "The Comparative Analysis of Organizations." HANDBOOK OF
ORGANIZATIONS (March):692.

Vacin, Gary Lee
1972   "A Study of Interorganizational Relations between the Cooperative Extension Service and Members of its Organization Set." Ames, Iowa: Iowa State University. Unpublished Ph.D. dissertation.

Warren, Roland L.
1967a   "The Interaction of Community Decision Organizations: Some Basic Concepts and Needed Research." THE SOCIAL SERVICE REVIEW 41, no. 3 (September).
1967b   "The Interorganizational Field as a Focus for Investigation." ADMINIST RATIVE SCIENCE QUARTERLY 12 (December):396-419.

Warren, Roland L.
1968   "Interorganizational Study Project—Method of Procedure." Waltham, Massachusetts: Brandeis University, The Florence Heller Graduate School for Advanced Studies in Social Welfare.
1969   "The Concerting of Decisions as a Variable in Organizational Interaction." Evanston, Illinois: Northwestern University. A paper prepared for the conference on Interorganizational Decision Making.

White, Paul E., Sol Levine and George J. Vlasak
1971   "Exchange as a Conceptual Framework for Understanding Interorganizational Relationships: Application to Non-Profit Organizations." Baltimore, Maryland: The Johns Hopkins University.

White, Paul E. and George J. Vlasak
1970   "Inter-organizational Research in Health." Baltimore, Maryland: The Johns Hopkins University.
1971   "A Selected Bibliography Focusing on Interorganizational Research on Health, 1960-70." Baltimore, Maryland: The Johns Hopkins University.

Wilcox, Leslie D., Ralph M. Brooks, George M. Beal and Gerald E. Klonglan
1972   SOCIAL INDICATORS AND SOCIETAL MONITORING. Netherlands: A Jossey-Bass/Elsevier Book.

Yep, Benjamin
1970   "Voluntary Organizations and Their Cooperative Interaction Patterns on a State Level." East Lansing, Michigan: Michigan State University. Unpublished Ph.D. dissertation.

Yuchtman, Ephraim and Stanley E. Seashore
1967   "A System Resource Approach to Organizational Effectiveness." AMERICAN SOCIOLOGICAL REVIEW 32, no. 6 (December):891-903.

13

Labor and Peasant Movements as Sources of Voluntary Organizations and Instruments of Class Mobility

Henry Landsberger

Voluntary Organizations Based on Class and Status

The "voluntary" organizations with which we deal in this chapter are those growing out of the social movements of persons low in economic and political status. They are a reaction to that low status, generally intended to improve it or, at least, to protect it against loss. The word *voluntary* was put in quotation marks because the extent to which membership is voluntary in some organizations (e.g., trade unions) is empirically subject to variation and is therefore a problem to be investigated scientifically.

Let us make explicit various theoretical points implicit in this formulation—some well-known, others more novel. First, the above formulation is in accord with Blumer's famous division (Blumer 1951) between general movements that may either eventuate in specific movements or may eventuate in organizations. Thus the British working-class movement, which like the American may be said to have had its beginning toward the end of the eighteenth century, is best seen as being a result of a general mood of discontent on the part of skilled workers at the prospect of the loss of status threatened by new forms of commercial and industrial organization (Pelling 1963). This general concern gave rise to a number of specific anxieties, such as how to meet the problems of illness and death; of high priced and adulterated food; of wages and working conditions; and of political powerlessness. Finally, these anxieties in turn gave rise to attempts to establish certain specific organizations to deal with them: mutual aid or "friendly" societies; consumer cooperatives; trade unions; and labor parties respectively. In all this we follow, therefore, a well-known sociological tradition.

A second implication of focusing on the voluntary organizations of low-status individuals is the conviction that such organizations share at least some characteristics with other organizations also concerned, wholly or in part, with economic and political status (e.g., the American Medical Association), while still other characteristics of worker and peasant movements are specific to their *low* status members. It is around this aspect of low status and status concern generally that we will propose a series of hypotheses and generalizations.

It should be noted, more than incidentally, that some of these hypotheses and generalizations should also apply to other low status groups such as blacks (women? students?), although insofar as the low status of these groups is not

363

due to their relation to the processes of production—as is that of workers and peasants—there will be differences in the movements they produce. But in any case, from the point of view of the purposes of this symposium on voluntary action, we believe that voluntary organizations rooted in social movements based on low status are worthy of special study within the more general field of "voluntary acts and organizations."

Third, it is appropriate to note—from the point of view of the logical organization of the discipline of sociology—that collective, organized concern with status should be placed side by side and on an equal footing with the study of individual concern with status, thus forming a more balanced field of "social stratification and mobility."

The individual (on his own behalf or that of his children) can attempt to obtain "more"—material wealth, political power, prestige: whatever the dimensions—either by "going it alone" and ascending to another position, or by banding together with others similarly situated in order to improve the status of the present position. That, of course, is what Marxian theory is all about, with its emphasis on loss of status first, through the emiseration of the proletariat, but its (semifinal) rise in status through the dictatorship of the proletariat. C. Wright Mills, too, focused on the relative movement of entire classes, whether with or without organization.

But these and other Marxian and neo-Marxian writings have rarely been conceptualized as a logical and necessary complement and alternative to the aggregation of individual mobility. The writings of sociologists have focused far too much on individual mobility through movement from one position to another, and too little on collective mobility (a term used by Smelser and Lipset, who express regret that the phenomenon has been so little analyzed—Smelser and Lipset 1966). Collective mobility, achieved through improving the rewards of an existing position, makes less necessary, and is an alternative to, "mobility" in the more usual individual sense. As we shall note below, even certain concepts from the field of individual mobility are applicable to that of collective, position-mobility. As a matter of fact, a more complex, two-dimensional projection is logically necessary, since collective efforts can well have as their goal both the mobility of the position and/or the easing of individual movement between positions. Organizations of landless day-laborers agitating not for better pay, but for being given land, want to move from one social position to another, as do trade unions when pressing for a more open educational system to enable their children to ascend the social ladder. Conversely, an individual can seek, not mobility to another position, but to improve his present position through higher wages, and so forth. Figure 13-1 demonstrates the point. But our main concern is to point out that the kind of organizations we are interested in are within the general fields both of social stratification and social mobility and of voluntary acts and organizations.

Let us now highlight the characteristics of these kinds of organizations that

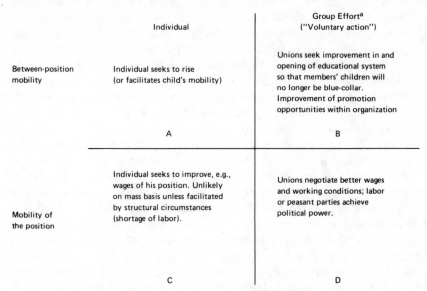

	Individual	Group Effort[a] ("Voluntary action")
Between-position mobility	Individual seeks to rise (or facilitates child's mobility)	Unions seek improvement in and opening of educational system so that members' children will no longer be blue-collar. Improvement of promotion opportunities within organization
	A	B
Mobility of the position	Individual seeks to improve, e.g., wages of his position. Unlikely on mass basis unless facilitated by structural circumstances (shortage of labor).	Unions negotiate better wages and working conditions; labor or peasant parties achieve political power.
	C	D

Figure 13-1. Schematic Representation of Position Mobility vs. Mobility between Positions; and Individual vs. Group Effort to Achieve These
[a]As discussed in the text: just as the aggregate of individual mobility, i.e., mobility in quadrants A and C are attributable both to changes in the structure of society and to the "openness" of society, so, too, the success of group efforts (B and D) will depend on structural changes as well as on group effort (indeed group effort will in part also depend on structural changes: see text).

are to a greater or lesser extent peculiar to it. A complete analysis of trade unions and peasant organizations is, for obvious reasons, out of the question.

Indeed, we cannot deal here even with two major definitional problems: (1) the issue of what shall be included under the concept of "movement" and "organization" (expressive vs. instrumental; relation to religious or nationalist movements which have status aspects); and (2) a more careful definition of, and attempts to measure, different dimensions of status. For this, the reader is referred to an earlier publication (Landsberger 1969, Chap. 1).

Societal Environment and Low-Status Movements

Idealistic and Materialistic Factors in the Growth of Working Class and Peasant Movements

Whatever may be true of other voluntary action organizations, the establishment of organizations among those toward the bottom of various status dimensions, defending their interest, in itself represents a notable structural social change. Yet it is usually but a partial reflection of structural changes that are even more profound. Such organizations are explicitly set-up to reallocate the major rewards of society—power and material wealth. Hence they generally meet with the hostility and resistance of those whose status along these dimensions is being threatened. Under these circumstances, the establishment of such organizations by groups who are by definition economically and politically weak, let alone the success of such organizations, often bespeaks of some kind of weakening of the old elites and/or some other major social change, such as the rise of new groups to power. The origin of such movements can therefore be analyzed, in part and with caution, as if they were potential revolutions or prerevolutionary situations of sorts. Thus, not only Smelser's value added model (Smelser 1963), which applies to any kind of collective behavior whether revolutionary or not, is useful to the study of these kinds of movements. Equally useful are models of revolution, such as the first stages of a "natural history" model, for example, as delineated by Crane Brinton (Brinton 1938, rev. 1965), or the more recent writings of Johnson (1966) and Arendt (1962).

All analysts—from de Tocqueville through Marx to the purely theoretically-oriented social scientists of today (or yesterday!)—are agreed that some room in the causal model must be left for objective, structural social changes as well as some room for changes in the subjective state, i.e., in the consciousness of those who organize and, indeed, in the consciousness of those against whom organization takes place.

Changes in Consciousness

On the side of the changing consciousness of workers and peasants, five points are particularly germane (we obviously cannot cover what is by now a debate which has lasted over 100 years).

First, the discontent on which these movements are based are now commonly conceptualized, in American sociological literature, as a quantitative gap between aspirations and reality, i.e., objective rewards (Davies 1962; Gurr 1970; though neither of these authors are exclusively interested in low-status discontent).

We do not agree, however, with the notion that a sudden downward trend in objective conditions, after a long upward trend (which had caused expectations to rise) is the only possible stimulant of discontent (Davies 1962). As a matter of fact, expectations can rise faster than a rising objective situation, thus also causing an increasing gap and discontent. Industrial disturbances have broken out throughout the early nineteenth century and unions have often been organized at times of rising prosperity not only because workers perceived that the situation was propitious for a successful movement, but because they subjectively felt left behind, relatively, even when their objective condition was improving, since the condition of employers was improving even faster (see the description of U.S. labor organizational activity in the early 1830s and early 1840s in Rayback 1966).

A steady downward trend, even if it is not preceded by a previous upward trend, can also cause the kind of discontent needed for the establishment of a movement. Such was the case of the Mexican peasantry prior to the revolution of 1910: their situation had steadily deteriorated (White 1969). What is necessary, then, for discontent is an expanding gap between reality and aspirations, no matter how produced.

Second, we believe that the worldwide, secular diffusion of the ideals of equality, of the dignity of the human person and related long-term value changes, have been a factor in increasing aspirations among those of low status, thereby widening the gap between reality and expectations, and making those of low status more ready to act in concert to improve their lot in life. Analysis of early peasant movements in Europe (e.g., the English peasant uprising of 1381, and the demands presented during the German Peasant Wars of 1525) indicates that memories of a more egalitarian state preceding feudalism definitely played a role in motivating the peasantry, no matter what the immediately preceding circumstances (Landsberger 1969, p. 34). It may be that these broad ideals, rooted far in the past, surfacing clearly in the philosophic movements of the eighteenth century and, of course, in the French Revolution, were peculiarly Western. Perhaps they then spread out from the West to other continents as the European powers built up their colonial empires. Or it may be that these values are also indigenous to other cultures. In any case, egalitariansim and related values are ever more evident both inside and outside Europe and North America and form one of the bases of the protest movements of "the lower classes" throughout the world. The movements among America's black citizens are clearly in part due to the spread of an egalitarian ideology, and not due to any worsening of their objective condition in the late 1950s and early 1960s.

Third, it is notable that Marxian and European writings generally (e.g., Touraine and Pecaut, 1970) are much less concerned than U.S. sociologists with the "size of the gap" and much more with the quality of the definition of the situation, and of themselves, sustained by those low in status. This dates back to Marx's distinction between "class in itself" vs. "class for itself." The latter indicates, according to Marx, a more profound appreciation of the total structure of society, in which the worker is not only aware that he is similarly situated to other workers, but in which he is "for" his own class and "against" those who are now seen categorically as class enemies. Such qualitative changes in perception (whether caused by the educational efforts of the vanguard and/or by changes in the objective situation) greatly influence the kind of movement workers want to have, the goals they want it to achieve in the short and in the long run, and so forth.

While many essays have been written on the shifting bases of worker loyalty (e.g., Moore 1967), few empirical facts are known about how many workers and peasants have had one, other, or none of the many alternative visions, ideologies, and utopias available to them since the beginning of the nineteenth century, and to what degree these visions have changed. Workers and peasants from the Mediterranean countries are credited with cherishing anarchistic, or syndicalist views (ownership and control of factories by workers) rather than envisaging a relatively centralized control of the economy, as under Marxism. The fact that the state did so little for these low status groups is sometimes credited with the explanation for their anarchistic leanings (Hobsbawm, 1959). The fact that so many worked in small, simple establishments is held to explain the popularity of syndicalism. United States workers and their unions, of course, are considered as widely, though never quite unanimously, accepting capitalism and only striving for improvements within it. Many authors have commented on this fact, ascribing it in part to differences in values and beliefs about mobility (not necessarily differences in objective mobility rates) but more usually to material reasons such as a high standard of living and social causes such as ethnic heterogeneity (Wilensky, 1966).

We very much agree that the quality of working-class consciousness, and not only quantitative gaps in aspirations, are profoundly necessary to an understanding of the kinds of organizations workers and peasants will support.

Fourth, it is clear that Marx and, even more, Lenin were correct that neither workers nor—quite especially—peasants easily become sufficiently conscious of their status and the potential for changing it through organization, without the proselytizing influence of an outside "vanguard." To join together voluntarily and organize sufficiently to attempt to remedy concrete local grievances is certainly within the scope of the peasantry. The industrial working classes, at least of Europe, had sufficient indigenous organizational capacity to form even national trade union movements with primarily economic goals (Kassalow 1969).

But to become conscious of the interlocking nature of political and economic power, and of the need to form a broadly based movement to displace traditional or bourgeoise elites per se—precisely the kind of higher consciousness of "class for itself" which we have just discussed—is not a style of thinking that emerges from the "lower strata" themselves. Indeed, it may be so foreign to them that they do not accept it even when the indoctrination attempt is made. The failure of the Russian student *narodniki* movement of the 1870s, the failure of Hugo Blanco in Peru in the 1960s and of SNCC in the U.S. rural South—these are all examples of the same phenomenon. Industrial workers are or were more susceptible to a broad revolutionary ideology, but there, too, it was limited always, and decreased over time, particularly if elites were at all yielding and reform minded. Thus broad ideologies of discontent are carried by middle-class intellectuals, whose role we examine briefly below.

Fifth, and returning to the question of the consciousness of a gap between aspirations and reality, it remains to define more precisely what the content of the gap is, i.e., aspirations for what? Implicit in our definition is that status concern may be over political status (as in the case of the British Chartist movement) as much as over economic aspirations (Bendix 1961). We believe that economic and political concerns are indeed central to these organizations. But it has also occurred, though less frequently, that discontent and aspirations deal with what might be termed, however vaguely, issues of "human dignity" or even religious status. Certainly past European peasant movements have concerned themselves with such matters.

Structural Changes: The Faltering Opposition of Elites

Changes in the relation between their aspirations and objective structural position may determine the state of discontent and consciousness of the organizing lower classes. But it is changes in the objective position and in the ideology of other classes which largely determine the possibility of success of organizing attempts. For consciousness is not, after all, enough to ensure successful organizing—let alone successfully reaching the goal of the organization. These three are very different phenomena: consciousness, organization, and success.

Structural changes, particularly changes in the economic system, have two kinds of effect: on existing elites, which are largely (though not invariably) hostile; and on the creation of new social groups, some of which may look to urban and rural low status groups for support.

As in the case of revolutions that do not succeed unless the old elites have in any case been badly weakened, so too in the case at least of peasant movements: these do not prosper unless the power of the traditional land-owning elite has already been undermined in some way. Perhaps it has been weakened by a disastrous foreign war, as in the case of Bolivia's Chaco War (1929-32), permitting the peasantry to slowly gather strength from 1936 onwards. Perhaps the large land owners have simply become a very small and isolated group as they have become richer and richer (often through becoming involved in international commodity trade) and are now surrounded by disaffected smaller land owners whom they have displaced. Francisco Madero, Mexico's first revolutionary president, was of this kind. Perhaps new industrial elites or more modern agricultural elites are overtaking the traditional elite, as in the case of Peru from the late 1950s onward (Craig 1969). Perhaps agriculture in general is in a state of decline. In any case, peasants do not suceed in organizing unless their enemies have already been weakened for reasons independent of the peasantry.

The situation is very different in the case of the organization of industrial workers in the developed countries and the noncolonial countries generally. While industrial workers may or may not have been helped by outside groups such as urban intellectuals, it is clear that their opponents—industrial entrepreneurs and managers—were not in a state of decline. Yet the movements did succeed.

The explanation is a two-fold one. First, there was, after all, a loss of relative status on the part of the employer in the course of the industrial revolution. A rapidly expanding working class had to be reckoned with at the end of the nineteenth century in Germany and Great Britain, for example, whereas it did not at the beginning when organizing attempts began. The power of the industrial magnate may have grown in absolute terms between 1850 and 1950. But it probably grew less fast than that of the working class. Hence an accommodation had to be arrived at and in view of an expanding and prosperous industrial sector, the sharing of power and wealth was relatively painless. In this lies the fundamental difference from the agricultural sector, which is generally stagnant and declining so that resistance to redistribution is much fiercer. In industry, however, the redistribution of power and wealth occurred and occurs in the context of rapidly increasing total power and wealth, and was thus easier to accept—as well as necessary to accept in order to avoid chaos. This holds true also for modern plantation-type agriculture which—as in the case of Peruvian sugar plantations—accepted unions of agricultural workers relatively early (Cotler and Portocarrero 1969).

Second, it is interesting to note that industrial labor organizations often do make their biggest gains when their opponent is, indeed, temporarily weakened. United States labor did so during the Depression of the 1930s (when, too, it received legislative aid of incalculable importance from liberal urban intellectuals). German labor secured gains (e.g., in the area of joint decision-making) after the political right was temporarily weakened in the period immediately following the collapse of Germany in 1918; and French labor improved its position after 1945, when employers were prostrate (Kassalow 1969).

Nevertheless—and we have already drawn attention to the fact—high-powered opposition to the movements of low status people is almost inevitable and we may be excused for not dwelling on this obvious point within the confines of this chapter. Economic victimization (i.e., discharge, eviction, and later "blacklisting"); the use of police power; strong-arm methods by privately hired goons; legal restrictions: all are standard tactics used against just about all working class and peasant movements in just about all ages in just about all countries. More interesting, therefore, are instances in which opposition is not so much vanquished, as illustrated above, but where it is less than complete to the formation of, and the goals of, associations of those low in status.

Typically, and insofar as any entity is more tolerant than another, it may well be the government rather than the employers or landlords directly involved. Often these are governments representing the more progressive, "realist" (Kerr et al. 1960) elements of traditional elites, and not governments supposedly representing more liberal elements. In England, for example, Disraeli and the Conservative Party in some ways did as much as, or more than, Gladstone and the Liberals to elevate the status of the worker. Earlier, in the 1840s Lord Shaftesbury, a Tory, had sponsored the first factory legislation. In Germany, Bismarck introduced social security; and Chile's 1925 labor code owes as much to the cogitations of the Catholic Conservatives in the 1910s as to members of the Liberal Alliance (Morris 1966).

Whether done only to saddle the new urban employer with heavier costs, (as was reputed to be the motivation of at least some Tories in England) or to "dish the Socialists" and defuse a potential revolution (as was reputed to be Bismarck's in the 1880s), the fact is that many ruling groups have yielded betimes, even if others have not.

We have repeatedly hinted above at the fact that structural changes produce allies for those low in political and economic status. Let us now examine this phenomenon more closely.

The "Allies" of Low-Status Movements: Partners in the Role-Set

Some time ago, Evans (1966) applied the concept of "role-set" to the level of organizations, renaming it "organization-set." The concept had originally been elaborated by Merton at the level of the individual role in order to indicate how important, to an understanding of any one role, is the understanding of other roles with which it necessarily interacts. However, this transposition of the concept to a higher level is not only applicable to specific interorganizational relationships such as those between a union and an employer. It also applies to more vague, and far broader entities such as movements and classes. In particular, in the case of low-status groups, their fate often can not be understood without reference to the position and activities of other, higher groups who orient their behavior toward lower status groups.

Marx and all later generations of Marxians have very clearly understood the importance of this point and of its subtle variations, depending on the society concerned. Lenin in particular, pondering the course which a revolution might take in Russia, realized that the Russian bourgeoisie at the beginning of the twentieth century was far too weak either to make its own revolution (as it had been able to do in England) or to defend it, and to govern, once the "bourgeoise" revolution against the remnants of Russian feudalism had taken place. He calculated, therefore, that working-class support would be necessary to, and would be sought by, the middle class and that its presence could be made to lead straight into the second proletarian revolution.

In point of fact, only rarely has a property-owning bourgeoisie of the classic

Marxian type allied itself for any length of time with an industrial working class or peasantry. The agitation which led to the passage of the 1832 Reform Act (which extended voting rights in England to some of the new urban middle class but not to the working class) was perhaps one of the few examples of this kind of alliance.

Much more likely is a situation in which a group of individuals (whether civilian or military) of, admittedly, better than low status, but definitely *not* an integral part of the ongoing economic and political system, takes a critical view of it. Needing mass support they turn to the peasantry, the working class and perhaps to other available groups as well. Young army officers in Latin America such as Peron in Argentina, or members of the *Union Patriotica Militar* in Venezuela in the 1945-48 period, by no means limited their search for support to low-status groups, even though they definitely included such groups. These alienated groups—often loosely referred to as "intelligentsia"—may or may not be very radical in orientation. That depends on the system which they oppose. The Congress Party which founded one sector of the Indian Trade Union Movement (the All-Indian Trade Union Congress) was only in part "radical" except in the sense of wishing to end British rule. The Bolivian *Movimiento Nacional Revolucionario* (MNR) was radical to the extent of nationalizing that country's tin mines and expropriating large land owners but not really much beyond that point, and even land reform was an afterthought rather than an integral part of its program. Those Russian dissenters from the Czarist regime who had substantial interest in the working class (Mensheviks and Bolsheviks) and peasants (Social Revolutionaries) were clearly more revolutionary, but the German socialists were less so, and British socialists and the Chilean Cristian Democrats even less.

But what these groups all do share, given precisely the fact that they do not have a real basis of power—no property, no overwhelming prestige from position or family connection—is their need for a mass base in order to gain political leverage. The "intelligentsia" offers to provide organizational and ideological leadership for low-status movements, brokering with the environment, and so forth, to back up its demand. Also, as a *quid pro quo* it incorporates into its program items which would have the effect of raising their clients' status—items which are, or are thought to be, desired by low-status groups: the nationalization of industries and expanded welfare programs in the case of the British Labour Party and that country's working class; land-reform in the case of *Accion Democratica* and the peasantry of Venezuela. While some of this program content would have been incorporated by the "intelligentsia" in any case (both groups may have many goals in common, for example) weakening the present elite) other parts of the program are often specifically accepted (at least for the time being!) to attract low-status groups, even against the intelligentsia's better judgment. Thus Communist parties in agrarian economies, from Lenin onwards, have frequently de-emphasized that collectivization would follow the expropriation of large estates (e.g., in the 1964 Chilean presidential elections) because the party knew this would not be popular with the peasants they were trying to attract.

The kind of support which is "demanded" in return for these offers is not, of course, necessarily confined to voting. This is particularly the case where, as in Latin America, voting is only one way in which "power capability" can be demonstrated and influence on decisions thereby obtained (Anderson 1967). Other ways of showing strength are political strikes, street demonstrations, and acts of violence used more as signals of strength than for what they accomplish intrinsically.

We should note four characteristics of these allies of low-status groups. First, the use of the word *intelligentsia* or *intellectuals* may hide more than it reveals. Those, for example, who have studied this kind of "exchange" between middle-class politicians and peasants in Eastern Europe are impressed with the fact that the intellectuals are really not one, but many different groups, and that their motivation and composition varies over time. Daniels, analyzing Russia, separates the early creators of idea systems whom he does regard as intellectuals (the "literary intelligentsia," active chiefly before the Emancipation in 1861), from what he calls the "quasi-intellectuals," for whose creative and even logical reasoning powers he clearly has far less respect than he does for their courage and energy (Daniels 1961).

Second, and however idealistic and altruistic their rhetoric, group mobility-striving is in turn an element that motivates these allies at least in part. Daniels sees this group as taking on the appearance of education and intellectuality only because they have no other road to status: they lack wealth and they are essentially not good enough to earn their living as creative intellectuals. Since they also disdain "practical work" they thus become "a frustrated and resentful member of the intellectual proletariat" (Daniels 1961, pp. 272-73). The changes these "quasi-intellectuals" advocate on behalf of their low-status clients would invest them with a good deal of power as policy-makers, technicians, and bureaucrats, displacing those who currently wield that power. This is presumably not an accidental aspect of the programs they advocate. And if change is slow in coming, they have often found in the past establishment politics via the leadership of peasants' or socialist parties a lucrative business. Seton-Watson makes it clear that not only intellectuals, but also small-town traders, business-men and public officials sponsor such parties, to whom the label "intelligentsia" is not even remotely applicable (Seton-Watson 1967, pp. 41, 227). The same could be said of France in connection with its working-class parties. The materialism and opportunism of their leaders was part of the reason why the early working-class movement wanted to have no part of the political process (Lorwin 1954).

In many of the ex-colonial countries, westernized urban intellectuals, as they grew in number, increasingly wanted to displace the colonial powers. They organized and directed trade union movements to provide a mass base for an essentially nationalist, independence movement (India, Kenya, North Africa, as described by Millen 1963). The organizing task was, of course, facilitated by the fact that employers were also foreigners. The colonial elites were unnerved both by the rising cost (interpreted broadly) of maintaining colonial hegemony after 1945, added to the ideological disrepute in which colonialism was increasingly held. After the exit of the colonial powers, westernized intellectuals took over—but often did not last long unless they had genuine mass support (Huntington 1968, p. 440).

Third, low-status groups are often aware of the dubious benefit to themselves of help received from other classes and of the dubious motivations involved. The role of intellectuals in the West and Central European socialist parties was a subject of hot debate by these movements themselves (Brin 1928), while in Russia, the first and most famous Workers Council (the St. Petersburg Soviet of 1905) also showed considerable hostility toward intellectuals and their interminable polemics and sought at one point to limit their power to intervene, though Trotsky, an intellectual par excellence, did play a substantial role in the St. Petersburg Soviet (Anweiler 1958, p. 65). In the United States, the late Selig Perlman was perhaps the most famous intellectual known for his criticism of the role of intellectuals in working-class movements! (Perlman 1928, especially Chaps. 2-5).

Fourth and finally, we may note here an interesting parallel between individual and group mobility. Turner some years ago drew attention to the fact that mobility can be structured both as a "contest," and as a system of "sponsorship" by status superiors. His contrasting cases were the United States and England respectively, and Turner linked the differences to differences in ideologies about mobility and to different methods of selection in the educational system (Turner 1960).

The point we wish to make here is that the idea of "sponsored" mobility is very meaningful at the level of groups and classes. At the level of detail, however, there are substantial differences. Thus the criterion of the elite concerning whom to select (in this case: which group to sponsor) is not that of how "to make the best use of the talents in society," but (in the political realm) which group might add most power and has interests closest to one's own. In the economic realm sponsorship also occurs: in the developing countries, there is increasing recognition even by oligarchic elites that the poverty of the masses of the population limits the market for products, and therefore their own prosperity. Similar reasoning has been found by the author (very occasionally!) in the Deep South, where local white merchants and bankers may support black voluntary organizations such as cooperatives, designed to increase the prosperity of the black population, because the bankers' own prosperity is safeguarded through such organizations.

We end this section by summarizing its main points in the form of hypotheses. Let us reemphasize, however, that—more systematically perhaps than in the case of any other kind of voluntary organization—the establishment of movements of peasant and industrial workers is: (1) a reflection of very broad societal changes involving changes in values and ideologies; (2) a decline, for various technical, economic, and political underlying reasons in the power of established elites against whom these movements are directed (especially in the case of peasant movements and of working-class movements in preindependent colonial countries); and (3) the appearance—again, for complex reasons—of new groups who are not yet, or who are no longer, fully within the system and are therefore disposed to help organize those low in status against the "establishment." Our hypotheses are the following:

1. The desire on the part of groups low in economic and political status to form voluntary organizations to raise or defend their status increases as the "gap" between aspirations and reality increases.
2. Such an increase may be caused by any combination of rising aspirations, falling objective status, aspirations rising faster than reality even though objective rewards also rise, and so forth.
3. The worldwide spread of the value of egalitarianism has been exerting a lifting influence on aspirations, thereby increasing the "gap" and the desire to organize. The example of the developed countries, conveyed through the media of mass communication, have had a similar effect, but one which needs to be conceptually distinguished.
4. Outside groups, especially rising urban middle-class and specially "intellectual" groups, frequently reinforce the process of making the perceived gap larger.
5. There are also substantial differences, over time and between societies, in the quality of the vision of society sustained by those low in status, and this of course, affects the kinds of movements and organizations they establish and join, especially the goals of such organizations. Differences in values, but more important, differences in social and economic structure and in the development process of each society, accounts for these qualitative differences between movements from one society and another.
6. There is a good deal of agreement that comprehensive, apocalyptic class-conflict perceptions of society are sustained: more by industrial workers than by peasants; more at critical moments early in the capitalist industrialization process and not, as Marx thought, late in that process. European peasants were at one time likely to have apocalyptic visions of a religious kind, but this is no longer likely as societies everywhere are more secularized.
7. Radical goals and interpretations of society are more likely to come from outside workers and peasants than to appear spontaneously from within on any large scale.

8. On the whole and spontaneously (e.g., assuming a reasonable degree of flexibility in the system to make concessions) workers and peasants would form organizations having rather limited, concrete, reformist goals. In the case of some peasants (or landless laborers) the goals may be "reactionary" and in that sense revolutionary: a return to communal or individual small proprietorship, where efficiency might dictate a more industrial form of agricultrual production (a point recognized by Marx and Lenin).

Concerning now the success of workers and peasants in establishing organizations, this depends on the strength of the resistance rather than on the strength of the organization.

1. In the case of peasant movements (but not those of industrial workers) successful establishment is frequently linked with the decline of a section of the land-owning class. Sometimes this decline is in economic terms: it is weakened by a change in crops, or in technology, or a general decline in agriculture. But more frequently, the weakening is in the form of political isolation, which deprives the land-owning class of the effective use of that force on which land ownership frequently, ultimately, rests.
2. Centralized states are particularly subject to dramatic shifts: they either manage to repress movements or are toppled by them. Barrington Moore brings out this point in his comparison of China and India (Barrington Moore 1966).
3. In the case of working-class movements, successful establishment of interest organizations is more likely than in the case of peasants. In part, this is due to factors within the working class itself: their greater proximity to each other, education, modernity of outlook, and so forth, as compared with peasants.
4. But chiefly, greater success on the part of workers is due to their greater bargaining power: they are simply less easily replaced than peasants, and would find it easier to get alternative employment at least in large cities.
5. Also of great importance in the greater success of working-class movements is the fact that employer resistance to worker organization is likely to be less: there is less of a status gap; industry is likely to be more prosperous and can therefore afford (and pass on to consumers) benefits granted, and so on.
6. Insofar as establishment of worker organization depends on government consent—and it invariably and very crucially does—governments are more likely to permit the early establishment of organizations of workers than of peasants. Partly, this is due to the fact that workers can exert more of a threat of violence closer to governments; partly because it is a constituency that is "mobilized," i.e., made conscious, earlier, and therefore can be won over. However, in later stages of development, as the peasantry also awakens, it too must be given the right to organize.

7. Urban groups without mass following will be particularly eager to see workers and peasants organized. If a working class exists, they will think first of organizing it; if it does not (as Russia in the 1870s) they will go to the country to organize. The relationship between intellectuals and both constituencies is likely to be an uneasy one.

Our main conclusion for purposes of this symposium is that the growth of this kind of voluntary association cannot be understood except through an understanding of very complex changes in its environment and in society as a whole. They are a reflection of the process of differentiation, specialization, and egalitarian integration both at the level of values and the level of structures.

With this we conclude what is intended as a suggestive, and not in the least an exhaustive or systematic, analysis of some of the relations between working-class and peasant movements and their environment at the time of their origin. We now jump straight ahead to the other end of the time continuum for an even briefer look at what the future seems to hold for this kind of movement.

The Future: The End of Low-Status Movements?

A movement, and certainly a formal organization dedicated to getting "more" for its members—power, prestige, income, education—presumes an environing society in which the more privileged groups and/or the government voluntarily permit, or are forced to permit, collective efforts of this kind, directed in part against these two entities themselves, by the underpriviledged and their allies. It presumes, in essence, a reasonably open competitive political system.

As one looks at the more than 130 sovereign nations today, it is clear that such competitive systems are likely to be very much in the minority, and there is no overpowering reason to expect anything else.

As has been noted many times, the larger of the presently reasonably open societies—the United Kingdom, West Germany, Japan, the United States, France—did not permit, or in any case did not have, powerful working-class or peasant movements during the early and most painful part of the industrialization process. Such movements, and democracy in general were a luxury which came later. That alone would be cause to expect that most of these 130 nations might likewise not have flourishing movements of this kind. For the great majority of them are attempting to enter upon the "take-off" stage of economic development; they are not in its later phases. The aim—even, or especially, of the governments genuinely dedicated to benefiting those in low status ultimately—is to temporarily centralize power and material wealth, not to distribute them.

More important is the fact that competition and struggle between groups, institutions, and organizations are today simply not seen as the most rational path toward the solution of any problem, whether it be the economic problem of the distribution of output between consumption and investment; and within consumption, between classes; or whether it is the political problem of distribution of power; the cultural problem of the distribution of education; or the sociomoral problem of the distribution of honor and prestige. It seems likely that many sociologists who advocate the universal functional utility of conflict are implicitly thinking only of capitalistic societies. One sees few writers who advocate that organized (nonviolent) competitive conflict between different interest groups would be healthy for Cuba and China, for example.

Not only are the few remaining traditional, oligarchic states against fostering the growth of independently powerful peasant and working-class movements. And not only, today in 1971, are the military regimes against them, as in Greece, Brazil, and Argentina, and the semimilitary regimes of the Dominican Republic and Guatemala. But so are regimes which, with greater or less sincerity, see themselves as explicitly dedicated to uplifting the poor of their nation, such as Cuba. That process is still by and large envisioned as taking place under a master plan, and such master plans cannot be allowed to suffer interference from free-wheeling trade unions and peasant groups who have their own consumption needs and not the national interest in long-term investment, and the nation as a whole, at heart.

This is obviously so in the case of countries which are confessedly socialist, as is Poland, the Soviet Union, and China. These countries differ substantially among each other. They differ in the extent to which material incentives as opposed to moral incentives are used to stimulate production in industry; or the extent to which land is taken out of private hands and agricultural production collectivized; or the extent to which consumption is sacrificed to investment (Cuba is said to be investing between 25 and 30 percent of its national income). But whichever of the alternatives is chosen, while obviously of crucial importance to the low-status groups involved, is evidently not a decision in which the independent organizations of these groups play a major part. All these problems are symbolized by the policy issues which Cuba has had to face in the last twelve years, as so vividly described in Leo Huberman and Paul Sweezy's SOCIALISM IN CUBA. Especially their last chapters are a very critical appraisal of the entire socialist world on the score of voluntary participation: and these two writers are warm friends, and not enemies, of the socialist world (Huberman and Sweezy 1969). The relevant decisions are made, at best, with the long-run good of these groups in mind, but never with the direct participation of these groups in organized form.

Perhaps most intriguing in this respect is the fate of the trade unions in those countries in which it looked, for a time, as if such movements would flourish. We refer to the ex-colonial countries of Africa and Asia where nationalism, not socialism or communism was the guiding ideology. Working-class movements seemed originally to show strength there. In their early stages, they were often nourished by the labor movements of the metropolitan countries (Great Britain, France, and Holland). But even more importantly, they were stimulated by those essentially middle-class groups who were fighting for independence and needed well organized mass support. (Once again, the group mobility aspirations of these middle-class elements—often lower-level civil servants and professionals—should not be overlooked as an element underlying their more idealistic nationalism.) During the forties and fifties, Tunisia, the British East African colonies and mandates (Kenya and Tanzania), French West Africa, Ceylon, Indonesia, and, of course, India, all showed a very considerable degree of working-class organization despite the fact that these countries were and are primarily agricultural, and even though one could clearly detect structural weaknesses as well (see Millen 1963; and Galenson 1959).

Today, it is clear that the exigencies of development in a setting of poverty, and the need to achieve national integration in the face of centrifugal forces, are leading most of these countries to some form of centralized and even dictatorial government. In such systems, associations of low-status groups cannot expect to have the freedom to gather strength, even if their bargaining power were such that they could if given the freedom. Generally, the political trend seems to have been a three stage one: the exhilaration and freedom of independence; followed by a tightening of controls under a charismatic nation-founding leader (Nkrumah, Sukarno, Bourguiba, Ben Bella); followed, most recently, by a wave of military regimes. While not a great deal of information is available on the precise status of trade union and peasant movements under the new regimes, one's general impression is that their power is far less than it was in the last few years of the colonial regimes. That power turns out, then, to have been transitory: dependent on the unique combination of the relative tolerance of the colonial authorities on the one hand, (strange though it may seem to say so), and the temporary need which certain middle-class elements had for mass organizations until they could seize power under the doctrine of nationalism. (For Africa, see Ioan Davies, 1966.)

Insofar as those of low status advance, it will be as a result of the unilateral action of the new middle-class elites, whether civil or military, and not by virtue of their own independent association. For a very stimulating schematization of the manner in which the type of elite (socialist, nationalist, middle class, dynastic, colonial) affects the structure of trade union movements, the collective bargaining process, the reward system, government policies, and so forth, the reader should consult Clark Kerr, et al., INDUSTRIALISM AND INDUSTRIAL MAN. We thoroughly agree with the generalizations presented by the authors and for that reason, see no reason to recapitulate them here. There is now, however, a passé quality about this brilliant book, written in 1960 and based primarily on developments in the 1950s (Kerr et al. 1960).

The independent organizations of low-status groups are, therefore, progressively more repressed in the ever increasing number of noncompetitive political systems whether right or left, civilian or military, developed or underdeveloped. And on top of this, in the few remaining competitive systems, they have undergone a degree of quantitative change which is tantamount to a change in quality. It, too, is a form of death, not through repression, but by atrophy from co-optation or simple transformation.

These societies are, for one reason or another, the richer ones. As the status of their working classes has floated upward[1] toward the middle class (at least absolutely, if not relatively) their organizations—labor parties and trade unions— are likewise ceasing to possess any distinctive characteristics to the extent they once did. In the case of the political parties, they cannot and do not remain pure in class membership. (We refer to the Social Democratic Party of Germany, Britain's Labour Party, etc.) For they would become extinct as shrinkage takes place in the proportion of blue-collar workers, and as shrinkage occurs even if we include all those of lower ranks in any organization, whether blue or white collar, as Dahrendorf would have us define class.

Nor do the trade unions, the economic manifestation of the working-class movement, today have characteristics differentiating them basically (as distinct from superficially) from the organizations of other economic role incumbents concerned with pay, working conditions, job security, and the limitation of entry rights. Admittedly, trade unions are superficially distinct in that they are often larger than other bodies of this kind; they do press their economic claims more explicitly in highly visible negotiations with highly visible employers and industries. Unlike some other entities such as the AMA or the NEA and American Federation of Teachers, unions perform no other (e.g., professional) functions apart from that of defending and increasing the economic status of their members. And their members do continue to be among those with lower status. But the characteristics which once distinguished the working-class movements here and in other Western countries are no longer present or are present only in highly attenuated form. High degree of involvements of those who were members (both behaviorally and in terms of enthusiasm and emotional pitch); a low degree of bureaucratization, of centralization and hierarchy in organization; the feeling of being part of a larger movement and being a movement in combat; occasional visions (or frequent ones: depending on the society—more frequent in Germany and France than in the United States) of substantial changes in the structure of society—all these have given way to the so-called mature union, described by some and mourned by others (Ross 1964; footnote 3 of Ross' article contains references to those who "mourn," such as Paul Jacobs, Sidney Lens, Paul Sultan, B.J. Widick, and others). In terms of sheer militancy—at least, as measured by strike statistics—there has been a very substantial decline indeed (Ross and Hartman 1960, especially Chapter 5).

This "embourgeoisement" of the organization is paralleled, of course—indeed, it is a reflection of—the "embourgeoisement" of the individual worker. There are admittedly sectors of the working class that continue to be disaffected: for example, some parts of the black working class. In the auto industry, black unions rivaling the UAW have sprung up in certain locals, and studies of unemployed black workers are particularly poignant in portraying their continuing disaffection (Leggett 1968). There may also be occasional eruptions of militancy: France in the summer of 1968 is often cited, but it is now three years later and nothing much seems to have happened since then. There may also be eruptions of white working-class backlash against black claims (by definition, an admission that these white workers are not at the bottom of the totem pole). But none of these, in our opinion, alter the basic picture that a class conscious, working-class movement with revolutionary potential such as was envisaged in the early part of this century is over and done with: atrophied by success in economically developed societies. As Goldthorpe and his colleagues have correctly pointed out: this by no means implies that unions as such will disintegrate, and that working-class people will become precisely like others in lifestyles and values (Goldthorpe et al. 1969). But clearly, this is not "the movement" in the old sense.

The future of these movements is, therefore, gloomy or at least unspectacular. Reactionary dictatorships will repress them even without conceding anything more than minimal improvements. "Peoples' Democracies" in the process of development may be striving with more sincere intent to create a society of greater equality and greater wealth. But independent associations of their peasant and working class are not going to be permitted. In developed capitalist societies, these movements will change to the point of losing their unique characteristics: as a result of substantial success in the case of industrial workers; as a result of disappearance in the case of the peasantry. The new poor will in some ways have an easier time organizing than did their predecessors. Oppression of their organizations is minimal as compared with those of the early nineteenth century. But in other ways, they will have greater difficulties, because they lack the focus that work and the work place provided for the earlier movements.

Note

1. We use the phrase "floated upward" with its passive connotations advisedly, even though it may be exaggerated. But there is considerable doubt and controversy whether, even on those economic dimensions which have been, after all, their central interest, union organization has much effect in the long run in changing the position of its members vis à vis higher status groups. The chief effect of unions may well be to widen the gap between organized and unorganized workers. In other words, unintended mobility through structural changes may be greater than those which can be achieved by purposive collective action (Chamberlain 1958).

References

Anderson, Charles W.
1967 POLITICS AND ECONOMIC CHANGE IN LATIN AMERICA. Princeton, New Jersey: Van Nostrand Company.

Anweiler, Oskar
1958 DIE RAETEBEWEGUNG IN RUSSLAND, 1905-1921. E.J. Brill, Leiden.

Arendt, Hannah
1962 ON REVOLUTION. New York: Viking Press.

Bendix, Reinhard
1961 "The Lower Classes and the 'Democratic Revolution.' " INDUSTRIAL RELATIONS 1, no. 1 (October 1961): 91-116.

Blumer, Herbert
1951 "Collective behavior." In PRINCIPLES OF SOCIOLOGY. Edited by A.M. Lee. New York: Barnes and Noble.

Brin, Hennoch
1928 "Zur Akademiker und Intellektuellenfrage in der Arbeiterbewegung." Ph.D. thesis, Faculty of Philosophy, Switzerland: University of Basle.

Brinton, Crane
1965 ANATOMY OF REVOLUTION. Englewood-Cliffs, New Jersey: Prentice-Hall.

Chamberlain, Neil W.
1958 LABOR. New York: McGraw Hill Book Company.

Cotler, Julio and Felipe Portocarrero
1969 "Peru: Peasant Organizations." In LATIN AMERICAN PEASANT MOVEMENTS. Edited by Henry A. Landsberger. Ithaca, New York: Cornell University Press.

Craig, Wesley
1969 "Peru: The Peasant Movement of La Convención." In LATIN AMERICAN PEASANT MOVEMENTS. Edited by Henry A. Landsberger. Ithaca, New York: Cornell University Press.

Daniels, Robert V.
1961 "Intellectuals and the Russian Revolution." AMERICAN SLAVIC AND EAST EUROPEAN REVIEW 20, no. 2 (April 1961): 270-78.

Davies, Ioan
1966 AFRICAN TRADE UNIONS. Harmondsworth, England: Penguin Books Ltd.

Davies, James C.
1963 HUMAN NATURE IN POLITICS. New York: John Wiley & Sons.
1962 "Toward a Theory of Revolution." AMERICAN SOCIOLOGICAL REVIEW 27, no. 1: 5-19.

Evans, William
1966 "The Organization-Set: Toward a Theory of Interorganizational Rela-

tions." In APPROACHES TO ORGANIZATION DESIGN. Edited by James D. Thompson. Pittsburgh: University of Pittsburgh Press.

Galenson, Walter (ed.)

1959 LABOR AND ECONOMIC DEVELOPMENT. New York: John Wiley & Sons.

Goldthorpe, John, David Lockwood, Frank Beckhofer and Jennifer Platt

1969 THE AFFLUENT WORKER IN THE CLASS STRUCTURE. London: Cambridge University Press.

Gurr, Ted R.

1970 WHY MEN REBEL. Princeton, New Jersey: Princeton University Press.

Hobsbawm, Eric

1959 PRIMITIVE REBELS. Manchester: Manchester University Press.

Huberman, Leo and Paul Sweezy

1969 SOCIALISM IN CUBA. New York: Monthly Review Press.

Huntington, Samuel P.

1968 POLITICAL ORDER IN CHANGING SOCIETIES. New Haven, Connecticut: Yale University Press.

Johnson, Chalmers

1962 PEASANT NATIONALISM AND COMMUNIST POWER. Stanford, California: Stanford University Press.

1966 REVOLUTIONARY CHANGE. Boston, Massachusetts: Little, Brown & Co.

Kassalow, Everett M.

1969 TRADE UNIONS AND INDUSTRIAL RELATIONS: AN INTERNATIONAL COMPARISON. New York: Random House.

Kerr, Clark et al.

1960 INDUSTRIALISM AND INDUSTRIAL MAN. New York: Oxford University Press.

Landsberger, Henry A., ed.

1969 LATIN AMERICAN PEASANT MOVEMENTS. Ithaca, New York: Cornell University Press.

Landsberger, Henry A. and Cynthia H. deAlcantara

1970 "Ten Sources of Weakness and Cleavage in Latin American Peasant Movements." In AGRARIAN PROBLEMS AND PEASANT MOVEMENTS IN LATIN AMERICA. Edited by Rodolfo Stavenhagen. New York: Doubleday-Anchor Books.

Leggett, John C.

1968 CLASS, RACE, AND LABOR: WORKING-CLASS CONSCIOUSNESS IN DETROIT. New York, Oxford University Press.

Lipset, Seymour Martin

1961-62 "Trade Unions and Social Structure: I & II." INDUSTRIAL RELATIONS 1, nos. 1 and 2: 75-89, 89-110.

Lorwin, Val R.

1954 THE FRENCH LABOR MOVEMENT. Cambridge, Massachusetts: Harvard University Press.

Maslow, A.H.

1954 MOTIVATION AND PERSONALITY. New York: Harper and Row.

Millen, Bruce H.

1963 THE POLITICAL ROLE OF LABOR IN DEVELOPING COUNTRIES. Washington, D.C.: Brookings Institution.

Moore, Barrington Jr.

1966 SOCIAL ORIGINS OF DICTATORSHIP AND DEMOCRACY: LORD AND PEASANT IN THE MODERN WORLD. Boston: Beacon Press.

Moore, Wilbert

1967 "Notes for a General Theory of Labor Organization." In ORDER AND CHANGE: ESSAYS IN COMPARATIVE SOCIOLOGY, New York: Wiley & Sons, Inc.

Murray, Henry A.

1938 EXPLORATIONS IN PERSONALITY. New York: Oxford University Press.

Olsen, Mancur

1968 THE LOGIC OF COLLECTIVE ACTION. New York: Schocken Books.

Pelling, Henry

1963 A HISTORY OF BRITISH TRADE UNIONISM. Harmondsworth, England: Penguin Books.

Perlman, Selig

1928 A THEORY OF THE LABOR MOVEMENT. New York: Macmillan.

Rayback, Joseph G.

1966 A HISTORY OF AMERICAN LABOR. New York: The Free Press-Collier-Macmillan Co.

Ross, Arthur M.

1964 "Labor Organization and the Labor Movement in Advanced Industrial Society." VIRGINIA LAW REVIEW 50, no. 8 (1964): 1359-85.

Ross, Arthur M., and Paul T. Hartman

1960 CHANGING PATTERNS OF INDUSTRIAL CONFLICT. New York: John Wiley & Sons.

Seidman, Joel, Jack London, Bernard Karsh and Daisy L. Tagliacozzo

1958 THE WORKER VIEWS HIS UNION. Chicago, Illinois: University of Chicago Press.

Seton-Watson, Hugh

1967 EASTERN EUROPE BETWEEN THE WARS, 1918-1941. New York: Harper and Row.

Smelser, Neil J.

1963 THEORY OF COLLECTIVE BEHAVIOR. New York: Free Press of Glencoe.

Smelser, Neil J. and Seymour Martin Lipset (eds.)
1966 SOCIAL STRUCTURE AND MOBILITY IN ECONOMIC DEVELOP-
MENT. Chicago, Illinois: Aldine Publishing Company.
Tannenbaum, Arnold S.
1964 "Unions." In HANDBOOK OF ORGANIZATIONS. Edited by James G.
March. Chicago, Illinois: Rand McNally and Company.
Tannenbaum, Arnold S., and Robert L. Kahn
1958 PARTICIPATION IN UNION LOCALS. Evanston, Illinois: Row, Peterson
and Company.
Thompson, E.P.
1964 THE MAKING OF THE ENGLISH WORKING CLASS. New York:
Pantheon.
Touraine, Alain and Daniel Pecaut
1970 "Working Class Consciousness and Economic Development in Latin
America." In MASSES IN LATIN AMERICA. Edited by Irving L.
Horowitz. Fairlawn, New Jersey: Oxford University Press.
Turner, Ralph H.
1960 "Sponsored and Contest Mobility and the School System." AMERICAN
SOCIOLOGICAL REVIEW 25, no. 6: 855-67.
White, Robert A., S.J.
1969 "Mexico: The Zapata Movement and the Revolution." In LATIN AMER-
ICAN PEASANT MOVEMENTS. Edited by Henry A. Landsberger. Ithaca,
New York: Cornell University Press.
Wilensky, Harold L.
1966 "Class, Class Consciousness and American Workers." In LABOR IN A
CHANGING AMERICA. Edited by William Haber. New York: Basic
Books.

14

The Impact of the Voluntary Sector on Society

David Horton Smith

Having now looked at a few facets of the impact of voluntary action from the level of the individual up to the level of social movements, let us take a final step up to the highest currently applicable level of impact of voluntarism—on society as a whole. In looking at impact on all of the previous system levels, it is all too easy to get lost among the "trees," thus losing sight of the "forest." In our view, the "forest" is the larger context of social meaning that voluntary action has in human society. By *social* we mean to include all aspects of social structure and culture here, and by *society* we mean to include not just American society or any other particular society, but all of mankind, past, present, and (hopefully) future.

The "voluntary sector" refers to all those persons, groups, roles, organizations, and institutions in society whose goals involve primarily voluntary action. The term "voluntary action" is treated at length in the first volume of this series (VOLUNTARY ACTION RESEARCH: 1972), so that we shall not elaborate on its meaning here. Suffice it to say that, roughly speaking, it includes what one is neither made to nor paid to do, but rather what one does out of some kind of expectation of psychic benefits or commitment to some value, ideal, or common interest. The voluntary sector may be roughly delineated in a negative way by contrasting it with the commercial or business sector (sometimes called the "private sector") and with the government or public sector. Another way of describing the voluntary sector is by saying that it is the total persisting social embodiment (in the form of norms, expectations, customs, and ways of behaving) of voluntary action in society.

Our question here is, simply, what impact does the voluntary sector as a whole have on society? There is not sufficient research information to permit one to do an aggregate analysis, building up a picture of the whole by systematically combining the parts—the kinds of impacts of voluntary action at different system levels we have been examining in part in prior chapters. Instead, we can only do the very sketchiest global analysis, based on a loose inductive logic and general theoretical considerations. In making this very brief and simplistic analysis, we are again more interested in suggesting some lines of possible future research and theory than in being exhaustive or thorough.

Another way of looking at what we are calling the impacts of the voluntary sector is to see the processes behind these impacts and to term them the

387

"functions" or "roles" of the voluntary sector. These processes are not necessary features of the voluntary sector in any given nation, let alone in all nations. But they do represent what the voluntary sector can do and often has done in the past in particular societies at particular times. This is an attempt to help delineate more clearly why there is a voluntary sector in society, much as one might elsewhere discuss the role of government institutions or business or even the family in society. Like all of the latter, of course, the role of the voluntary sector changes over time in a given society and even in human society as a whole. Several of the chapters of Part One of this volume suggest some major aspects of these changes in the voluntary sector over time. Nevertheless, the impacts of the voluntary sector we discuss briefly below are suggested as very general aspects of the voluntary sector in human society, and hence they are present to at least some degree as long as there is a voluntary sector.

First, one of the most central impacts of the voluntary sector is to provide society with a large variety of partially tested social innovations, from which business, government, and other institutions can select and institutionalize those innovations which seem most promising. The independent voluntary sector is thus the prototyping test bed of many, perhaps most new social forms and modes of human relations. Where business and government, science and technology are active in the creation and testing of technological innovations, the independent voluntary sector specializes in the practical testing of social ideas. Nearly every function currently performed by governments at various levels was once a new social idea and the experiment of some voluntary group, formal or informal—this is true of education, welfare, care for the aged, building roads, even fighting wars (volunteer citizen militias).

In sum, the voluntary sector has tended to provide the social risk capital of human society. It has been sufficiently free of the kinds of constraints that bind business (the constant need to show a profit) and government (the need to maintain control and, in societies with effective democracies, the need to act in accord with a broad consensus) so that its component elements (particular voluntary groups or even individuals) can act simply out of commitment to some value or idea, without needing to wait until the payoffs for that kind of activity can be justified in terms appropriate to mobilizing economic or governmental institutions. It is thus the most "error-embracing" and experimental component of society (see Smith with Dixon 1973).

Second, another central impact of the voluntary sector on society has been the provision of countervailing definitions of reality and morality—ideologies, perspectives, and worldviews that frequently challenge the prevailing assumptions about what exists and what is good and what should be done in society. The voluntary sector is that part of society which, collectively, is most likely to say that "the emperor has no clothes." Voluntary groups of various kinds are distinctive among human groups in the extent to which they develop their own ideologies and value systems. If these definitions of reality and morality are sufficiently compelling to people, voluntary groups grow into huge social movements and can change the course of history, both within a given nation (e.g., the abolitionist movement in the early and middle nineteenth century of the United States) and across human society as a whole (e.g., Christianity, Buddhism, democracy, communism).

This kind of impact of the voluntary sector is related to the previous one, but where the former kind of impact emphasized experimentation with social innovation in practice, the present impact emphasizes instead ideological and moral innovation. Where the previous point focused on the social risk capital role of the voluntary sector in society, the present point focuses on the role of the voluntary sector as a gadfly, dreamer, and moral leader in society. Voluntary groups of various kinds are concerned with the generation and allocation of human commitment in the deepest sense. In the process of doing this, the voluntary sector as a whole provides moral and ideological leadership to the majority of human society, and often calls into question the existing legitimacy structures and accepted social definitions of reality of particular societies.

A third major impact of the voluntary sector on society is to provide the play element in society, especially as the search for novelty, beauty, recreation, and fun for their own sake may be collectively organized. Again because the voluntary sector is not constrained generally by such values as profit, control, and broad social consensus, voluntary groups can form in terms of literally thousands of different kinds of common interests. A full array of common interest groups (especially expressive rather than instrumental ones) in an elaborated but still evolving voluntary sector permits (in principle) nearly all individuals to find at least one group that will be satisfying to them. If there is no such group, one or more individuals may form one, if they wish, to reflect their own needs and vision of the play element. Such a group may be formal or informal, large or small, permanent or transient, open or closed, and so forth.

To speak of the play element here is not to speak of something trivial and unimportant. As society becomes increasingly complex and work activity is increasingly structured in terms of large bureaucracies, people's unsatisfied needs for play, novelty, new experience, and all manner of recreation tend to increase. The kind of easy interchange and blending of play and work that could be present in more traditional economies tends to be lost. Under such circumstances, voluntary groups often provide a window of variety and intrinsic satisfaction in an otherwise rather boring or at least psychically fatiguing world of work and responsibility.

Fourth, the voluntary sector also has a major impact on the level of social integration in society. Partly through directly expressive groups, whose aims are explicitly to provide fellowship, sociability and mutual companionship, and partly through the sociability aspects of all other kinds of collective and interpersonal forms of voluntary action, the voluntary sector helps in a very basic way to satisfy some of the human needs for affiliation, approval, and so on. In advanced industrial and urbanized societies, where the family and kinship as well as the local community and neighborhood play a markedly reduced role in providing social integration, affiliations based on common interests can become very important to the individual. Indeed, without the latter kind of voluntary sector-based common interest affiliations, the resulting rates of individual social isolation in society would lead to even more anomie, alienation, and a variety of attendant social and psychological problems than are now the case. Obviously, the voluntary sector has not been the whole solution to the root problem of social isolation in modern society, yet voluntary groups do play a demonstrable and important part in the solution. And with the feeling of being accepted as a person that the voluntary sector provides (or can provide) to a significant proportion of the population in modern societies goes the correlative provision of positive affect, a major component of human happiness and the quality of human life.

Another aspect of the role of the voluntary sector in providing social integration is the social adjustment "buffering" function that many kinds of voluntary groups provide. When numerous individuals of a certain social and cultural background are for some reason uprooted from their customary societal niches, new voluntary groups frequently emerge to provide these individuals with an insulated or "buffered" special environment for part of their time. Typical examples would be the numerous immigrant associations that sprang up in the United States as a result of successive waves of immigration from various countries (Handlin 1951) or the kinship oriented voluntary associations that emerged to ease the adjustment of rural West Africans to life in large cities (Little 1965).

These kinds of social adjustment oriented voluntary groups do not, however, emerge only in the case of physical/geographical changes on a large scale. The voluntary sector also provides a social adjustment "mechanism" to ease the shocks of social dislocations and rapid social changes of all sorts. The voluntary groups involved may cater to a former elite that has been disenfranchised or deprived of its former holdings (e.g., the association of maharajahs of India, which arose to fight for "maharajah's rights" when the Indian Congress stripped them of their traditional privileges and land, substituting a moderate annual stipend). Or the voluntary groups involved may represent a deprived category of persons who are attempting to adjust to changed social conditions that are more conducive to their sharing equitably in the good life as lived in their society (e.g., the early labor unions or black power groups, striving for recognition of their right to exist and to fight for the betterment of the conditions of their constituencies).

On another level, the voluntary sector plays an important integrative role by linking together individuals, groups, institutions and even nations that otherwise would be in greater conflict, or at least competition, with each other. (This and other impacts of voluntary groups are discussed further in Smith, 1966.) At the community level, a variety of voluntary associations will each tend to have as members a set of two or more individuals representing differing and often opposing political, religious, cultural, or social perspectives and backgrounds. The co-participation of this set of individuals in the same voluntary association can have significant moderating effects on the relationships among these individuals. Similar integrative effects can be found at national levels where several groups from different parts of the country and/or different social and cultural perspectives participate together in a common federation or other national voluntary organization. And at the international level, the joint participation of voluntary groups from otherwise conflicting nations in some transnational federative organization may well have important long range effects on the relations between the countries involved and on the possibilities of peace in the world, as Skjelsbaek suggests in Chapter 5.

A fifth kind of general impact of the voluntary sector involves the opposite of the first one, which dealt with the social innovation role of voluntarism. In addition to providing a wide variety of *new* ideas about social behavior, the voluntary sector also is active in preserving numerous *old* ideas. Voluntary action and voluntary organizations have played a major role in history in preserving values, ways of life, ideas, beliefs, artifacts, and other productions of the mind, heart, and hand of man from earlier times so that this great variety of human culture is not lost to future generations. For example, there are in the United States numerous local historical societies that specialize in preserving the history of particular towns and areas. There are nonprofit voluntary organizations that run local museums, libraries, and historical sites. And there are a number of voluntary organizations whose primary function it is to preserve the values of cultures or subcultures that no longer have any substantial power or importance in American society, but that nevertheless represent a way of life of significant numbers of people at some period in history or somewhere around the world (e.g., American Indian groups, in some instances, or immigrant ethnic associations that persist long after the ethnic group involved has been thoroughly assimilated into American culture). The role of municipal, state, and national governments in supporting museums and historical sites grows from the roots of earlier non-profit, non-governmental support of such "islands of culture."

Another aspect of the belief/value preservation role of the voluntary sector involves voluntary associations as educational experiences, especially where these associations are attempting to pass on to their members or to the public at large some body of beliefs and values originating in the past. In part this would include many of the activities of most religious sects and denominations, especially insofar as one focuses upon their socialization and indoctrination activities (e.g., catechism classes, "Sunday schools," Hebrew day schools, etc.). In part this function also includes all manner of more strictly educational voluntary organizations, from Plato's Academy (see Peterson and Peterson 1973) to modern Great Books Discussion Groups and so-called "Free Universities."

The various levels of government in the contemporary world have largely taken over the task of education on a broad scale, yet voluntary organizations still are active in supplementing government-run educational systems by filling in the gaps and by prodding these systems to improve or take on responsibility for the preservation of additional knowledge or values. For instance, voluntary civil rights and black liberation organizations have taken the lead in educating both blacks and whites in the United States regarding black history and accomplishments. Gradually, under the pressure of such voluntary associations in the past several years, the public educational system in the United States has been changing to accommodate a more accurate and complete picture of black history, although the process is by no means finished yet. Similar examples could be given with regard to other content areas as well (e.g., women's history, American Indian history, etc.).

A sixth major impact of the voluntary sector is its embodiment and representation in society of the sense of mystery, wonder, and the sacred. Neither the business nor government sectors in modern society have much tendency to be concerned with such matters. Many would say that religion today *is* very much a big business; and both business and government support science in a substantial way. Yet precisely in those areas where religion and science almost meet, where the borders of religion are receding under the pressure of an ever-expanding science, the business and government sectors are often *least* involved. Voluntary associations and non-profit foundations/research organizations are the only groups experimenting seriously with new forms of worship, non-drug induced "consciousness expansion" and the "religious experience," the occult, investigation of flying saucers, extra-sensory perception, etc.

The "heretics" of both science and religion are seldom supported in their work directly and consciously by the business or government sectors. Only through voluntary action and the support of the voluntary sector have the major changes in man's view of the supernatural and its relation to the natural tended to come about in the past. The same has also been true, by and large, for major changes in man's view of himself and of the natural universe in the past. The dominant economic and political (and religious) systems of any given epoch are seldom very receptive to the really new visions of either the natural or supernatural world (e.g., Galileo and Copernicus; Jesus). Voluntary action is thus the principal manner in which a sense of the sacred, the mysterious, and the weird can be preserved and permitted some measure of expression in our otherwise hyper-rational contemporary society.

A seventh impact of the voluntary sector results from its ability to liberate the individual and permit him or her the fullest possible measure of expression of personal capacities and potentialities within an otherwise constraining social environment. All societies have their systems of laws, customs, roles, and organizations that box people in and limit their opportunities for personal expression and personal development. The full extent of societal limitations on people has just begun to be realized in recent decades, spurred in part by the "liberation" movements of women, blacks, the poor, the "Third World" and other disadvantaged or disenfranchised groups. The primary embodiments of these societal barriers and boxes have generally been the economic and governmental systems, although other major institutions of society have played a role as well (e.g., education, the family, religion, etc.).

Voluntary associations and groups, on the other hand, have long been a primary means of at least partially escaping these barriers and boxes. Through participation in voluntary action a wide variety of people have been able to find or to create special social groups that would permit them to grow as individuals. This kind of personal growth has many relevant aspects, but can be summed up generally as "self actualization," to use a term from Maslow (1954). For some this means intellectual development, the process of becoming increasingly analytical, informed, and self-conscious about the nature of one's life situation and problems. When this occurs for a whole category or group of people, the process is often referred to as "group conscienticization" or "consciousness-raising" (e.g., among blacks, women, the poor). Seldom does such special personal growth occur on a broad scale outside voluntary groups and movements.

For others, self-actualization through voluntary action takes the form of developing otherwise unused capacities, talents, skills or potentials of a more active and practical sort. For many kinds of people, depending on the stage of social, economic, and political development of a society, voluntary associations and voluntary action offer the only feasible opportunity for leadership, for learning to speak in public, for practicing the fine art of management, for exercising analytical judgment, etc. Until very recently in American society, for instance, neither blacks nor women nor the members of certain other disadvantaged groups could hope to develop fully their capacities through the occupational system of the economic or government sectors. Only in voluntary groups of their own making could they seek any kind of fulfillment and self expression, bound as they were (and in part continue to be) by the prejudices and discrimination of the dominant white, male, Anglo-Saxon Protestants in our society. However, this situation is not unique to the United States. There are similar and even different forms of prejudice and discrimination in *all* other societies, varying only in degree and the particular social groups singled out for attention. And in all societies voluntary associations also offer the disadvantaged some chance of enhanced self-development, though these associations must sometimes meet in secret as underground groups if the society in which they are operating is oppressive and does not respect the right of free association.

Voluntary action potentially offers unique opportunities for personal growth and realization of personal potentials not only for those people whom society otherwise deprives, but also for *all* the members of society in certain directions. No matter how free, open, egalitarian, and highly developed the society, there are always limitations of some sort placed on the development of each person by his particular social environment. Any major decision to follow a certain line of personal occupational or educational development, for instance, automatically forecloses a number of other alternatives, or at least makes them highly unlikely. Voluntary associations, however, exist (or can exist) in such profusion and variety that they can provide otherwise missed personal development opportunities to almost any person at almost any stage of life. This is as true for the school teacher who always wanted to learn to fly (and who can join a flying club to do so even at age 60), as it is for the airline pilot who always wanted to write novels (and who can join a writer's club to work toward this end).

Of course, not every person will find the appropriate voluntary association for his or her personal growth needs to be available at the time it is needed. But the voluntary sector as a whole, nevertheless, still serves in some significant degree this general role of providing substantial numbers of individuals in society with otherwise unavailable opportunities for self actualization and self fulfillment.

An eighth major impact of the voluntary sector in society is one of overriding importance, relating directly to the first and second impacts discussed above. We are referring to the impact of the voluntary sector as a source of "negative feedback" for society as a whole, especially with regard to the directions taken by the major institutions of society such as government and business. Without "negative feedback," any system is dangerously vulnerable to destroying itself through excesses in one direction or another. Thus, however uncomfortable and irritating they may be at times, voluntary associations and the voluntary sector are absolutely vital to the continuing development of a society.

This systemic corrective role of the voluntary sector is, of course, not carried out by *all* voluntary associations, any more than all voluntary associations are concerned with the play element, value preservation, or the sacred. Yet the small cutting edge of the voluntary sector that does perform the role of social critic is extremely important, usually bearing the responsibility for the continued existence and future growth of the rest of the voluntary sector. In societies where a sufficient number and variety of voluntary groups are *un*able to play effectively their roles as social critics, the dominant governmental and economic institutions may well take over and suppress the entire voluntary sector (e.g., Allen 1965).

In the contemporary United States there are numerous examples of voluntary associations and groups playing this systemic corrective role. All of the cause-oriented, advocacy, and issue-oriented groups tend to fall into this category, from the environmental movement to the civil rights movement and women's liberation. The tactics and strategy of such groups cover a broad range from rather traditional lobbying, through demonstrations and "be-ins," to direct remedial action such as "ecotage" (sabotage of notable corporate polluters and other "environmental undesirables").

Some of the more imaginative and innovative approaches have been developed in an attempt to modify the business sector, rather than focusing solely on the government sector. For instance, there have been in-depth investigations by Ralph Nader and his associates of particular companies' practices and their relationship to the public interest (e.g., for First National City Bank of New York and for DuPont), counter-management stockholder activity in the public interest (e.g., Project G.M.), dissenting annual reports written to present a full public accounting of a corporation's activities harmful to the general public interest and welfare, class action suits brought by voluntary groups against manufacturers and developers, etc.

When looked at in the particular, such activities (which vary markedly in their success) often seem fruitless and doomed to failure, given the power of the organizations and systems being challenged. Yet when we see these activities of voluntary groups in a larger context, when we sum up these numerous activities attempting to modify and improve the dominant systems and organizations of our society, they take on a very important general meaning. Even if many or most of such system correction attempts by voluntary groups should fail, the continual and expanding pressure being brought to bear by the voluntary sector on the central institutions of society is still likely to have a salutary long term modifying influence. When the leaders of the business and governmental sectors *know* that "someone is watching," that they will eventually have to account to the public interest for their actions, this awareness encourages greater attention to the public interest rather than merely to narrow, private interests.

When for one reason or another the voluntary sector is not able to operate effectively as a systemic corrective (either because of its own inadequacies or the failure of the leaders of dominant institutions to listen and change accordingly), the usual result in human history has been a broad social revolution (not just a palace revolution or simple coup). When the dominant institutions of any society have ignored for too long or too often the voices of the public interest as expressed by elements of the voluntary sector, revolutionary and usually underground voluntary groups arise and make concrete plans to overthrow the existing system completely. The American, French, Russian, Chinese, Cuban, and other revolutions all attest to this pattern.

Thus, when the voluntary sector cannot make itself heard adequately through the permissible communication and influence channels in a society, certain voluntary groups and movements tend to arise to revamp the whole system, establishing whole new institutional arrangements with their corresponding new channels of influence and communication. Not surprisingly, these new channels generally favor those kinds of persons and groups who were unable to be heard previously (although the kinds of people formerly dominant often end up in as bad a position or worse than that faced by the formerly disadvantaged prior to the revolution). This cycle will tend to repeat itself until a society reaches a point where it is effectively and continuously self-correcting, through the activities of a strong and social change-oriented voluntary sector, and where its major institutions are basically operating primarily in the public interest of *all* of its citizens (not just its white, male, Anglo-Saxon Protestants, or their equivalents in some other societies than the United States and the British Commonwealth).

The ninth major impact of the voluntary sector worth mentioning here is the support given by the voluntary sector specifically to the economic system of a society, especially a modern industrial society. Voluntary associations of many kinds provide crucial kinds of social, intellectual, and technical linkages among workers in numerous occupations: professional associations increase the effectiveness of most kinds of scientists, engineers, technicians, etc., just as manufacturers' and trade associations support the growth of whole industries. And various kinds of labor unions play their part as well, although many businessmen would question the degree to which they "support" the economic system. But labor unions only seem non-supportive of the economic system when the latter is viewed narrowly from the point of view of an employer interested solely in profit maximization. Labor unions ultimately have to be deeply concerned with the viability of the economic system and the productivity of their own members if they are to survive.

This economic support role of the voluntary sector is usually lost sight of because so many people tend to view all kinds of economic self-interest and occupationally related voluntary associations as integral parts of the business sector. In fact, these kinds of voluntary organizations are quite distinct from the business sector itself, however close their relationship might be to business corporations and occupational activities. The primary purpose of business corporations is to make a profit for their owners, whether they are actually involved in running the corporation or not. On the other hand, economic self-interest voluntary associations have as their primary purpose the enhancement of the long term occupational and economic interests of their member-participants. While corporation employees and professionals are *paid* in salaries, wages or fees for their participation, the members of economic self-interest voluntary associations themselves *pay* for the privilege of belonging to and benefiting from these associations.

The tenth major impact of the voluntary sector we shall note is a rather subtle one: the voluntary sector constitutes an important *latent* resource for all kinds of goal attainment in the interests of the society as a whole. Put another way, the voluntary sector represents a tremendous reservoir of potential energy that can be mobilized under appropriate circumstances for broad societal goals. The role of the voluntary sector in revolutionary situations is but one example of this latent potential. The activity of voluntary association networks in more limited disaster situations is a more common example (Barton 1970). The voluntary sector and its component associations, groups, and channels of communication and influence make possible the mobilization of large numbers of people on relatively short notice for special purposes (usually in the common interest) without resorting to economic rewards or legal coercion as activating forces. Such a latent potential in the voluntary sector is especially important when neither economic nor political-legal forces can feasibly be brought to bear to resolve some widespread problem situation.

The latent potential of the voluntary sector can be viewed in another way as well. Voluntarism is based on a *charitable grants economy* (donations of time, money, etc.) as contrasted with the *coercive grants economy* (taxation) on which the government sector operates or the *market economy* on which the business sector operates. Both of the latter types of economy work well for certain kinds of purposes, but neither works well for the accomplishment of *all* kinds of purposes in society. In the same way, there are many kinds of purposes and activities (several of which are implicit in the nine major impacts of the voluntary sector reviewed above) for which the charitable grants economy tends to work best.

Now the important latent potential of the voluntary sector is that, under appropriately compelling circumstances (i.e., for the "right" value, goal or ideal), the money, goods, real property, and services mobilized by the voluntary sector through the charitable grants economy can completely overwhelm all considerations of the coercive grants economy and the market economy. For certain goals and ideals, a large majority of society can be induced to "give their all" and to do so gladly, willingly, and voluntarily. This does not occur very often, to be sure, nor does it last very long. But the latent potential is there in any society at any time. With the right spark—usually a charismatic leader with an idea and an ideal—the course of history can be changed in these brief, rare periods of almost total societal mobilization through the leadership of the voluntary sector.

The Negative Side

In describing the foregoing ten types of impact that the voluntary sector tends to have in some degree in any society, we have emphasized the positive contributions that voluntary action makes to society. However, as with any form of human group or activity, voluntary action and the voluntary sector are by no means always positive in their impacts. For every one of the ten types of impact we have noted, there can be negative consequences in certain circumstances and with regard to certain values. Thus, when voluntary associations experiment with new social forms, the failures can often be harmful to specific people and organizations. When alternative definitions of reality and morality are offered, these can be evil as in the case of Nazi Germany and its ideology as generated by the Nazi party, a voluntary association. When voluntary groups focus on the play element, their fun can become mischievous as in the case of a boys' gang that wrecks a school "just for kicks." When social clubs provide a warm and close sense of belonging to their members, they can also create deep dissatisfaction in people who would dearly like to belong but are excluded from a particular club or kind of club.

In the same way, voluntary groups striving to preserve some beliefs or values from the past may be holding on to anachronisms that would be better left to the pages of history books. Clubs whose members chase around seeking flying saucers and little green men from Mars might more profitably spend their time and energy elsewhere with more satisfying results. Organizations that arouse the full potentials of black people—who must then go out into the real world and face a harsh reality of bigotry and discrimination—may or may not be doing them a favor. The kinds of systemic corrections being suggested by cause-oriented and advocacy groups may not be conducive to the greatest good of the greatest number. Economic self-interest voluntary groups often tend to ignore the public interest in favor of an exclusive and selfish private interest. And the latent potentials of the voluntary sector can be mobilized to do evil as well as to do good for one's fellow man.

Conclusion

What then? Our answer is clear: All the more reason to begin a thorough study of the impact of the voluntary sector and voluntary action at all system levels, in all kinds of societies, in terms of all kinds of possible value standards. What we have seen in the foregoing chapters of Part Two of this volume and what we have suggested as major impacts of the voluntary sector in this chapter only scratch the surface of a very large area for research. We have tried harder to demonstrate what voluntary action *might* do in various areas, rather than what it actually *does* do. We have done more to illustrate the breadth of the present topic than to present a definitive synthesis of the way things are, based upon empirical research. In most areas and for most types of voluntary action we simply do not know what the impacts are because no relevant research exists.

Yet at many levels and in many topical areas the possible impacts are extremely important to human society, past, present and future. Therefore, we would argue that evaluation of the impact and effectiveness/ineffectiveness of all types of voluntary action (see Smith et al. 1972) is one of the highest priority areas for future research on voluntary action. We seem to have much less empirical evidence bearing on such impact questions than we have for almost any other area or subfield of voluntary action research. This situation can be remedied only by a great deal more future commitment to impact/effectiveness research on the part of voluntary action scholars (including the Association of Voluntary Action Scholars itself), voluntary organizations and movements, and funding agencies of all kinds. We sincerely hope this joint commitment will be forthcoming in the next few years.

References

Allen, William Sheridan
1965 THE NAZI SEIZURE OF POWER. Chicago: Quadrangle Books.
Barton, Allen H.
1970 COMMUNITIES IN DISASTER. Garden City, New York: Anchor Books, Doubleday and Company.
Handlin, Oscar
1951 THE UPROOTED. New York: Grosset and Dunlap.
Little, Kenneth
1965 WEST AFRICAN URBANIZATION: A STUDY OF VOLUNTARY ASSOCIATIONS IN SOCIAL CHANGE. Cambridge, England: Cambridge University Press.
Maslow, Abraham H.
1954 MOTIVATION AND PERSONALITY. New York: Harper and Row.
Peterson, Sophia, and Virgil Peterson
1973 "Voluntary Associations in Ancient Greece." JOURNAL OF VOLUNTARY ACTION RESEARCH 2, no.1, 2-16.
Smith, David Horton
1966 "The Importance of Formal Voluntary Organizations for Society." SOCIOLOGY AND SOCIAL RESEARCH 50, 483-92.
Smith, David Horton, with John Dixon
1973 "The Voluntary Sector." Chapter 7 in Edward Bursk, ed., CHALLENGE TO LEADERSHIP: MANAGING IN A CHANGING WORLD. New York: The Free Press, Macmillan and Co.
Smith, David Horton, Richard D. Reddy, and Burt R. Baldwin
1972 "Types of Voluntary Action: A Definitional Essay." Chapter 10 in David Horton Smith et al., eds., VOLUNTARY ACTION RESEARCH: 1972. Lexington, Mass.: Lexington Books, D.C. Heath and Co.

Index

ACTION, 275
Activism, impact of, 304–305
Activists:
  characteristics of student, 303–304
  student, defined, 300
Addicts Anonymous, 213
Adjustment (social), mechanism for, 390
Advocacy, 37, 273, 394, 398
Age-sets, 14, 20
Agriculture, U.S. Department of, 351
Alaska Native Brotherhood, 19, 21
Alchoholics Anonymous, 213, 214–216
Allies of low-status groups, 371–373
American Friends Service Committee,
  191–192
American Student Union, 141
Anomia, 196, 212
Anonymity, 151–152
Aristocrats, 17
Associations:
  collegiate, 129–142
  hybrid, 245
  village, 31–32
  voluntary, *see* Voluntary associations
Athens, 35, 37–38
Attitudes:
  influences on, 177–178, 186, 191–192,
    194, 307
  stability of, 171
  toward citizen participation, 277–278,
    280, 282
  toward low-status organizations, 366

Bands, 9, 12, 22
Bath, the Roman, 43
Behavior, effect of volunteering on, 202–
  204, 221–222
Beliefs, effect of volunteering on, 198–199,
  220
Benevolency, 149, 154
Black Nation of Islam, 210
Boxers, the, 30
Boy Scouts, 78
Brainwashing, 173–174
Buddhism, 30

Caste system, 20, 33–35, 44
Characteristics:
  of secret societies, 152
  of student activists, 303–304
  of voluntary associations, 12, 181–182,
    243–244
  of working-class movements, 380

Charity, 149
China, 15, 20, 29–33, 34, 44–45
Cities, 19, 32
  early, 14
  FVO in, 22
    See also Urbanization
Citizen participation, 165–166, 259–287
  roles in, 277–280
Civil rights work, 190
Clans, 11, 19, 20, 31, 33
Clientage, 42–43
Clubs, 15, 397–398
  benefit, 35
  Greek, 35–38
  mental health, 217–219
  political, 36, 39
  Roman, 39
  social, 21, 35, 397–398
Co-ops, British, 77–78
Co-optation, 248–249, 263, 337, 338
Collectivity orientation, 57, 59, 62, 63, 64,
  66, 67, 90
College:
  impact of, 177–179
  student: population ratio, 129
Collegia, 39–41
Comilla Cooperative, 211
Communication, 85–86
  network, 57–59, 62, 64–65
Communist party, 30, 195, 372
Community Action Agency (CAA), 273
Community service volunteers, 199–200
Conscienticization, group, 393
Conspiracies, 36, 66
Convergence hypothesis, 91–93, 95
Conversion effects, 210, 222
Convocation, 18
Cooperation (interorganizational), 247
  model of, 346–352
  types of, 338, 340
Cooperatives, 67, 77–78, 211–212
Coordination (organizational), 243–244
  defined, 349–350
  models of, 342–345, 350
  preconditions for, 339
  types of, 342–345
Corporations (Roman), 39
Corrective role of voluntary associations,
  394–396
Council of Federated Organizations
  (COFO), 138
Credit associations, 21, 32
Cults, 15, 30, 34, 39, 40

401

About the Contributors

Robert T. Anderson, with doctorates in both anthropology (Berkeley) and sociology (Sorbonne), is an anthropologist who specializes in the study of complex societies. Since 1960 he has taught at Mills College, where he holds the Edward Hohfeld Chair in Anthropology. Among his publications are *Traditional Europe* (1971) and *Modern Europe* (1973).

Nicholas Babchuk, a Professor of Sociology at the University of Nebraska-Lincoln, is the coauthor of *The Voluntary Association in the Slum*, and has published frequently in various scholarly journals. Currently, he is serving as an Associate Editor of *The Sociological Quarterly*, the *Journal of Voluntary Action Research*, and has served in the past as an Associate Editor of *Sociological Inquiry*.

Burt R. Baldwin, Assistant Professor of Sociology at Central Connecticut State College, coedited *Voluntary Action Research: 1972*. He is currently engaged in research on the problem of incidence and prevalence of voluntary organizations.

Don Dillman is Assistant Professor of Sociology and Director of the Public Opinion Laboratory at Washington State University. Published articles include work in the area of public values, population redistribution policy, and mail and telephone data collection methods. Current research includes an analysis of voluntary association influences on citizens' public values.

John Dixon is Director of the Center for a Voluntary Society. From 1965-1968 he managed the Washington education and public relations offices of Xerox Corporation. Before that he served as a foreign service officer with the U.S.I.A. for the U.S.-U.S.S.R. Cultural and Scientific Exchange Agreement; and spent seven years as a special assistant to R. Buckminster Fuller.

Gerald E. Klonglan is Professor of Sociology at Iowa State University, Ames, Iowa. He is the author of over 100 articles and research monographs focusing on community organization and social change. He has recently coauthored *Social Indicators and Societal Monitoring* and is currently co-director of a research program to develop a methodology for applying social indicators to community development.

Henry A. Landsberger is Professor of Sociology and Research Professor in the Institute for Research in the Social Sciences, University of North Carolina at Chapel Hill, N.C. He is the editor of books on peasant movements, the Catholic church in Latin America, and comparative complex organizations, and the author of articles in these and other fields, including the labor movement, rural co-operatives and Latin American politics.

Charles L. Mulford, Associate Research Professor and Associate Professor of Sociology at Iowa State University, is author and coauthor of over 30 articles, monographs and professional papers in community power structure analysis, complex organizations and instigated social change.

Virgil Peterson, Director of University Honors and Associate Professor of English, West Virginia University, is an Editorial Associate for *Victorian Poetry*. He is the author of studies of literature, education and voluntarism.

Richard D. Reddy, a member of the Department of Sociology at the State University of New York at Fredonia, is the Associate Editor of the *Journal of Voluntary Action Research*. He coedited *Voluntary Action Research: 1972.*

Jack C. Ross, Associate Professor of Sociology, Memorial University of Newfoundland, is coauthor of *Black Belonging*, and several articles on sociological theories of voluntary associations.

Alvin J. Schmidt is Associate Professor of Sociology at Concordia College, Seward, Nebraska. He has authored articles appearing in the *Journal for the Scientific Study of Religion, Journal of Voluntary Action Research*; and other periodicals. He is currently engaged in research examining the correlates of fraternal organization affiliation of State legislators from four states.

Kjell Skjelsbaek, Acting Executive Director of the International Peace Research Institute, Oslo, has been a visiting scholar at the Mental Health Research Institute at the University of Michigan, Ann Arbor. He has contributed to several international journals and readers.

David Horton Smith, Director of Research for the Center for a Voluntary Society in Washington, D.C., and Associate Professor of Sociology at Boston College, is Editor of the *Journal of Voluntary Action Research* and President of the Association of Voluntary Action Scholars. He coauthored *Becoming Modern*, with Alex Inkeles, and coedited *Voluntary Action Research: 1972*. He has written numerous articles on all phases of voluntary action and the voluntary sector.

Hans B.C. Spiegel, Professor of Urban Affairs at Hunter College of the City University of New York, has taught at the University of Pennsylvania, Springfield College, and Columbia University. No stranger to Washington, Dr. Spiegel is a former Deputy Assistant Commissioner of the U.S. Urban Renewal Administration; he also helped plan VISTA as a member of the Presidential Task Force in the War Against Poverty and the Model Cities Program as a staff member of the Presidential Task Force on Urban Problems. He has been assigned research tasks, many in citizen participation, from several federal departments, including HUD, HEW, and Labor.

Athena Theodore, Associate Professor of Sociology at Simmons College, Boston, edited *The Professional Woman*, and has authored various articles and papers in the areas of voluntary action, social change, and the status of women. Among her articles are "Social Change and Voluntary Action" which appeared in *Voluntary Action Research: 1972.*

W. Keith Warner, Professor of Sociology at Brigham Young University, has authored and coauthored several articles and other writings relating to voluntary associations and other kinds of organizational phenomena, including a chapter in *Voluntary Action Research: 1972.*

Benjamin Hong Yep, Assistant Professor of Sociology and Extension Sociologist at Iowa State University, developed the Applied Model of Interorganizational Relations and has presented this model to the staffs of the United States Public Health Service, U.S.D.A., and the U.S. Office of Civil Defense.